Baltimore Publishing Company

The Memorial Volume

A History of the Third Plenary Council of Baltimore...

Baltimore Publishing Company

The Memorial Volume
A History of the Third Plenary Council of Baltimore...

ISBN/EAN: 9783744747158

Printed in Europe, USA, Canada, Australia, Japan

Cover: Foto ©ninafisch / pixelio.de

More available books at **www.hansebooks.com**

His Holiness Pope Leo XIII.

THE
MEMORIAL VOLUME

A HISTORY

— OF THE —

THIRD PLENARY COUNCIL

OF BALTIMORE,

NOVEMBER 9–DECEMBER 7, 1884.

BALTIMORE:
THE BALTIMORE PUBLISHING COMPANY,
No. 174 West Baltimore Street.
1885.

COPYRIGHT
BY THE BALTIMORE PUBLISHING CO.,
1885.

Press of The Baltimore Publishing Co.

MEMORIAL VOLUME

— OF THE —

THIRD PLENARY COUNCIL

OF BALTIMORE.

APPROBATION.

We give our most cordial approbation to the enterprise of The Baltimore Publishing Company, The Memorial Volume of the Third Plenary Council of Baltimore, and we trust that it will meet with the hearty co-operation of the faithful.

✠ JAMES GIBBONS,
Archbishop of Baltimore.

APPROBATION.

We give our most cordial approbation to the enterprise of The Baltimore Publishing Company, The Memorial Volume of the Third Plenary Council of Baltimore, and we trust that it will meet with the hearty co-operation of the faithful.

✠ JAMES GIBBONS,
Archbishop of Baltimore.

Most Rev. Archbishop Gibbons.

PREFACE.

THE BALTIMORE PUBLISHING COMPANY, in presenting this volume to the public, trust that its typographical appearance and the careful manner with which its matter has been prepared will be appreciated. It is a work which every Catholic family should possess.

The sermons of the bishops during the council form, of course, one of the chief features of the work. In their crude form, as reported by stenographers, they have been extensively published, both at home and abroad; thus showing the world-wide interest taken in the acts of the council. The dignified Pastoral Letter which follows them has also received no small share of public attention, and its patriotic tone and wise counsels have commended it even to citizens of other creeds.

With regard to the preliminary matter, it is only necessary for us to say that it has been prepared with the greatest care. The first article consists of the Prize Essay on "The Catholic Church in the United States," and will be found a good condensed summary of our Church's origin and growth in this country. Then come a chronicle of the preceding Councils of Baltimore, based on the Latin records; a history of the Third Plenary Council's public acts; an account of the grand reception tendered by the citizens of Baltimore to the members of the Council; the congratulations to the Most Rev. Apostolic Delegate; the acclamations; a list of the members of the Council; a list of the deceased members of the Second Plenary Council;

outline sketches of the lives of the American prelates; and the Pastoral of the Most Rev. Archbishop of Baltimore to the clergy and laity of his archdiocese. The facts in the sketches of the prelates' lives are authentic. The whole work is embellished by portraits of the prelates and other illustrations.

CONTENTS.

Dedication,	1
Approbation of Archbishop Gibbons,	2
Preface,	3
Illustrations,	7
"The Catholic Church in the United States." Prize Essay by John A. Russell, A.B.,	9
"The Councils of Baltimore." By Hugh P. McElrone,	29
The Third Plenary Council of Baltimore,	46
The Reception to the Members of the Council by the Citizens of Baltimore,	52
Congratulating the Apostolic Delegate,	65
The Acclamations,	68
Members of the Council—A list of their Names,	70
Deceased Prelates of the Second Plenary Council,	80
Lives of the Present American Prelates—Outline Sketches, Giving the Authentic Facts,	82
Pastoral Letter of the Most Rev. Archbishop of Baltimore to the Clergy and Laity of his Diocese,	111

SERMONS.

"The Church in Her Councils." By Most Rev. Patrick John Ryan, D.D., Archbishop of Philadelphia,	1
"The Catholic Church Equally Opposed to Anarchy and to Despotism, the Guardian of Society, the Defender of True Liberty." By the Right Rev. John Ireland, D.D., Bishop of St. Paul, Minn.,	11
"De Mortuis—Our Deceased Prelates." By the Most Rev. M. A. Corrigan, D.D., Coadjutor Archbishop of New York,	33
"The Priesthood." By the Most Rev. W. H. Elder, D.D., Archbishop of Cincinnati,	43
"The Unity of the Church." By the Right Rev. J. F. Shanahan, D.D., Bishop of Harrisburg,	59

"The Missions for the Colored People." By the Right Rev. W. H. Gross, D.D., Bishop of Savannah, Ga., ... 71

"University Education Considered in its Bearings on the Higher Education of Priests." By Right Rev. J. L. Spalding, D.D., Bishop of Peoria, Ill., ... 75

"The Necessity of Revelation." By the Right Rev. R. Gilmour, D.D., Bishop of Cleveland, ... 103

"Indian Missions." By the Most Rev. C. J. Seghers, D.D., Archbishop of Oregon City, ... 114

"Christian Marriage." By the Right Rev. M. J. O'Farrell, D.D., Bishop of Trenton, N. J., ... 120

"The Observation of Feasts." By the Right Rev. S. V. Ryan, D.D., Bishop of Buffalo, N. Y., ... 132

"Faith and Reason." By the Right Rev. J. A. Watterson, D.D., Bishop of Columbus, ... 142

"The Catholic Church in the United States." By Right Rev. Bernard J. McQuaid, D.D., Bishop of Rochester, . . . 161

"The Sacrifice of the Mass." By Right Rev. E. Fitzgerald, D.D., Bishop of Little Rock, Ark., ... 177

"Thanksgiving Day." By Right Rev. J. L. Spalding, D.D., Bishop of Peoria, Ill., ... 186

"Catholic Societies." By Right Rev. J. J. Keane, D.D., Bishop of Richmond, Va., ... 190

"The Church and Science." By Right Rev. Thomas A. Becker, D.D., Bishop of Wilmington, Del., ... 209

"The Catholicity of the Church." By Right Rev. James O'Connor, D.D., Vicar Apostolic of Nebraska, ... 214

"The Sanctity of the Church." By Right Rev. John Hennessy, D.D., Bishop of Dubuque, ... 224

"The Work of the Council." By Right Rev. J. L. Spalding, D.D., Bishop of Peoria, ... 245

"The Blessed Virgin Mary, under the Title of the Immaculate Conception, Patroness of the Church in the United States." By Right Rev. F. S. Chatard, D.D., Bishop of Vincennes, ... 255

Pastoral Letter of the Third Plenary Council.

The Cathedral Organ.

ILLUSTRATIONS.

1. His Holiness Pope Leo XIII. Frontispiece.
2. Most Rev. James Gibbons, Archbishop of Baltimore and Apostolic Delegate.
3. His Eminence John Cardinal McCloskey, Archbishop of New York.
4. George Calvert, Lord Baltimore, Founder of Maryland and Religious Freedom in America.
5. Most Rev. John Carroll, First Archbishop of Baltimore.
6. Most Rev. John J. Williams, Archbishop of Boston.
7. Most Rev. P. J. Ryan, Archbishop of Philadelphia.
8. Interior View of the Cathedral, Baltimore.
9. Exterior View of the Cathedral, Baltimore.
10. Exterior View of the Seminary where the Private Sessions were held.
11. View of the New Cathedral Organ.
12. Most Rev. M. A. Corrigan, Coadjutor Archbishop of New York.
13. Most Rev. W. H. Elder, Archbishop of Cincinnati.
14. Most Rev. Michael Heiss, Archbishop of Milwaukee.
15. Most Rev. P. A. Feehan, Archbishop of Chicago.
16. Most Rev. P. W. Riordan, Coadjutor Archbishop of San Francisco.
17. Most Rev. F. X. Leray, Archbishop of New Orleans.
18. One Group of Five Archbishops and Bishops.
19. Fourteen Groups, Nine Each, of Bishops and Other Members of the Council.

Cardinal McCloskey

THE CATHOLIC CHURCH IN THE UNITED STATES.

PRIZE ESSAY.

BY JOHN A. RUSSELL, A.B.

WERE it given to some seer of the tenth century to address the future American Church in the person of the monk who came out from Ireland to Christianize Iceland, he would use language full of hope and promise, yet not unmixed with sorrow and regretful anticipation. He would tell of a northern nation converted to Christianity from gross idolatry, and taught in the arts and the science and the literature of Christian Europe; and he would add that that Christianity was wiped out of existence by the extinction of the race which professed it. The next chapter of his prophecy would open on the coast of San Salvador on that October day when, after months of battling with the ocean's storms, Columbus planted the cross of the Crucified One on the shores of the newly found continent; and before that chapter were finished he would have recorded the humiliation and ingratitude which were the portion of the same Columbus before his eyes were closed in death. Joy and sorrow, toil and suffering, hope and even despair would be his themes ere he would tell the story of the firm foundation of the American Church. And that tale would scarcely be ended before he would have to modify it with recitals of the storms which the Church had to buffet and the trials which she had to undergo before her priests were venerated and her children respected as was their due. Marking as the opening of the Third Plenary Council does the beginning of a new era in the Catholic history of America, an excellent opportunity is afforded to look back and take a retrospect of what that seer might have told by anticipation. Such is the object of this monograph,—briefly to consider the Rise and Progress of the Catholic Church in the United States.

I.

Catholicity is nothing new in America. Away back in the eleventh century, before England had fallen under the dominion of Danish kings, while the monk Gerbert occupied the chair of Peter under the title of Sylvester II, and just after the combined Christian princes of Spain had routed the armies of Almanzor, the Moor, there were Norse settlements in Iceland and on the shores of the North American continent, where altars were raised to the true God, and where priests chanted His praises and people adored Him with a fervor unexcelled in any of Europe's strongholds of faith. As early as the year 1000, missionaries were working for the conversion of Iceland. They found their task neither tedious nor difficult; and in the course of sixteen years the stone gods of the Vikings were overturned, and in their stead were erected altars to Him who, loving all, redeemed all. Nor did the work end here. Not contented with the limits placed by a small island, the sons of men who had taken refuge from a tyrant on the high seas once more boldly struck out, and following the coast of the mainland, penetrated to Vinland, now New England. There is proof positive that the colonists in Vinland maintained their profession of the faith in which their fathers and brothers believed. Thus was Catholicity implanted in America at an early date; thus were priests employed; and thus was the flock developed which was watched over by the Bishop of Garda. There was no lack of progress on the part of the Icelandic Church, which, founded at a time when Europeans were anxiously and fearfully awaiting the Milennium, promised to become one of the brightest jewels of the Roman crown.

All things earthly seem forced to run in a mad race towards dissolution. The Norse colonies within the shadow of the Arctic circle were no exception to this general rule. For a time they prospered, and with them the religion of their inhabitants. But by one of those terrestrial changes which can never be sufficiently accounted for, the gulf stream shifted its course and left Greenland and Iceland bereft of that influence which had tempered the rigor of the polar gales. The climatic changes attendant upon the fluctuation of the gulf stream turned Iceland and Greenland into barren wastes, habitable only by rude and hardy tribes. The Norse colonies were wiped out, and by the extinction as a race of those who professed Catholicity in the North, the history of the Norse-American Church was closed forever. Thus ended one period of the Church in America. That period was as separate and distinct from any which followed, as it was original and independent of any that went before. It bequeathed to later ages no influences, and it left behind it no effects other than the ruined altars and the half obliterated inscriptions subsequently discovered in Greenland and Vinland.

It was not long, comparatively, until the next epoch of American Catholicity began. Columbus came in 1492, and his return to Spain with tales of his wonderful discovery and of the strange races to whom the true God was an unknown Being and His worship a mystery, marked the beginning of the new era. Earnest men began to assert and skeptical ones to half admit that perhaps there were yet nations to be won over to Christ and to be marshaled under His banner. Brave souls followed in the wake of Columbus, and every vessel that left the ports of Spain brought with it to America one or more of those intrepid missionaries who were born for higher things than ordinary men, and who braved old ocean's storms and the trials and tortures which they could only faintly imagine, in behalf of the cause of Christ. Half a century's work wrought a great change. By the middle of the sixteenth century Ponce de Leon, the missionaries who accompanied and fell with Narvaez, the companions of De Soto, and the Dominicans who followed under Father Carcer, had all left their imprint on the soil of Florida, Alabama and Mississippi, and their influence in the hearts of the Indians who basked in the rays of an almost tropical sun. Farther west the devoted Franciscan, Andrew de Olmos, was at work in Mexico, and in the North Jacques Cartier and his followers forgot not the religion which they had known in sunny France. And thus it followed that before the beginning of the seventeenth century that portion of the American continent lying east of the Mississippi river had been traversed by a band of missionaries, not great in numbers, but strong in ardor and perseverance. The reports of the successes of this forlorn hope found many eager students in the novitiates and seminaries of Europe, and it was not long until new spirits were enlisted in the work of Christianizing the savages of America. No history can be more interesting, no romance more fascinating, no tragedy more touching than the record of the lives and the labors, the trials and the sufferings of the early missionaries in America. Nearly three centuries have passed away since they advanced through the West and the South,—the pioneers of civilization and the heralds of faith. To-day their missions still exist among the few Indians who linger about Sault-Ste.-Marie and the islands of Green Bay; while at this distant time traditions of the "Black Robes" are fondly treasured up by the wild, roving Indians of the North. On the moss-grown trees we yet see the carved cross, surmounted by the characteristic motto, A.M.D.G., to remind the traveler that he treads upon ground hallowed by the footsteps of saints. Thus the stately pines of the Saginaw Valley, the tall cedars of Sault-Ste.-Marie and the giant oaks and the gnarled cherry trees of the Green Bay region all bear witness to the zeal and the burning piety of the early Jesuit missionaries. Those grand old woods formed the cathedral arches through which re-echoed the solemn tones of the *Tantum Ergo*. Those silent oratories were the scenes of fasts and weary watches, all offered to the Most High for the conversion of the degraded Indians. Through those woods men of piety and genius and noble birth trod their uncertain way from one scene of torture to another. Sacrificing all that was great in the eyes of the world, all that promised a life of ease and comfort and luxury, they crossed the bleak Atlantic and made their way up the St. Lawrence to Montreal. There they separated. Some few remained to minister to the spiritual wants of the post. Others went south, never to return. Some, again, went to the wild shores of Lakes Huron and Superior, where they labored and suffered until, when their thankless task was finished, they offered up their pure and well-tried souls to their Creator. A goodly number succumbed to the tortures of barbarous Indians. The wild shrieks of the Iroquois formed the fitting requiems of Brebœuf and Daniel. The sainted Marquette and the venerable Menard, worn out by toil and age and torture, knelt down to pray beside some giant tree; and there, far from the land of their birth, far from all that was near and dear to them, they passed away. Where their relics lie concealed only the great recording angel knows.

Nor did the work of these men die with them. They studied

George Calvert, First Lord Baltimore.

the nature of the country, its features and its resources, and all these they incorporated into their contributions to that great and reliable source of American history, the "Relations de Jésuites." To the early missionaries, then, we owe much. To them we owe the civilization of almost every portion of the country. Their missions in lands made fertile by the blood of martyrs, have grown great. The mission of Sault-Ste.-Marie is now an episcopal see. The mission of Kaskaskia has grown to a metropolis, known the world over. For their labors we can never repay them; for their troubles no eulogium can be a sufficient recompense; for their faults, if they had any, a merciful God has given pardon.

But it is not yet of these that this necessarily brief sketch must treat. It must pass over in silence works worthy of being graven on plates of brass and written on stone with a stylus of iron in order that due attention may be paid to a later and, to Catholics of the present day, a more important period. The growth of the Catholic Church in the United States, prior to the Revolution, was not that of the sturdy oak, whose roots grow stronger and thicker with each succeeding year. It was rather like the mosses which cluster round the trunk, and which, beautiful though they may be, are easily uprooted. We must look, then, for the real birth of the existing American Church to a later period than that which is glorified by the labors of the early missionaries; we must pass on to that period which began just before the first episcopal see was established in America, when the priests were few and those few worn by toil and service.

II.

Before the thirteen original States had thrown off the garb of adolescent dependence and had assumed the toga of independent manhood, the various missions which comprised the American Church were attached to the jurisdictions of the parent nations. Florida was administered from Spain; the priests of the Northwest owed ecclesiastical obedience to superiors in France; the Jesuit missionaries looked to Rome for counsel and direction; while the few priests who were stationed in the States on the Atlantic coast received comparatively little attention from the Vicar Apostolic of London. The change from dependence to independence on the part of the colonies wrought a corresponding change in the government of the American Church. The feeling against the parent nation was so strong at the close of the Revolution that there was a manifest impropriety in having the American clergy derive their ecclesiastical authority from the English vicar apostolic. This dignitary was represented in the colony of Maryland by the Rev. Father Lewis, who had been Superior of the American Mission of the Society of Jesus before the suppression of the Order. A change was speedily effected. In 1784 the regular clergy of the United States, who numbered not more than thirty at most, united in a petition to the Holy See for the appointment of a superior or vicar apostolic, who should have all the necessary faculties of a bishop. Rome had anticipated the request of the clergy of the then promising American mission; and the Sacred Congregation was already discussing the propriety of an episcopal appointment for the new country, when the petition of the clergy was presented. A favorable answer was at once returned, and with it came the official notice of the appointment of the Rev. John Carroll as superior. He was already nearly fifty years of age. A native of Maryland, he had been educated in England and France, and had been a member of the Society of Jesus until the issuance of the famous brief of Clement XIV. In obedience to that mandate he dissolved his connection with the order at Bruges, and after tarrying in England for a brief period he returned to his native land. There he found a state of affairs which was interesting from whatever point it was viewed. Politically, all was anxiety and dissatisfaction at the manner in which the mother country had dealt with the colonies. Little evidence of religious life existed. The priests were few, their charges onerous, and the conditions under which they worked were not always favorable. He took up his residence with his mother at Rock Creek, ten miles from the present city of Washington. From a chapel on her estate he ministered to the spiritual wants of the Catholics of the surrounding country. On the breaking out of the war of 1776 he espoused the cause which was ennobled by the services of his illustrious relative of Carrollton. From the first he was ardent in his support of the principles of the Revolution. He early recognized the incompatibility of the English temperament with that of the American colonists; and he felt that perfect religious freedom might be implanted in the nation to be formed if the war had a successful outcome. His learning and his judgment were early recognized, and during the war he was appointed one of four commissioners to visit Quebec in the hope of gaining the active co-operation of the Canadians, or at least of obtaining from them a promise of neutrality. The commissioners failed in their first purpose, because the Canadians remembered that the New England colonies had included among their grievances against the British crown the "intolerable tyranny of the King of England in allowing the practice of the Popish religion in Canada." But Father Carroll secured, by his entreaties, the neutrality of our northern neighbors, before he returned to Maryland to resume the active charge of his Rock Creek Mission.

Such, briefly, was the career of John Carroll, priest of the Society of Jesus, up to the time of his appointment as superior of the American clergy. The choice gave universal satisfaction, for Father Carroll was respected by Protestants and Catholics alike. He at once entered upon the duties of his new and, in some respects, unique dignity. The Church at that time was not strong nor were its adherents of the most fervent character. The lack of priestly ministrations and counsel had resulted in many cases in causing whole settlements to become lukewarm. These Father Carroll sought to reach. The first difficulty that stood in his way was the lack of priests. This was partially obviated by the immigration of a number of priests from Europe. Pastors were at once sent to parishes in New England, the Carolinas and Kentucky, in which State there was a Catholic population of four thousand souls. For himself, in spite of his dignity, he worked from early morning until late at night in the cause of religion. Journeys for the administration of the sacraments were made to the most distant parts of the district, over which he had authority. The priests in almost all cases became imbued with the fervor of their superior, and redoubled their efforts in the vineyard of the Lord.

For five years Father Carroll occupied the position of superior of the American clergy. In 1789, the prosperity and rapid growth of the Church suggested the propriety of the appointment of a bishop. The authority of the vicar general was not sufficiently extensive; and his lack of some powers was the cause of insubordination on the part of a few priests, who refused to bow before any but an episcopal mandate. The clergy applied to Rome for the foundation of an American see, and soon received a favorable answer, coupled with the privileges of selecting the see and nominating its first incumbent. The choice was soon made and forwarded to Rome. By a bull of November 6, 1789, Pope Pius VI designated the city of Baltimore as the Episcopal see, and appointed John Carroll Bishop and Pastor of its Cathedral Church. This was more than Dr. Carroll had expected. Fearing lest his position as superior of the American clergy might suggest the choice of his name, he was careful to frustrate every movement that might lead to his nomination. But he accepted the call and in the summer of 1790, he sailed for England. Arrived there he presented himself before Right Rev. Charles Walmsley, Vicar-Apostolic of London, for consecration. The ceremony took place in the private chapel of a wealthy Commoner, Thomas Weld, who proffered his hospitality to Bishop Carroll during his stay in England. When he had been vested with all the power and dignity of his office, the bishop sailed for the country to which he was now bound by a stronger tie, to which he stood in a holier relation, than any man had stood before. He appreciated his responsibilities and bent every effort toward making his administration successful for the Church. Before leaving England he had arranged with the Sulpicians who were driven from France, for the establishment of a theological school in his see, in order that he might draw on the rising generation in America for laborers in the vineyard. He attended personally to all the duties, clerical and otherwise, of his office, a task which entailed no small amount of labor. From all parts came requests for priests and complaints of insufficient attention, occasionally varied by a dispute between a clergyman and his congregation. All these matters Bishop Carroll had to adjudicate. He sought not only to conserve and consolidate the existing Church, but also to extend it. A number of fortuitous circumstances assisted him in carrying out his generous design. On the dying out of that opposition to the Society of Jesus which had wrung from Pope Clement the bull of suppression, the exiled and separated Fathers of the order were called from the seclusion in which they had spent years. Through the halls of seminaries and educational institutions, through the corridors of prisons and jails, through the forests and the morasses of half-known lands

Most Rev. John Carroll, First Archbishop of Baltimore.

rang the permission of the Holy See for the establishment of the order. The words were sweet music in the ears of the noble disciples of Loyola, and in a brief time the society was once more ready for the strife, weak and wounded, it is true, yet still full of courage and hope. Bishop Carroll needed all the help possible to enable him to carry out his work; and he was not slow in enlisting in his support the men who spend half a lifetime in learning how to do the greatest good in the other half. But the Jesuits were not the only forces who came to his aid. Infidel ascendancy in France had filled the religious heavens with dark and lowering clouds. Persecution was going on in some places, and in other localities no one knew how soon the lash would be applied. This state of affairs resulted in the emigration to America of a number of brilliant ecclesiastics, who offered their services to Bishop Carroll. The aid was opportune, and from these recruits, the American Church has selected such names as Matignon, Cheverus and Richard for veneration. Ten years go by quickly, and when they are past it is only in rare instances that it can be said that any special good has been done during their continuance. But the decade which followed the consecration of Bishop Carroll was prolific in good. Its beginning saw a Church without an episcopal head, without sufficient workers to attend to its wants, without either schools or seminaries in which to train the Catholic youth of the young republic. The opening of the present century witnessed as the head of the American Church a man possessed of the most consummate administrative ability. The number of priests had increased and with them flocks had grown in extent and devotion. All promised well for the Catholic Church in America at the beginning of the initial year of the nineteenth century. The Church was consolidated and the efforts of the pastors were directed to a common end. All was harmony and every one was filled with a desire for the growth of Catholicity. Young men came forward to perform the sacred duties of the ministry, and by the year 1810, there were in the country nearly one hundred priests, in charge of as many congregations. A new life was breathed into the American Church, formed as it had been from a spiritual rib of the almost dormant religious Adam of the Old World.

Rome was not insensible to the advances in the new world, and at an early date the Sacred Congregation of the Propaganda saw that the burthen borne by Bishop Carroll was too heavy for even his strong and willing shoulders. Some years before Rev. Leonard Neale, president of Georgetown College, had been made coadjutor to the Bishop of Baltimore, *cum jure successionis*. But instead of alleviating the cares of Bishop Carroll this new move only sought to enlarge his usefulness by allowing him to look over portions of his field which had been hitherto neglected. The Diocese of Baltimore then included that entire portion of the United States lying south of the St. Lawrence river and the Great Lakes. It stretched from Michigan to Florida and from Maine to Missouri. It included among its charges the civilized Indians of Maine and the savages of the Northwest territory; and as if all these did not entail sufficient responsibility, a portion of the West Indies owed spiritual allegiance to the Bishop of Baltimore. With the increase of the American Church the burden became too great for one man, and a division was made. Dr. Carroll was raised to the dignity of Archbishop, and four suffragan dioceses were created with their respective sees at Philadelphia, Boston, New York, and Bardstown, in Kentucky. The bishops appointed to fill the episcopal chairs thus created were: Dr. Egan, for Philadelphia; Dr. Cheverus, for Boston; Dr. Concannon, for New York, and Dr. Flaget, for Bardstown. All were holy ecclesiastics, whose earnest labors had rendered them in every manner worthy of the dignity with which they were honored. Three of the appointees (for Dr. Concannon died in Naples just before the time he intended to sail for America) presented themselves in St. Peter's Church, Baltimore, for consecration on the Sunday preceding and the Sunday following the Feast of All Saints in the year 1810. After their consecration Archbishop Carroll took the occasion of their presence to hold a conference on matters relating to the discipline and the future government of the American Church. The conference over, the Archbishop was relieved of much of the anxiety attendant upon the administration of so extensive a diocese, and he devoted his spare time and the remnant of his enormous energy to building up the educational and charitable institutions attached to the primatial see, and for five years the destinies of the American Church were guided by this holy man in a spirit of prudence and judgment.

The year 1815 was ebbing out when John Carroll, priest, patriot, and successor of the Apostles, was stricken with sickness unto death. In spite of his eighty years, in spite of his labors and privations, in spite of the length of the period he had figured in American ecclesiastical affairs, there were many who thought that the end was not yet. But they were mistaken. Representatives of the gay society with which he often mingled, and the expounders of strange creeds to whom he was a living sermon and who loved him as one of their own, gathered about the death-bed of the primate and joined in the prayers for the departing soul, to which the dying lips made clear and unequivocal response. Within the shadow of St. Peter's, stretched on the floor that he might die the more humbly, and with "*Miserere mei*" on his lips, the American patriarch passed away on the 9th of December, 1815.

There are at long intervals men whose lives are the keys to movements and whose existence furnishes the index to the history of the circles in which they moved. Such a man was Dr. Carroll. He became head of the American Church at a time when its future successful existence was little more than a hope; and he closed his eyes with the satisfaction that he had been instrumental in the realization of that hope. He was the embodiment of those religious principles and that holy energy which marked the early periods of Catholicity in the United States. No apology is, therefore, required for giving to him so large a portion of the space devoted to a period of which he was the central figure.

III.

There were a few who feared that when the directing hand of Archbishop Carroll was removed from the American Church its progress would not be as great or as rapid as it had been. But the destinies of the Church of Christ depend on no human agencies, and the greatest saint who may rule that Church is only the instrument of the Omnipotent. The removal by death of the venerable archbishop was, no doubt, a great blow to American Catholics. Every one felt as if he had lost a personal friend, as indeed he had. But all knew that the only proper way to do honor to the memory of the patriarch was to follow in his footsteps and to walk in the path which he had marked out. The Church continued to grow. Its numbers were increased by immigration from the Old World and conversion in the New. At times scandal was given by insubordinate priests, who felt that Archbishop Carroll's successors, the Most Revs. Leonard Neale and Ambrose Marechal, were not possessed of the firmness which had characterized the rule of the first bishop of the United States. In this, however, they were mistaken and the scandal given by rebellious ecclesiastics of Charleston, Norfolk and Philadelphia was in part repaired by an exposition of the true character of the rebellious men. The Sees of Charleston and St. Louis were added to the suffragans of the See of Baltimore. The See of Charleston was presided over by Bishop England, who had been called from the parish of Bandon, Ireland, to assume the direction of the Church in the Carolinas. He was a man possessed of the most penetrating judgment, and he was early struck with the necessity of co-operation on the part of the bishops. There were evils prevalent in all the existing dioceses which threatened to mar the harmonious existence of the American Church. One of these was the system of lay trusteeism, which had a tendency towards the disruption of congregations. There were other evils of as great magnitude which had to be coped with. United action was necessary, a uniform rule was desirable. In order to arrive at such unity it occurred to Bishop England that a council of prelates would be of incalculable assistance by facilitating the interchange of opinions and ideas. He communicated his plan to the Metropolitan, Archbishop James Whitfield, with the result that the latter issued an invitation to all the prelates under his jurisdiction to meet in the first Provincial Council of Baltimore in the autumn of 1829. The occasion was a memorable one, marking as it did the beginning of uniformity in the discipline of the American Church. Besides Archbishop Whitfield there were present at this council Bishops England, Flaget and Rosati and the two Fenwicks, who filled the Sees of Boston and Cincinnati. The council sat for several days, and embodied its work in thirty-eight decrees, which subsequently received the approbation of the Holy See. No little prudence and forethought was required of the assembled prelates. They were legislating for the half million Catholics of our day and perhaps for as many more who should succeed them before another council was held. The bishops did not betray their trust, and as a consequence their decrees have received uniform respect and commanded unvarying obedience during all the years that have elapsed since their formulation.

Besides dealing with other important matters the decrees tended towards checking the abuses attendant upon lay-trusteeism and towards the establishment of a Catholic book concern.

It was in the '30's that that incessant stream of immigration, which has since continued with uninterrupted vigor, began to flow from Ireland. Seven centuries of persecution had so worked upon the Irish mind that even when O'Connell wrung from the British government the deed of Irish religious independence, there were many who feared that the concession was made for some occult purpose. Across the sea they saw an independent and a prosperous land, which held out a constant invitation to all who sought escape from tyranny, and who yearned for freedom. The invitation was accepted, and from that day to this the Irish race has been furnishing more than its share of intellect and genius and talent to the American Church. The influx of so many immigrants did much to increase the number of American Catholics. They crowded into the cities, and made their uncertain way into the western regions of the country; and wherever they went they brought with them their priests and erected their altars. Changes took place; new dioceses were created, and in some cases the incumbents of old ones resigned their charges, while others passed to their reward. In the course of time the advisability of holding a second council became apparent, and it was convened in 1837 by Archbishop Whitfield, who had presided over the first assemblage of American prelates. The council effected changes in the methods of episcopal nominations, and devoted much of its time to a discussion of missions for the conversion of the negroes of Liberia and the Indians of the Northwest. By general consent both these charges were confided to the Society of Jesus, which took up the work with alacrity, and resumed among the Indians the missions which had been commenced by the school of Jogues and Menard, and they did not relinquish them until 1850, when one of their number, Rev. John Baptist Miege, was raised to the episcopal dignity, and the Indian Territory made a vicariate apostolic. During the years that followed, provincial councils were convened at Baltimore at intervals of four or five years, and the wisdom and the piety which marked the councils when they represented the nation continued to be their characteristic when other archiepiscopates were formed, and Baltimore ceased to be the only seat of an American archbishop. Important suggestions were made at these councils with regard to discipline, and not the least important of their acts was the declaration of the seventh Council of Baltimore (convened in May, 1849), that the definition by the Pope of the Immaculate Conception of the Blessed Virgin Mary as a dogma of the Roman Catholic Church would be looked upon with great satisfaction by the prelates. In the newly created provinces provincial councils were likewise held, and decrees formulated which received the sanction of the Holy Father. But these decrees had a binding force which was purely local in character. They failed to bear that authority with which the decrees of the Baltimore provincial councils were stamped when those bodies legislated for the entire American Church. This circumstance caused the American prelates to enter into a quiet but earnest movement looking towards the holding of National Councils. The result of the movement was that a summons was issued to all the bishops of the United States to meet in the Cathedral Church of the city of Baltimore on the 9th of May, 1852, for the discussion of questions affecting the interests of the Church in this country.

No such gathering had been before witnessed in the history of the American Church. Among its attendants were six archbishops and twenty-six bishops, all of whom were presided over by the Most Rev. Francis Patrick Kenrick, who had been transferred from the See of Philadelphia only a few years before. The entire episcopacy was present, from the Archbishop of Baltimore, to the Bishop of Monterey, who had to travel across the continent. Austere Jesuits, silent Trappists, bearded Franciscans and learned Benedictines represented their orders, and a dozen religious orders were present in the person of their superiors. The council was in session for a number of days, and the principal result of its labors was a request to the Holy See to establish eight new bishoprics, to raise San Francisco to an archiepiscopal see, and to constitute Upper Michigan a vicariate apostolic. This increase of the episcopacy was rendered necessary by the rapid growth of the Catholic population. Bishops no longer found themselves able to attend to the requirements of a large district, for the population had become concentrated and the trading posts of fifty years before had grown into promising cities. The calls for episcopal ministrations were so many that the increase in the number of bishops was fully justified by the exigencies of the times. The pastoral letter of the council was prepared by Archbishop Kenrick. It abounds in good counsels and directions to Catholics for their proper conduct, and has been characterized by many as the most truly apostolical document which ever emanated from such a body. The decrees of the council were, with some slight amendments, approved by the Roman Congregations, and the approval returned in the following year in an apostolic letter of the Holy Father. It had been originally intended that a National Council of the bishops of the United States should be held every ten years. In 1862, when the time came for the second Plenary Council, the country was in the midst of internecine strife. A civil war had dismembered the nation, and it was next to impossible for the prelates of the North and South, and the East and the West, to meet in National Council. At the close of the war, when the embers of sectional animosity had ceased to glow, preparations were begun for the postponed assembly. Martin John Spalding was then the successor of Archbishop Carroll, and a worthy one he was. He was the son of one of the oldest families of Maryland, and had been baptized by the apostolical Father Nerinckx. After some years of study in the seminary at Bardstown, Kentucky, he was sent to Rome to study theology and philosophy. His public defence of theses for the doctor's cap was so able an exhibition as to win for the young scholastic the encomiums of all who were present at his examination. Made coadjutor to the Bishop of Louisville in 1848, he succeeded the venerable Bishop Flaget on that prelate's death in 1850. On the death of the Archbishop of Baltimore in 1864, he was elevated by Papal rescript to the most dignified position in the American Church. This was the man who was commissioned Apostolic Delegate to the second Plenary Council held in 1866. That event exceeded the first council in magnificence, as much as the first council had been in advance of any religious event known before in this continent. In the sunshine of that October morning on which the council opened, six archbishops, thirty-seven bishops, three mitred abbots, and the representatives of thirteen religious bodies, followed by upwards of one hundred theologians, moved reverentially through the crowds which lined the streets of Baltimore, from the archiepiscopal residence to the metropolitan church. No such sight had been witnesssed on earth since the Council of Trent. Those who knew not Catholic unity were astonished that such an event could take place in a country which had been divided by civil war only a few months before. They could not understand how, after a strife which had dismembered the most powerful of the sects, the prayer of the Northern priest could be wafted to heaven on a cloud of incense with the petition of his Southern brother. They knew naught of what Father Ryan, in his address at the council, called "that faith in one Holy, Catholic and Apostolical Church which for fifteen centuries, from the Council of Nice to the second Council of Baltimore, has expressed the faith of her children." The solemn sessions of the council were conducted on a scale of the most solemn magnificence, while at the private sessions the questions engrossing the attention of the prelates are said to have been discussed with unequalled intelligence and judgment. It was not long until the decrees of the council, to which Cardinal Cullen alluded as a mine of theological learning, received their binding force from Rome, and at the Vatican Council of 1869, they were referred to as monuments to the correct judgment and thorough learning of those who took part in their formulation. They are unique in ecclesiastical legislation, and in all cases exhibit a desire on the part of the legislators to conform as far as possible with the usage of the Church on all points.

IV.

In our opening lines the assertion was ventured that the history of the Catholic Church in the United States would not be found to be unmixed with sorrow and persecution. Up to this point only the pleasing phases of that history have been dwelt upon. The outlines of the picture have been drawn, and the coloring laid in perhaps imperfectly. The toning now remains to be added,—the shadows are yet to be filled in, that the picture may form a true and a just whole.

As far back as 1830, a peculiar class of French and German refugees came to the hospitable shores of America. They brought with them little that was good and much that was vicious. Expelled from their native lands for their connection with secret societies which threatened the existence of the government, they sought to re-establish their infamous associations in this country. They were, in a great measure, successful. Their combinations were ostensibly directed against citizens of foreign birth, but were in reality meant as a persecution to the American arm of the Catholic Church. An intense popular feeling against Catholics was worked up, and unjustly. In spite of the fact that Catholics had shed their blood as freely in the days of the Revolution as their Protestant fellow-citizens, in spite of their hitherto unquestioned patriotism, in spite of their earnest protestations of thorough and uncompromising loyalty, an influential party became embued with the idea that they owed obedience to the Pope of Rome, who could be looked upon in no other light than as a foreign potentate. The party became known and flourished as the "American," and later as the "Know-Nothing" party. The embers of the excitement smouldered with an occasional outburst such as that which led to the destruction by incendiaries of the Convent of Mount St. Benedict, at Charlestown, Mass., when scores of young ladies escaped only at the peril of their lives. In 1852 the flames broke out afresh. The number of the French and German refugees had already been augmented by the arrival of a numerous band of Italian anarchists whom fear of the law's strong arm had driven from Italy. They re-formed their societies of Carbonari in America, and used all possible means to excite the passions of the American people against the Church. An opportune occasion for an exhibition of malevolence was soon presented. Monsignor Bedini, the Pope's nuncio to Brazil, had been commissioned by the venerable Pius IX to visit the United States and to personally convey to President Pierce and his Cabinet expressions of the Pope's warmest regard for the Executive and the nation over which he ruled. The visit of the Pope's nuncio was the red rag to the infuriated Italians, who had scarcely ceased conspiring against the nuncio's master within the very walls of his own city. The revolutionary papers attacked and villified the visitor, and at Cincinnati his life was threatened by a mob. Gavazzi and his German confreres preached death to the priest, and it was only by cutting short his intended stay in the United States, that the monsignor escaped with his life. But the hissing of the serpents which had been warmed at the American breast had their effect. The doctrine was heralded to the nation that

America was for Americans, and that foreigners, and especially Catholic foreigners, were engaged in treasonable plotting against the existence of the government. The whole country became inflamed. A secret society having as its end the extinction of the Catholic Church in America was formed, and its members were bound by oaths deep and dark. The party proscribed those who did not belong to it, and its members regarded as an enemy every man who could not give the password known only to the initiated. Brilliant intellects were fettered by the chains of prejudice, and they succumbed to the malign influence. The wild fanaticism practiced and preached defies the descriptive powers of human pen. No one but its victims could tell of its malevolence, and in a number of cases their tongues were hushed in death. To use the words of one who took part in the struggle, "Know-Nothingism was something worse than civil war; it was a struggle into which all the worst elements of politics and religion entered." It denounced and insulted every dignitary of the Catholic Church, from the first Pope of Rome to the humblest acolyte who served Mass in the church of the rudest hamlet.

The campaign of 1855 was conducted in several States with great acrimony. In Louisville, Kentucky, in Ellsworth, Maine, and in several other places, the culmination was reached in outrages on Catholics. The facts are well known to students of American history, who have blushed at the dishonor cast upon our country's fame and the unworthy acts done in the name of liberty. But in the year 1859, Virginia dealt the first blow to the supremacy of the "American" party by prostrating it in that State, and their power began to wane. Their purposes were no longer occult; their designs were no longer hidden. By the beginning of the year 1860 they had returned to the nothingness from which they had sprung.

But Know-Nothingism is not the only evil with which the Catholic Church has had to contend in the United States. For thirty years and more the Catholic population of this country has been forced to pay tribute to a system of godless education of which not one can conscientiously take advantage. The Catholic protests against paying for the education of other than their own children were made in the earliest days of the Know-Nothing era, and were hurled back as arguments in favor of the enmity of Catholics to free institutions.

But Know-Nothingism has passed away, and the school question still remains in all its glaring injustice. Millions of money are annually taken from Catholics for the support of schools in which they have no interest. The Catholic considers it unfair to tax him for the support of schools from which all ideas of religion are excluded, nor can he accept those in which a false religion is taught; for between godlessness and error the choice is only slightly in favor of the latter. The fight has been an earnest one on both sides. It has elicited and is to-day drawing forth the most solid arguments in favor of the Catholic doctrine. Some day the quarrel will be ended, some day justice will be done.

V.

We have seen, briefly, the history of the Church up to the close of the second Plenary Council. We have viewed its struggles and its successes, and have alluded to the persecution through which its children have had to pass. But since the last Plenary Council great changes have been effected and great advances made. The body spiritual has increased until the Catholic Church in the United States numbers seven millions of adherents. The favor of the Holy See has been shown by the appointment of an American cardinal. The growth of the Church has been exemplified by the erection of stately cathedrals and magnificent temples. Peace and war, love and enmity, prosperity and hardship have all caused her truths to become known and her counsels to be followed. Her relations with the republic have ever been of the most amicable character. The Church which built up and sustained San Marino, Andorra, Venice and a host of Old World republics could have no differences with a government more perfect than any of these had been. Her priests have marched and fasted, her sons have shed their blood on the battle-field, her daughters have carried solace and comfort to wounded bodies and lacerated hearts, with as much if not more devotion than have their fellow-citizens of other sects. And with the beginning of this third Plenary Council the American Church stands ready for a new era of activity, clad in a stronger mail of faith than ever before, with a brighter buckler of hope, with a more perfect shield of charity.

But could no other Church have done this? "O unconquerable Church of Rome! Church of all lands and all races, of all centuries and all seasons, with the same unvarying faith, the same priesthood, the same sacrifice, the same sacraments for the king and the peasant, the most learned philosopher and the most unlettered of men, for the Crœsus and the Lazarus; what Church but thou could have a mission for this land of ours, where Providence has gathered men of every race and tongue, and shown the very helplessness of schism and error by their utter incapacity to mould men into one homogeneous Christian body, instinct with faith, hope, and life that is in charity? This dost thou accomplish, O Catholic Church of America, and it is wonderful in our eyes."[1]

[1] John G. Shea, *American Catholic Quarterly Review*, vol. ix. p. 481.

The Cathedral, Baltimore.

THE COUNCILS OF BALTIMORE.[1]

BY HUGH P. McELRONE.

I.

FEW and scattered were the Catholics of the republic in the year 1791. The most of them perhaps were in the Diocese of Baltimore. It was therefore only natural that the Right Rev. John Carroll, its first Bishop, should have had the honor of presiding over the first ecclesiastical tribunal which adopted regulations for the Church in the United States; for the Province of Baltimore included at that time all the broad thousands of miles which are now divided into several provinces and many dioceses.

Accordingly, shortly after his appointment to the see, by episcopal summons, dated October 27, 1791, the Bishop of Baltimore called together his ecclesiastical dependents, and the synod met on November 7. It is curious to note at this day how small was the body assembled to legislate for what has developed into the mighty Church of America. The record contains the following names, besides that of Bishop Carroll: Very Rev. James Pellentz, Vicar-General; Revs. James Frambach, Robert Mollineux, Francis A. Fleming, Francis C. Nagot, John Ashton, Henry Pile, Leonard Neale, Charles Sewall, Sylvester Boarman, William Elling, James Vanhuftel, Robert Plunkett, Stanislaus Cerfoumont, Francis Beeston, Laurence Gressel, Joseph Eden, Louis C. Delavau, John Tessier and Anthony Garnier.

The legislation of the synod, which was apparently not sent to Rome for approval (at least there is no record of the fact), was highly approved by the first Provincial Council. Bishop Carroll was indeed worthy of all praise for the labor he bestowed upon the work, he taking the initiative in, if not indeed originating, all the decrees that were passed. Session first was occupied by

[1] Revised from articles in THE CATHOLIC MIRROR.

religious ceremonies, but the evening session of the day on which the synod assembled regulated the conditions of the Sacraments of Baptism and Confirmation. The whole of the next day was consumed in completing the decree on the Eucharist. Penance, extreme unction and matrimony were dealt with on the 9th. But the chiefest work was done on November 10, the fourth and last day of the synod. It was mostly devoted to issuing rules for the clergy to observe in the performance of their functions. The last decree of the little synod, the results of whose efforts were immediately felt, bore on the Paschal Communion, reinforcing the decree, "Omnis utriusque sexus," of the Lateran Council. Finally the bishop announced that Rev. John Ashton had been designated his coadjutor, and then, after a "Te Deum" was sung, the synod adjourned.

With not less approval did the Provincial Council of 1829 mention the articles of ecclesiastical discipline put forth by the then Archbishop Carroll, of Baltimore, in conjunction with the coadjutor bishop and the Bishops of Philadelphia, Boston, and Bardstown, Kentucky. The first article bears upon priests going from one diocese to another; the second on regulations for the secular and regular clergy; the third on the Scriptures, approving the Douay Bible; the fourth on parochial registers; the fifth on baptism; the sixth on sponsers; the seventh on the material for celebrating Mass; the eighth on matrimony, ordering the ceremony to be performed in churches where possible; the ninth directs pastors to warn their flocks against indulging in going to theatres or other public entertainments of a bad character, and reading immoral fables called novels—especially prohibiting the perusal of works which attack our holy religion.

The tenth article should be remarked upon at some length. The ridiculous charge has been frequently made that the Church has changed her attitude since the revolution of 1848 in regard to secret societies and their great prototype, Freemasonry. There are grounds for the charge to rest upon, astonishing as they may seem to Catholics. A passage from one of Joseph de Maistre's letters from St. Petersburg intimating that the operations of the Illuminati (the Nihilists of those days) were not unfavorable to the spread of the Catholic Church in Russia, has been garbled and extensively quoted in Protestant journals. Maistre never put the matter in the way the Church's enemies make it appear that he did, but even if he did we are not disposed to regard him as an authoritative Catholic writer. However, the tenth article of the disciplinary rules promulgated by Most Rev. John Carroll, Archbishop of Baltimore, and his suffragan bishops, in 1810, just about the period that Maistre wrote, effectually disposes of this calumny. In it they enjoin upon priests not to administer the Sacraments of the Church to those who belonged to Freemasonry, no matter in what shape they might put their connection with the condemned society.

These are the beginnings of ecclesiastical legislation in the United States. They are adduced first, in order to contrast how few were those ecclesiastics who took part compared to the host which attended the third Plenary Council; and secondly, to show how the legislation of the Church of this country, even as far back as 1791 and 1810, when Catholics were weak in numbers and she was unknown and despised, was pitched in the high and independent tone and firm attitude as to the verities of religion which has ever since marked the American Church and gained it admiration throughout the world.

II.

Nineteen years passed along after the promulgation of the disciplinary rules by Archbishop Carroll and his suffragans in 1810 before it was thought necessary to call together the growing episcopate of America to consult upon our Church affairs. The population had been increasing slowly but steadily, and to the list of bishops, which, on the former occasion, included only three besides the coadjutor of the archbishop, had been added a man of singular energy of character and a scope of genius which forecast the brilliant future of the American Church—Right Rev. John England, who was consecrated Bishop of Charleston (his diocese then including North and South Carolina and Georgia) in 1820. It was chiefly through his exertions that the first Provincial Council, which was really National, since it included the United States so far as they were mapped out into diocesan lines, was convened. In constant communication with Rome, the trusted adviser of the Propaganda, and the regular correspondent of the Propagation

Society, of Lyons, France, he was naturally looked upon, in effect, as the channel of connection between the centre of religion and the promising republic of the western hemisphere.

Accordingly, by letters issued in December, 1828, Most Rev. James Whitfield, who had been consecrated Archbishop of Baltimore, May 25, 1828, as the successor of Archbishop Marechal, summoned the following prelates to the first Provincial Council: Right Rev. Benedict J. Flaget, Bishop of Bardstown, Kentucky, consecrated November 4, 1810; Right Rev. John England, Bishop of Charleston, South Carolina, consecrated September 21, 1820; Right Rev. Edward Fenwick, Bishop of Cincinnati, consecrated January 13, 1822; Right Rev. Joseph Rosati, Bishop of St. Louis, consecrated March 25, 1804; Right Rev. Benedict Fenwick, Bishop of Boston, consecrated November 1, 1825; Very Rev. William Matthews, Vicar Apostolic and Administrator of Philadelphia, consecrated February 26, 1828. Among those who were designated as assistant theologians may be mentioned the choice of the Bishop of Bardstown, Rev. Francis Patrick Kenrick, who was also one of the secretaries of the Council, and the choice of Bishop England, Rev. Simon Gabriel Bruté—both names which, later on, shone high in the galaxy of the American episcopate—the former destined to preside over our first Plenary Council.

On the fourth day of October the council held its first session. That and the following four days were devoted to the reading of Papal documents, and to the unfolding of the Roman Church's views in regard to America by Bishop England. Ten days were then spent in a careful consideration of disciplinary rules, which are embodied in the "Concilia Provincialia Baltimori," 1851. They include not only an amplification of Archbishop Carroll's wise regulations, but also contain additions chiefly from Bishop England, the fruit of extended and most active observation. The number of these decrees is thirty-eight. They embrace nearly the whole field of Catholic discipline, and not only the prompt approval of them by the Roman Congregations, but also the endorsement and continuation of them by subsequent councils of American prelates, show how well they were framed and how singularly fortunate they were in meeting the anticipated needs of succeeding times.

One of the evils which Bishop England early recognized and vigorously worked against was the practical unaccountability of priest to bishop, and in turn of layman to priest. Things were generally in a loose state, many unworthy priests who had been sent out of Europe taking up their abode in various places, either without the authorization of the spiritual rulers or else on false pretences, and thus creating scandal among the community at large. There were few native priests; most of them came from foreign parts; and in this another drawback lay. A large part of them were the French refugees from the terrors of the French Revolution. Good and holy men they were, and their exertions were recognized as bearing the best fruits. But they were believers in monarchy; and their horror of republicanism was increased by the sad hardships which the unworthy French republicans had inflicted upon themselves and by the memory of the cruel scenes which they had witnessed. But slightly acquainted with our language, the genius of our institutions and the temper of our people, they often gave vent to sayings that were magnified and distorted by the enemies of the Church, and this had a great deal to do with the preservation of England's Puritan Tradition in this country. Accordingly we find this our first Provincial Council occupied largely with the subjects indicated.

After making several regulations in regard to the administration of the Sacraments, another matter is touched upon. It has been charged that the Church's policy has greatly changed on the subject of the danger to Catholic youth from education in mixed schools. Certainly the evil is aggravated now by the vast expansion of the system, but as far back as 1829 we see no difference in the tone of the prelates—that is, measured by the lesser danger at that day. The thirty-third, thirty-fourth and thirty-fifth decrees deal with the matter in no honied tones. Wherever parochial schools are possible, they are ordered to be opened, and Sunday-schools are insisted upon as an absolute necessity; when a school is found in which Catholic doctrines or moral principles are attacked, it is the duty of the pastor in its neighborhood to prohibit attendance at it by the children of his flock.

In the beginning of the following year these decrees were returned as approved by the Propaganda Congregation and the Pope. A most favorable impression was made upon the Church at large.

c

III.

It was only four years after the first Provincial Council that a pressing need was felt for a new one. Accordingly, in the last days of October, 1833, in obedience to the summons issued some months before, the prelates of the United States and their theologians assembled once more in the metropolitan city to consult on the affairs of the Church.

One of the most interesting features in the history of the Councils of Baltimore is the notation of the names of ecclesiastics and of their positions, who afterwards rose to high places in the Church. To use a military expression, the illustrious prelates, who have gained a place in the world-wide history of the universal Church, did not reach their stations by the mere force of precedence; they won their spurs by hard work. In addition to those who attended the last council we find: Right Rev. John Dubois, Bishop of New York, consecrated on the 29th of October, 1826; Right Rev. Michael Portier, Bishop of Mobile, consecrated November 5, 1826; both of whom failed to attend the former council because of the delay in their return to this country from Rome; Right Rev. Francis Patrick Kenrick, Bishop of Arathensia and coadjutor of the Bishop of Philadelphia, consecrated June 6, 1830; Right Rev. Frederick Résé, Bishop of Detroit, consecrated October 6, 1833; Right Rev. John B. Purcell, Bishop of Cincinnati, consecrated October 13, 1833; the last being the successor of Right Rev. Edward Fenwick, then dead. Among the assistant theologians may be mentioned several names which are still familiar to our ears: Revs. Peter Fredet, William McSherry, Samuel Eccleston, Andrew Byrne (the first student in the seminary established by Bishop England in Charleston), John Hughes and Simon Bruté.

The most important business before this small but illustrious assembly was the erection of new dioceses and settling the boundaries of the old. The Pope, Gregory XVI, by a bull issued in the July of the following year, approved the decrees on these subjects. For instance, the Diocese of Boston, which is now a flourishing province with many suffragan sees, included the six States of New England—"that is" says the bull, "Massachusetts, Maine, New Hampshire, Rhode Island, Connecticut and Vermont."

The Diocese of New York comprised not only the whole of that Empire State, but also the counties of Sussex, Bergen, Morris, Essex, Somerset, Middlesex and Monmouth in New Jersey. Virginia and West Virginia were subject to the Archbishop of Baltimore. The Diocese of Philadelphia consisted of the whole State of Pennsylvania, of Delaware, and seven counties in New Jersey. It needs only the mention of these facts to call attention to the contrast now afforded by the numerous compact sees which cover all this territory.

Among the other notable decrees passed and approved at Rome are two placing the Indian and Negro missions under the special charge of the Society of Jesus. Another decree called for a correct edition of the Rituale Romanum, and the last fixed the date for the opening of the next council—the third Sunday after Easter in the year 1837. The second Provincial Council adjourned October 27, 1833.

IV.

There was no increase in the number of prelates who attended the third council. Its decrees, as were those of the preceding Council, are signed by ten names. Archbishop Whitfield had passed to his reward, and Archbishop Eccleston had succeeded, and he presided over the assemblage. Dr. C. I. White, one of America's most learned scholars, was the associate secretary of the council, and a great deal of its labor fell upon him.

All the sessions of this council were short, and the time of it extended only from the 17th to the 22d of April, inclusive. The decrees that it passed are printed upon three pages, and are confined in their scope to clerical and liturgical regulations. The Roman Ritual of the Sacred Congregation recommended by Pope Gregory XVI at their request for an authoritative version was adopted.

In 1836 Bishop England, on being invited to do so, addressed a series of letters to the Propagation Society of Lyons, which had been most generous in its contributions to the cause in America, on the progress and the state of the Church in this country. He estimated the Catholic population at 1,500,000, after having consulted all the authorities within his reach and having employed the most careful inquiry. According to the calculations which he adduces there should have been at least 3,900,000 Catholics in the United States—a loss of 2,400,000. Among the various causes which he assigned for this defection there are prominently placed by him—unworthy priests, foreign priests, who did not understand the nature of our people, and a scarcity even of the material that could be got. In the first class were many who simply disgraced the name and created the greatest scandals; others, who, though honest enough, lacked that polish and refinement which enable one to take a place in society; for the strange theory prevailed in Europe that Americans were rude and uncultured, perhaps lived in log huts and dressed in homespun, and that any kind of priests would do for them; the consequence of which opinion was that many of the priests at that time not only repelled non-Catholics, but did much by their manners to drive Catholics from the Church. Many of the foreign priests were French, the objections to whom have been stated. In order to meet these wants measures were adopted in this council looking to a provision of means for educating native priests; and the beginnings made then have developed, under the watchful care of the zealous and vigilant succession of prelates who have ruled the American Church, until to-day we see in America a band of priests whom it would be hard to match in any country of the world.

Some of the Papal rescripts approving the council's decrees were not received until 1841, after the next council was held.

V.

It is now seemed a settled matter that councils should be held every three years. Accordingly, in 1840, 1843, 1846 and 1849 four councils followed the others so happily and successfully planned by the great brain of Bishop England. When the fifth met he was absent from the list of prelates—gone to that bourne whence no traveler returns. Archbishop Eccleston presided over the four councils now under consideration.

Little was done except to confirm and strengthen precedent legislation, and to add such regulations as the needs of the day demanded. The steady increase in the prelates is, however, observable. Thirteen signed the decrees of the 1840 council, and the following ones bear the signatures of fifteen (sixteen counting Bishop England's place filled by the administrator of the diocese,

Very Rev. R. S. Baker), twenty-three, and twenty-five, respectively. Right Rev. Francis Patrick Kenrick appears as the Bishop of Philadelphia, and Right Rev. John Hughes as Bishop of New York; Right Rev. John McCloskey, Bishop of Albany, and Right Rev. Martin John Spalding, Bishop of Lengonensis *in partibus*—all of them names which require only to be mentioned now, for they are household words throughout the United States. Among the attendant theologians are also many names since become familiar throughout the land for theological lore and ripe scholarship, as also for having attained high ecclesiastical stations. For instance, the Revs. Boniface Wimmer, Joseph S. Alemany, C. I. White, J. F. Wood, John Loughlin, Michael Heiss, Bernard O'Reilly, William H. Elder, C. L. Pise and others—some of them dead, some of them living to-day—but all of them so well known that it requires only the mention of their names. Thus, it will be seen that the episcopate was steadily gaining, not only in numbers, but in the quality of the material composing it; and a number of wise theologians were growing up, ready to add their lore to its assembled deliberations.

The decree issued in 1810 by the then few prelates in America against secret societies has been mentioned. The seventh decree of the fourth council repeats and reinforces the disciplinary article of Archbishop Carroll and his suffragans. Members of these societies were deprived then as now of participation in the Sacraments, and pastors were urged to exhort the faithful not to join them. This was in 1840, still a good while before the Catholic Church is said to have changed her policy in regard to secret societies and under a Pope before Pius IX, who, the enemy alleges, was scared by the revolution of 1848. To Catholics no proof was needed; but we would like to ask our friends the enemy how they will overcome the fact of these decrees, which were duly approved at Rome by Gregory XVI?

The other decrees of these councils related chiefly to clerical regulations, as, for instance, forbidding one clergyman to trespass upon the parish of another. Only five decrees were passed by the sixth council, and the last one merely fixed, as usual, the date of the following meeting. One thing, however, makes it notable. Pope Gregory XVI had died, and Pius IX, under whose fostering care the rapid growth of the Church in the succeeding thirty years was witnessed in this country, had succeeded and for the first time addressed his American followers through the Archbishop of Baltimore. Even thus early, when he had just mounted the Papal throne, and although his letter is very short, he manifests his love and admiration for the vigorous young Church of the West, destined, in his prophetic opinion, to make up for the melancholy losses in Europe. The energy of our episcopate, considering the difficulties they had to struggle with and the vast extent of country covered by their dioceses, moves him to wonder, which he freely expresses—and, indeed, Pius IX's favorites were always the American Bishops, American Catholics—the nation itself. "I am more truly Pope in America than in any other country," he used to say. The Roman cardinals called Bishop England, on account of his untiring industry and celerity of movement, the "steam bishop." Pius IX knew him well before Charleston's great bishop died—several years anterior to the Pope's succession to the throne; and the tradition of him who was the originator of the American councils and his brother prelates yet remained. A new generation was now at hand, but they were worthy heirs of the robes worn by those rugged heroes, our first bishops, who metaphorically fought their way into the United States and cleared the paths for those that followed them.

Although the dogma of the Immaculate Conception of the Blessed Virgin was not defined by the Holy See until five years after the holding of the seventh council, we find recorded here a letter from the Pope inculcating devotion to her in the Immaculate Conception; and the two first decrees relate to this grand, glorious and pious subject. In them the Catholics of America are urged to pay particular devotion to the Holy Mother of God in the Immaculate Conception, and our country placed under her special protection. It is notable to behold this unanimous demand, as it were, of the American episcopate for the promulgation of the dogma. They, in common with their brethren throughout the Catholic world, asked that it be made a doctrine of the faith, and when five years had passed the Holy Father acceded to the wishes of his children by solemnly promulgating it. It is an illustration of how wise and cautious the proceedings of the Holy See are. It does not originate anything; it waits until a question is raised, and when the universal voice is for its approval or condemnation it speaks, guided by the counsels of the Holy Ghost.

The last decree of the council fixed the date of the first Plenary or National Council for 1850, but the subsequent delays necessitated by providing for the divisions of provinces and dioceses, and the appointments of rulers thereof, prevented it from assembling before 1852.

VI.

At the conclusion of the seventh Provincial Council (and it must be remembered that these councils were really national) a petition to the Holy Father was adopted asking the erection of new archdioceses, with the reservation of primatial powers to the metropolitan See of Baltimore.[1] The petition was accepted, and the consequence was the erection of six provinces out of the single original archdiocese which had for half a century covered the whole country. In these, various Provincial Councils were held to adopt regulations suitable to the wants of their people. In doing so, however, it speedily became obvious that much confusion would follow from the fact that varying rules prevailed in each of the provinces. It was necessary that some central landmark, as it were, should be set up as a guide for all. Hence, having received letters as Delegate Apostolic from the Holy See, the Archbishop of Baltimore issued a call, November 21, 1851, to the other archbishops and their suffragans, for the first Plenary Council of the United States to assemble in the following May.

Archbishop Eccleston, who had presided over several of the Provincial Councils, had passed away, and the Most Rev. Francis Patrick Kenrick occupied the primatial see. Let us note the other archbishops and the order in which they are ranked: Most Rev. Francis N. Blanchet, Archbishop of Oregon; Most Rev. Peter Richard Kenrick, Archbishop of St. Louis; Most Rev. Anthony Blanc, Archbishop of New Orleans; Most Rev. John Hughes, Archbishop of New York; and Most Rev. John B. Purcell, Archbishop of Cincinnati. There were twenty-three bishops, among whom is notable the Right Rev. John McCloskey, Bishop of Albany—now our illustrious cardinal—and Right Rev. Martin John Spalding, Bishop of Louisville, afterwards Archbishop of Baltimore.

The council lasted eleven days—from the 10th to the 20th of

---

[1] Ut Sedes Metropolitana Baltimorensis Primatus honore gaudeat, cui Sedes omnes, tam Metropolitanæ quam Episcopales in Fœderatis Americæ Septentrionalis Statibus et Territoriis, subjaceant.

May inclusive. There were many weighty questions to be considered, and the first that came before the body was the lack of uniformity in the provincial decrees of the preceding two or three years. Accordingly the second decree bears upon this point by extending the decrees of the seven Provincial Councils of Baltimore to all the dioceses of the Federal Union. There were in all twenty-five decrees. The majority relate to ecclesiastical discipline, such as re-adopting the Rituale Romanum approved by the first Provincial Council, fixing the periods during which a bishop might, for various reasons, absent himself from his diocese, exhorting bishops to consult, when possible, aged, learned and experienced priests in their dioceses before promulgating rules and regulations, etc. Among the decrees may be noted the following: The 9th provides that priests coming from Europe to settle in the United States should be required to show credentials from the bishops of the dioceses whence they come in order to obtain a station from the American bishop to whom they applied. The 11th orders the bans of marriage to be published in all the dioceses without fail, and exhorts the clergy not only to be emphatic in doing so, but to diligently seek out whether any grave obstacles exist in each case. The 13th deals with the school question. In it the bishops in their respective dioceses are earnestly exhorted to take into grave consideration the great and increasing evil of youth growing up ignorant of God and the teachings of His Church; and, if it was possible, to establish a school by the side of every church. The next decree provides that each province should have at least one seminary for training priests and supplying the thin ranks so inadequately filled by the recruits from Europe.

Among the acts of this our first Plenary Council was the establishment of a sodality to pray for the conversion of non-Catholics. A petition was forwarded to the Holy Father asking that indulgences be granted to the prayers offered up; to which the late glorious Pope replied with his accustomed benignity, freely bestowing upon them the treasures of heaven.

At the time the council was held there was in this country a Catholic population of about 4,000,000. It would be a moderate estimate to say that a much larger number than this had been lost to the Church. As will be seen above the prelates recognized this melancholy fact. They speak of the great and increasing evil

of youth being allowed to grow up in a godless state; and they devote a decree to the subject.

Between the first and second Plenary Councils lies a long, troubled and bloody chapter of American history. Not that the quarrels of men can effect the calm course of the Church, but material obstacles necessarily intervened. In the meantime there were held three truly Provincial Councils in Baltimore; but the design is to treat only those of national extent, and we pass on to the second Plenary Council.

VII.

In coming to treat upon the second Plenary Council, one feels that we are touching almost contemporary history. It is within the recollection of thousands now living, and it would be useless to dwell upon it to the extent that its importance will demand and will receive hereafter. However, there are some things in connection with it which should be noticed here in order to contrast it with the former councils.

But before going into any details about it, let us observe the difference between the Catholic Church, which retains the spirit as well as the doctrines of her Founder, Jesus Christ, and the false sects which could only imitate the human passions of their earthly founders. From 1861 to 1865, the United States were torn by one of the fiercest civil wars on record. In that terrible struggle Catholics were not backward on either side. They were found in the forefront of the battle in the Federal and in the Confederate armies; on every field their blood was freely poured out for the cause they had espoused. But while Catholic met Catholic hilt to hilt in defence of what each side considered to be their country and its rights, they were ready to kneel as brothers in the same Church; they never dreamed of importing their quarrels into the calm sanctuary of the Lord. So, while armies marched and the sword flashed up and down the land, the Church of America remained one, undivided, indivisible. There were a Presbyterian Church North and a Presbyterian Church South; a Methodist Church North and a Methodist Church South; and, strange as it may sound, these divisions hated each other even worse than the sectaries hated the Papists. What more decisive proof can be adduced to show that the Church has the spirit of that Christ who prayed that His followers might in religion, be united even as the Father and He were united? And what more decisive proof can be adduced to show the falsehood of the jarring sects, ready to split in two during those very trials which God sends upon the wicked earth to try men's souls?

Scarcely had the echoes of war died away when the Most Rev. Martin John Spalding, Archbishop of Baltimore, on the 19th of March, 1866, issued a call, as Apostolic Delegate of the Holy See, to the archbishops and bishops of the United States to assemble in this city for the purpose of consulting on the affairs of the Church. The date for the council had been fixed for 1862, but, as the letter says, it could not then be held on account of the disturbed state of the times. In response to the call, there met in the autumn of 1866 seven archbishops, thirty-seven bishops, one administrator, one procurator, and two mitred abbots. Among the notable things which we find recorded in the names of those taking part in this council are these: The present Apostolic Delegate and Archbishop of Baltimore, Most Rev. James Gibbons, acted as assistant chancellor to the chancellor, Rev. Thomas Foley; while Father Corcoran, the chief secretary of the third Plenary Council just closed, was the chief secretary of the second. The theologians included such well-known names as these: Revs. J. L. Spalding, P. J. Ryan, Edward Fitzgerald, F. X. Weninger, S.J., A. M. Toebbe, N. J. Perché, Francis McNierny, J. B. Brouillet, M. Marty, T. A. Becker, B. J. McQuaid, F. X. Leray, J. Benoit, T. F. Hendricken, D. Manucy, T. Mullen, A. S. Healy, John McElroy, S.J., etc., who are known now from Maine to Texas for their intellectual acquirements and the high stations they occupied or occupy in the Church.

The second point to which we desire to call particular attention is the completeness of the body of decrees passed by the second Plenary Council as compared with the precedent ones. They take up a volume as large as that which includes all those of the councils which we have been reviewing in these pages. The first portion is a thorough digest of Christian doctrine and the second a summary of discipline for the American Church. For the convenience of those who desire to refer to the volume, it is arranged in chapters and sections and indexed fully. Everything about it bears the stamp of Archbishop Spalding's commanding genius, assisted by the scholarly talents of his brother prelates and the theologians of the council. Well might Archbishop Corrigan, in his sermon on "Our Deceased Prelates" (given elsewhere in full) speaking of Archbishop Spalding, exclaim: "The generation to come will have reason to bless his memory for all that he accomplished for the Church in America."

Title X of chapter IV, p. 243, contains a specially interesting decree. The council was swift in recognizing the immense change brought about by the emancipation of the slaves, and this long and careful decree relates to efforts for their conversion. It begins by reciting the well-known fact that Protestants have never converted a heathen people and by dwelling on the deplorable condition of the manumitted negroes, plunged in darkness and Fetichism. Each archbishop is exhorted to make a careful study of the situation in regard to the blacks in his province and to take such steps as he thinks proper to Christianize this unfortunate people. It will be remembered how this decree and the consequent acts of Provincial Councils excited the ire of a bigoted part of the American press, and how a certain New York pictorial "Journal of Barbarism" libelled the clergy of the American Church until the indignant protests of the fair-minded American people compelled it to desist. In order to show the calm and temperate tone of the prelates, in such striking contrast to the disturbed feelings on both sides at that time, a part of the council's pastoral letter is quoted:

"We must all feel that in some manner a new and most extensive field of charity and devotedness has been opened to us by the emancipation of the immense slave population of the South. We could have wished, that in accordance with the action of the Catholic Church in past ages, in regard to the serfs of Europe, a more gradual system of emancipation could have been adopted, so that they might have been in some measure prepared to make a better use of their freedom than they are likely to do now. Still the evils which must necessarily attend upon the sudden liberation of so large a multitude, with their peculiar dispositions and habits, only make appeal to our Christian charity and zeal, presented by their forlorn condition, the more forcible and imperative. We urge upon the clergy and people of our charge the most generous co-operation with the plans which may be adopted by the bishops of the dioceses in which they are, to extend to them that Christian education and moral restraint of which they stand in such need. Our only regret in regard to the matter is, that our means and opportunity of spreading over them the protecting and salutary influences of our holy religion are so restricted."

There is not a thoughtful man in America to-day who will not endorse this wonderfully sagacious forecast of the American bishops. The truth is, the Church has the experience of ages; she is not moved by the evanescent passions of the moment; but, guided from on high, she moves forward calmly and steadily; her prelates catch her spirit and "like stars to their appointed heights they rise."

Parochial and industrial schools are recommended, nay, commanded, where possible, in two decrees. The relations of Church and State are luminously explained. Many of the popular theories of to-day are condemned, Spiritism (falsely called Spiritualism) being described as the work of Satan and his attendant demons. In conclusion we quote the weighty words of the council on the newspaper press:

"We cheerfully acknowledge the services the Catholic press has rendered to religion, as also the disinterestedness with which, in most instances, it has been conducted, although yielding to publishers and editors a very insufficient return for their labors. We exhort the Catholic community to extend to these publications a more liberal support, in order that they may be enabled to become more worthy the great cause they advocate. We remind them that the power of the press is one of the most striking features of modern society; and that it is our duty to avail ourselves of this mode of making known the truths of our religion and removing the misapprehensions which so generally prevail in regard to them."

To reinforce the above, the letter of Pope Pius IX, February 12, 1866, is adduced, in which he speaks of the evil secular press which is animated by a diabolical hatred of our holy religion, and of the necessity of having a Catholic press to counteract the mischievous influence of those who have seized upon the art invented by a Catholic and turned it into an engine of destruction against the Church.

The last decree of the council is devoted to the recommendation of the erection of fifteen new episcopal sees.

There were many interesting questions canvassed in this council and in regard to which there are contained in the volume before us[1] several letters back and forth between the Roman Congregations and the American prelates. But we have already outrun our limits, and must close by noting the impulse which the council gave to the progress of the Church in America. In a period of eighteen years the number of the hierarchy has doubled; the number of priests has risen from about 3,000 to about 8,000; churches, from 3,500 to 8,500; while the Catholic population, which was 5,500,000 in 1866, is to-day over 8,000,000—some placing it as high as 10,000,000.

[1] "Concilii Plenarii Baltimorensis II. Acta et Decreta." Editio Altera Mendis Expurgata. Baltimore, MDCCCLXXX.

THE THIRD PLENARY COUNCIL.

THE third Plenary Council was formally opened in the Cathedral of Baltimore on Sunday, November 9, and continued for four weeks, closing on Sunday, December 7, 1884.

A conference of the American bishops had been held in Rome the preceding year, at which, under the guidance of Congregations of Roman cardinals, the *schema* of our third National Council were prepared, and the Most Rev. James Gibbons, D.D., Archbishop of Baltimore, was appointed by our Most Holy Lord, Leo XIII, Pope, as Apostolic Delegate, to preside over the august assemblage which recently closed in Baltimore.

The number of prelates who took part was nearly double that of those who attended the second Plenary Council. The members were divided in rank as follows: Fourteen archbishops, sixty bishops, five visiting bishops from Canada and Japan, seven abbots, one prefect apostolic, eleven monsignors, eighteen vicars general, twenty-three superiors of religious orders, twelve rectors of seminaries, and ninety theologians. A large number of clergymen from all parts of the country participated in the ceremonies.

I.

At 9.30 A.M. of the opening day the prelates met at the archiepiscopal residence, and being joined by the clergy, moved in solemn procession through the streets to the Cathedral. The following was the order observed: Cross-bearer carrying the processional cross; seminarians of St. Sulpice; regular clergy; secular clergy; chanters; theologians of the council; officials of the council; superiors of religious orders; rectors of theological seminaries; Very Rev. and Rt. Rev. monsignors; Rt. Rev. mitred abbots; Rt. Rev. bishops; Most Rev. archbishops; censer-bearer carrying the censer; archiepiscopal cross-bearer between two acolytes; assistant priest of the Most Rev. Apostolic Delegate; Most Rev. Apostolic

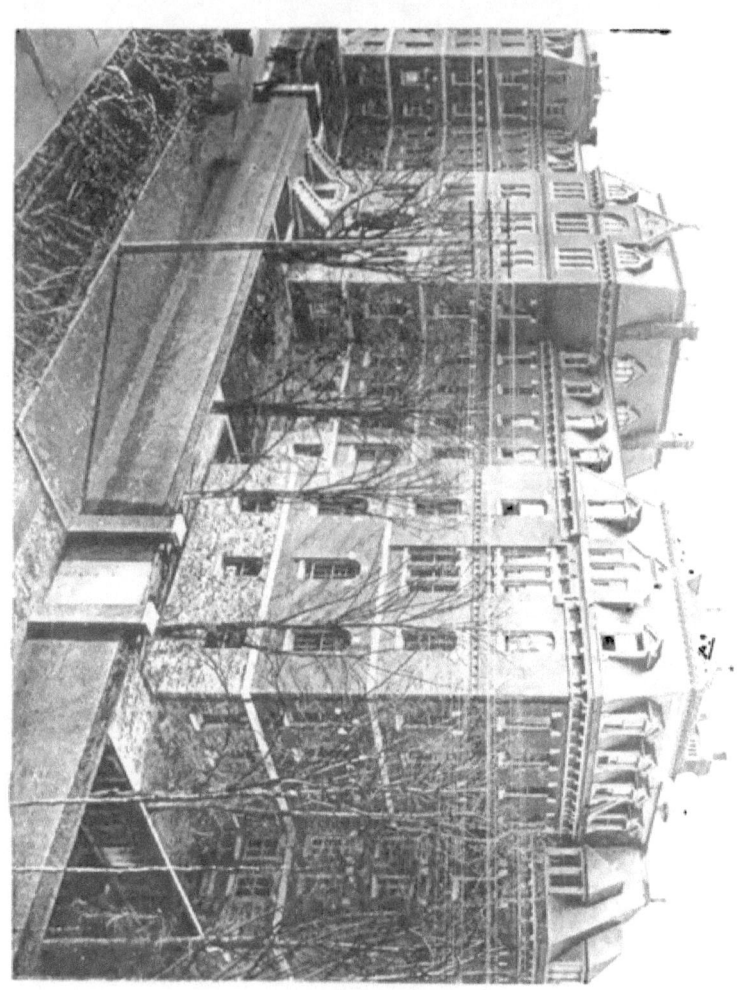

Delegate between his deacons of honor; insignia-bearers of the Most Rev. Apostolic Delegate.

The seminarians, Rev. clergy and chanters were vested in cassock, surplice and biretum; the Rev. regular clergy in the habit of their respective orders; the theologians in amice, alb, cincture, red stole and red chasuble; the officials of the council, superiors of religious orders, rectors of seminaries and monsignors in surplice (or rochet), amice, red cope and biretum; the Rt. Rev. mitred abbots in the habit of their respective orders, red cope and plain white mitre; Rt. Rev. bishops and Most Rev. archbishops in rochet, amice, red cope and plain gold mitre; the assistant priest in surplice, amice, red cope and biretum; the deacons of honor in amice, alb, cincture and red dalmatic; the Most Rev. Apostolic Delegate in amice, alb, cincture, red stole, red cope and precious mitre.

During the procession the hymns *Veni Creator Spiritus* (The Hymn to the Holy Ghost), *Ave Maris Stella* (The Hymn to the Blessed Virgin), and the Psalms 80, 83 and 86 were sung by the Rev. clergy and choir.

The Most Rev. Apostolic Delegate on reaching the altar sang the Prayer to the Holy Ghost, and to the Blessed Virgin, Patroness of the Cathedral. Pontifical High Mass was celebrated by the Most Rev. Peter Richard Kenrick, D.D., Archbishop of St. Louis, in presence of the Most Rev. Apostolic Delegate, who occupied the throne at the Gospel side of the sanctuary.

At the end of the Mass the Most Rev. celebrant retired to the sacristy, accompanied by his attendant ministers. The Most Rev. Patrick J. Ryan, D.D., Archbishop of Philadelphia, then ascended the pulpit and preached the opening sermon, the subject being: "The Church in Her Councils."

After the sermon the ceremonies proper to the opening session were begun. They were as follows: Antiphon and psalm by the choir; prayer by the Apostolic Delegate; litany of the saints by the choir; prayer by the Apostolic Delegate; Gospel by the deacon; hymn, *Veni Creator*, by the choir; address by the Apostolic Delegate; formal opening of the council; reading of preliminary decrees which regard the rules to be observed in the council, etc., etc.; roll of members called; profession of faith made by all the members of the council; announcement of the date of the following session; Papal Benediction by the Apostolic Delegate; return of the procession to the archiepiscopal residence.

II.

On the Sundays during the council, the public ceremonies in the evening consisted of Pontifical Vespers, sermon and Benediction of the Blessed Sacrament. On the Mondays, Tuesdays, Wednesdays and Fridays of each week the public ceremonies in the evening consisted of a sermon and Benediction of the Blessed Sacrament. Every Sunday and Thursday except the first Thursday, there was a solemn session of the council, at which the two houses of the bishops and theologians met and passed upon the decrees. The following are the dates of the sermons preached by the prelates and given elsewhere, except the two in Latin: Sunday, November 9, 10.30 A.M., "The Church in her Councils," by Most Rev. P. J. Ryan, D.D., Archbishop of Philadelphia; 7.30 P.M., "The Unity of the Church," by Right Rev. J. Shanahan, D.D., Bishop of Harrisburg; Monday, November 10, "The Church—the Support of Just Government," by Right Rev. J. Ireland, D.D., Bishop of St. Paul; Tuesday, November 11, "The Church and Science," by Right Rev. T. A. Becker, D.D., Bishop of Wilmington; Wednesday, November 12, "The Necessity of Revelation," by Right Rev. R. Gilmour, D.D., Bishop of Cleveland; Thursday, November 13, "De Mortuis—Our Deceased Prelates," by Most Rev. M. A. Corrigan, D.D., Coadjutor Archbishop of New York; Friday, November 14, "Indian Missions," by Most Rev. C. J. Seghers, D.D., Archbishop of Oregon; Sunday, November 16, 10.30 A.M., "The Priesthood," by Most Rev. W. H. Elder, D.D., Archbishop of Cincinnati; 7.30 P.M., "The Higher Education of the Priesthood," by Right Rev. J. L. Spalding, D.D., Bishop of Peoria; Monday, November 17, "Faith and Reason," by Right Rev. J. A. Watterson, D.D., Bishop of Columbus; Tuesday, November 18, "Christian Marriage," by Right Rev. M. J. O'Farrell, D.D., Bishop of Trenton; Wednesday, November 19, "The Observation of Feasts, etc.," by Right Rev. S. V. Ryan, D.D., Bishop of Buffalo; Thursday, November 20, "De Sacerdotio—The Holy Priesthood," by Most Rev. J. S. Alemany, D.D., Archbishop of San Francisco; Friday, November 21, "The Missions for the Colored People," by Right Rev. W. H. Gross, D.D., Bishop of Savannah; Sunday, November 23, 10.30 A.M., "The Sacrifice of the Mass," by Right Rev. E. Fitzgerald, D.D., Bishop of Little Rock; Monday, November 24,

Most Rev. Michael Heiss, D.D.

"The Catholicity of the Church," by Right Rev. J. O'Connor, D.D., Vicar-Apostolic of Nebraska; Tuesday, November 25, "Catholic Societies," by Right Rev. J. J. Keane, D.D., Bishop of Richmond; Wednesday, November 26, "The Progress of the Church in the United States," by Right Rev. B. J. McQuaid, D.D., Bishop of Rochester; Thursday, November 27, "De Dignitate Sacerdotali—The Dignity of the Holy Priesthood," by Most Rev. M. Heiss, D.D., Archbishop of Milwaukee; "Thanksgiving Day," by Right Rev. J. L. Spalding, D.D., Bishop of Peoria, Ill.; Friday, November 28, "The Blessed Virgin Mary, Patroness of the Church in the United States," by Right Rev. F. S. Chatard, D.D., Bishop of Vincennes; Sunday, November 30, 10.30 A.M., "The Sanctity of the Church," by Right Rev. J. Hennessy, D.D., Bishop of Dubuque; Thursday, December 4, 10.30 A.M., "The Papacy," by Rev. W. Wayrich, C.SS.R.; Sunday, December 7, 10.30 A.M., "The Work of the Council," by Right Rev. J. L. Spalding, D.D., Bishop of Peoria, Ill.

At St. Alphonsus's Church, which was used as a pro-Cathedral, the following sermons were preached in the German language: November 9, Sunday evening, the Most Rev. Michael Heiss, D.D., Archbishop of Milwaukee. Subject, "The Councils of the Church—Their History and Their Usefulness;" November 12, Wednesday evening, Rt. Rev. Martin Marty, O.S.B., D.D., Vicar Apostolic of Dakota Territory. Subject, "The Church—Her Indestructibility and Infallibility;" November 14, Friday evening, Rt. Rev. Caspar H. Borgess, D.D., Bishop of Detroit. Subject, "The Church—Her Unity and Sanctity;" November 16, Sunday evening, Rt. Rev. Joseph Dwenger, D.D., Bishop of Fort Wayne. Subject, "The Church—Her Apostolicity and Catholicity; or, The Reformation is in Principle a Denial of the Divinity of Christ;" November 19, Wednesday evening, Rt. Rev. Francis Xav. Krautbauer, D.D., Bishop of Green Bay. Subject, "The Church in America—Especially the German Element;" November 21, Friday evening, Rt. Rev. Joseph Rademacher, D.D., Bishop of Nashville. Subject, "Catholic Schools—Their Necessity to the Child and their Influence on Society;" November 23, Sunday evening, Rt. Rev. Henry Joseph Richter, D.D., Bishop of Grand Rapids. Subject, "The Indissolubility and Sanctity of Matrimony;" November 26, Wednesday evening, Rt. Rev. Kilian C. Flasch, D.D., Bishop of La Crosse. Subject, "The First

Precept of the Church;" November 28, Friday evening, Rt. Rev. Winand Michael Wigger, D.D., Bishop of Newark. Subject, "The Love of the Most Sacred Heart of Jesus to Man;" November 30, Sunday evening, Rt. Rev. Aegidius Junger, D.D., Bishop of Nesqually, Washington Territory. Subject, "Mary, the Mother of Jesus, is our Spiritual Mother."

III.

On the last day of the council, Sunday, December 7, there was a procession as on the first. White vestments were worn during the procession and the Pontifical High Mass, which was that of the Most Holy Trinity, celebrated by the Most Rev. M. A. Corrigan, Coadjutor Archbishop of New York; and red vestments during the closing session. At the end of the Mass, Right Rev. J. L. Spalding preached the sermon, on "The Work of the Council." After the sermon, the bishops and prelates in the sanctuary, and all the other members of the council in the sacristy, exchanged the white vestments worn during Mass for those of a red color (this color being symbolical of the tongues of fire which descended on the Apostles on Pentecost Sunday).

The closing ceremonies of the council were as follows: 1. Prayers, Hymn, Psalms, etc., similar to those of the First Session, were sung. 2. The decrees not yet voted on, were proposed to the Fathers of the Council. 3. All the decrees were signed. 4. Roll of members called. 5. Acclamations chanted. 6. Kiss of Peace given. 7. *Te Deum* by the choir. 8. Closing Prayers. 9. Papal Benediction by the Most Rev. Apostolic Delegate. 10. Return of the procession to the Archiepiscopal residence and to St. Alphonsus's Hall as on Sunday, November 9.

IV.

What the decrees of the council are will not be made known in an official form until they have received the approval of the Roman Congregations and the Holy Father. It is, however, well understood that the principal object of the meeting was to devise means for a gradual introduction of canon law into this country. It is reported that one-tenth of the pastors will be made irremovable rectors; that ecclesiastical courts will be established, consisting of two, four, or six clergymen, to be known as consultors, according to the size of the diocese, and these courts will have considerable powers as advisers; that the consultors and irremovable rectors will, when occasion arises, select three names, out of which the Pope, after considering any objections which the bishops of that province may make to one or all the names, will select one as bishop, or send all back for reconsideration. Other important decrees were passed, such as one adopting a universal catechism, the profits on the sale of which is to be devoted to the maintenance of Catholic schools; the selection of a single Catholic newspaper in each province for special support; longer terms for the education of priests, and the establishment of a Catholic university for which funds have been provided; and various other measures which will all be made known in a clearer and more definite form when the decrees are published.

The pastoral letter of the council, which is printed at the conclusion of this volume, has been received by the American public in the most cordial manner. Comments of the secular press could be quoted by the score praising the broad, patriotic, and enlightened views of the prelates and the sterling character of the Christian counsel which they give to the eight or ten million of the faithful, of whose spiritual affairs they have charge.

A new chapter has been added to the history of American Catholicity; and it is one of which every member of this great council may well feel proud to the last day of his life. By their labors they have gained the more loving allegiance of the Catholic laity, and a higher degree of respect and honor from their fellow citizens of other creeds.

THE RECEPTION.

AT the Concordia Opera House, on Thursday evening, November 20, the citizens of Baltimore tendered a grand reception to the members of the third Plenary Council. Among the seven hundred or eight hundred present in the hall were many of the notabilities of official and judicial life.

Seated on the stage were Archbishops Gibbons, of Baltimore, and Williams, of Boston; Hon. W. J. O'Brien, who presided as chairman, Judge William M. Merrick and Mr. Charles J. Bonaparte. At nine o'clock, the Hon. William J. O'Brien called the assemblage to order and said:

Most Rev., Right Rev. and Rev. Sirs—The Catholics of Baltimore have availed themselves of your presence in our city at the third Plenary Council to tender to you this evening's reception. It is with great pleasure that they testify their high respect for you personally and their devotion to our Holy Mother Church. I now introduce Mr. Charles J. Bonaparte, who will address you.

Mr. Charles J. Bonaparte then advanced to the front of the stage and spoke as follows:

Reverend Prelates—The Catholics of Baltimore, in whose name I address you, express, by their gathering to-night, the interest felt, not by Baltimoreans or Catholics only, but by citizens of all our States and thoughtful men of every creed, in the third Plenary Council of the American Church. This interest arises less from curiosity regarding the details of your work, the particular measures which your wisdom may devise to define the teaching or perfect the discipline of the Church, than from the living proof which your meeting affords of its harmony, its vitality, its steady, unvarying growth in the great nation of the New World. Catholics compare with a just pride in their religion this reunion with its predecessors; note the new sees grown up where was yesterday a wilderness, the provinces become too large for the guidance of a single hand, the thousand churches risen from their foundations since last the bishops of the United States met to take counsel; the monasteries, asylums, convents, colleges, hospitals, schools, then unthought of, now active and prosperous; and they feel a reasonable confidence that as the past has been, so will be the future, that the Church in our country is destined, under God's providence, to live and to purify our people. Of this hope, which you share with us, I need say no more; let me dwell for a moment on the reasons why our fellow-citizens who, unhappily, differ from us in belief; or, at least, those qualified by education and reflection to appreciate the drift of men and things around us, may look on your meeting as of grave and joyful significance.

In our day and country two classes of thinking men contemplate the phases of life and thought portrayed in the manners of the times with ever-increasing anxiety. Many see, with alarm and distress fast deepening into silent despair, religious faith in themselves and others fading into a dim uncertainty as to everything beyond the world of sense. These men are skeptics, involuntary skeptics, as to everything. They would believe in a God, but they find only a possibility of His existence in physical science, and His alleged revelation as doubtful for critics as Himself; they would believe in their own immortality, but they can only hope it is real; they feel, too clearly for their happiness, that with the fundamental doctrines of Christianity they give up the quickening spirit of modern civilization, but the light which shows the abyss at whose brink they stand, reveals no way of escape. They have seen the religions they may still formally profess, qualify and make meaningless one tenet after another, concede this point, silently abandon that, try vainly to compromise over and over again with a constantly advancing spirit of materialism and negation, until the very idea that there can be any fixed, immutable religious truth, has become strange to them. And, while they have lost so much, they have gained nothing. The followers of Luther or Calvin could believe in a reformed Church; the disciples of Voltaire or Rousseau could believe in a regenerated society; but modern agnostics can believe nothing, not even that they were wrong before.

Others look less below the surface of things; they are troubled by phenomena in which the first class recognize outward symptoms of the same deep-seated evil. On all sides they note in the

American people a blunting of the sense of justice; a growing dimness of our moral sight; an inability to distinguish clearly and promptly between right and wrong; a tendency to resolve ethics into mere blind sentiment; in short, a distortion and maiming of the national conscience. It is not that we have among us bad men, and that these do after their kind; this but proves the inherited frailty of our human nature; it is that we seem no longer to know bad men and wicked acts when we see them, or to know how to deal with them if we do. We live in an age of condoned dishonor, of prosperous fraud, when brazen guilt need fear no reproach, if only it has paid. That wealth and what wealth brings should be gained through baseness; vast fortunes be built up on falsehood and deceit and breach of trust, the perversion of justice, the debauchery of public servants, is, after all, what is seen everywhere, and has been seen always, and must be seen while men remain men; but that those who thus for profit trample on divine precept and evade human law should be met by the voices of public opinion, the guardians of public morals, with a faltering denunciation, a halting reproof, an indignation but half kindled and dying out almost before it has flickered; that their fruitful sins should be forgotten before they are cold, and the sight of their scandalous prosperity awaken but admiration and envy—these things reveal a canker eating into the heart of the nation. Many indisposed to more abstruse speculation, yet feel this and are startled by it, and cast around their eyes for some guide in morals who at least knows his mind and dares to speak it.

To both classes we declare that which they elsewhere vainly seek. The creed of the Catholic Church is founded on no theory in physics or psychology, and she makes no treaty with such theories. She teaches not what she thinks from reasoning, but what she knows from an ever-present, unceasing revelation. With her facts hypotheses, however plausible or ingenious, must square themselves as best they may; it is not her business to point out their inconsistencies or to correct their errors. She does not so much condemn them as disregard them; she believes, not indeed because, but although what she believes may be, humanly speaking, impossible. And she has no fear of the future; as all the speculations of idealist metaphysicians have never made one man doubt for one moment the reality of his own existence or that of the visible universe, so no proof, however conclusive in seeming, that our spiritual life is a dream, eternity a blank, the Gospel a myth or a forgery, can touch her, who lives and breathes and has her being in the reality and truth of all these things. Sure of her mission, she shrinks from none of its responsibilities. Her religion is no abstraction; it is a practical rule of life. She is not content with a passive assent to her claims; her children must heed her voice and do her work at all times and in all places, on the days of labor as on the day of rest, by the family hearth, in the forum, in the mart no less than within the temple and before the altar. Every act or thought, however minute or private, is subjected to her scrutiny and may merit her rebuke. She would not merely invite, but compel men to do right; and what is right she always knows and is always ready to say.

You are fortunate, venerable Fathers, in the time of your meeting. At this moment we discharge the grave duty imposed on us all by our form of government, of choosing our chief ruler.

Thoughtful and patriotic men throughout the country are now reminding us of the principles on which our polity is founded. That the happiness of a republic depends on the virtue of its citizens; that the suffrage is not a privilege to be abdicated or bartered away, but a trust to be sacredly filled; that no man has a right to give his conscience into the keeping of any party or faction, or to surrender himself for a season to the promptings of blind prejudice or selfish greed; that hypocrisy and calumny and falsehood in every shape are no less mean and hateful during a political campaign than before or after it; these truths they would now have us call to mind. And should not your assembling aid to recall them? True, the Catholic Church has no politics; she knows nothing of candidates or platforms, of administrations or policies, of tariffs or currencies; she is mute on every question as to which honest men may honestly differ, and no more tells her children what ticket they shall vote than what food they shall eat or what clothes they shall wear. But, as she demands that they shall eat with temperance, that they shall dress with decency, so she requires of them to vote with an unclouded judgment, with an undrugged conscience, with the good of the country as their motive, with the fear of God before their eyes. She does not meddle with the things of Cæsar, but honor and truth, good faith and public spirit, loyalty to our rulers, candor and charity towards our fellow-men; these are not the things of Cæsar, they are hers and she will have them, of all that belong to her; no man can be at once a good Catholic and a bad citizen.

To your assembly are turned, now when our wants are most sorely felt, the eyes of those who seek, amid the baseness and injustice which political agitation brings as scum to the surface of our national life, the forces left among us which yet make for righteousness. They greet you as shepherds who will do battle with the ravening wolves of selfishness and avarice—as physicians, who will cure the spreading ulcer of dishonesty and falsehood. We, who speak for them, are here to tell you that we recognize the immensity of your task, and our obligation to aid you in our humbler sphere. What you shall determine your spiritual children will accept with reverence and observe with loyalty. They leave with confidence to your wisdom the means by which the good cause may be made to prosper; but they ask with earnestness and humility of Almighty God, who illumines your minds and strengthens your purpose, that through this council He may make the American people more worthy of His priceless gift—their civil and religious liberty.

The chairman then introduced Judge William M. Merrick, who spoke as follows:

Most Reverend Archbishops, Right Reverend Bishops, and Members of the Third Plenary Council—To you, the accredited representatives and guardians of the spiritual interests of eight millions of American Catholics, the Catholic citizens of this community have deputed me to extend their cordial welcome, and to express their profound gratification at your presence in our midst. The assemblage of any body of men, voluntary or authoritative, for the purpose of promoting the advancement of their fellow-beings, whether in the industrial, the social, the scientific, the political or the moral order, must always be an event of importance and of interest. The measure of the importance of the assemblage is the importance of subject-matter with which they are charged, and the interest felt in it depends largely upon the character and capacity of the delegates who have been brought together. How great then must be the importance, how profound the interest, how vivid the sympathy which attach to this august body, charged to consider of the social, the moral and the spiritual welfare of the millions now existing, and of the countless millions who hereafter, in this republic, will regulate their lives and frame their immortal hopes in accord with the teachings of the Catholic Church.

Recognizing, as we do, that the motives which have wrought to bring about this council are the binding together in good will, for good purposes, of the clergy and the laity of the Church in America, and the infusion into its membership of a more vigorous spiritual life; and that self-forgetfulness, self-denial, self-sacrifice are the moral attributes which you individually cultivate, we tender to you in your official character our veneration, and to your personal characters our affectionate esteem and fraternal greeting. Neither the adulation of individuals, nor of official station, nor anything which savors of pandering to spiritual pride on the one hand, nor of servile dependence on the other, can have place in the greetings which the Catholic laity tender to the Catholic clergy. Such inducements would be as distasteful to yourselves as they would be unworthy of those on whose behalf I speak.

This reception then has its whole significance in, and is meant to represent the idea of, the cordial relations which exist between the Catholic clergy of America as a body, and the Catholic laity as a body; of the unity of sentiment which forms the bond between the one and the other, and of our desire to manifest before the world our just sense of the benefits conferred upon society—upon humanity—by the Catholic clergy of this country, who, while steadily inculcating the precepts of faith, and encouraging the growth of the spiritual life, and thereby aiding us to fit ourselves for transit to a higher and happier sphere, moreover bear a most important part in advancing civilization, in stimulating and promoting learning and the arts; and by example and precept assist and encourage the laity in the due performance of all those duties which make men the true-hearted citizens of a free republic, fully abreast with the progressive spirit of the age. Nothing is more generally misunderstood than the teachings and the tendencies of the influence of the Catholic Church upon republican institutions; and doubtless this council has been looked upon by many with pious alarm, lest it prove a congress convened to make insidious war against American freedom. Very many well-intentioned men fail to understand how loyalty to the State can co-exist with obedience to the Church, and simply because they do not know that the jurisdictional limits of the Church are rigorously confined to the domain of faith and morals. But if, instead of darkening counsel, candid thought were directed to the Church's incessant teaching of the Redeemer's answer—"Render unto Cæsar the things that are Cæsar's, and to God the things that are God's," and to its fundamental tenet of the universal brotherhood of man; and that in order to be our Saviour it was necessary for the Holy One first to become our Brother, it would necessarily be admitted that the doctrine of non-intervention with forms of government is a cardinal doctrine of the Catholic Church, and that its preaching of the brotherhood and equality of men, and its salient precepts of self-abnegation and self-sacrifice for the sake of our fellow-men, are the very radicals out of which all political freedom in modern times has grown. Need I, in proof, refer to the historic fact, which stands out clear and vivid in spite of all calumny, that the Catholic clergy of this country have never interfered with its political agitations? Was there ever an occasion on which any portion of the Catholic clergy passed any resolve upon any political issue or for or against any candidate for public favor? Need I recall to memory the time when this country was torn with civil strife, and agonized through four years of deadly conflict, how that, while in many other Church organizations there was dissension, separation and denunciation, the Catholic Church kept aloof from either side; its clergymen inculcating forbearance, counselling peace and extending the consolations of religion without stint, and in the unity of faith, to all without distinction? Individual clergymen entertained and acted upon their individual opinions as citizens on either side, but never acted as heated partisans on any side. The present occasion especially warrants me in recalling one illustrious instance in affirmative proof of the natural sympathy of the Church with our institutions.

I refer to your great predecessor, sir—to the Most Rev. John Carroll, the first Archbishop of Baltimore, the companion and intimate friend of Washington, a zealous advocate of American independence, and the author of that beautiful prayer published by authority, and recited publicly every Sunday in our churches, in which we say: "Let the light of Thy divine wisdom, direct the deliberations of Congress, and shine forth in all their proceedings and laws, framed for our rule and government, so that they may tend to the preservation of peace, the promotion of national happiness, the increase of industry, sobriety and useful knowledge, and may perpetuate to us the blessings of equal liberty." Yes! here is an authentic teaching of the American Catholic Church, found in the prayer that the acts of our national government may be directed by the light of divine wisdom, to the perpetuation of our American liberty. Surely when the invocation suggested to his flock by the first Primate of America, and sanctioned by the unbroken usage of his successors, goes up, through the revolving years, from the earnest hearts of millions of Catholic citizens, for the perpetuation of the blessings of equal liberty, the imputation of hostility to republican institutions, in the teachings or in the *spirit* of the Catholic Church, has been thereby met, and effectually refuted. The unexampled growth of the Catholic faith in this country, moreover, proves that it flourishes best in an atmosphere of perfect freedom of thought and opinion, of free discussion and untrammelled action. Just one hundred years ago, in November, 1784, the venerable prelate, whose name I have mentioned, received official notification of his appointment as the spiritual superior of the Catholic clergy of the United States; by which act the Church in America became an organized body, in place of consisting of scattered and dependent missions. At that time the Catholics numbered about 16,000 in Maryland, about 7,000 in Pennsylvania, and a very few thousand in other States, not counting the Canadian French and their descendants in the territory to the westward of the Ohio, and on the borders of the Mississippi.

At this centennial date more than eight millions may be computed within the republic. This could not have come to pass were free thought and free institutions uncongenial to the development of the Church. It must be obvious then to anyone who will reflect for a moment upon these suggestions, that even the inferior motives of temporal advantage concur with those of the highest and noblest type in binding the cause of human liberty with that of revealed religion.

But not only is the spirit of the Church in accord with the largest liberty of citizenship; it has nothing to fear, nor does it shrink from the greatest freedom of philosophic and scientific inquiry. At the foundation of Christianity it encountered all the ancient schools of philosophy in turn; Stoic, Pythagorean, Epicurean, and the rest. And all along the tract of its early history the successive speculative opinions which it encountered, and the successive heresies of prominence which it combatted and overthrew, had their support in the subtlest operations of the acutest intellects of those times.

The Church did not hesitate to encounter its adversaries in the very field of human reason which they selected. Excelling them in the use of their own weapons, it converted those weapons into instruments of its own triumph, and with a wise magnanimity it has preserved and been really the only means of preserving the memory of those schools and systems from oblivion. It has made the learning of those schools the monument of its own glory; and in its turn has been and is now the patron of intellectual development.

One of the tenets of the Epicurean school still survives, and remains in a modified form among the most dangerous impediments to faith. I mean the opinion that the distance between Divinity and man is so great that He has no concern, or rather sympathy, with humanity, and that therefore any and all creeds and religious requirements, whether for the regulation of our conduct here or as incentives to effort for immortal happiness, are without sanctions to uphold them and are utterly fruitless. Another, more ignoble, but at this immediate present far more captivating error, is that arising out of an illogical application of the doctrine of evolution, to which recent investigations in material philosophy have lent an exaggerated importance. In the progress of inquiry perverted intellectual pride has stepped in to suggest that man's own greatness is enhanced by denying his dependence upon a creating God, and by ascribing his origin and his powers to some obscure moving cause, out of which his present state and the present condition of other things in their order are emanations. Being persuaded that he is the best teacher of revealed religion who has sounded the depths of human philosophy, and that he will be the most devout Christian who has learned the utter insufficiency of philosophy to illuminate his pathway through the unknown, the Church through its ministers has not for an instant avoided the challenge to enter the field of historic and philosophic inquiry, and to invite and stimulate its laity to do the same. No matter how far the telescope of the astronomer may penetrate; no matter how many immeasurable worlds may be proved to exist beyond those now dreamed of, it knows that God is still there, and the more and more overwhelming is the necessity for His presence; no matter how minute and how perfect in the descending scale the organisms which the microscope discloses, yet more and more it demonstrates that only the constructive and sustaining powers of a divine Architect are capable of causing these harmonious developments. But with or without a law of development, reason must pause before some final and impulsive point. Failing at last the intellect must turn to revelation for aid. And then steps forward the Church, repeating to reason one of its own forgotten truths, that the *finite* cannot measure the infinite, that the less cannot prescribe a law to the greater. And with reason thus baffled and humbled she addresses the heart: Can it be an indignity or a degradation to receive a favor from one whom you have loved, from one whom you know to be prompted by an immeasurable love for yourself? Behold if there were the sting of dependence in creation it is taken away by the brotherhood of redemption; and man is lifted by gratuitous aid to an immortal rank far higher than the wildest dreams of intellectual pride could ever reach. The law of love reconciles science with religion, man with his Maker. I have thus ventured, on this festal occasion, and although these topics have been exhaustively treated from the pulpit by two eminent bishops during the sittings of this council, to refer to the harmony between patriotism and religion, and between science and revelation, for the especial purpose of emphasizing the feeling and the conviction of the laity as to the true attitude of the Catholic clergy of America toward these questions, so that it may be fully understood how well grounded are the interest we feel in the deliberations with which you, venerable men, are now engaged, and our confident assurance that the regulations which you may formulate will not fall short of the exigencies of the times, and will tend to the vast enlargement of your field of wholesome influence upon religion and upon society.

One hundred years ago there were nineteen priests in Maryland and five in Pennsylvania; of these, four, through age and infirmity, almost entirely unfit for any service. Oh! if that feeble and devoted band could have seen, as perhaps in the visions of Christian confidence and hope they did see, this vast gathering of archbishops, bishops and mitred abbots, what would have been their exultation. We, the descendants of the men whom they taught and succored, here on the soil consecrated by their humble labors, in the enjoyment of the heritage of liberty and religion which we have received, calling to mind that past to make us more sensible of the countless blessings of the present, again welcome you, venerable Fathers and dear friends, to the hearts and firesides of a grateful people.

When Judge Merrick sat down Mr. O'Brien said: "I have now the honor to present to you Archbishop Williams, of Boston, who will make the reply on behalf of the prelates." Archbishop Williams said:

Ladies and Gentlemen—Your representatives, in their address to the prelates of the third Plenary Council of Baltimore, welcome them to your hearts and to your firesides. We have reason to believe in the sincerity of this welcome, judging by the past, as the prelates of former councils have already proved the whole-souled heartedness of the Catholics of Baltimore. We of the present council have already proved it for ourselves. The open house of your respected and well-beloved archbishop; of your numerous and generous clergy, and of so many of your distinguished laity have already told us that Baltimore still treasures the old traditions, and that no matter how numerous may be the members of a council, the Catholics of this city will always have a welcome for them in their hearts and at their firesides.

And we on our side bring to your city feelings different from those we should carry to any other city of this great republic. Here we find our Mother Church. Here we find the home of him who, one hundred years ago, was appointed over the young Church of the United States, with less than thirty thousand Catholics, and less than thirty priests, and to-day his illustrious successor, in his venerated Cathedral, surrounded by a numerous, pious and well-educated clergy, as Apostolic Delegate presides over a third Plenary Council, with thirteen archbishops, sixty bishops, seven mitred abbots, Roman prelates, thirty-five superiors of religious orders, eleven

Most Rev. John J. Williams, D.D.

heads of theological seminaries, and nearly one hundred theologians chosen from every portion of our great country. Such a growth in a single century is unparalleled; and yet the greater portion of it has taken place in the last half century. The Catholic Church does not look upon this growth as one of its glories. It is the glory of our country and of its government which has attracted men from every nation to our shores. Here they found peace from persecution, deliverance from laws that oppressed them. Here they are welcome and admitted to all the rights of citizenship. But the glory of the Catholic Church in this country is that in the face of this wonderful increase it has not yet been found wanting. It is impossible to realize all that had to be done to meet the wants of these millions of Catholics who have poured into these United States during the last fifty years. The priests to be found or ordained, the churches to be built, the schools, the hospitals, the asylums to be provided, the dioceses to be erected, the ecclesiastical provinces to be established, and all this to be done with judgment and with wise forecast for the future. But the wisdom and untiring zeal of the bishops and their clergy, with the continued and unlimited generosity of the faithful were ever ready to meet whatever was necessary; and the success of their united efforts is as wonderful as the increase which called them forth. But why do I recite these events? Because in Baltimore this work of the Church began, in Baltimore it was carried out. In the Councils of Baltimore, under the leadership of your noble archbishops and the guidance of the Holy See, have been framed those wise regulations which have directed the young Church of America and enabled her to carry out successfully her difficult mission.

Well may you cherish your venerable Cathedral of Baltimore. Other cathedrals larger and more costly may be built, but this Mother Church has memories and glories which can never belong to another. Here was the scene of the labors of those old champions of the early Church; here their voices resounded in times gone by, and filled her dome with the power of their eloquence. These champions are nearly all gone. But to our joy, one of them has returned again to Baltimore to speak to us the traditions of glorious days, and aid us by his wisdom and experience. Although advanced in years he has still all his mental vigor and physical vitality. Another there is, who is with us only

in spirit, our Cardinal Prince. His presence here would have made
our joy complete,—and how fittingly, how gracefully, how eloquently
he would answered your address and expressed the satisfaction
of the prelates of this council at the reception you have given
them this evening. In conclusion, allow me to recall one more
reason why all Catholics, and indeed all lovers of their country,
should cherish the name of fair Maryland. It is the memory of
that noble inheritence left you by your fathers who, having left
England to find peace in the exercise of their religion, and having
come to these shores, not only left, but established as far as lay
in their power, what here they found—*freedom to worship God.*

CONGRATULATING THE APOSTOLIC DELEGATE.

AFTER the signing of the decrees at the last public session of the third Plenary Council, Sunday, December 7, 1884, the Most Rev. Peter R. Kenrick, of St. Louis, who is the senior archbishop of the hierarchy, advanced to the foot of the altar, and, half facing the Apostolic Delegate, thanked him for the able manner in which he had presided over the deliberations of the council, and the clergy and laity of Baltimore for their hospitality, which he said the members would always remember with feelings of pride and happiness. Of the work of the council he said it would be sure to be followed with beneficial results. "More than a half century," continued the venerable speaker, "has passed since the first Plenary Council, when I stood beneath the dome of this cathedral a silent spectator of the deliberations of that body. I had never seen a more sublime sight. It was not this grand old building, nor the gorgeous vestments, nor the dulcet strains of the music which seemed to come from heaven that inspired me; it was that assemblage of men, from all parts of the country, with different ideas and sentiments, but with one common end in view—the good of our Church." The archbishop spoke with great emotion when he referred to the pleasant memories of the two former Plenary Councils, of both of which he was a member. He is now over seventy-seven years.

When he had resumed his seat Archbishop Gibbons, moving to the edge of the platform, replied to the address of the Archbishop of St. Louis, saying:

I cannot sufficiently express the thanks I feel, Most Reverend, Right Reverend and Reverend Fathers, for the sentiments uttered by your venerated representative, the Most Rev. Archbishop of St. Louis. Whatever success has attended my part of the work I attribute, under God, to your kind forbearance and unfailing benevolence towards me. Mindful of the words of the Apostle, you have not despised my youth.

I have witnessed the proceedings of the greatest deliberative bodies in the world—I have listened to debates in the House of Commons, the French Chambers and both Houses of Congress; I have attended provincial, national and ecumenical councils—but never did I witness more order or decorum, more earnest debates joined with unfailing courtesy; never did I witness a more hearty acquiescence in the voice of the majority than in the third Plenary Council of Baltimore. Venerable Fathers, we have met as bishops of a common faith; we part as brothers bound by the closest ties of charity. We have met, many of us strangers to one another; we part as dearest friends. Though differing in nationality, in language, in habits, in tastes, in local interests as was said to-day by the eloquent Bishop of Peoria, we met as members of the same immortal episcopate, having one Lord, one faith, one baptism, one God and Father of all. And if the Holy Father, whose portrait adorns our council chamber, could speak from the canvass, well could he exclaim: "Behold how good and how pleasant a thing it is for brethren to dwell together in unity." The words you have spoken in council, like good seed, are yet hidden from the eyes of man, but they will one day rise and bring forth fruit of sanctification. The decrees you have formulated will one day resound throughout the length and breadth of the land. They will foster discipline and piety; they will quicken the faith and cheer the hearts of millions of Catholics.

The joy with which we welcomed you to Baltimore, venerable Fathers, is equalled only by the sorrow we feel at your departure. The clergy and people of this city, whose honored guests you were, have cherished you with all the filial affection and reverence which the faithful of Ephesus had for the Apostle of the Gentiles, and their regret at your departure is as sincere as was that of the Christians of Ephesus at the departure of their beloved Apostle. They will follow you with their prayers and best wishes for your safe return and a long life of usefulness in your respective dioceses.

This is the last time that we shall assemble again under the dome of this venerable cathedral, with the portraits of God's saints looking down upon us, as the venerable archbishop has said. He has reminded us of our short tenure of life. But we are immortal. God grant that the scene of to-day may be a presage of our future reunion in the temple above not made with hands, in the company of God's living saints, where, clothed in white robes and palms in our hands, we shall sing benediction, and honor, and glory to our God forever.

THE ACCLAMATIONS.

AT the close of the council, it is usual for the Fathers to chant, in alternate choirs, certain Acclamations, which are at once a profession of their faith in the Church, of their good will toward their brethren, and of their best wishes for the peace and prosperity of the country and the welfare of their fellow-citizens. The following was the wording of these Acclamations in the third Plenary Council of Baltimore:

Chanter. To the most Holy and Undivided Trinity, eternal glory and thanksgiving!

Chorus. The Charity of the Father, the Grace of the Son, the Communication of the Holy Ghost, O Blessed Trinity!

Chant. To the most Blessed Mary, preserved from Original Sin, through the foreseen merits of her Son, the bountiful Patroness of these United States, praise and veneration!

Chor. Blessed be the Virgin Mother of God, conceived without Original Sin, who is the Tower of Ivory from which are suspended a thousand shields, the entire armor of the strong!

Chant. To our Holy Pontiff, Pope Leo XIII, happily reigning, the visible Head of the whole Church, and the true Vicar of Christ on earth, unfading prosperity, eternal memory!

Chor. May the Lord fulfill the petitions of our most Holy Father, and may He confirm all his judgments against the enemies of the most beloved Spouse of Christ, so that they may come to nought, like water that floweth away, and may they fail like the smoke which vanisheth!

Chant. To the most illustrious and most Reverend Archbishop of Baltimore, Delegate of the Apostolic See, by whose labor and exertions this Plenary Council has been assembled, directed, and brought to a happy issue, manifold graces with many years!

Chor. Manifold graces with many years! May the Lord grant him the reward of his work; may he receive an unfading crown of glory!

Chant. To the most illustrious and Rev. Archbishops and Bishops who have adorned this council by their learning and wisdom, a happy return to their flocks, long life, and all prosperity from God!

Chor. Everlasting peace, the most plentiful benediction of the Almighty, and a blessed reward of their labors!

Chant. To the Right Rev. Abbots, and Very Rev. Superiors of Religious Communities, and also to the Rev. Theologians, who, by their learning and labor, have aided the prelates in the management of the work, increase of grace, eternal happiness!

Chor. May the Lord grant them, according to His goodness, every perfect gift! May the God of wisdom, and the unfading Fountain of true light, illumine their minds with the light of heavenly glory, cherish them by His grace, and strengthen them in virtue!

Chant. To the Rev. Clergy of these States, and the whole flock of Christ, salvation and benediction from the Lord!

Chor. Show them, O Lord, Thy ways, and direct them in Thy truth, that they may not forget the works of the Most High, and that they may fulfill His Commandments!

Chant. To our great and cherished republic, supreme peace, full prosperity, and the overflowing benediction of Almighty God!

Chor. Grant peace, O Lord, in our days, because there is no one to fight for us but Thee, our God!

Chant. To all the people of these United States, unfailing peace, indissoluble concord!

Chor. Confirm, O God, what Thou has wrought in them, that all disturbance being removed, we may freely serve Thee with one heart and one soul!

Chant. To all the faithful departed, who have gone before us with the sign of faith, and repose in the sleep of peace!

Chor. Eternal rest grant to them, O Lord, and may perpetual light shine upon them!

Chant. And may we, as the Apostle commandeth, obey our prelates, and observe their commands, that with joy they may watch over us, as having to render an account of our souls!

Chor. So be it! so be it! amen! amen!

MEMBERS OF THE COUNCIL.

APOSTOLIC DELEGATE.

Most Rev. James Gibbons, D.D., Archbishop of Baltimore.

CARDINAL ARCHBISHOP.

His Eminence John Cardinal McCloskey, D.D., Archbishop of New York. (Absent through illness.)

ARCHBISHOPS.

Most Rev. Joseph S. Alemany, D.D., Archbishop of San Francisco.
Most. Rev. Michael A. Corrigan, D.D., Titular Archbishop of Petra and Coadjutor of New York.
Most Rev. William H. Elder, D.D., Archbishop of Cincinnati.
Most Rev. Patrick A. Feehan, D.D., Archbishop of Chicago.
Most Rev. Michael Heiss, D.D., Archbishop of Milwaukee.
Most Rev. Peter R. Kenrick, D.D., Archbishop of St. Louis.
Most Rev. John B. Lamy, D.D., Archbishop of Santa Fé.
Most Rev. Francis X. Leray, D.D., Archbishop of New Orleans.
Most Rev. Patrick W. Riordan, D.D., Titular Archbishop of Cabasa and Coadjutor of San Francisco.
Most Rev. Patrick J. Ryan, D.D., Archbishop of Philadelphia.
Most Rev. John B. Salpointe, Titular Archbishop of Anazanba and Coadjutor of Santa Fé.
Most Rev. Charles J. Seghers, D.D., Archbishop of Oregon City.
Most Rev. John J. Williams, D.D., Archbishop of Boston.

BISHOPS.

Right Rev. Peter J. Baltes, D.D., Bishop of Alton. (Absent through sickness.)
Right Rev. Thomas A. Becker, D.D., Bishop of Wilmington.
Right Rev. Caspar H. Borgess, D.D., Bishop of Detroit.
Right Rev. Dennis Bradley, D.D., Bishop of Manchester.
Right Rev. John B. Brondel, D.D., Bishop of Helena.
Right Rev. Francis S. Chatard, D.D., Bishop of Vincennes.

Right Rev. John J. Conroy, D.D., Titular Bishop of Curium.
Right Rev. Henry Cosgrove, D.D., Bishop of Davenport.
Right Rev. C. M. Dubuis, (Resigned) Bishop of Galveston. (Absent in France and sick.)
Right Rev. Joseph Dwenger, D.D., Bishop of Fort Wayne.
Right Rev. Louis M. Fink, O.S.B., D.D., Bishop of Leavenworth.
Right Rev. Edward Fitzgerald, D.D., Bishop of Little Rock.
Right Rev. Kilian C. Flasch, D.D., Bishop of La Crosse.
Right Rev. Nicholas A. Gallagher, D.D., Titular Bishop of Canopus and Administrator of Galveston.
Right Rev. Richard Gilmour, D.D., Bishop of Cleveland.
Right Rev. Louis De Goesbriand, D.D., Bishop of Burlington.
Right Rev. A. J. Glorieux, D.D., Vicar Apostolic Elect of Idaho.
Right Rev. Thomas L. Grace, D.D., Titular Bishop of Mennith.
Right Rev. William H. Gross, D.D., Bishop of Savannah.
Right Rev. James A. Healy, D.D., Bishop of Portland.
Right Rev. Thomas F. Hendricken, D.D., Bishop of Providence.
Right Rev. John Hennessy, D.D., Bishop of Dubuque.
Right Rev. John J. Hogan, D.D., Bishop of Kansas City and Administrator of St. Joseph.
Right Rev. John Ireland, D.D., Bishop of St. Paul.
Right Rev. Francis Janssens, D.D., Bishop of Natchez.
Right Rev. Ægidius Junger, D.D., Bishop of Nesqually.
Right Rev. John J. Kain, D.D., Bishop of Wheeling.
Right Rev. John J. Keane, D.D., Bishop of Richmond.
Right Rev. Francis X. Krautbauer, D.D., Bishop of Green Bay.
Right Rev. John Loughlin, D.D., Bishop of Brooklyn.
Right Rev. Joseph P. Machebeuf, D.D., Titular Bishop of Epiphany and Vicar Apostolic of Colorado.
Right Rev. Camillus P. Maes, D.D., Bishop Elect of Covington.
Right Rev. Patrick Manogue, D.D., Bishop of Grass Valley.
Right Rev. Dominic Manucy, D.D., Administrator of Mobile and Brownsville.
Right Rev. Martin Marty, O.S.B., D.D., Titular Bishop of Tiberias and Vicar Apostolic of Dakota.
Right Rev. John Moore, D.D., Bishop of St. Augustine.
Right Rev. Francis Mora, D.D., Bishop of Monterey and Los Angeles.
Right Rev. Ignatius Mrak, D.D., Titular Bishop of Antinoë. (Absent through sickness.)

Right Rev. Tobias Mullen, D.D., Bishop of Erie.
Right Rev. William G. McCloskey, D.D., Bishop of Louisville.
Right Rev. Lawrence S. McMahon, D.D., Bishop of Hartford.
Right Rev. Francis McNeirny, D.D., Bishop of Albany.
Right Rev. Bernard J. McQuaid, D.D., Bishop of Rochester.
Right Rev. John C. Neraz, D.D., Bishop of San Antonio.
Right Rev. Henry P. Northrop, D.D., Bishop of Charleston.
Right Rev. Eugene O'Connell, D.D., Titular Bishop of Joppa.
Right Rev. James O'Connor, D.D., Titular Bishop of Dibona and Vicar Apostolic of Nebraska.
Right Rev. Michael J. O'Farrell, D.D., Bishop of Trenton.
Right Rev. William O'Hara, D.D., Bishop of Scranton.
Right Rev. Patrick T. O'Reilly, D.D., Bishop of Springfield.
Right Rev. Joseph Rademacher, D.D., Bishop of Nashville.
Right Rev. Henry J. Richter, D.D., Bishop of Grand Rapids.
Right Rev. Isidore Robot, O.S.B., Prefect Apostolic of Indian Territory.
Right Rev. Stephen V. Ryan, D.D., Bishop of Buffalo.
Right Rev. Rupert Seidenbusch, O.S.B., D.D., Titular Bishop of Halia and Vicar Apostolic of Northern Minnesota.
Right Rev. Jeremiah F. Shanahan, D.D., Bishop of Harrisburg.
Right Rev. John L. Spalding, D.D., Bishop of Peoria.
Right Rev. John Tuigg, D.D., Bishop of Pittsburg and Administrator of Allegheny. (Absent through sickness.)
Right Rev. John Vertin, D.D., Bishop of Marquette and Saut Ste. Marie.
Right Rev. Edgar P. Wadhams, D.D., Bishop of Ogdensburg.
Right Rev. John A. Watterson, D.D., Bishop of Columbus.
Right Rev. Winand M. Wigger, D.D., Bishop of Newark.

VISITING PRELATES.

Most Rev. John J. Lynch, D.D., Archbishop of Toronto, Canada.
Most Rev. Cornelius O'Brien, D.D., Archbishop of Halifax.
Right Rev. James J. Carbery, D.D., Bishop of Hamilton, Ontario.
Right Rev. J. V. Cleary, D.D., Bishop of Kingston, Ontario.
Right Rev. Joseph T. Duhamel, D.D., Bishop of Ottawa, Ontario.
Right Rev. T. T. O'Mahony, D.D., Coadjutor Bishop of Toronto, Canada.
Right Rev. J. Osouf, D.D., Vicar Apostolic of Northern Japan.
Right Rev. John Walsh, D.D., Bishop of London, Canada.

PROCURATORS.

Very Rev. E. H. Brandts, Administrator of Covington.
Very Rev. John N. Lemmens, Procurator of the Administrator of Vancouver's Island.
Very Rev. R. Phelan, V.G., Procurator of the Bishop of Pittsburg.
Very Rev. F. H. Zabel, D.D., Procurator of the Bishop of Alton.

MITRED ABBOTS.

Right Rev. Maria Benedict, Trappist, Abbot, Abbey of Our Lady of La Trappe, Gethsemani, Kentucky
Right Rev. Frowenus Conrad, O.S.B., Abbot, New Engelberg Abbey, Conception, Missouri.
Right Rev. Alexius Edelbrock, O.S.B., Abbot, St. John's Abbey, Collegeville, Minnesota.
Right Rev. Fintan Mundwiler, O.S.B., Abbot, St. Meinrad's Abbey, Indiana.
Right Rev. Boniface Wimmer, O.S.B., Archabbot of St. Vincent's Abbey, Pa., and President of the American Cassinese Congregation.
Right Rev. Innocent Wolf, O.S.B., Abbot, Abbey of St. Benedict, Atchison, Kansas.

DOMESTIC PRELATES OF HIS HOLINESS.

Right Rev. Patrick Allen.
Right Rev. Leonard Batz. (Absent.)
Right Rev. Julian Benoit, V.G. (Absent.)
Right Rev. August Bessonies, V.G.
Right Rev. James A. Corcoran, D.D.
Right Rev. George Doane.
Right Rev. Thomas Preston, V.G., LL.D.
Right Rev. William Quinn, V.G.
Right Rev. Robert Seton, D.D., Apostolic Prothonotary.

PRIVATE CHAMBERLAINS OF HIS HOLINESS.

Very Rev. Henry Cluver, D.D.
Very Rev. John M. Farley.
Very Rev. John Sullivan, V.G.

SUPERIORS OF RELIGIOUS ORDERS.

Very Rev. A. Aigueperse, S.P.M.
Very Rev. M. Alberick, Trappist, Superior of New Melleray Abbey, Dubuque, Iowa.
Very Rev. John B. Bigot, S.M.
Very Rev. Leopold Bushart, S.J.
Very Rev. Theobald Butler, S.J.
Very Rev. Joseph Cataldo, S.J.
Very Rev. Nicholas Congiato, S.J. (Absent.)
Very Rev. Henry Drees, C.P.P.S.
Very Rev. Hyacinth Epp, O.M.Cap.
Very Rev. Cyrille Fournier, C.S.V.
Very Rev. Bonaventure Frey, O.M.Cap.
Very Rev. Robert Fulton, S.J.
Very Rev. Aloysius M. Gentile, S.J.
Very Rev. Lucas Gottbehœde, O.S.F.
Very Rev. Vincent Halbfass, O.S.F.
Very Rev. Isaac T. Hecker, C.S.P.
Very Rev. Alfred Leeson, S. St. J.
Very Rev. Joseph Lesen, O.M.C., D.D.
Very Rev. John J. Lessmann, S.J.
Very Rev. Michael D. Lilly, O.P.
Very Rev. William Lœwekamp, C.SS.R.
Very Rev. A. Mandine, C.M.
Very Rev. Pius R. Mayer, O.C.C.
Very Rev. Augustine Morini, O.S.
Very Rev. C. A. McEvoy, O.S.A.
Very Rev. James McGrath, O.M.I.
Very Rev. Theophilus Pospisilik, O.S.F.
Very Rev. John N. Reinbolt, S. Fr. M.
Very Rev. Damasus Ruesing, O.S.F.
Very Rev. Elias F. Schauer, C.SS.R.
Very Rev. Thomas Smith, C.M.
Very Rev. E. Sorin, C.S.C.
Very Rev. Thomas Steffanini, C.P.
Very Rev. James Strub, C.S.Sp.
Very Rev. Francis S. Vilarrassa, O.P. (Absent.)

SUPERIORS OF THEOLOGICAL SEMINARIES.

Very Rev. William Byrne, V.G., D.D., Superior of Mt. St. Mary's Seminary, Emmitsburg.
Very Rev. Patrick V. Cavanagh, C.M., Superior of the Seminary of Our Lady of the Angels, Buffalo.
Very Rev. James Corrigan, Superior of the Seminary of the Immaculate Conception, Newark.
Very Rev. Henry Gabriels, D.D., Superior of St. Joseph's Sulpician Seminary, Troy.
Very Rev. J. W. Hickey, C.M., Superior of St. Vincent's Seminary, Cape Girardeau.
Very Rev. John B. Hogan, S.S., D.D., Superior of St. John's Sulpician Seminary, Brighton, Boston.
Very Rev. William Kieran, D.D., Superior of the Seminary of St. Charles Borromeo, Overbrook, Philadelphia.
Very Rev. Alphonsus Magnien, S.S., D.D., Superior of the Seminary of St. Sulpice, Baltimore.
Very Rev. Nicholas A. Moes, Superior of St. Mary's Seminary, Cleveland.
Very Rev. George McCloskey, V.G., Superior of Preston Park Seminary, Louisville. (Absent.)
Very Rev. Theophile Pospisilik, O.S.F., Superior of the Seminary of St. Bonaventure, Buffalo.
Very Rev. Augustine Zeininger, Superior of the Seminary of St. Francis of Sales, Milwaukee.

THEOLOGIANS.

Rev. P. M. Abbelen, for the Archbishop of Milwaukee.
Rev. John C. Albrinck, for the Archbishop of Cincinnati.
Very Rev. John E. Barry, V.G. for the Bishop of Manchester.
Rev. Ferdinand Bergmeyer, O.S.F., for the Bishop of Vincennes.
Rev. Thomas Bonacum, for the Archbishop of St. Louis.
Rev. Henry A. Brann, D.D., for the Coadjutor Archbishop of San Francisco.
Rev. Thomas M. A. Burke, for the Bishop of Little Rock.
Rev. Richard L. Burtsell, D.D., for the Bishop of St. Augustine.
Rev. Thomas S. Byrne, for the Archbishop of Cincinnati.
Very Rev. Edward Cafferty, V.G., for the Bishop of Savannah.
Rev. Nicholas Cantwell, for the Archbishop of Philadelphia.

Very Rev. Thomas Casey, V.G., for the Bishop of Erie.
Rev. William F. Clarke, S.J., for the Administrator of Galveston.
Very Rev. P. J. Conway, V.G., for the Archbishop of Chicago.
Right Rev. J. A. Corcoran, D.D., for the Archbishop of Philadelphia.
Rev. Alfred A. Curtis, for the Archbishop of Oregon City.
Very Rev. Leo Da Sarracena, O.S.F., for the Bishop of Hartford.
Rev. Isidore Daubresse, S.J., for the Coadjutor Archbishop of New York.
Rev. Emil De Augustinis, S.J., for the Apostolic Delegate.
Rev. Januarius De Concilio, for the Vicar Apostolic of Nebraska.
Rev. Edmund Didier, for the Titular Bishop of Joppa.
Right Rev. Geo. H. Doane, for the Coadjutor Archbishop of Santa Fé.
Rev. Robert Doman, for the Bishop of Detroit.
Rev. Francis S. Dumont, S.S., for the Bishop of Richmond.
Rev. E. Durier, for the Archbishop of New Orleans.
Rev. Edward R. Dyer, S.S., D.D., for the Vicar Apostolic of Colorada.
Rev. John T. Gaitley, for the Bishop of Nesqually.
Rev. Joseph Giustiniani, C.M., for the Bishop of Monterey and Los Angeles.
Rev. Charles Goldsmith, S.T.B., for the Bishop of La Crosse.
Rev. F. Goller, for the Archbishop of St. Louis.
Rev. Thomas Griffin, for the Bishop of Springfield.
Rev. Matthew Harkins, for the Archbishop of Boston.
Rev. A. V. Higgins, O.P., S.T.M., for the Bishop of Columbus.
Rev. J. B. Hogan, S.S., D.D., for the Archbishop of Boston.
Very Rev. Michael Hurley, V.G., for the Bishop of Peoria.
Very Rev. Frederick Katzer, V.G., for the Bishop of Green Bay.
Rev. Benjamin J. Keiley, Ph.D., for the Bishop of Wilmington.
Rev. Jas. T. Keogh, for the Archbishop of Milwaukee.
Rev. Henry F. Kinnerny, for the Bishop of Providence.
Rev. Thomas S. Lee, for the Archbishop of New Orleans.
Very Rev. Christopher Linnenkamp, V.G., for the Bishop of Kansas City.
Rev. Bernard Loenikar, O.S.B., for the Vicar Apostolic of Northern Minnesota.
Very Rev. P. A. Ludden, V.G., for the Bishop of Albany.
Very Rev. Dwight E. Lyman, V.F., for the Bishop of Helena.
Very Rev. Thomas Lynch, V.G., for the Bishop of Burlington.
Rev. James F. Mackin, for the Archbishop of Oregon City.

Very Rev. Alphonsus Magnien, S.S., D.D., for the Apostolic Delegate.
Very Rev. Edward McColgan, V.G., for the Apostolic Delegate.
Rev. James McGolrick, for the Bishop of St. Paul.
Rev. Bernard J. McManus, for the Bishop of Harrisburg.
Very Rev. James T. McManus, V.G., for the Bishop of Rochester.
Rev. John McQuirk, D.D., LL.D., for the Titular Bishop of Curium.
Rev. Michael C. O'Brien, for the Bishop of Portland.
Rev. Joseph P. O'Connell, D.D., for the Bishop of Brooklyn.
Rev. James O'Reilly, for the Bishop of Leavenworth.
Rev. H. Pefferkorn, for the Bishop of San Antonio.
Rev. Charles Piccirrillo, S.J., for the Bishop of Natchez.
Right Rev. William Quinn, V.G., for the Coadjutor Archbishop of New York.
Rev. Peter A. Racicot, S.J., for the Archbishop of Santa Fé.
Rev. Thomas Rafter, for the Bishop of Grand Rapids.
Rev. Daniel J. Riordan, for the Coadjutor Archbishop of San Francisco.
Rev. William Robbers, for the Bishop Elect of Covington.
Rev. Henry L. Robinson, for the Bishop of Mobile.
Rev. J. A. Rochford, O.P., for the Archbishop of San Francisco.
Rev. George Ruland, C.SS.R., for the Archbishop of San Francisco.
Very Rev. Roger Ryan, V.G., for the Bishop of Dubuque.
Rev. Aloysius Sabbetti, S.J., for the Archbishop of Santa Fé.
Rev. Richard Scannell, for the Bishop of Nashville.
Rev. Emil Sele, D.D., for the Bishop of Louisville.
Very Rev. Elias F. Schauer, C.SS.R., for the Apostolic Delegate.
Rev. Charles Sigl, C.SS.R., for the Prefect Apostolic of Indian Territory
Very Rev. Anthony Smith, V.G., for the Bishop of Trenton.
Rev. Sebastian B. Smith, D.D., for the Bishop of Newark.
Rev. Joseph M. Sorg, for the Bishop of Buffalo.
Rev. J. A. Stephan, for the Vicar Apostolic of Dakota.
Very Rev. John Sullivan, V.G., for the Bishop of Wheeling.
Rev. T. P. Thorpe, for the Bishop of Cleveland.
Rev. A. Trevis, for the Bishop of Davenport.
Very Rev. James Trobec, for the Titular Bishop of Mennith.
Rev. A. Varsi, S.J., for the Bishop of Grass Valley.
Rev. John Waldron, for the Archbishop of Chicago.

Rev. S. Wall, for the Vicar Apostolic Elect of Idaho.
Very Rev. Thomas Walsh, V.G., for the Bishop of Ogdensburg.
Rev. E. P. Walters, for the Bishop of Fort Wayne.
Rev. Francis X. Weninger, S.J., D.D., for the Bishop of Marquette and Sant Ste. Marie.
Rev. J. J. Wedenfeller, for the Bishop of Charleston.
Very Rev. Moses Whitty, V.G., for the Bishop of Scranton.[1]
Rev. Wm. J. Wiseman, S.T.L., for the Coadjutor Archbishop of Santa Fé.

PROMOTERS.

Right Rev. Francis Janssens, D.D., Bishop of Natchez.
Right Rev. J. J. Kain, D.D., Bishop of Wheeling.

JUDGES OF EXCUSES AND COMPLAINTS.

Right Rev. Louis M. Fink, O.S.B., D.D., Bishop of Leavenworth.
Right Rev. Louis De Goesbriand, D.D., Bishop of Burlington.
Right Rev. John Loughlin, D.D., Bishop of Brooklyn.
Right Rev. William G. McCloskey, D.D., Bishop of Louisville.

CHANCELLORS.

Rev. George W. Devine.
Rev. John S. Foley, D.D.

SECRETARIES.

Right Rev. James A. Corcoran, D.D.
Very Rev. Henry Gabriels, D.D.
Rev. Sebastian G. Messmer.
Rev. D. J. O'Connell, D.D.

NOTARIES.

Right Rev. Robert Seton, D.D., Prothonotary Apostolic.
Very Rev. P. L. Chapelle, D.D.
Very Rev. John M. Farley.
Very Rev. Nicholas A. Moes.
Very Rev. P. A. Stanton, O.S.A., D.D.

---

[1] Towards the last his place was taken by Rev. Thomas F. Coffee.

Rt. Rev. E. O'Connell, D.D.   Rt. Rev. R. Seton, D.D.   Rev. James McCallen, S.S.

Very Rev. A. Morini, O.S.   Rt. Rev. Jas. A. Corcoran, D.D.   Rev. Thos. Honacum.

Very Rev. John Sullivan, V.G.
Very Rev. Frederick Wayrich, C.SS.R.
Rev. P. M. Abbelen.
Rev. J. L. Andreis.
Rev. Charles P. Grannan, D.D.
Rev. Matthew Harkins.
Rev. Henry Moeller, D.D.
Rev. Sebastian B. Smith, D.D.

MASTERS OF CEREMONY.

Rev. Thomas Broyderick.
Rev. Michael Kelly.
Rev. James McCallan, S.S.

CHANTERS.

Rev. Gabriel André, S.S.
Rev. William E. Bartlett.
Rev. Joseph Cassidy.
Rev. John B. Drennan.
Rev. Anthony Lammel.
Rev. John Marr.
Rev. Joseph O'Keefe.

DECEASED PRELATES OF THE LAST COUNCIL.

ARCHBISHOPS.

Most Rev. James Roosevelt Bayley, D.D., Archbishop of Baltimore.
Most Rev. Francis Norbert Blanchet, D.D., Archbishop of Oregon City.
Most Rev. John Martin Henni, D.D., Archbishop of Milwaukee.
Most Rev. J. M. Odin, D.D., Archbishop of New Orleans.
Most Rev. Napoleon J. Perché, D.D., Archbishop of New Orleans.
Most Rev. John Baptist Purcell, D.D., Archbishop of Cincinnati.
Most Rev. Martin John Spalding, D.D., Apostolic Delegate and Archbishop of Baltimore.
Most Rev. James Frederic Wood, D.D., Archbishop of Philadelphia.

BISHOPS.

Right Rev. Thaddeus Amat, D.D., Bishop of Monterey.
Right Rev. David W. Bacon, D.D., Bishop of Portland.
Right Rev. Frederic Baraga, D.D., Bishop of Marquette.
Right Rev. George Aloysius Carrell, D.D., Bishop of Covington.
Right Rev. Modeste Demers, D.D., Bishop of Vancouver's Island.
Right Rev. M. Domenec, D.D., Bishop of Pittsburg.
Right Rev. Henry Damian Juncker, D.D., Bishop of Alton.
Right Rev. Peter Joseph Lavialle, D.D., Bishop of Louisville.
Right Rev. Peter Paul Lefevre, Bishop of Detroit.
Right Rev. J. H. Luers, D.D., Bishop of Fort Wayne.
Right Rev. P. N. Lynch, D.D., Bishop of Charleston.
Right Rev. Augustus M. Martin, D.D., Bishop of Natchitoches.
Right Rev. F. P. McFarland, D.D., Bishop of Hartford.
Right Rev. John McGill, D.D., Bishop of Richmond.
Right Rev. James O'Gorman, D.D., Vicar Apostolic of Nebraska.
Right Rev. John Quinlan, D.D., Bishop of Mobile.
Right Rev. Amadeus Rappe, D.D., Bishop of Cleveland.
Right Rev. S. H. Rosecrans, D.D., Bishop of Columbus.

Right Rev. Maurice de St. Palais, D.D., Bishop of Vincennes.
Right Rev. John Timon, D.D., Bishop of Buffalo.
Right Rev. Augustin Verot, D.D., Bishop of St. Augustine.
Right Rev. Richard Vincent Whelan, D.D., Bishop of Wheeling.

ABSENT ON ACCOUNT OF ILLNESS:

Right Rev. J. B. Miège, D.D., Titular Bishop of Messenia, and (resigned) Vicar Apostolic of Nebraska.

The following is a list of eleven other deceased prelates who had either retired from active life before the second Plenary Council or else received episcopal consecration after that date:

Right Rev. Guy Ignatius Chabrat, D.D., Coadjutor Bishop of Bardstown, (now Louisville.)
Right Rev. Thomas Foley, D.D., Bishop of Chicago.
Right Rev. Thomas Galberry, D.D., Bishop of Hartford.
Right Rev. Celestine de la Hailandière, D.D., Bishop of Vincennes.
Right Rev. Joseph Melcher, D.D., Bishop of Green Bay.
Right Rev. John McMullen, D.D., Bishop of Davenport.
Right Rev. M. O'Connor, D.D., Bishop of Pittsburg.
Right Rev. Anthony Dominic Pellicer, D.D., Bishop of San Antonio.
Right Rev. Frederick Résé, D.D., Bishop of Detroit.
Right Rev. Augustus M. Toebbe, D.D., Bishop of Covington.
Right Rev. James Whelan, D.D., Bishop of Nashville.

LIVES OF THE AMERICAN PRELATES.

OUTLINE SKETCHES.

MOST REV. JAMES GIBBONS, D.D.,
ARCHBISHOP OF BALTIMORE AND APOSTOLIC DELEGATE.

Most Rev. James Gibbons was born in Baltimore, July 23, 1834. When very small he was taken to Ireland by his father and there received his first education. Entering St. Charles' College, Howard County, Md., on his return, he graduated in 1857. From St. Charles' College he was transferred to the Seminary of St. Sulpice and St. Mary's University, and was ordained, June 30, 1861. He was connected with several churches in the city of Baltimore, until the second Plenary Council, at which he acted as assistant chancellor; he was named to the Vicariate Apostolic of North Carolina, and consecrated titular Bishop of Adramyttum August 16, 1868. He was translated to the See of Richmond July 30, 1872; and appointed coadjutor to the Archbishop of Baltimore May 20, 1877, succeeding to the see October 3, of the same year. He presided over the third Plenary Council of Baltimore, November, 1884, as the Apostolic Delegate of the Holy See.

MOST REV. JOSEPH S. ALEMANY, D.D.,
ARCHBISHOP OF SAN FRANCISCO.

Most Rev. Joseph S. Alemany was born in Vich, Spain, in the year 1814, and ordained in Viatebo, Italy, in 1837. In 1840 he came to America, settling first in Mississippi. After a term of mission work in various States and Territories, he was consecrated Bishop of Monterey June 30, 1850, and translated to the See of San Francisco July 29, 1853, being its first Archbishop.

MOST REV. MICHAEL AUGUSTINE CORRIGAN, D.D.,

COADJUTOR ARCHBISHOP OF NEW YORK.

Most Rev. Michael A. Corrigan was born in Newark, N. J., August 13, 1839. He received his classical education at Mount St. Mary's College, Emmitsburg, Md., graduating in 1859. He was among the first students in the American College at Rome, when he made his theological course, being ordained September 19, 1863. On his return to America, he was assigned to a professorship at Seton Hall College, South Orange, N. J., being successively promoted to the vice-presidency and presidency. In 1868 he was appointed vicar general of the Diocese of Newark. He was consecrated Bishop of Newark May 4, 1873; and on October 1, 1880, was promoted to the titular Archbishopric of Petra and coadjutor to the Cardinal Archbishop of New Yor'

MOST REV. WILLIAM HENRY ELDER, D.D.,

ARCHBISHOP OF CINCINNATI.

Most Rev. William Henry Elder was born in Baltimore, Md., March 22, 1819. He received his education at Mt. St. Mary's College, Emmitsburg, Md., and in the Urban College of the Propaganda, Rome. He was ordained in Rome March 29, 1846, and, on his return to this country, was made director of the Theological Seminary of Mt. St. Mary's College. He was consecrated Bishop of Natchez May 3, 1857; appointed titular Bishop of Avara and coadjutor of Cincinnati, *cum jure successionis*, January 30, 1880; and succeeded to the See of Cincinnati on the death of Archbishop Purcell, July 4, 1883.

MOST REV. PATRICK A. FEEHAN, D.D.,

ARCHBISHOP OF CHICAGO.

Most Rev. Patrick A. Feehan was born in County Tipperary, Ireland, August 28, 1829. He was educated at Maynooth Seminary, and on coming to America was ordained at St. Louis, November 1, 1852. After a varied experience of mission work and pastoral charges, he was consecrated Bishop of Nashville, Tenn., November 12, 1865; and was promoted to the Archbishopric of Chicago, September 10, 1880.

MOST REV. MICHAEL HEISS, D.D.,

ARCHBISHOP OF MILWAUKEE, WIS.

Most Rev. Michael Heiss was born April 12, 1818, at Pfahldorf, Bavaria. After a course of theological training under such professors as Doellinger, Moehler and Goerres, he was ordained October 18, 1840. In 1842 he came to America, and was at first engaged in mission work in Kentucky and Ohio. He went to Milwaukee in 1844 when that see was created. From then up till 1865 he labored in Milwaukee, founding, with the assistance of Dr. Joseph Salzmann, St. Francis' Seminary, of which he was the first president. He was consecrated the first Bishop of La Crosse September 6, 1868; appointed coadjutor of Milwaukee and titular Archbishop of Adrianople March 14, 1880; and succeeded the late lamented Archbishop Henni on his death, September 7, 1881.

MOST REV. PETER RICHARD KENRICK, D.D.,

ARCHBISHOP OF ST. LOUIS.

Most Rev. Peter R. Kenrick was born in Dublin, Ireland, August 17, 1806. He was ordained March 6, 1832. He came to America and settled in Philadelphia in October, 1833. After re-

Most Rev. P. A. Feehan, D.D.

maining there eight years in successive charge of several parishes he was consecrated November 30, 1841, titular Bishop of Drasa and coadjutor to Right Rev. William Rosati, first Bishop of St. Louis; succeeded to the Bishopric in 1843; and was promoted to Archbishop in 1847.

MOST REV. JOHN B. LAMY, D.D.,

ARCHBISHOP OF SANTA FE, N. M.

Most Rev. John B. Lamy was born near Clermont, France, October 11, 1814. He received his preliminary education at the Seminary of Clermont and completed his theological studies at the Seminary of Montferrand, where he was ordained in December, 1838. He came to America in 1839, going first to the Diocese of Cincinnati, where he labored for eleven years building churches and establishing missions. He was consecrated Bishop of Santa Fé November 24, 1850, and arrived in his see the following year. In the year 1875 he was created Archbishop.

MOST REV. FRANCIS X. LERAY, D.D.,

ARCHBISHOP OF NEW ORLEANS.

Most Rev. Francis X. Leray was born at Rennes, France, April 20, 1825, where he received his secular education. He came to America in 1843, and having studied for a time in Vincennes, Ind., was, in 1849, sent to St. Mary's Seminary, Baltimore, where he completed his theological course. He was ordained at Natchez, Miss., March 19, 1852. In 1853 he succeeded the rector of Jackson, Miss., who had died of yellow fever during the epidemic of that year. In 1857 he was removed to Vicksburg. He was consecrated Bishop of Natchitoches, April 22, 1877; appointed coadjutor of New Orleans and Bishop of Janopolis, October 23, 1879; and succeeded the late lamented Archbishop Perché on his death in 1883.

MOST REV. PATRICK W. RIORDAN, D.D.,

COADJUTOR ARCHBISHOP OF SAN FRANCISCO.

Most Rev. Patrick W. Riordan was born in Chetham, N. B., August 27, 1841. He made his theological studies at the Louvain University, Belgium, and was ordained at Melines, June 10, 1865. On his return to America he went to Chicago, where he was professor of history and dogmatic theology in the Seminary of St. Mary of the Lake for two years. He then became the pastor of Woodstock, Ill.; was transferred to St. James', Chicago, and remained there until his consecration as titular Bishop of Casaba and coadjutor Archbishop of San Francisco, September 16, 1883.

MOST REV. P. J. RYAN, D.D.,

ARCHBISHOP OF PHILADELPHIA.

Most Rev. P. J. Ryan was born at Thurles, Ireland, February 20, 1831. He made his classical and theological courses in Dublin and in Carlow College, being ordained September 8, 1852. He came to America the same year, settling in St. Louis, where he was made professor of English literature in Carondelet Theological Seminary. After a varied experience in mission work and pastoral charges, during which he made two trips to Europe, he was consecrated titular Bishop of Tricomia and coadjutor of the Archbishop of St. Louis; promoted to the titular Archbishopric of Salamis in 1884, and was transferred to the See of Philadelphia November 11, 1884.

MOST REV. C. J. SEGHERS, D.D.,

ARCHBISHOP OF OREGON CITY.

Most. Rev. C. J. Seghers was born in Ghent, Belgium, December, 26, 1839. He was educated at the University of Louvain and ordained in June, 1863, at Mechlin. He was first stationed at Victoria, Vancouver's Island; was consecrated Bishop of Vancouver's Island June 20, 1873; was translated as coadjutor to the Archbishop of Oregon City by brief of December 10, 1878, and succeeded on the retirement of Most Rev. F. N. Blanchet, December 12, 1880. He has been transferred (1884) to Vancouver's Island at his own request.

MOST REV. JOHN B. SALPOINTE, D.D.,

TITULAR ARCHBISHOP OF ANAZANBA AND COADJUTOR OF THE ARCHBISHOP OF SANTA FE.

Most Rev. John B. Salpointe was born at St. Maurice, France, February 22, 1825. He received his preparatory education at the Seminaries of Agen and of Clermont-Ferrand, and made his theological course under the Sulpician priests at Montferrand, where he was ordained December 21, 1851. He spent three years in pastoral charges and five years as professor in the Clermont-Ferrand Seminary. In August, 1859, he came to America, and devoted himself to missionary work in the Diocese of Santa Fé. He was appointed Vicar Apostolic of Arizona in September, 1868, and consecrated June 20, 1869, and was promoted to be coadjutor to the Archbishop of Santa Fé in March, 1884, with the title of Archbishop of Anazanba.

MOST REV. JOHN JOSEPH WILLIAMS, D.D.,

ARCHBISHOP OF BOSTON.

Most Rev. John J. Williams was born in Boston, Mass., April 27, 1822. He went to the Sulpician College, in Montreal, in September, 1833, graduating in 1841. After a course in Seminary of St. Sulpice, Paris, he was ordained there in May, 1845. On his return to America he was appointed assistant at the Boston Cathedral, November 1, 1845; was made rector in 1855; took charge of St. James' in 1857, in which latter post he remained until his appointment as coadjutor Bishop of Boston, January, 1866.

He succeeded to the see February 13, 1866, and was consecrated March 11, 1866. He was promoted to the rank of Archbishop February 12, 1875.

RIGHT REV. PETER J. BALTES, D.D.,[1]

BISHOP OF ALTON, ILL.

Right Rev. Peter J. Baltes was born at Ensheim, in the Rhenish province of Bavaria, Germany, April 7, 1827. He came with his parents to America in 1833. His theological studies were made at the Sulpician Seminary, Montreal, Canada, where he was ordained May 21, 1853. His first mission was at Waterloo, Monroe county, Ill., whence he was sent to Belleville, St. Clair county, in 1855. He was consecrated Bishop of Alton January 23, 1870.

RIGHT REV. JOHN B. BRONDEL, D.D.,

BISHOP OF HELENA, MONTANA.

Right Rev. John B. Brondel was born at Bruges, Belgium, February 23, 1842, where he received his secular education. He made his theological studies at Louvain in the American College, and was ordained at Mechlin, Belgium, December 17, 1864. In 1866 he went to Washington Territory, succeeding the rector of Heilacoom the following year. In 1877 he was transferred to Walla Walla; returned to Heilacoom in 1878; and was consecrated Bishop of Vancouver Island, at Victoria, December 14, 1879. In 1883 he was appointed administrator of the Vicariate Apostolic of Montana, and on March 7, 1884, became the first Bishop of Helena.

RIGHT REV. CASPAR HENRY BORGESS, D.D.,

BISHOP OF DETROIT.

Right Rev. Caspar H. Borgess was born at Addrup, in the Grand Duchy of Oldenburg, Germany, August 1, 1826. Coming

---

[1] Bishop Baltes, on account of illness, did not attend the Council, but was represented by a procurator.

to America in 1834, he made his classical and philosophical studies in Philadelphia and at St. Charles' Seminary. He finished his education at St. Xavier's College, Cincinnati, where he was ordained December 8, 1848. For ten years he was stationed at Columbus, O., being appointed in May, 1859, as rector of St. Peter's Cathedral, Cincinnati, where he remained until his promotion to the See of Detroit. He was consecrated titular Bishop of Calidonia and coadjutor April 24, 1870, and succeeded to the Bishopric of Detroit December 31, 1871.

RIGHT REV. THOMAS A. BECKER, D.D.,

BISHOP OF WILMINGTON, DEL.

Right Rev. Thomas A. Becker was born in Pittsburg, Pa., December 30, 1832. He made his studies at the Propaganda College, Rome, being ordained in that city June 18, 1859. On his return to America he was assigned to Richmond, Va., whence he was sent to Martinsburg and Berkeley Springs; returning to Baltimore at the end of the late war, he was stationed at St. Peter's Church, and afterwards became professor of theology, ecclesiastical history and Sacred Scriptures in Mt. St. Mary's College, Emmitsburg. He acted as one of the chief secretaries of the second Plenary Council, being stationed at the Cathedral when it assembled. Afterwards Dr. Becker was at the Richmond Cathedral until his appointment in March, 1868, to the new Diocese of Wilmington, for which he was consecrated in the Baltimore Cathedral August 16, 1868.

RIGHT REV. DENNIS BRADLEY, D.D.,

BISHOP OF MANCHESTER, N. H.

Right Rev. Dennis Bradley was born in Ireland February 25, 1846, and was brought to Manchester, N. H., when a small boy (1854.) Having received his secular education in that city, and made his classical studies at Holy Cross College, Worcester, Mass., he entered St. Joseph's Provincial Seminary, Troy, N. Y., in 1867, and was ordained there June 3, 1871. Immediately afterwards he was assigned to the Cathedral at Portland, Me., where he remained for nine years, filling the offices of chancellor of the diocese and rector of the Cathedral. He was appointed pastor of St. Joseph's Church, Manchester, N. H., in June, 1880, being consecrated bishop in the same church, which is now his Cathedral, June 11, 1884.

RIGHT REV. FRANCIS SILAS CHATARD, D.D.,

BISHOP OF VINCENNES, IND.

Right Rev. Francis S. Chatard was born in Baltimore, Md., December 13, 1834. He was educated at Mt. St. Mary's College, Emmitsburg, Md., and was ordained at the Trinity ordination at Rome in the year 1862. He was successively vice-rector and rector of the American College in Rome. He was consecrated Bishop of Vincennes May 12, 1878.

RIGHT REV. HENRY COSGROVE, D.D.,

BISHOP OF DAVENPORT, IOWA.

Right Rev. Henry Cosgrove was born at Williamsport, Pa., December 19, 1834. He received his education at St. Mary's Seminary, and was ordained August 27, 1857. He was first appointed to St. Margaret's Church, Davenport, Iowa, and after a long experience of mission and pastoral work, was consecrated Bishop of Davenport September 14, 1884.

RIGHT REV. JOHN JOSEPH CONROY, D.D.,

TITULAR BISHOP OF CURIUM.

Right Rev. John J. Conroy was born at Greagafulla, Queen's County, Ireland. He came to America, settling in New York, in 1832. He made his classical, philosophical and theological studies at the College of St. Sulpice, Montreal, and at Mt. St. Mary's College, Emmitsburg, Md., being ordained at Fordham, N. Y., May 21, 1842. He remained at St. John's College, in that place, until March, 1844, when he was appointed pastor of St. Joseph's, Albany. He was designated Bishop of Albany July 7, 1865, and consecrated October 15, of the same year. Having resigned October 16, 1877, he was transferred to the titular See of Curium, March 22, 1878.

RIGHT REV. JOSEPH DWENGER, D.D.,

BISHOP OF FORT WAYNE.

Right Rev. Joseph Dwenger was born in the State of Ohio in 1837. He entered at an early age the Congregation of the Precious Blood; completed his studies at Mt. St. Mary's of the West, Cincinnati, and was ordained, with papal dispensation, September 4, 1859. He was engaged in teaching till 1862; for six years in pastoral work; and from 1868 to 1872 devoted himself exclusively to preaching missions and giving retreats. He was nominated Bishop of Fort Wayne February 10, 1871, and consecrated April 14, of the same year.

RIGHT REV. LOUIS M. FINK, D.D.,

BISHOP OF LEAVENWORTH, KAN.

Right Rev. Louis M. Fink was born at Triftersberg, Bavaria, July 12, 1834. He received his elementary and most of his higher education at Ratisbone. Coming to America in 1852, he joined the Benedictine Order of St. Vincent's, Pa., where he finished his studies and was ordained in May, 1857. He was successively stationed at Bellefonte, Pa.; Newark and several other places in New Jersey; St. Joseph's, Covington; and St. Joseph's Chicago, which latter he left in 1868 to be placed at the head of St. Benedict's College and to act as pastor of the congregation in charge of the Fathers at Atchison, Kan. He was consecrated Bishop of Encarpia and coadjutor to Right Rev. John B. Miége, S.J., then Vicar Apostolic of the territory east of the Rocky Mountains. He was transferred to the newly created See of Leavenworth May 22, 1877.

RIGHT REV. EDWARD FITZGERALD, D.D.,
BISHOP OF LITTLE ROCK, ARK.

Right Rev. Edward Fitzgerald was born at Limerick, Ireland, October 28, 1833. He came to America with his parents in 1849 and immediately entered the preparatory Seminary of St. Mary, Barrens, Mo. In 1852 he was admitted into the Seminary of Cincinnati, and in 1855 he was sent to Emmitsburg, Md., to finish his studies. He was ordained August 22, 1857, and placed in charge of St. Patrick's, Columbus, O., where he remained till his consecration as Bishop of Little Rock, February 3, 1867.

RIGHT REV. KILIAN C. FLASCH, D.D.,
BISHOP OF LA CROSSE, WIS.

Right Rev. Kilian C. Flasch was born at Retzstadt, Bavaria, July 16, 1837. He was brought to America in June, 1847, and was sent to school to the Fathers of the Holy Cross, South Bend, Indiana, completing his education for the priesthood at the Seminary of St. Francis de Sales, near Milwaukee. He was ordained December 16, 1869, and consecrated Bishop of La Crosse, August 24, 1881.

RIGHT REV. NICHOLAS A. GALLAGHER, D.D.,
BISHOP ADMINISTRATOR OF GALVESTON, TEXAS.

Right. Rev. Nicholas A. Gallagher was born at Temperanceville, Belmont county, Ohio, February 19, 1846. He made his classical, philosophical and theological studies at Mt. St. Mary's Seminary, Cincinnati, and was ordained December 25, 1868, at Columbus. He was appointed administrator of the Diocese of Columbus October 8, 1878, and transferred to the administration of Galveston, Texas, January 10, 1882, being consecrated April 30, 1882.

RIGHT REV. L. DE GOESBRIAND, D.D.,
BISHOP OF BURLINGTON, VT.

Right Rev. L. De Goesbriand was born in France August 4, 1816. He received his theological education at St. Sulpice, Paris, where he was ordained July 17, 1840. He came to America, arriving in Cincinnati in the month of September of the same year. He labored on the missions of Northern Ohio till 1847, when he became vicar general of Cleveland on the creation of that diocese, at which post he remained until his appointment to the newly created See of Burlington, of which he was consecrated Bishop October 30, 1853.

RIGHT REV. THOMAS L. GRACE, D.D.,
TITULAR BISHOP OF MENNITH.

Right Rev. Thomas L. Grace was born in Charleston, S. C., November 14, 1814. He was educated at the College of the Minerva, Rome, and was ordained in that city December 21, 1839. On his return to America he was stationed at Memphis, Tenn., where he remained fourteen years. He was consecrated Bishop of St. Paul, Minn., July 24, 1859. He resigned the See of St. Paul April 31, 1884, and was appointed to the titular See of Mennith November 13, 1884.

RIGHT REV. RICHARD GILMOUR, D.D.,
BISHOP OF CLEVELAND.

Right Rev. Richard Gilmour was born in Glasgow, Scotland, September 28, 1824, and came with his parents to America in

1829. When eighteen years of age he was converted to the Catholic faith. He studied for the priesthood at Mt. St. Mary's Seminary, Emmitsburg, being ordained August 30, 1852. For five years he labored on Missions in Ohio, Kentucky and Virginia; in 1857 he was appointed pastor of St. Patrick's, Cincinnati, retaining this post for eleven years; from March, 1868, to July, 1870, he taught at Mt. St. Mary's of the West; then took charge of St. Joseph's, Dayton, where he remained until his appointment to the Bishopric of Cleveland. He was consecrated April 14, 1872.

RIGHT REV. W. H. GROSS, D.D.,
BISHOP OF SAVANNAH, GA.

Right Rev. W. H. Gross was born in Baltimore June 12, 1837, his father having come from Alsace in colonial times and his maternal grandfather being one of the exiles from Ireland in 1798. He was educated at St. Joseph's College and joined the Redemptorists in 1857. He was ordained March 12, 1863, by Archbishop Kenrick, and was stationed successively in New York and Boston, and engaged in mission work until he finally became Superior of the Redemptorist Home in Boston. On September 2, 1873, he was appointed to the See of Savannah.

RIGHT REV. JOHN HENNESSY, D.D.,
BISHOP OF DUBUQUE.

Right Rev. John Hennessy, D.D., is a native of the County Limerick, Ireland, where he made his preparatory studies. Coming to America, he finished his classical and theological courses at St. Louis, and was ordained November 1, 1850. After having spent three years in the mission he was appointed professor of theology in the Diocesan Seminary of St. Louis, where he spent four years, part of the time as vice-president and part of the time as president of the seminary. He spent six years as pastor in St. Joseph, Missouri. In 1866 he was appointed Bishop of Dubuque, and consecrated September 30.

RIGHT REV. JAMES A. HEALY, D.D.,

BISHOP OF PORTLAND, MAINE.

Right Rev. James A. Healy was born near Macon, Ga., April 6, 1830. He received his secular education at Flushing, Long Island, Burlington, N. Y., and Holy Cross College, Worcester, Mass., graduating in 1849. He made his theological course at Montreal and Paris under the priests of St. Sulpice, and was ordained June 10, 1854. He was secretary of Right Rev. J. B. Fitzpatrick until 1866, and pastor of St. James', Boston, until 1875, in which latter year, on the 2d of June, he was consecrated Bishop of Portland.

RIGHT REV. THOMAS F. HENDRICKEN, D.D.,

BISHOP OF PROVIDENCE, R. I.

Right Rev. Thomas F. Hendricken was born in Kilkenny, Ireland, May 5, 1827. He was educated at Maynooth and was ordained in Dublin April 25, 1853. He immediately came to this country, settling first in Providence, R. I., but soon afterwards removing to Waterbury, Conn., where he remained for eighteen years. He was consecrated the first Bishop of Providence April 28, 1872.

RIGHT REV. JOHN J. HOGAN, D.D.,

BISHOP OF KANSAS CITY AND ADMINISTRATOR OF ST. JOSEPH.

Right Rev. John Joseph Hogan was born in the Diocese of Limerick, Ireland, May 10, 1829, where he received his secular education. He came to America in 1848, studied philosophy and theology in the Diocesan Seminary of St. Louis, and was ordained April 10, 1852. He was successively pastor of St. James', Potosi, St. Michael's, St. Louis, and St. Columbanus', Chillicothe, all in Missouri. On September 13, 1868, he was consecrated Bishop of St. Joseph; and on September 10, 1880, he was transferred to the newly created See of Kansas City, still retaining the administration of the Diocese of St. Joseph.

RIGHT REV. JOHN IRELAND, D.D.,

BISHOP OF ST. PAUL, MINN.

Right Rev. John Ireland was born in Ireland, September 11, 1838, but came to this country in 1849. He was educated in France and ordained in St. Paul, December 21, 1861. He was consecrated Coadjutor Bishop of St. Paul, December 21, 1875, succeeding to the see on the resignation of Right Rev. Thomas L. Grace, in August, 1884. His earnest work in the cause of temperance has gained for him the soubriquet of the "Father Mathew of the West."

RIGHT REV. FRANCIS JANSSENS, D.D.,

BISHOP OF NATCHEZ, MISS.

Right Rev. Francis Janssens was born at Tilburg, Holland, October 17, 1843. He studied in the seminaries of his diocese and in the American College, Louvain, Belgium, and was ordained at Ghent, December 21, 1867. He came to this country and was stationed at the Richmond, Va., Cathedral, where he remained until he was consecrated Bishop of Natchez, May 1, 1881.

RIGHT REV. ÆGIDIUS JUNGER, D.D.,

BISHOP OF NESQUALLY, WASH. TER.

Right Rev. Ægidius Junger was born at Burtscheid, Rheinprovinz, Prussia, where he received his secular education. He made his classical studies at the Gymnasium of Aix-la-Chapelle, and his theological course at the Louvain University, Belgium, and was ordained at Malines, July 26, 1862. Coming to America the same year, he was appointed to the mission of Walla Walla, in the Diocese of Nesqually, November 6. The next year he was appointed rector at the Cathedral of Vancouver, Washington Territory. He was consecrated Bishop of Nesqually, October 28, 1879.

Most Rev. P. W. Riordan, D.D.

RIGHT REV. JOHN JOSEPH KAIN, D.D.,

BISHOP OF WHEELING, W. VA.

Right Rev. John Joseph Kain was born at Martinsburg, W. Va., May 31, 1841, of Irish parents. He received his primary education in his native town; made his classical studies at St. Charles' College, Md., and his theological course at St. Mary's Seminary, Baltimore. Ordained July 2, 1866, he was stationed at Harper's Ferry, where he remained for nine years, having charge of nine or ten counties in Virginia and West Virginia. He was consecrated Bishop of Wheeling May 23, 1875, succeeding Bishop Whelan.

RIGHT REV. JOHN J. KEANE, D.D.,

BISHOP OF RICHMOND, VA.

Right Rev. John J. Keane was born at Ballyshannon, County Donegal, Ireland, September 12, 1839. He was brought to America when seven years of age, his family settling in Baltimore in 1848. He received his elementary education in Baltimore schools; made his classical studies at St. Charles' College, Howard county, Md., and his theological course at St. Mary's Seminary, Baltimore. He was ordained in 1866, immediately after which he was stationed at St. Patrick's Church, Washington, where he remained twelve years. He was consecrated Bishop of Richmond August 25, 1878.

RIGHT REV. F. X. KRAUTBAUER, D.D.,

BISHOP OF GREEN BAY, WIS.

Right Rev. F. X. Krautbauer was born in the parish of Bruck, near Ratisbon, Bavaria, in 1824. He made his studies in Ratisbon and at the University of Munich, returning to the Seminary at Ratisbon and being ordained July 16, 1850. He came at once to America, his first charge being St. Peter's, Rochester, N. Y. In 1858 he became Vicar General of the Diocese, which post he retained for one year, relinquishing it for the purpose of accepting the chaplaincy of Notre Dame in Milwaukee, where he remained for sixteen years. He was appointed Bishop of Green Bay in February, 1875, being consecrated on the 29th of the following month.

RIGHT REV. JOSEPH P. MACHEBEUF, D.D.,

VICAR APOSTOLIC OF COLORADO.

Right Rev. Joseph P. Machebeuf was born at Riom, France, August 11, 1852. He received his secular education in the Christian Brothers' schools and the College of Riom, and his theological course at the Seminary of St. Sulpice, Montferrand. He was ordained December 25, 1836, and was assistant priest in the Diocese of Clermont for three years. He came to this country in 1839; labored first in Sandusky City, Ohio; accompanied Right Rev. J. B. Lamy, the newly appointed Vicar Apostolic of New Mexico, as his vicar general to the West. In October, 1860, he was sent to Colorado as a missionary, and built the first church in that territory, at Denver. He was consecrated Bishop of Epiphany and Vicar Apostolic of Colorado August 16, 1868.

RIGHT REV. MARTIN MARTY, D.D.,

VICAR APOSTOLIC OF DAKOTA.

Right Rev. Martin Marty was born at Schwyz, Switzerland, January 12, 1834. He made his studies in the Jesuit Colleges of Schwyz and Fribourg and in the Benedictine Abbey of Einsiedeln, of which last he became a member May 20, 1855. He was ordained September 14, 1860. In September, 1860, he came to America, settling at the Benedictine Priory in Spencer county, Indiana, of which he was appointed the first abbot in September, 1870. He went to Standing Rock, Dakota Territory, in 1876, to labor as a missionary among the natives, and was appointed Vicar Apostolic of Dakota, August 8, 1879, and consecrated titular Bishop of Tiberias, February 1, 1880.

RIGHT REV. CAMILLUS P. MAES, D.D.,

BISHOP OF COVINGTON, KY.

Right Rev. Camillus P. Maes was born at Courtrai, West Flanders, Belgium, March 13, 1846. He made his classical studies in the college of that city, and his theological course at the Seminary of Bruges and the American College, Louvain, being ordained for the Diocese of Detroit, December 18, 1868. On coming to America, he was stationed as pastor of Mount Clemens, Detroit, 1869; of St. Mary's, Monroe, 1871; of St. John's, same city, 1873, becoming the secretary of the Diocese of Detroit in 1880. He was appointed to the vacant See of Covington, in September, 1884.

RIGHT REV. PATRICK MANOGUE, D.D.,

BISHOP OF GRASS VALLEY, CAL. AND NEV.

Right Rev. Patrick Manogue was born at Desart, County Kilkenny, Ireland. He received his elementary education in Callan, and soon after came to America and settled in New England. He made his theological course at St. Mary's of the Lake and the Sulpician Seminary, Paris, where he was ordained in 1861. After twenty years of labor on mission work and in pastoral charges, he was consecrated coadjutor Bishop of Grass Valley in 1881; and promoted to the Bishopric in March, 1884.

RIGHT REV. D. MANUCY, D.D.,

ADMINISTRATOR OF MOBILE, ALA., AND OF THE VICARIATE APOSTOLIC OF BROWNSVILLE, TEXAS.

Right Rev. D. Manucy was born at St. Augustine, Fla., December 20, 1823, where he received his secular education. He entered Spring Hill College, Mobile, in 1842, and was ordained August 15, 1850. In the November of the same year he was sent to Warrington, Fla., to organize a congregation and build a church; in March, 1853, was transferred to Apalachicola; in April, 1855, was called to the Cathedral of Mobile as assistant; in December, 1861, was put in charge of the Church of St. Vincent de Paul; and in January, 1865, was transferred to St. Peter's Church. He was consecrated bishop December 8, 1874, and sent to Texas to organize the Vicariate Apostolic of Brownsville, and in December, 1883, was made Bishop of Mobile, taking charge of his see on Passion Sunday, March 30, 1884.

RIGHT REV. FRANCIS MORA, D.D.,

BISHOP OF MONTEREY AND LOS ANGELES, CAL.

Right Rev. Francis Mora was born near Vich, Spain, where he received his secular education, making his theological studies in the seminary of that city. In 1854 he volunteered to come to the mission of California with Right Rev. Thaddeus Amat, by whom he was ordained at Santa Barbara, March 19, 1856. He was successively rector of several churches, becoming finally rector of the Pro-Cathedral of Los Angeles, February 1, 1863, and vicar general in 1865. He was consecrated August 3, 1873, Bishop of Mossynopolis and Coadjutor of Right Rev. Thaddeus Amat, *cum jure successionis*, and on the death of Bishop Amat, May 12, 1878, he succeeded to the See of Monterey and Los Angeles.

RIGHT REV. JOHN MOORE, D.D.,

BISHOP OF ST. AUGUSTINE, FLA.

Right Rev. John Moore was born in Delvin, County Westmeath, Ireland, June 27, 1835. In 1848 he went to Charleston, S. C., studying successively in the Collegiate Institute and the Seminary of St. John the Baptist in that city. He completed his studies in the College of Cambrée, France, the Roman College and the Propaganda College. He was ordained in Rome, April 9, 1860; was assistant at the Charleston Cathedral for five years; and was for twelve years pastor of St. Patrick's and vicar general of the diocese. He was consecrated Bishop of St. Augustine, Fla., May 13, 1877, as the successor of Bishop Vérot.

RIGHT REV. TOBIAS MULLEN, D.D.,

BISHOP OF ERIE.

Right Rev. Tobias Mullen was born in Flushtown, County Tyrone, Ireland, March 4, 1818. Having received his elementary education in the national schools, he entered Maynooth in 1840. Three years later he came to America and was ordained September 1, 1884. He was consecrated Bishop of Erie, August 2, 1868.

RIGHT REV. BERNARD J. M'QUAID, D.D.,

BISHOP OF ROCHESTER, N. Y.

Right Rev. Bernard J. McQuaid was born in New York City, December 15, 1823. He was educated at Chambly, Canada, and Fordham College and Seminary, New York. He was ordained in the Cathedral of New York, July 16, 1848, and after twenty years of experience in mission work and pastoral charges, was consecrated Bishop of Rochester, July 12, 1868.

RIGHT REV. WILLIAM GEORGE M'CLOSKEY, D.D.,

BISHOP OF LOUISVILLE, KY.

Right Rev. William George McCloskey was born in Brooklyn, New York, November 10, 1823. He made his classical studies in St. Mary's College, his theological course in the seminary, and was ordained in the Cathedral of New York by Archbishop Hughes in 1852. Having spent one year on the mission in New York as the assistant of his brother, the Very Rev. George McCloskey, he returned to the "Old Mountain" as one of its professors. In 1857 he became director of the Seminary and professor of moral theology and Sacred Scripture. In December, 1859, he was appointed by Pope Pius IX the first president of the American College, which that Pontiff had just founded in Rome. After presiding over this institution Dr. McCloskey was appointed to the See of Louisville and consecrated May 24, 1868.

RIGHT REV. LAWRENCE S. M'MAHON, D.D.,

BISHOP OF HARTFORD, CONN.

Right Rev. Lawrence S. McMahon was born at St. John, N. B., December 26, 1835, but was brought to Boston, Mass., in the following year. He made his theological studies at Aix, in Provence, France, and at Rome. He was ordained in the latter city, March 24, 1860. On his return to America he successively served at the Boston Cathedral, as a chaplain in the army, and as pastor of New Bedford. He was appointed Vicar General of the Diocese of Providence in July, 1872, and was consecrated Bishop of Hartford, August 10, 1879.

RIGHT REV. FRANCIS M'NEIRNEY, D.D.,

BISHOP OF ALBANY.

Right Rev. Francis McNeirney was born in New York City, April 25, 1828, where he received his secular education at private schools. Having made his classical studies in Montreal College, and his theological course in the seminary of the same city, both under charge of the Sulpician Fathers, he was ordained August 17, 1854, in St. Patrick's Cathedral, New York. He was secretary of Archbishop, subsequently Cardinal McCloskey, from 1854 to 1872; was appointed titular Bishop of Rhesina and coadjutor of Albany, December 22, 1871; was consecrated April 21, 1871; appointed administrator of Albany, February 19, 1874, becoming Bishop of the see by right of succession, October 12, 1877.

RIGHT REV. HENRY PINCKNEY NORTHROP, D.D.,

BISHOP OF CHARLESTON, S. C., AND ADMINISTRATOR OF NORTH CAROLINA.

Right Rev. Henry P. Northrop was born in Charleston, S. C., May 5, 1842. He received the rudiments of his education at Georgetown College, D. C. (1853-6), whence, on his health failing, he was sent to St. Mary's College, Emmitsburg, graduating in 1860. Entering the seminary the same year, he studied there four years, going thence to the American College in Rome, where he was ordained in June, 1865. For some months he was on duty at the Church of the Nativity, New York; was one year at St. Joseph's, Charleston; four years at Newbern, N. C.; six years assistant at St. John's Pro-Cathedral, Charleston, and pastor of Sullivan's Island; and one year pastor of St. Patrick's Church, Charleston. He was made titular Bishop of Rosalia and Vicar Apostolic of North Carolina, January 8, 1882. By brief dated January 27, 1883, he was transferred to the See of Charleston, as the successor of Right Rev. P. N. Lynch, still retaining the administration of the Vicariate of North Carolina.

RIGHT REV. JOHN C. NERAZ, D.D.,

BISHOP OF SAN ANTONIO, TEXAS.

Right Rev. John C. Neraz was born at Anse (Rhône) France, January 12, 1828. He received his preliminary education at the Seminary of St. Jodard (Loire), and made his theological course in the Sulpician Seminary of Lyons. He came to America in 1852 and was ordained in Galveston, Texas, March 19, 1853. After a succession of mission and pastoral charges he was appointed administrator, then Bishop of the Diocese of San Antonio, being consecrated May 8, 1881.

RIGHT REV. EUGENE O'CONNELL,

TITULAR BISHOP OF JOPPA.

Right Rev. Eugene O'Connell was born near the cities of Kells and Navan, County Meath, Ireland, June 18, 1815, where he received his secular education. He made his theological course in the Royal College of St. Patrick, Maynooth, where he was ordained in June, 1842. After discharging missionary duties in several parishes and being a professor in All Hallows College, he sailed for California, arriving in 1851. He was for a year in charge of the natives of Santa Inez; for three years at the Seminary of St. Thomas, near San Francisco, returning in 1854 to All Hallows. The Archbishop of San Francisco recalled him in 1861, when he was created Bishop of Flaviopolis and Vicar Apostolic of Marysville. He was translated to the See of Grass Valley (composed of Northern California and Nevada), March 22, 1868, of which charge he was relieved at his own request March 17, 1884, being then appointed titular Bishop of Joppa.

RIGHT REV. M. J. O'FARRELL, D.D.,

BISHOP OF TRENTON, N. J.

Right Rev. M. J. O'Farrell was born in Limerick, Ireland, December 2, 1832. He was educated at All Hallows, Dublin, and St. Sulpice, Paris, being ordained in his native city, August 18, 1855. Having labored on missions for thirteen years, he was stationed at St. Peter's Church, New York, from 1868 to 1881. He was consecrated the first Bishop of Trenton, November 1, 1881.

RIGHT REV. JAMES O'CONNOR, D.D.

VICAR APOSTOLIC OF NEBRASKA.

Right Rev. James O'Connor was born in Queenstown, Ireland, September 10, 1834. He came to Philadelphia in 1838, and there completed his preparatory studies at the Seminary of St.

Charles Borromeo. In January, 1843, he entered the College of Propaganda, at Rome, where he studied philosophy and theology, and returned to the United States in 1848. He commenced his missionary labors in the Diocese of Pittsburg, under his brother, who had been made its first bishop in 1843. He was rector of St. Michael's Seminary for about seven years, vicar general and administrator of the diocese for one year, and, in 1862, returned to Philadelphia. He was then appointed professor of philosophy and ecclesiastical history at St. Charles' Seminary, and, soon after, rector, which position he retained till June, 1872, when he resigned and was appointed pastor of St. Dominic's Church, Hohmsburg. He was consecrated Bishop of Dibona and Vicar Apostolic of Nebraska, August 20, 1876.

RIGHT REV. PATRICK T. O'REILLY, D.D.,

BISHOP OF SPRINGFIELD, MASS.

Right Rev. Patrick T. O'Reilly was born in Ireland, December 24, 1833. He was sent to this country when a small boy. He made his classical studies at St. Charles' College, near Ellicott City, and his theological course at St. Mary's Seminary. He was ordained, August 15, 1857. After much experience of mission work and pastoral charges, he was appointed Bishop of Springfield in June, 1870, and was consecrated September 25, 1870.

RIGHT REV. JAMES RADEMACHER, D.D.,

BISHOP OF NASHVILLE, TENN.

Right Rev. James Rademacher was born in Clinton County, Mich., December 3, 1840. He made his classical, philosophical and theological studies at St. Vincent's College, Westmoreland county, and at St. Michael's Seminary, near Pittsburg, Pa., being ordained August 2, 1863, in the Cathedral of Fort Wayne, Ind. He was in charge of Attica, Fountain County, Ind., and a number of smaller missions for seven and a-half years; in Columbia City for eighteen months; at St. Mary's Chapel, Fort Wayne, for eight years, and at St. Mary's Church, Lafayette, Ind., for three years. He was consecrated Bishop of Nashville, June 24, 1883.

RIGHT REV. HENRY J. RICHTER, D.D.,

BISHOP OF GRAND RAPIDS, MICH.

Right Rev. Henry J. Richter was born in Neuenkirchen, Grand Duchy of Oldenburg, Germany, April 9, 1838. In 1854 he came to America. He studied at St. Xavier's College, Cincinnati; St. Thomas' Seminary, Bardstown, Ky.; St. Mary's Seminary, Cincinnati, and at the American College, Rome, in which city he was ordained in 1865. On his return to America he was made president and vice-rector of St. Mary's Seminary, Cincinnati, which post he retained until 1870, when he became pastor of St. Lawrence's and chaplain of the Sisters of Charity at Cedar Grove. He was consecrated Bishop of Grand Rapids, April 22, 1883.

RIGHT REV. ISIDORE ROBOT, D.D.,

PREFECT APOSTOLIC OF INDIAN TERRITORY.

Right Rev. Isidore Robot was born near Avallon, France, July 17, 1837. Having joined the Benedictine Order, he came to America in 1873 and took charge of a mission in Louisiana. In 1875 he settled in Indian Territory, and founded the Sacred Heart Mission. He was raised to the dignity of Abbot in 1877, having received charge of the Prefecture Apostolic of Indian Territory, first created by the Holy See, May 14, 1876.

RIGHT REV. STEPHEN VINCENT RYAN, D.D.,

BISHOP OF BUFFALO, N. Y.

Right Rev. Stephen B. Ryan was born in Ottawa, Canada, January 1, 1825, but was brought, when a child, by his parents to Pottsville, Pa. In 1846 he entered St. Charles' Seminary, Philadelphia, and in 1844 went to Missouri to join the Lazarist Community, finishing his studies at Cape Girardeau and the Barrens, and being ordained at St. Louis in 1849. He was then engaged as professor, president, and visitor to the communities at St. Mary's College, Barrens, St. Vincent's College, Cape Girardeau, and the mother house in St. Louis, until the latter was transferred in 1868 to Germantown, Pa. He was consecrated Bishop of Buffalo in the cathedral of that city, November 8, 1868.

RIGHT REV. RUPERT SEIDENBUSH, D.D.,

VICAR APOSTOLIC OF NORTHERN MINNESOTA.

Right Rev. Rupert Seidenbush was born at Munich, Bavaria, October 13, 1830. He came to America in 1850, and joined the Benedictine Order. Having finished his theological studies at St. Vincent's, Westmoreland, Tenn., he was ordained in June, 1853. After having worked on the missions in the Dioceses of Pittsburg, Erie, Tennessee and Newark, N. J., he was recalled as prior to St. Vincent's Abbey in 1863. In 1866 he was elected Abbot of the newly erected Abbey of St. Louis (now St. John's), Minn., and blessed May 30, 1867. In the year 1875 he was nominated titular Bishop of Halia and Vicar Apostolic of Northern Minnesota, and consecrated May 30.

RIGHT REV. JEREMIAH F. SHANAHAN, D.D.,

BISHOP OF HARRISBURG, PA.

Right Rev. Jeremiah F. Shanahan was born at Silver Lake, Susquehanna County, Pa., July 17, 1834. His early studies were made in the local schools, the Academy of Binghampton, N. Y., and St. Joseph's College, Pa., and his theological course at the Seminary of St. Charles Borromeo, Philadelphia. He was ordained July 3, 1859, and immediately appointed rector of the preparatory Seminary of the Philadelphia Diocese, where he remained until his appointment of the new See of Harrisburg. He was consecrated in the Cathedral of Philadelphia, July 12, 1868.

RIGHT REV. JOHN TUIGG, D.D.,

BISHOP OF PITTSBURG AND ADMINISTRATOR OF ALLEGHENY.

Right Rev. John Tuigg was born in County Cork, Ireland, in 1822, and received his education at All Hallows College. He came to Pittsburg in 1850, and was ordained in the May of that year. He was first stationed at the Pittsburg Cathedral, then was the pastor of Altoona, where he remained until appointed to the See of Pittsburg, March 19, 1876, when that diocese was divided. On August 3, 1877, the Diocese of Allegheny was temporarily reunited to that of Pittsburg, and he was appointed administrator of it.

RIGHT REV. JOHN VERTIN, D.D.,

BISHOP OF MARQUETTE AND SAUT SAINTE MARIE.

Right Rev. John Vertin was born at Carniolia, Sclavonia, July 17, 1844, where he received his secular education. Coming to America in 1863 he made his philosophical and theological course in the Seminary of Milwaukee, Wis. He was ordained August 31, 1866, and labored on missions in several States until September 14, 1879, when, having been appointed to the see, he was consecrated Bishop of Marquette in place of Bishop Mrak, who had resigned the previous year.

RIGHT REV. J. L. SPALDING, D.D.,

BISHOP OF PEORIA, ILL.

Right Rev. J. L. Spalding was born at Lebanon, Ky., in 1840. He received his education at St. Mary's College, in Kentucky; at Mt. St. Mary's, Emmitsburg, Md., and at St. Mary's, Cincinnati, where he graduated in 1859. In the fall of the same year he went to Louvain, Belgium, and after studying there five years was ordained. Having spent a year in Rome, he returned to Kentucky, and was made secretary to the Bishop of Louisville. At the end of three years was appointed to organize a congregation among the colored Catholics of Louisville, and he there built for them a church, school house and pastoral residence. He remained in charge for two years, when he was appointed chancellor of the diocese. In 1872 he went to New York to write a life of Archbishop Spalding. When this work was done he remained in the city as assistant at St. Michael's Church, a post he held until his appointment to the newly-created Diocese of Peoria. He was consecrated May 1, 1877.

RIGHT REV. EDGAR P. WADHAMS, D.D.,

BISHOP OF OGDENSBURG, N. Y.

Right Rev. Edgar P. Wadhams was born at Lewis, Essex County, N. Y., May 21, 1817. Having received his secular education in the Middlebury College, he made his theological course at St. Sulpice Seminary, Baltimore, and was ordained in Albany, January 15, 1850. He was stationed in several churches in succession, becoming rector of the Albany Cathedral and vicar general of the diocese in 1866. He was appointed Bishop of Ogdensburg, February 15, 1872, and consecrated, May 5, 1872.

RIGHT REV. JOHN AMBROSE WATTERSON, D.D.,

BISHOP OF COLUMBUS, O.

Right Rev. John A. Watterson was born in Blairsville, Indiana County, Pa., May 27, 1844. He began his education in his native town's parochial school and in St. Vincent's College, near Latrobe, Pa., completing his classical, philosophical, and theological courses at St. Mary's College, Emmitsburg, Md., and was ordained at St. Vincent's Abbey, August 8, 1868. On the invitation of Dr. McCaffrey, he returned to Mount St. Mary's as professor of classics, and was a few years afterwards raised to the chair of theology. In September, 1878, he was elected president of the college and seminary, and on March 14, 1880, was appointed Bishop of Columbus, Ohio, to succeed Right Rev. Sylvester H. Rosecrans. He was consecrated by Archbishop Elder in the Cathedral of Columbus on the 8th of the following August, the twelfth anniversary of his ordination.

RIGHT REV. WINAND M. WIGGER, D.D.,

BISHOP OF NEWARK, N. J.

Right Rev. Winand M. Wigger was born in New York, December 9, 1841, and received his secular education at St. Francis' College. He entered Seton Hall Seminary, South Orange, N. J., in 1860, where he remained two years, after which he was sent to a college in Genoa, Italy. He was ordained June 10, 1865. On his return to America he was appointed assistant in the cathedral parish, Newark; became successively rector of St. Vincent's, Madison; St. John's, Orange, and St. Theresa's, Summit. He was consecrated Bishop of Newark, N. J., October 18, 1881.

RIGHT REV. A. J. GLORIEUX, D.D.,

VICAR APOSTOLIC-ELECT OF IDAHO.

Right Rev. A. J. Glorieux was born at Dottignies, West Flanders, Belgium, February 1, 1844. He was educated at the College of Courtrai, Belgium, from 1857 to 1863; made his philosophical and theological courses at the American College, Louvain, from 1863 to 1867; was ordained at Malines, by his Eminence Cardinal Sterckx, on August 17, 1867; and left Belgium for Oregon October 13, 1867. He had charge of the Southern Missions of Oregon for two years; became rector of St. Paul, French Prairie, in 1869; took charge of St. Michael's College, Portland, on the 28th of August, 1871, and remained in that position until appointed Vicar Apostolic of Idaho in 1884.

Most Rev. Francis X. Leray, D.D.

PASTORAL LETTER

— OF THE —

MOST REV. ARCHBISHOP OF BALTIMORE,

— ON THE —

THIRD PLENARY COUNCIL,

TO THE CLERGY AND LAITY OF HIS DIOCESE.

JAMES GIBBONS, by the grace of God, and the favor of the Apostolic See, Archbishop of Baltimore and Apostolic Delegate.

TO THE CLERGY AND FAITHFUL OF THE ARCHDIOCESE OF BALTIMORE:

Venerable Brethren of the Clergy, and Dearly Beloved Children of the Laity:—Our Holy Father, Leo XIII, out of his paternal solicitude for the welfare of all the faithful committed to his care, has desired all the Bishops of the Church in the United States to assemble in Plenary Council, to consider the best means for promoting the salvation of souls in this portion of our Lord's vineyard; and because of the infirm health of his Eminence, the Cardinal Archbishop of New York, who was so well qualified to preside, not only on account of his high office, but also of his nature wisdom and weight of merits, his Holiness was pleased to appoint us, to convoke by his Apostolic authority, the Third Plenary Council of Baltimore, and to preside over the same as Apostolic Delegate.

We therefore, dearly beloved brethren and children, now make known to you, that in virtue of this authority, we have, by our letters of date March 27, of this year, convoked the Third Plenary Council to convene in our Metropolitan Church at Baltimore on the ninth day of November, in this year of our Lord, 1884.

Eighteen years have now elapsed since the last Plenary Council was held, and we have reason to be devoutly thankful to God for the steady progress which religion has made in the United States since that period. It cannot fail to be a source of consolation and benefit to the chief Pastors of the Church of America to meet again after so long an interval, to recount their trials, their hopes and their success in their respective fields of labor, to interchange views, to enlighten one another by mutual counsel, and to derive that strength and confidence which result from the reunion of earnest men engaged in the same holy mission.

The steady expansion of the hierarchy and of the faithful during the last two decades of years naturally calls for the enactment of special statutes to meet the exigencies of the times, and our gradual transition from a missionary state to the fixed and normal condition of the Church, demands an adjustment of legislation more suitable to our improved situation.

Every State and Diocese of the Union will be represented at the approaching Council by Prelates and Priests; and although they are descended from divers nations, and speak every European tongue, they are all united by the bonds of a common faith, and animated by the spirit of fraternal charity, having "one Lord, one faith, one baptism, one God and Father of all." (Ephes. iv.) To them may be truly applied the words of the Psalmist: "Behold how good and how pleasant a thing it is for brethren to dwell together in unity." (Ps. cxxxii.)

The object for which this Council is summoned, as you are well aware, is not to formulate new dogmas of faith; for the only doctrine we preach to you is "the faith once delivered to the saints." (Jude i, 3.) Nor will our deliberations have any political significance, since we have no political grievances to redress nor political aspirations to gratify. The Church of God has no direct relations with politics; political intrigues form no part of her divine mission; the kingdom of Christ and of His Church "is not of this world." (John xviii.) She "renders to Cæsar the things that are Cæsar's, and to God the things that are God's." (Matt. xxii.)

The enactment of salutary laws for the promotion of piety and sound morals, the correction of abuses, the establishment, as far as practicable, of greater uniformity in ecclesiastical discipline, the development of the Christian commonwealth, the quickening and strengthening of the bonds of charity which should bind us all as members of the Christian family, to our God, and to each other—these are the signal blessings at which we aim in assembling together.

You know, brethren of the laity, that by our ordination as Priests, and consecration as Bishops, we are irrevocably dedicated to your service. Whether we preach the word, or administer the sacraments, or celebrate the sacred mysteries, or erect temples of worship, it is for your sakes that these labors are accomplished: Our Lord "gave some to be Apostles, and some Prophets, and some Evangelists, and others Pastors and Doctors, for the perfecting of the saints, for the work of the ministry, for the building up of the body of Christ." (Ephes. iv.)

If we meet in Council, our object is to make you more upright citizens, by becoming holier Christians; for "righteousness exalteth a nation, but sin maketh nations miserable." (Prov. xiv.)

We have all, both clergy and people, been redeemed by the same blood of Jesus Christ; we are all in the same bark of Peter, and are steering for the same eternal shores; we have all the hope of the same heavenly inheritance. As our spiritual interests are the same, so should we be actuated by the same zeal for the advancement of religion.

We, therefore, rely on your generous coöperation, and invoke your pious interest in the successful issue of the Council. We are sure, Brethren of the clergy, and Children of the laity, that following the traditions of your fathers, you will joyfully welcome and hospitably entertain, the prelates and clergy who will be your honored guests during the Council, and that you will emulate in this regard the veneration of the primitive Christians of whom the Apostle writes: "You received me as an angel of God, even as Christ Jesus." (Gal. iv.)

"We beseech you especially, brethren, through our Lord Jesus Christ, and by the charity of the Holy Ghost, that you help us by your prayers for us to God." (Rom. xv.) "Praying at all times in the spirit . . . that speech may be given us, that we may open our mouth with confidence, to make known the mystery of the Gospel, for which we are ambassadors." (Ephes. vi.) Pray that God may enlighten the minds, purify the hearts and direct the will of the assembled prelates, that all our acts may contribute to His glory, the propagation of His Church, and the sanctification of its members. May our legislation tend to the stability of the commonwealth, and the maintenance of the peace and tranquility of our beloved country. May the Supreme Legislator, the source of all light, be the sole Suggestor and Guide of our judgments, so that we may in nowise stray from the path of equity. May we so temper justice with charity, that our decisions may be approved by Him by whom "kings reign and lawgivers decree just things." (Prov. xiv, 34.)

With the view of obtaining the divine light by union of prayer, we deem it advisable to ordain and promulgate the following exercises of devotion for this archdiocese:

1. The collect *de Spiritu Sancto* will be added in the Mass by the priests of the archdiocese henceforward till the close of the Council.

2. All the religious communities of both sexes will recite, daily, the hymn of the Holy Ghost, *Veni Creator Spiritus.*

3. The Litany of the Saints will be publicly recited in the parish churches, either before or after the High Mass, on every Sunday, till the first Sunday of November inclusive.

This Pastoral Letter will be read in all the churches of the archdiocese on the Sunday after its reception.

Given at our residence in Baltimore on the Feast of St. Augustine, 1884.

✠ JAMES GIBBONS,
Archbishop of Baltimore, Apostolic Delegate.

A. A. CURTIS,
    Secretary.

SERMONS

DELIVERED DURING THE SESSIONS

—OF THE—

THIRD PLENARY COUNCIL

OF BALTIMORE.

Most Rev. P. J. Ryan, D.D.

The Church in Her Councils.

SERMON OF MOST REV. PATRICK JOHN RYAN, D.D.,

ARCHBISHOP OF PHILADELPHIA.

> "And Jesus coming spoke to them, saying: All power is given to Me in heaven and in earth; going, therefore, teach ye all nations; baptizing them in the name of the Father and of the Son and of the Holy Ghost; teaching them to observe all things whatsoever I have commanded you: and, behold, I am with you all days, even to the consummation of the world."—*St. Matthew*, c. *xviii*, v. *18, 19 and 20*.

IT is not without emotion and embarrassment that I presume to address you on the occasion of the opening of this great council. It is difficult to rise to an adequate conception of the importance and the majesty of this scene. In you, Most Reverend Apostolic Delegate, I behold represented the mighty headship of Peter, whom Christ placed supreme pastor over His flock and made the rock on which He built His Church, and because of which the falling rains and rising floods and pelting storms have beaten in vain—and "that house fell not, because it was founded on a rock." And in you, venerable Fathers of the Council, I behold the successors of the other Apostles — unshorn of a single prerogative essential to the Apostolate, as that Apostolate, according to Christ's express words, was to continue until the consummation of the world. I behold you as pillars supporting and adorning the great temple of God, your mitres indicating, like Corinthian capitals, the particular order of sacred architecture in which you belong. I behold you assembled with a power direct from God, not deputed, but ordinary, for the Holy Ghost Himself has placed you "bishops to rule the Church of God." I salute you as a portion of the great senate of the kingdom of God on this earth assembled to and heart as the eight beatitudes of the Sermon on the Mount?— "On this rock I build My Church, and the gates of hell shall not prevail against it." "He that will not hear the Church, let him be to thee as the heathen and the publican." "He who hears you hears Me, and he who despises you despises Me." "As the Father sent Me, so also I send you." "All power is given to Me in heaven and in earth; go ye, therefore, and teach all nations; and behold I am with you all days until the consummation of ages." This identity with Christ is confirmed by this expostulation to the persecutor, Saul: "Saul, Saul, why persecutest thou Me?" Now, Saul did not persecute Christ in His sacred Person, but he did it in His mystic body, the Church, and hence Christ said: "I am Christ whom thou persecutest." As if He said: "He who despises you despises Me, and he who strikes you strikes Me." We find here more than justified St. Paul's comparison of the union of Christ with His Church to the union of husband and wife. And not only did he identify the Church with Himself, but He identified it also with the other two persons of the Holy Trinity. "He who despises you despises Me, and he who despises Me despises Him that sent Me;" therefore, for the syllogism is perfect, he who despises you despises Him that sent Me—God the Father. And again, He said He would send God the Holy Ghost to abide with them forever, to be to them a Spirit of truth and consolation—another Paraclete—to be the very life of the future Church, as man's soul is the life of his body. This identification of the Church with God the Holy Ghost is expressly mentioned by the Apostles after their last council in Jerusalem, when they said: "It seemeth good to the Holy Ghost and to us."

The Church so identified with God has a twofold mission—a mission of verification and sanctification. In the first she bears witness to the facts of our Lord's life and the doctrines He taught, and in the second she sanctifies in His name the individual and society; and these ends she attains in great part through her councils. "You shall bear witness to Me in Jerusalem and in all Judea and Samaria, and to the uttermost ends of the earth." Her testimony to Him is written in the blood of her martyrs. For a martyr is not a man who merely dies for an opinion or a conviction; a martyr means a witness, one who dies, testifying what he has seen or heard.

Now Christianity is a religion of facts, and the eye-witnesses and ear-witnesses of the events of our Lord's life died declaring these things to be facts, and have continued to do so, as the Church continued to live. As the sun in the firmament to-day, were he able to speak, or testify to what he saw, could say: "I was there when He made the blind to see and the lame to walk and the deaf to hear and the dumb to speak, and raised the dead to life; my rays beamed on His thorn-crowned head when Pilate exclaimed to the multitude, 'Ecce Homo!' I saw the men tear the garments from His body and nail Him to the gibbet, and as they were about to expose Him to the multitude, I, like Noe's son, averted my face of light and cast the mantle of darkness over my exposed and expiring Lord—'from the sixth hour, when there was darkness over the whole earth, until the ninth hour.' My evening beams fell on His silent sepulchre, and on the morning of the third day, when He arose, I poured a flood of golden light into His vacant grave. I saw Him ascend from Mt. Olivet until He passed above the domain of my light into 'the glory which He had before the world was made.' I have seen the persecutions which His followers endured in every age for 1900 years." In like manner, beloved brethren, is the Church a witness, in every age, to the great facts on which Christianity is founded. The Church of the first century was the Church of the second, and so until the present century. Her bishops meet in council, bringing together the traditions of their different Churches, and preserving unbroken the chains of testimony. Unbroken, because, to use an admirable illustration, which I heard in the closing sermon of the council held here eighteen years ago, as the breaking of the Atlantic cable at any point would prevent the transmission of a message from Europe, so, if the chain of testimony be not unbroken, we cannot know with certainty the great fundamental facts of Christianity. She, too, can say: "In the persons of the Apostles, I was there when He performed His miracles. In Peter and John I looked into His vacant sepulchre and testified to the great central fact of His resurrection, and for nearly 1900 years have I chanted my 'Alleluias' over the place where they laid Him. I have testified to Him in the person of my first martyr, Stephen, and my cloud of witnesses has grown thicker and more crimson as it has passed along the firmament of time. I stood in the

Coliseum by Ignatius when the lions bounded upon him and pulverized that noble 'wheat of Christ.' I was in Rome with Peter and at Corinth and Athens with Paul. I was down in the Catacombs, where even the sun's rays could not shine, and testified to my buried and risen Lord. I stood by the throne of the Cæsars when my son Constantine mounted its steps. I went out in the persons of the missionaries. I was a witness to Him 'in Jerusalem and in all Judea, and to the uttermost ends of the earth.' '

Such is the Church as Christ prophesied it should be. Where is it to-day, for it lives with the communicated vitality of God the Holy Ghost, who abides in it? Where is it to-day? Look around and see it represented in part in this great council. How glorious it is, how real, how living! Alive with the life of God and strong with the strength of God, and beautiful with the beauty of God. To it to-day may He say in the words of Scripture: "Thou art made exceedingly beautiful, because of My own beauty, which I have put upon thee." Not beauty in the mere external pomp of ritual, not in the sheen of these golden mitres, or the splendor of precious vestments. These are but the variegated garments of the King's daughter: not even in the inner individual sanctity of any who wear them, but in their official position as representatives of God, "because of My own beauty, which I have put upon thee.'

But the mission of the Church is not only to testify to facts, but also to sanctify the individual and society. She acts on the world through her sovereign head, the Pope, through her bishops on their several dioceses, and through her councils. These councils are chiefly of four kinds—the Ecumenical, or General Council, consisting of the Sovereign Pontiff in person or representative and the bishops of the world; the Plenary Council, like the present one, composed of an Apostolic Delegate and the bishops of a particular country; the Provincial Council, consisting of an archbishop and the bishops of a particular section known as his province; and the Diocesan Council or Synod, composed of the bishop and priests of a particular diocese. Now the Church in these councils acts for the benefit of society in three different ways: First, indirectly, by preserving the purity and certainty of great truths, which give certain motive to morality; secondly, by the reformation of morals amongst her own children; and thirdly, by her solicitude for the poor and suffering members of society. The purity of faith she preserves especially by her Ecumenical Councils. The decisions of such councils she regards as unerring. A tribunal like the Supreme Court of a State or of the United States takes cognizance only of overt acts, and may be final without being infallible. But when there is a question of legislating for the intellect itself, how can a decision which may be wrong settle a doubt? Now, certainty of faith is all-important for purity of morals. If I have only a vague opinion of the future life, of hell and heaven, and of my personal responsibility for the sins of my life, this opinion will never stand the test of a great temptation. Hence there must be an unerring mode of solving doctrinal doubts. The logical connection of faith with morals is almost ignored in our day. Formerly the cry was "justification by faith alone." Now it is justification by works alone, no matter what men believe, as if works did not depend on faith for their great motives.

Secondly, she discharges her mission to society by the reformation of abuses that arise amongst the clergy and laity, and this she does in both general, plenary, provincial and diocesan councils. If she does not always succeed in such reformation, we must remember that the influences of the Church, though necessary, are not necessitating. She no more than her spouse can paralyze that tremendous power—free will. Satan in heaven, Adam in paradise and Judas Iscariot at the Last Supper, with all the sanctifying influences around them, most miserably sinned. No man can deny, from an examination of her ethical teaching and sacramental system, as well as from the facts of history, that the Catholic Church has the power to sanctify, and has sanctified, individuals and society. By that power she evangelized, civilized and sanctified Europe in the past. By it she led captive to the feet of Jesus Christ the conquerors of the Roman Empire in the persons of the Northern invaders of Southern Europe. She has the power, and has used it, but she will not and cannot force men to hear and heed her. The individuals and nations that have heard her and neglect her teachings are much more difficult to convert than those who know her not. I believe that she never had a grander mission in all her history than she has to-day to the noble, generous and fair-minded American people. And in regard to certain parts of Europe only God knows how much worse they would be without her influence. And whilst her faith remains there is left the power to bring back these men to the true standard of Christian morality.

A third mode by which she discharges her mission to society is by the amelioration of the condition of the poor and suffering of our race, and in this great work also she acts in her councils and in imitation of her Founder. The trite saying that "one-half of the world does not know how the other half lives" was particularly true before the coming of Christ. Poverty was virtually a crime and a degradation. Even the divine Plato, the most naturally Christian perhaps of all the pagan philosophers, in his regulations for a model republic would have the poor expelled if they became so numerous as to disturb the peace of the prosperous. Everywhere in the pagan world was poverty persecuted, when an angelic voice was heard above the pastures of Palestine addressing some poor shepherds in these words: "Fear not, for I bring to you glad tidings of great joy that shall be to all the people, for this day is born to you a Saviour, who is Christ the Lord in the city of David, and this shall be a sign to you: you shall find the child wrapped in swaddling clothes and laid in a manger." The Saviour of the poor, He came in poverty, and defied poverty by uniting His Divinity to it. Soon the kings of the East came, and wealth, royal wealth, was found at the feet of poverty. The first words He spoke in His sermon on the Mount were, "Blessed are the poor." During life He often had not where to lay His head. He died in the embrace of poverty, and as in life He had not place to lay His head, neither had He after death, for they laid Him in a sepulchre that belonged to another. He made care for the needy the condition for obtaining eternal happiness, and neglect of the poor, He said, would be punished with eternal exclusion from the kingdom of God. He will give His benediction or malediction to the children of men acccording to this criterion—"I was hungry and you gave Me meat, thirsty and you gave Me to drink, naked and you clothed Me." So that His identification with poverty, commencing in Bethlehem, shall continue for all time. We behold this solicitude for the poor continued in the apostolic days. St. Paul and St. Barnabas were particularly charged, as the former tells us, to take care of the poor, which thing, he says, we were careful to do.

The Church continued this great work through pontiffs, bishops, and priests in her councils. Thus we find the Council of Cæsarea, in 313, commending and praising the assistants of the bishops, especially for their care of the poor. The Council of Aix, in 816, commanded that all ecclesiastical foundations of monks and canons should provide for a certain number of the poor, the sick, widows and strangers. A Council of Lyons in 558, commanded that the clergy should keep lists of the poor in their districts, so that they might be aided. The Council of Ravenna, in 1113, ordered that four or six men should be annually elected, whose business it should be to collect for the poor, and granted forty days' indulgence to all contributors on the conditions always required for indulgences, that the persons gaining them should be contrite for their sins. The Council of Trent granted extensive powers to bishops to visit the sick poor in hospitals, and we well know the devotedness of bishops and priests to such work.

Now, beloved brethren, this care for the poor is not only a divine and ecclesiastical law, but it is the highest wisdom of the political economist. "One-half of the world does not know how the other half lives," but that other half will soon let them know and assure them that they do not intend to live so any longer. Christian kindness to the poor and the working men and women, and the inculcation of patience in poverty, after the example of our Lord, are the best securities against the communism and anarchy that seem to threaten society. In the same manner did the Church act in regard to prisoners and slaves. We know how cruelly both of these classes were treated before the appearance of the divine Prisoner in the hall of Pontius Pilate. We know how captives were dragged at the chariot wheels of Roman conquerors and imprisoned in dungeons into which the white light of heaven was not permitted to enter until a Christian emperor decreed that the darkness should be dispelled and the captives see the sun.

The Church in the Councils of Chalcedon, in 541, and Orleans, in 549, provided for the visitation of prisoners, according, says the Council of Chalcedon, "to the traditions of the Fathers," showing that it had always been the custom. So in regard to slaves the Councils of Chalon-sur-Saone, in 550, Celchet, in England, in 816, London, in 1102, and Armagh, in Ireland, in 1172, provided for their gradual emancipation. The Council of Armagh liberated all the

English in Ireland who were held as slaves. How salutary was the effect on society of such authoritative action on the part of the Church.

To sum up what I have said: Because society in our day needs regeneration, and morality needs a firmer basis than mere natural honor and integrity, which so easily yield to strong temptation; because Christ is the great Regenerator and the name of Jesus the only name under heaven by which society, like the individual, can be saved; because the institution called the Church is inseparably connected with Christ, being in truth Himself continued; because she has in her councils ever sustained morality by increasing faith in the dogmas that give it life and motive; because she has in these councils endeavored to correct moral abuses within her fold; because by her principles and institutions she has ameliorated the condition of the poor and the unfortunate and taught them contentment with their lot—therefore have we ground of hope that she will be a great conservative power in this young and promising republic, and that the council that here represents her comes most opportunely in the order of God's providence to sustain it. But we must remember, brethren, that it is the supernatural element that is most potent in producing and preserving the good that we seek, for "unless the Lord guard the city they labor in vain who guard it." Therefore let us ask God's blessing on the deliberations of this great council. Let all—bishops, priests and people—"adore and fall down before the Lord who made us, for the Lord is our God; we are His people and the sheep of His pasture." Let the faithful people cry out, "Send forth Thy light and Thy truth, that they may lead us and those who govern us to Thy holy mountain and unto Thy tabernacles." Let bishops and priests between the porch and the altar cry aloud, "Spare, O Lord, spare Thy people; preserve human society from the fierce delirium of its passions." Let bishops, priests and people ask God in profound supplication that the sacrifice of the Mass just offered may be borne by the hands of His holy angel —even the angel of His great council—to His sublime altar in the heavens and in sight of His Divine Majesty, that the partakers of it may be filled with every grace and celestial benediction, and that the Holy Spirit in whose honor it has been offered "may come and fill the hearts of the faithful, enkindle in them the fire of His love, and thus renew the face of earth."

Most Rev. C. J. Seghers, D.D.   Most Rev. John B. Lamy, D.D.

The Church—The Support of Just Government.

SERMON OF RIGHT REV. JOHN IRELAND, D.D.,

BISHOP OF ST. PAUL, MINN.

"Let every soul be subject to higher powers: for there is no power but from God; and those that are, are ordained of God."—*Rom., c. xiii, v. 1.*

I DO not, I think, mistake the feelings of many of my fellow-countrymen in presence of the Plenary Council now holding its sessions in Baltimore, when I ascribe to them the desire that a statement be made as to the bearings of the Catholic Church in her teachings and her practical acting towards civil society, and notably, perhaps, towards the form of government for society which obtains in the United States of America. Whether they examine or not the claims of the Church to their spiritual allegiance, they know her to be, from the number of her adherents, her closely organized forces, the consistency of her principles in doctrines and morals, a great power in the land, a most important factor in forming the destinies of the commonwealth; and, with reason, they believe it to be their right to inquire what the results may be from the continued growth and development of her influence among the citizens of the republic.

The American people have had their false prophets who strove to create prejudice against the Catholic Church. Again and again from sectarian pulpit and popular rostrum has the accusation gone forth that she is the evil genius of society and of government, and that loyalty to her means disloyalty to their free institutions.

I respect too much my fellow-countrymen not to be glad, when the occasion offers, to declare to them the truth and to guard them against deceiving tongues. I love too deeply the Catholic Church and the American republic not to be ever ready to labor that the relations of the one with the other be not misunderstood. It is true, the choicest field which providence offers in the world to-day to the occupancy of the Church is this republic, and she welcomes with delight the signs of the times that indicate a glorious future for her beneath the starry banner. But it is true, also, the surest safeguards for her own life and prosperity the republic will find in the teachings of the Catholic Church, and the more America acknowledges those teachings, the more durable will her civil institutions be made. I speak beneath this cathedral dome no less as an American citizen than as a Catholic bishop. The Church is the mother of my faith, the guardian of my hopes for eternity: America is my country, the protectress of my liberty and of my fortunes on earth. I could not utter one syllable that would belie, however remotely, either Church or republic, and when I assert, as I now solemnly do, that the principles of the former are in thorough harmony with the interests of the latter, I feel in the depths of my heart that I speak the truth.

You will permit me to put before you the principles of Catholic theology relating to civil society. These principles will be the proof that the Church, equally opposing anarchy and despotism, is the sure guardian of society, the sure defender of true liberty.

Man is by nature a being fashioned for society—"*civile animal.*" His instincts, his needs demand society; they demand the guarantees and the encouragements of society. He depends for very existence and for growth to mature life upon the family, the first of social units; individual and family again depend for the enjoyment of their most sacred rights upon the higher social form—the State. It is the superior authority of the body politic that secures to all "life, liberty and the pursuit of happiness." The great movements which improve and elevate the human race spring from the emulation which society supplies, and are carried to success through the reduction of separate forces under the law of unity, which is the eternal principle of order, beauty and power. The absence of social organization introduces warfare with his fellows as man's permanent condition, paralyzes his energies for good, consecrates barbarism. Man, as a rational, perfectible being, is impossible outside of society. But society means a central authority, a government, and here we are confronted with the great problem underlying all social philosophy—

the constitution of society upon principles which, while guarding it from anarchy on the one hand, will guard it with no less jealousy from despotism on the other. Anarchy is the total disruption of the social frame-work. Authority is needed to avert the evil; but authority suggests the danger of an evil no less fatal, the abuse of authority or despotism, which, under pretense of warding off riotous ruin, crushes out with iron heel the rights it was instituted to preserve. Anarchy and despotism are the Scylla and the Charybdis of the civil community. Death awaits it from either and will come as surely and as swiftly from one as from the other.

Never in history was the difficulty of the social problem felt as keenly as it is to-day. Society is most unstable; it reels on its foundations as if drunken through wild passion. At one moment its bulwarks are on the point of being shattered into a thousand fragments amid the clamorings and violences of Communists and Nihilists; at another we behold it rushing madly with a shriek of despair into the deathly grasp of military Cæsarism, or worshiping idolatrously the irresponsible absolutism of the State. Doctrinaires have lied to society. Hearkening to them, it has renounced the principles of life with which its divine Author had endowed it, and it is paying the penalty. What those principles are, the Church, the faithful custodian of the revelation of God, tells us. Her teaching saves society.

Modern social theorists, led by Hobbes and Rousseau, assert that by nature men are free from all social obligations, society being nothing more than a voluntary pact among themselves, having no existence, no powers except as derived from their own consent. The powers of society, mere concessions from individuals, are revocable at will, and bind so far only as individuals are pleased to recognize them. Society is a simple aggregation of men for mutual protection—rather a necessary evil; obedience is not a moral duty; authority is a creature of the aggregation, the members of which in consequence, whether they are the governing or the governed, remain equal in rights of all kind, social as well as natural. With these theorists God counts for nothing in society; He gives nothing to society, and social affairs need have no reference to Him.

All this is false. Only atheists and materialists may legitimately with their principles propose absurdities of the kind. The pagans of old never uttered the like; their cities and empires were sacred to the Divinity. Reason proclaims that society is not a voluntary pact among men: it exists by the force of nature, and consequently, by the command of the Author of nature. God may no more be removed from society than He may be from any part of the cosmos. As He made man for it, so He ordained it, and willing the means together with the end He conferred upon society the authority needed for its preservation. Society is not a simple organization of individuals; it is a moral entity of itself, a complete organism, having its own life and its own authority not derived from and independent of individual members. Society is superior to individuals. Obedience to it is obedience to God. Those who govern, invested with power communicated by God, are the superiors of those over whom they are placed.

The forgetfulness of the divine origin of society and of government leaves no choice for the State between anarchy and despotism.

"By Me," says divine Wisdom, "kings reign and lawgivers decree just things. By Me princes rule and the mighty decree justice." St. Paul teaches: "There is no power but from God: and those that are, are ordained of God. Therefore, he that resisteth the power resisteth the ordinance of God. . . . For he is God's minister to thee for good." The Church repeats the teachings of Scripture and sets forth the practical consequences. In his Encyclical on Socialism in 1879, the present Pontiff, Leo XIII, condemns the modern atheistic theory of society. "By a new sort of impiety, unknown to the pagans," he writes, "States constitute themselves independently of God, or of the order which He has established. Public authority is declared to derive neither its principle nor its power from God, but from the multitude, which, believing itself free from all divine sanction, obeys no laws but such as its own caprice dictates." . . . "They (the Socialists) never cease proclaiming that all men are equal in all things; and hence kings have no right to command them, nor laws any power to bind unless made by themselves and according to their own inclinations. But, on the other hand, the Gospel teaches that all men are indeed equal, inasmuch as all have the same nature, all are called to the sublime dignity of children of God. . . . But an inequality of rights and powers emanates from the Author of nature Himself, of whom all paternity is named in heaven and on earth. . . . As in the Church He has instituted a diversity of degrees and offices, so too He has established in civil society different orders in dignity, in right and power, so that the State, like the Church, might form one body composed of many members, some more noble than others, but all necessary to one another, and all laboring for the common good." The words of the Encyclical, in view of what has already been said, need no comment. It is plain that the equality which the Pontiff denies is the social or political equality which excludes the distinction between the governing and the governed, and annihilates society. When power is given by God, they who exercise it are for the time being superior to those over whom it is exercised, however equal in rights they may be as men under the law of nature. Leo XIII refers again to social questions in a later Encyclical of 1884. He reproves the assertions of the Naturalists that "each one is by nature free;" that "no one has the right to command others;" that "to wish to subject men to the authority of any one, unless that authority has come to him from themselves, is to do violence to them." In saying that no one is "by nature free," the Pontiff means that no one is by nature free from the laws of society, no more than he is free from parental authority or other restrictions to which nature subjects him. In asserting the right of some to command others, he does not imply that some men have this right as something proper or peculiar to them from nature; he speaks of the acquired social right belonging to all legitimately constituted rulers in society. The words of both Encyclicals, wrested from the context which indicates clearly their limitation to political and social matters, have been to a large extent misconstrued by the public press of both continents, and I quote them at some length that you may correctly understand them.

I have stated the teaching of the Church on the origin of society and of government: this teaching is the potent breakwater against anarchy, the sure foundation of authority in society.

Society is as a city built upon the mountain within whose bosom burn a thousand volcanic fires. There are ten, thirty, fifty millions of human beings, differing from, opposed to, one another in inclinations and interests. Mutual sacrifices are required, sacrifices often most severe, that union in one body politic be possible. The passions of men know in their fury no control: they must be abated. The poor envy the rich; inferiors hate superiors; the proud seek to rise upon the ruins of their fellows; the strong oppress the weak; humanity must be diverted from these evil tendencies. To repress passion, to obtain that individual interest be sacrificed to that of the common weal—this is the mighty task which devolves upon authority. Under the ægis of authority, there is order and peace: authority displaced, it is the reveling of crime and chaos.

Authority—do we pause to notice facts too patent?—loses day by day its sacredness, its power. Socialists and Nihilists, whose lodges honey-comb Europe, have named authority the enemy—the enemy which they are sworn to combat. The Commune of Paris mocked it and spat upon it amid the lurid glare of burning palaces and the savage uproar of murderous riot. Things are better in America. Yet Socialism has immigrated to America; the mob occasionally rules our cities; a spirit of lawlessness is visible in the population; laws seem made to be broken, and crowds gather around the voting booth to elect to office men pledged to disregard the edict of the legislator. The question is opportune: whither is society drifting? what protection will society be able henceforward to afford to life, liberty, and rights the most sacred?

Authority is the safeguard; but if authority is to be something more than an idle name or a lifeless shadow, we must establish it upon grounds that will insure reverence and obedience.

Will the appeal be to right in government and to duty in subject? Assuredly not, if society is cut off from God, if government has no power, no right but what it has received from the people constituting it. If society, as atheistic theorists hold, is but the voluntary aggregation of individuals, and not an ordinance of God, if the governing power has no consecration beyond the free acknowledgment of the governed, what right is or can be violated when the individual disobeys, or even withdraws altogether from, the pact? No one may complain when all are equal. The "sacred right of insurrection," as rebellion, just or unjust, has been too often termed, whether against certain laws, or a certain government, or society at large, is the inalienable possession of each person. Indeed, there is never rebellion, because there exists no authority above the individual himself. Rousseau's theory of society is political Protestantism, the supremacy of the individual; and as in Protestantism there can be no religious heresy, so in Rosseau's principles there can be no social rebellion. The ruler who would constrain the individual is a tyrant, assuming power not vested in him. The majority of his fellows, were they in the name of number to strive against him, are tyrants. Mere numbers give no power over others, except the power such as robbers and murderers claim. Right does not and cannot exist under the terms of the "Social Contract." No wonder is it that authority is called the enemy. No wonder is it that the French Revolution, with all the horrors of Jacobinism, followed the spread through France of Rosseau's teachings. The statue of the Genevan philosopher, standing out from his sarcophagus in the Pantheon, represents him befittingly as holding in his right hand a burning torch. It is the torch of revolution, of social destruction and social ruin.

Perhaps self-interest will take the place of duty and compel men to submit to authority. The vainest of illusions! Why, it is self-interest that begets opposition to law and authority. Talk of self-interest to the ambitious, the vengeful, the licentious! Talk of self-interest to the millions hopelessly doomed to unceasing labor, to suffering and to want! Talk of self-interest to the many who bear the burdens of society, while the glitter and the pleasure belong to the few! Say, if you wish, that whatever becomes of the present time and the present individual, the ultimate interest of the race, the general good of the commonwealth, is secured by this labor and this suffering. Philosophers may in their easy chairs dream of such remote results; the masses do not make sacrifices for them.

Will physical force be invoked? This is on occasions a convenient and effective solution of the difficulty. Cannon and dragoons will do much towards scattering a mob; prison and exile will thin the ranks of rebels; the silence of death may be called peace. But what is physical force if not despotism most execrable, a hundred times more galling and degrading than the wildest anarchy? Order purchased by despotism is too high-priced that we should desire it. Besides, it will be of but short duration. Despotism intensifies opposition; it stimulates hidden plottings and terrible reactions. Governments, alas! too often lend a helping hand to social atheism, fancying that armies and bayonets will suffice for their maintenance. "And now, O ye kings, understand: receive instruction, you that judge the earth. . . . . When His wrath shall be kindled in a short time, blessed are all they that shall trust in Him." A godless people will swiftly demolish the stoutest bastiles.

Well, in the name of God's Church, I will say whither the appeal shall be made. Tell men that there is a God in Israel, that authority is divine, that God's majesty encircles with its rays the legislators and rulers of nations. Tell them that they who govern on earth are indeed human, but that back of them stands the Eternal, making their laws His own, whom to serve is kingly honor, towards whom reverence is highest duty. God is the Creator of man, his Master, and God's will is our supreme guidance. Then make the appeal to man's conscience, that divine sense in him which re-echoes the divine command, the sole moral power on earth, the sole power that can repress passion, whether in the individual or in society. Make the appeal to conscience—the sacrifice is sweet; there is peace in obedience; the sword may seek its scabbard.

The Church teaches with St. Paul that disobedience to civil law is a sin. "He that resisteth the power, resisteth the ordinance of God, and they that resist purchase to themselves damnation. . . . Wherefore be subject of necessity, not only for wrath, but also for conscience' sake." In the eyes of the Church loyalty to country is loyalty to God; patriotism is a heavenly virtue, a high form of holy obedience; the patriot dying for his country wears the halo of the martyr. The Catholic Church commands, blesses, consecrates patriotism. The true Catholic must needs be the truest patriot.

Nations, did they but know what is for their welfare, should have written in letters of gold the Encyclicals of Leo. His words will save society. High above the storm that threatens devastation to all social fabrics his voice rises, even as the voice of the Master amid the winds of Genesareth, bidding us not to fear, and indicating the means of salvation. And thus will it ever be. So long as Peter's throne rests on the Vatican, so long will testimony be given to truth, and the principles of order and authority will be proclaimed to the nations of the earth.

And now, authority secured, I will speak the word which

in your hearts you desire to hear from my lips, which will sound as magic to your ears—a word, the inspiration of a thousand battle-fields, which names the dream of nations, the ideal to them of temporal grandeur and felicity—liberty! Did you think that in my zeal for authority I was forgetting liberty? Believe me, I, too, love liberty. With deep emotion I speak the word, and I speak it this evening with most confident affection, because, standing in a Catholic pulpit, I can establish it upon ever-enduring foundations—the eternal principles of divine truth.

Do not imagine a conflict between liberty and authority. License sacrilegiously calls itself liberty, "making liberty a cloak for malice;" despotism dares usurp the holy name of authority, and the conflict is between license and authority as it is between despotism and liberty. Liberty and authority are one. Liberty presupposes and follows from authority; authority has liberty for its object. Liberty is the untrammeled use of one's powers and faculties; it is, so to speak, the ownership of itself; hence, we all cherish it. It is, at the same time, the possibility of self-expansion and self-aggrandizement—the spring of movement and progress in society; hence, nations consider it their most precious inheritance. But that this ownership of self, this expansion of one's faculties, be possible, protection is required against the invasion of the wayward and the malefactor; authority gives this protection. Authority, furthermore, combines into one force the energies of the many, and renders individual rights the more fruitful and progress the more certain. Liberty, outside of authority, is the freedom of wild beasts to devour one another. "Appoint, O Lord," says the Psalmist, "a lawgiver over them, that they may know themselves to be men." Authority impeding liberty! Do the hillsides, nature's barriers, by confining within their bed the waters of the mighty Mississippi lest they divide over adjacent lowlands into shallow and murky marshes impede their free and majestic flow or diminish their strength and beauty in their course to the ocean? Who they are that should dread authority St. Paul tells us in the Epistle to the Romans, from which I have already quoted: "Wilt thou, then, be afraid of the power? Do that which is good, and thou shalt have praise from the same; for he is God's minister to thee for good. But if thou do that which is evil, fear, for he beareth not the sword in vain: an avenger to execute wrath upon him who doeth evil." The sacrifices which authority demands from the good and the well-disposed in the community are a hundredfold compensated for in the advantages they obtain and the security accorded to them. While authority is sacred, liberty is safe; when authority is assailed, a death-blow has been leveled at liberty.

"There is no power but from God; and those that are, are ordained of God." The same principle of Catholic teaching which consecrates authority confines it to just limits. If civil power is from God, it is to be used for the purposes intended by God—the preservation of society, the defence of rights of individuals and families. Beyond those purposes rulers have no power, and, when their acts unjustly invade the rights they were appointed to protect, they are in opposition to God.

The Catholic Church the enemy of liberty! This has been said, but with what truth I will ask you to judge after I will have made a few further statements as to her principles on civil authority, and the use to be made of it.

Authority, I have said is from God, and civil governments rule by right divine. But remark in what way, according to Catholic teaching, civil governments are constituted. God does not appoint for a people a particular form of government, as he has done for instance in the case of the Church, nor does he select the particular men who are to wield authority. All this is remitted to the people. They select the ruler and make choice of the form of government: God vests in the people's candidates the sovereignty, subject to the conditions and limitations with which they have circumscribed it. There are no kings or rulers by divine right in the sense that specified men or families are directly called by God to reign, or that specified governments are authorized by Him. Rulers govern by the will of the people, and derive their just powers from the consent of the governed in the sense that the consent, the choice, of the governed is the condition upon which heaven conveys authority.

The principle of the intervention of the people in the selection of their government is the primary constituent of civil liberty. The people decide for themselves in what manner sovereignty shall be exercised over them: they are parties to the contract with their rulers. They decree whether the full sovereignty shall be confided to one person or divided between several; whether a ruler shall hold office for a number of years or for his life-time; whether his sovereignty shall be concluded with himself or transmitted by him to his heirs. Room is made for an absolute monarch, for a king with lords and commons, for a president with senators and representatives, as the nation may see fit to elect. "There is no prohibition to nations, the rules of justice being otherwise observed," says Leo XIII in his Encyclical of June, 1881, "to choose for themselves that sort of government which befits their temper or accords with the traditions and customs of their race." Republic, monarchy, empire — all fare alike before the Church; the authority in all is divine, and obedience towards all is obligatory.

Let me, however, make some observations in order that Catholic teaching be in nothing misunderstood. The choice once made, the conditions of the government once traced, the people cannot, at will, through mere whim or fancy, dethrone their rulers or revoke their constitutions. Stability is an essential element of order in society, and changes, without the gravest reasons, destroy stability. Society, a divinely ordained institution, may not commit suicide; no right is conceded to prince or to people, to the multitude collectively or distributively, that tears down instead of building up the social frame-work. When mention is made of the intervention of the people, we are to understand the people at large, as they express the general national will, not individuals singly or parcels of individuals. Once chosen directly or indirectly by the people and invested with divine power, civil rulers are, in fact and right, the superiors of those whom they govern, and they should act for the general good as their consciences dictate; they are not the mere mouth-pieces of subjects to repeat their orders, the mere servants of their constituents to obey their whims. The sovereignty resides in them, and not in the people, and upon them lies the responsibility for the proper exercise thereof.

Listen now, while I repeat in the words of the "Angel of the Schools" the principles of the Church on the use and the extent of sovereignty: "Law is a rule dictated by reason, the aim of which is the public good, and promulgated by him who has the care of society." "The will to have the force of law must be guided by reason. In this sense only can the will of a sovereign be said to have the force of law; in any other sense it would not be law, but injustice." "Human laws, if they are just, are binding in conscience, and they derive their power from the eternal law from which they are formed." "Laws may be unjust in two ways, either by being opposed to the common weal or by having an improper aim, as when a government imposes upon its subjects onerous laws, which do not serve the common interest, but rather cupidity and ambition; or on account of their author, as when one makes a law beyond the power vested in him. Such laws are rather outrages than laws." "The kingdom is not made for the king, but the king for the kingdom; for God has constituted kings to rule and govern, and to secure to every one the possession of his rights; such is the aim of their institution; but if kings, turning things to their own profit, should act otherwise they are no longer kings but tyrants." (St. Thomas, "De Leg. et de Reg. Princ.," *passim*.) Never were words more grand written on civil liberty than those penned by Aquinas. According to the principles laid down by him, all power is from God: God grants no power to rulers against Himself. His own laws, the supreme dictates of righteousness and goodness, must never be violated. In their official, as well as in their private life, rulers are subject to them. God is "the King of kings and the Lord of lords," and nations, as well as individuals, are His creatures. Human laws contradicting the divine have no binding power: "They are rather injustices than laws." The "higher law" limits all civil power. Even the monarch who could say in his mightiness, "I am the State," had to hear the solemn monition: "Hitherto thou shalt come, and thou shalt go no further." Amid apparent absolutism an impregnable citadel remains to liberty—the conscience, whose cry of war against tyranny has never been stilled in the world since the first prince of the Church exclaimed in Jerusalem: "If it be just in the sight of God to hear you rather than God, judge ye." Nor is this all. Civil power in the hands of rulers is a trust, the aim of which is the public good; reason must direct its use. The good pleasure of the sovereign does not make law. The State is not for the ruler, but the ruler is for the State. The maxim of the Roman poet is false—that "the human race lives for the profit of the few." In the intent of the trust the ruler becomes the servant of the people, and when he does not serve them, but heeds rather his ambition, his pride, his cupidity, he is a tyrant, and his laws are "injustices," "outrages." Equally despotic is the ruler who violates the conditions upon which he was chosen by the people as their superior; he is bound as much as they by the fundamental laws, written or traditional, by the charter or constitution of the nation. Authority deserves obedience only when "deriving its power from the eternal law." Otherwise the nimbus of divine majesty vanishes from the ruler's brow. The human remains; the human demanding to reign is despotism, and obedience to it were slavery. This, assuredly, is civil liberty—law "a rule dictated by reason, the aim of which is the public good." This is liberty in its truest, fullest measure. Liberty we take to be the alliance of social protection and individual rights with as little curtailment of the latter as the case may permit. The Catholic definition of law is the consecration of this alliance.

The zeal of theologians for liberty goes farther than to call the edicts of despotism injustices and outrages, and to declare that they do not bind in conscience. A revolution, the dethronement of power, the Church holds, and rightly, to be a fearful occurrence. Society quakes from the shock to its deepest foundations; with difficulty will it ever recover its equipoise; and yet, when despotism lowers its heavy hand over a people, and representation, counsel and entreaty fail to ward it off, the nation—rather than let liberty die for evermore—may, we are told, rise up with all its might and, in a supreme effort for life, hurl against despotism the thunders of war. This right belongs not to an individual nor to a few; the people only may say when the time for insurrection has come. "In extreme circumstances," says Balmes, "non-resistance is not a dogmatical prescription. The Church has never taught such a doctrine; if any one will maintain that she has, let him bring forward a decision of a council or of a Sovereign Pontiff to that effect. St. Thomas of Aquin, Cardinal Bellarmine, Suares, and other eminent theologians were well-versed in the dogmas of the Church; and yet, if you consult their works, so far from finding this doctrine in them, you will find the opposite one." "Bossuet and other authors of repute," Balmes adds, "differ from St. Thomas, Ballarmine, and Suares; and this gives credit to the opposite opinion, but does not convert it into a dogma. Upon certain points of the highest import the opinions of Bossuet suffered contradiction."

Those principles of Catholic teaching are the very core of the tree of civil liberty. They give us the substance, nothing that is merely external and superficial, as we too often receive where professions are the loudest. The world is easily deceived: words win above realities. Liberty is bidden to cast the veil of its name now over anarchy and again over despotism. Be the name what it may, there is no liberty where law is not the dictate of reason, and where it is there needs must be liberty. External forms of government, so far as true liberty is concerned, are largely accidental: they neither create nor necessarily impede liberty. The spirit of the people is of incomparably greater importance than the form of their government. An empire or a monarchy may secure the fulness of liberty to the subject, and despotism may reign in a republic. The republic may in the name of brutal numbers, ignore justice, prostitute to private ends the public power, trample under foot the rights of minorities, and with liberty's own wand crush out her life. An American publicist says of representative democracy: "The tyranny of the majority is worse than the tyranny of one man or a few men, because it has no restraint." Gibbon says of the expiring republic of Rome: "The provinces, weary of the oppressive ministers of the republic, were willing to submit to the authority of a single master;" and never were the rights of minorities and of individuals more unscrupulously sacrificed than in the recent republics of a Gambetta in France and a Castelar in Spain. The foulest form of despotism—Statolatry or the deification of the State—is a temptation of all forms of government. The despotic State, be it called monarchy or republic, allows no higher authority than itself; it assumes to be the supreme arbiter of right and wrong, of the spiritual and the temporal, controlling the school and the Church, thought and conscience, as it does army maneuverings and real estate taxation, and refusing the recognition of all right, except what its own will authorizes. It is the most complete incarnation of despotism. The pagan State was nearly always constituted on this basis, and consistently with the doctrine the "*patria*" received divine honors. Our own too popular maxim, "*Vox populi, vox Dei*," is a form of Statolatry, implying that the sovereign people can never do wrong, and that their will is the highest law. Modern political Socialism, now so vigorously striving in the very name of liberty for supremacy, goes beyond the claims of the pagan State, asserting that the State is all in all, and the individual nothing—the individual having no right to own property, to speak, to think, to train his children except as the State directs and allows in the supposed interest of the common good. Never, perhaps, more than in our century has it been necessary to keep before the minds of men the vital principles of civil liberty.

The value of Catholic principles is not realized by considering their intrinsic truth and beauty. We have to consider, in addition, the power of the living organism which thinks them and proclaims them. The principles of civil liberty taught by the Church can never become in the world a dead letter: they are never allowed to be forgotten by men. No tyrant can shelve them with the tomes on whose pages they might be inscribed, as he would the sayings of philosophers, beyond the reach and the hearing of his subjects. They palpitate with the vigorous life of mother Church, whose noble progeny they are. Their voice surges in far-reaching waves from the Encyclicals of Popes, the lectures of doctors, the sermons of humblest pastors. It reaches down to the poorest peasant and to the most oppressed slave, and begets in their souls a sense of right, a spirit of personal dignity and of manly independence. It passes through the serried ranks of satellites which encircle the throne of the tyrant and rings into his ear notes of terror, reminding him of the penalty of despotic wrong-doing. It reaches through every age and over every land. The spirit of liberty is Catholic and immortal, because its parent and guardian is the Church Catholic and immortal.

Objection has been raised in the name of the State against the Catholic Church as if she interfered with the duties of citizenship by dividing the allegiance of subjects. No less a name than that of William E. Gladstone has been connected with this objection. We cannot but wonder that it was ever raised. There is no ground for it. "Render to Cæsar the things that are Cæsar's, and to God the things that are God's"—this is a supreme rule of Catholic policy. Reserving strictly to her own direct jurisdiction the things that are God's, the Church has never sought—she can never without manifest contradiction seek—to interpose in the things that are Cæsar's. The temporal administration, the practical methods of government, are matters for the State exclusively.

The Church simply proclaims the principles of justice and of morality which are binding upon men, whether as individuals or as communities. To bid her be silent is to make the State supreme alike in morals and in secular concerns, and to remove all restraint from despotism. No remedy would be found in substituting for the teaching of the Church the individual conscience uninstructed save by the light of private reason. This on the one hand would establish each individual the judge of the State and open the door to anarchy, and on the other by leaving the individual alone and unprotected it facilitates the triumph of despotism over the country. There is gain both for authority and for liberty in the existence of a spiritual power which, in God's name, gives final sentence upon principles of religion and of morals.

Among the brightest pages of history, and the most honorable for the human race, are those which tell the battles of the Church in defence of liberty. She fought for the possession by herself of liberty. Never did the Catholic Church bend the neck under the yoke of temporal prince. She held directly from Christ, and she permitted no sovereign of earth to rule over her. The ambition of tyrants was ever to enslave the spiritual power. In imperial Rome the ruler was at the same time *"imperator"* and *"pontifex"*—the high-priest and the commander-in-chief of the armies. The pagan union of the two powers was often coveted in Christendom. Henry IV, in Germany, took upon himself to dispose of the bishop's crozier as he would of the vassal's sword. Henry II, in England, allowed in his kingdom no rights to the Church not deriving from his own will. This was the tyranny in later years of Henry VIII, King and Pope of England, and in our own days, of Chancellor Von Bismarck, of Prussia, whose May laws make the State as powerful in the sanctuary as in the military garrison or the revenue bureau. The victory always remained with the Church; it was no more her own victory than the victory of civil liberty. It was not the hatred of religion that led rulers to war with the Church: it was the hatred of liberty. They could not brook the existence of a power independent of them, to which their people could appeal, which reminded subjects that there is a limit to the authority of masters. Cæsar was not omnipotent, so long as the Church refused him "the empire of minds," and he raged against the Church. Fortunately a Canossa ever awaited him, and liberty was saved to the world. "But for the intervention of the Papacy," says a Protestant writer in the *Edinburgh Review*, alluding to the excommunication of Henry IV by Pope Gregory VII, "the vassal of the West and the serf of Eastern Europe would, perhaps, to this day be in the same state of social debasement, and military autocrats would occupy the place of paternal and constitutional governments."

The Church fought the battles of personal liberty against slavery and serfdom. The "rights of man" were first made known to the world by her Pontiffs and her councils. Her dogma of a common brotherhood under the one divine paternity struck to the ground the manacles which heartless man was always too willing to impose upon his weak fellow. No social law or feudal caste could long resist the example of the great Church that never refused her own dignities to slave and serf, and that placed them, when her own princely insignia waved from their shoulders, in social rank above the highest lord and lady in the land. "In 1167," says Voltaire, "Pope Alexander III declared in the name of the council that all Christians should be exempt from slavery." "This law," adds the same writer, "alone should render his memory dear to all people." In the same spirit Gregory XVI, during our own century, raised his powerful protest against the African slave trade, and led the way to the total abolition of negro slavery in civilized lands.

The Church fought the battles of civil liberty. During the Middle Ages she was recognized as the arbiter of nations: her Popes judged and deposed sovereigns. They always acted in the interest of the people, in the interest of civil liberty. Report comes to us that Philip, Henry, Frederick, oppresses his subjects—this the usual tenor of the pontifical letters bringing sovereigns to trial, and telling the world in thundering tones that right is above might, and that despotism is a crime of high treason against society. The solemn condemnation of a Barbarossa or a Henry sufficed to thrill all Christendom with the spirit of liberty, and to awaken from their slumbers all rights of humanity, whether in high or low estate. The result was that in the Middle Ages, as Montalembert expresses it, "the world was bristling with liberty. The spirit of resistance, the sentiment of individual right, penetrated it entirely; and it is this which always and everywhere constitutes the essence of freedom." Feudalism was at the time strongly entrenched in Europe, and opposed powerful obstacles to the development of liberty. The Church was alone capable of resisting its influences. "If the Christian Church had not existed," says Guizot ("Hist. de la Civil.," 2e leçon), "the entire world would have been delivered up to mere material force. The Church alone exercised a moral power." Hume himself writes ("Hist. of the House of Tudor") that without the Papacy "all Europe would have fallen very early into one or many caliphates, and would have submitted infallibly and disgracefully to Turkish sway and to Oriental oppression and stupefaction."

Strange fortune of the Catholic Church! She battled for centuries in giant warfare, and saved Europe to liberty, and yet the accusation has gone abroad against her that she befriends despotism and crushes out free institutions. Her work for liberty, for civilization, for progress was culminating in the beginning of the sixteenth century, when Protestantism appeared on the horizon and the credit of a long and tedious work of ages has been awarded to the new religion.

Protestanism did nothing for liberty. It introduced into the world no one new principle that favored liberty. Its claim to private judgment in religion was religious anarchy; if it was anything in civil and political matters, it was political anarchy, the reaction from which always leads to despotism. Protestantism is not an organized force, and its contribution of positive power to any cause must necessarily be next to nothing: whatever is seemingly done under its sway is done by other causes than itself. It weakened the elements of resistance to the encroachments of despotism by dividing them, and as a fact despotism followed everywhere in the wake of its earliest advances. Never during Christian ages, except in Protestant countries, was the subjection of the spiritual to the temporal an accomplished fact. The Protestant prince was made the head of the Church in his realm, and he ruled souls as well as bodies. Henry VIII became the keeper of the consciences of the people of England; his daughter Elizabeth demanded more servile obedience from her bishops than from her lieutenants and her sheriffs, and Gustavus Adolphus was equally despotic over the Church in Sweden. In Protestant Germany the political maxim prevailed, "*cujus regio illius religio*," and every petty prince shaped out in his cabinet dogmas and rules of morals which subjects had to accept or lose their heads. The doctrine of passive resistance, according to which a prince, however despotic, can never be dethroned, was brought into its greatest prominence by Anglican divines under James I, and however much Guizot, a Protestant, praises the Reformation, he is compelled to confess that as a fact "absolute monarchy triumphed simultaneously with it throughout Europe." No; Protestantism retarded instead of advancing the growth of liberty. If in later times liberty has asserted herself in Protestant lands, she but recovered by her own energies her pristine vigor, and wherever to-day she thrives her strength comes to her from the principles proclaimed and defended during the whole course of the Christian era by the Catholic Church.

The relations of political to civil liberty I take to be as those of a means to an end. I call political liberty the diffusion of the State sovereignty among large numbers of the citizens, and the intervention as direct as it may be made of the people in the affairs of the government. The republic is the special embodiment of this liberty. The presumption is that the people will guard with great care their civil liberty—the free, untrammeled enjoyment of their rights—by giving personal attention to the government rather than by abdicating the whole sovereignty into the hands of one ruler. The general principles bearing upon authority, which I have so far explained, remain inviolate. The representatives of power, once placed in office, no matter how numerous they be, or how brief their term of authority, are for the time being the superiors of the community, and hold their power from God within the limitations assigned to their several charges by the constitution.

Do you ask the attitude of the Catholic Church towards a republican form of government? The reply is substantially given in what I have heretofore said on the rights of the people. The Church teaches that the choice of constitutions and of rulers lies with the people. Whether they will have an empire, a monarchy or a republic it is their own privilege to decide, according as their needs may suggest or their desires may lead. The Church is from her own principles without a voice in this matter. This is the emphatic declaration of Pope Leo in his Encyclical of June, 1881.

It is for the people to speak; for the Church to consecrate and enforce their will. When the people have under due conditions constituted a government over themselves, whatever form in itself legitimate this government may have, the Church commands obedience to it. It is the Catholic doctrine that in America loyalty to the republic is a divine virtue, and resistance to its laws a sin crying to heaven for vengeance. The republic in America will receive from the Church all the honor and respect due to the representative of divine authority in temporal matters, and her prayer for the republic will be that it may secure to the people what its professions permit them to expect—the largest possible share of civil liberty.

I lose all patience when I hear prejudice still surviving to the extent to assert that the Catholic Church is not the friend of free institutions. Could her teachings be more explicit? Has her history belied those teachings? The soul, the life of a republic, is an intense love of civil liberty: has not the Church ever labored to create and strengthen this love? Have not her efforts been always in the direction of personal dignity, and of the rights of the individual? Did not the Middle Ages under her guidance gradually emerge from Roman despotism and barbarian feudalism into the possession of political liberty, so that we may truly say she started the nations on the road to the highest forms of liberty? What power but the Church, by the abolition of slavery and serfdom, widened the ranks of freemen and citizens? Were not her bishops parties to all the charters of liberty wrenched from absolute monarchs? Were not parliaments and trial by jury the institutions of Catholic ages? Were not the fueros and communes of the Middle Ages the freest forms of municipal *regimes*? Are not the names of the Italian republics of Genoa, Pisa, Sienna, Florence, Venice familiar to all students of history? Does not Switzerland, that classic land of mountain liberty, shoot into remote Catholic centuries the roots of her republican institutions? I may add in all truth, if the world is to-day capable of enduring and understanding political liberty, it is due to the Church's long and painful parturition of European civilization. I presume our Radicals wonder that the hordes led by Attila and Genseric were not at once educated by the Church into the intricacies of parliamentary debate and presidential campaigning. The action of the

Church in the world is as the action of God, strongest when mildest, sowing seeds in due season, and awaiting due season to reap the harvest, educating nations as a parent educates its child. This much certainly is manifest from her history, that she encouraged the fullest development of personal freedom and personal rights, and that so far as political liberty is compatible with civil liberty, and avoids anarchy no less than despotism, the Church will rejoice in its widest expansion.

I do not say that Catholics the world over will profess, or that Catholics of all past ages would have professed, my own love and admiration for the republican form of government. The choice of governments the Church leaves to nations, and as in all questions left to free discussion, men differ. Catholics in other places see matters from peculiar standpoints; they judge from experiences near to them; they may, too, be influenced by public opinion or prejudices in their several countries. This much, however, I know, that if they prefer other forms they are not compelled in their choice by Catholic principles or Catholic history. This much too, I know, that I transgress no one iota of Catholic teaching when I speak forth my own judgment this evening, and salute the republic as the government I most cordially cherish.

The great Augustine ("De Lib. arbitrio") wrote: "If the people are serious and temperate; and if, moreover, they have such a concern for the public good that each one would prefer the public interest to his own, is it not true that it would be advisable to enact that a people should choose their own authorities for the administration of their affairs?" and the answer given is, "certainly." Remark the conditions: "If the people are serious and temperate," etc., etc. The one fear for the republic is that it gives more freedom than poor humanity deserves or can endure. No form of government as much as a republic demands wisdom and virtue in the people. The many control the ship of State; the many, consequently, must be able to control their own passions, else swift shipwreck awaits it. Rome lost her liberties when the Romans had lost the stern morality of their early history. Virtue is but a name, where religion, the deep sense of man's obligations to God, is not deeply imbedded in the hearts of the people. To Americans, then, who love the republic, I fearlessly say, your hope is in the Catholic Church, because she is the mighty power to-day to resist unbelief and vice. Do you not see that outside of the Catholic Church the most important doctrines of Christianity are melting away, and that a moral chaos is threatening, most vital virtues said to be no longer of significance, and the fount of all social life, the family, breaking up under the pressure of violent passion? The most valued aids to the republic from the Church are not her direct enunciations on liberty, but her powerful labors in the cause of religion, of purity, of honesty, of all the heavenly virtues that build up the Christian man and the Christian family.

Republic of America, receive from me the tribute of my love and of my loyalty. I am proud to do thee homage, and I pray from my heart that thy glory may never be dimmed — *Esto perpetua!* Thou bearest in thy hands the brightest hopes of the human race. God's mission to thee is to show to nations that man is capable of the highest liberty. Oh! be ever free and prosperous that liberty triumph over the earth from the rising to the setting sun. *Esto perpetua*—but forget not that religion and morality can alone give life to liberty and preserve to it a never-fading youth. Believe me, thy surest hope is from the Church which false friends would have thee fear. Believe me, no hearts love thee more ardently than Catholic hearts, no tongues speak more loudly thy praises than Catholic tongues, and no hands will be lifted up stronger and more willing to defend thy laws and thy institutions in peace and in war, than Catholic hands. Again— *Esto perpetua!*

Most Rev. Michael A. Corrigan, D.D.

Archbishop Perché; for Archbishop Henni, of Milwaukee; Archbishop Blanchet, of Oregon City; Archbishop Wood, of Philadelphia.

Besides these, memory turns, with fond regret, to a long list of Right Reverend prelates, who were all present at the late Plenary Council, and who have since, one by one, passed away, namely: Bishop Timon, of Buffalo; Bishop Lavialle, of Louisville; Bishop Baraga, of Marquette; Bishop Carrell, of Covington; Bishop Juncker, of Alton; Bishop Lefebre, of Detroit; Bishop Demers, of Vancouver; Bishop Luers, of Fort Wayne; Bishop McGill, of Richmond; Bishop O'Gorman, of Omaha; Bishop Whelan, of Wheeling; Bishop McFarland, of Hartford; Bishop Bacon, of Portland; Bishop Martin, of Nachitoches; Bishop Verot, of St. Augustine; Bishop De Saint Palais, of Vincennes; Bishop Rappe, of Cleveland; Bishop Domenec, of Pittsburgh; Bishop Amat, of Monterey; Bishop Rosecrans, of Columbus; Bishop Lynch, of Charleston; Bishop Quinlan, of Mobile.

We mourn, moreover, the loss of the Rt. Rev. Dr. Miége, prevented by illness from attending the last National Synod, and who departed this life only a few months ago; and we mourn as well eleven other prelates who had either retired from active duty before the celebration of the second Plenary Council, or who received Episcopal consecration after that date, namely: The Rt. Rev. Dr. Chabrat, Coadjutor of Bardstown; Rt. Rev. Bishop Résé, of Detroit; Rt. Rev. Dr. O'Connor, of Pittsburgh; Rt. Rev. Bishop Whelan, of Nashville; Rt. Rev. Bishop De la Hailendiere, of Vincennes; Rt. Rev. Bishop Melcher, of Green Bay; Rt. Rev. Bishop Galberry, of Hartford; Rt. Rev. Bishop Foley, of Chicago; Rt. Rev. Bishop Pellicer, of San Antonio; Rt. Rev. Bishop McMullen, of Davenport; Rt. Rev. Bishop Toebbe, of Covington.

As we repeat each well-known name, hosts of pleasant memories come crowding on the mind just as by-gone scenes are awakened to new life by some sweet strain of once familiar music. Venerable forms loom up again before us with the paternal kindness, the distinguished presence, the winning ways we knew so well of old; and while the vision lasts we seem to hear a still, small voice saying: "To-day for me, to-morrow for thee," or the echo of the words spoken by the wise woman of Thecua to the king on his throne: "We all die, and fall down into the earth, like waters that return no more."

"Star differeth from star in glory." The bishops, whose virtues we commemorate, differed in gifts of mind, in habits of thought, in nationality, in early training, in personal experience, in almost everything else but their common faith. This golden bond united them to each other and to us. There was still another point of resemblance and another link that bound them all together—the participation in the divine work of the Good Shepherd which was laid upon them all.

We cannot attempt this morning to review the lives of forty prelates one by one; but we can at least give a passing glance at their labors, and so realize to some extent how much we owe them.

"Nothing in this world," says St. Augustine, "is more difficult, more laborious, more perilous than the office of a bishop; yet nothing more blessed in God's sight if the work be so executed as our heavenly Commander enjoins." "The bishop," he continues, "is not for himself, but for those to whom he preaches the divine word and dispenses the holy sacraments."

From its very nature, therefore, the episcopate is a name not so much of honor as of labor and of burden. Among the heathens, for instance, at this very hour, to the devoted bishops, who carry their lives in their hands, the episcopate is a name of untold hardship and of peril. Apart from open persecution, it is a name of consuming anxiety, even in so-called Catholic countries where the free action of the Church is hampered by the State, the outward splendor of the office but too often concealing a hidden yet a bitter bondage. Once more: even when the Church is free, and religion has long been established, the episcopate is still a name of awful responsibility on account of the great multitudes of souls to be cared for.

In our beloved country, dear brethren, although the edge of the sword, the jealousy of interfering governments, and swarming Catholic populations, as in Europe, have thus far been wanting; yet our deceased prelates have certainly not been exempt from the trials of their office. Let me recall to mind a single characteristic fact. Of the two and forty chief pastors whose loss we deplore no fewer than twenty-three were the first bishops of their sees, that is, founders of new dioceses, and if the term may be used, pioneers of religion. Now, if we consider all that the life of a pioneer implies, in overcoming difficulties, in creating resources, in facing hardships, privations, unknown dangers, in displaying untiring steadiness of purpose, energy and courage, carried even often to heroism, the humble pioneer stands before us an humble missionary no longer, but transfigured with shining light, in all the majesty, the supernatural loveliness, the glory of an apostle. Yet such were the labors, more or less, such the lives of all our deceased prelates, and from this chair of truth we may well proclaim our deep indebtedness for the work they accomplished.

We owe their memory lasting thanks, dear brethren, because they achieved: (1.) great results, (2.) In a short time, (3.) In spite of many difficulties.

And, first of all, a vast work was given them to do. Take, for instance (as a typical case, although by no means one of the most embarrassing), the case of your late Archbishop, and my beloved predecessor, Bishop Bayley. Named first Bishop of Newark, he found a diocese with twenty-five priests and as many churches, but unprovided with a single house of learning, with no religious orders, no charitable institutions, except a small frame building, rented as a temporary orphan asylum, under the care of five Sisters of Charity. The field was large and inviting, the harvest not only not ripe, but the seeds hardly yet planted. Situated between two great cities, the new bishopric received the surplus of an overflowing tide of immigration rich, indeed, in prospective blessings, like the inundations of the Nile, but bringing also multitudinous wants demanding instant attention. To meet and direct the rising flood it was necessary to multiply, first of all, the number of devoted laborers; then religious orders had to be introduced as auxiliaries, so that churches, schools, hospitals, asylums, might be erected everywhere. I need not dwell on the results accomplished. Suffice it to say that such was the growth of religion that a single parish had to be divided eighteen times over in as many years—thirty-six priests doing duty in a district where a few years previously three stood watch and guard over the interests of souls.

From the Atlantic let us pass to the distant Pacific coast. It is not yet half a century since a Canadian Missionary, Father Francis Norbert Blanchet, afterwards bishop and archbishop, penetrated the wilds of Oregon, where, at that time, there was neither church nor priest. At the date of his consecration, in 1843, his entire clergy consisted of the distinguished Father De Smet and four other devoted Jesuit Fathers. But remember the size of his vicariate. It embraced 375,000 square miles, a tract of territory larger than England, France and Italy put together, or than all our Atlantic sea-board States, from Maine to Florida, both included. With all our actual appliances for annihilating distance, this would still constitute an immense field of labor. What must have been the toil of traversing it before the building of railroads forty years ago, on foot or on horseback.

Leaving now our sea-coasts, separated from each other by thousands of miles, let us pass to the interior and recall the labors of another pioneer and founder—the Most Rev. Archbishop Henni. During the sixth Provincial Council of Baltimore he was nominated to the See of Milwaukee, then a far distant frontier city, in which the Holy Sacrifice had been offered for the first time only seven years before. At his installation he found in his new diocese four priests, four or five churches and about 8,000 faithful people. At his death there were 185 clergymen, 258 churches, 125 schools, 200,000 Catholics, and these figures whould be still larger had not the diocese meanwhile been divided and subdivided.

But all this, and much more of the same character that could be added, is a familiar tale to you, dear brethren, who, to use the phrase of Cardinal Barnabo at the opening of the American College, Rome, live in a country "in which cities are not built, but improvised." What elsewhere is the steady, gradual and progressive growth of centuries had to be accomplished here in a single lifetime.

The country advanced with more than giant strides. The Church had to keep equal pace, if not, indeed, to lead the march of progress. In justice to the dead, may we not say that their work was most successfully, as well as expeditiously, accomplished? Take the Seminary of St. Charles, at Overbrook, that monument of the late noble-hearted Archbishop of Philadelphia. In point of elegance of construction, of comfortable accommodation, and of architectural beauty, is there in the Catholic world a finer seminary? And as regards system and organization, thoroughness of equipment, attention to sanitary laws and personal comfort, may not many institutions of benevolence and charity established under the auspices of our deceased prelates compare quite favorably, to say the least, with the very best productions of Europe?

Thus far we have seen that the bishops had a vast work to do, and to do it quickly. "Being made perfect in a short space they fulfilled a long time." There remains a third consideration—they had to discharge their labors in the midst of many obstacles.

First of all, there was the manifest want of funds. They had no princely patrons, no overflowing coffers to depend on, but only the mites of the poor and the living springs of Christian charity.

Next there was the want of men—of a numerous and well-trained clergy. In a diocese in which all things are duly ordered, according to the law of the Church; where the bishop is surrounded by vicars-general, canons and a competent staff of other officials; where all the duties of routine labor are equally distributed, and each department of work has its own head, its own organization, the task of presiding is rendered comparatively easy; just as a commander-in-chief rules and directs an army. But with us, hitherto, instead of attaching to himself a corps of officials and so lightening his own labors, the bishop gave the first thought to the pressing needs of souls, and hence he was obliged to do the work of many others single-handed and unassisted. All the difficulties of the diocese meanwhile came swelling up to him, as a pyramid rises to its apex.

New issues, with new complications not contemplated in ordinary ecclesiastical jurisprudence, were continually forming, so that the chief pastor, besides attending to a large correspondence and the discharge of episcopal functions, was compelled to act as theologian, parish priest, architect, lawyer, financier—"to become all things to all men, to gain all to Christ." In the language of St. Augustine, he was emphatically not for himself, but for others—the servant of the servants of God.

Nor must we omit to notice another serious difficulty incidental to a country so large and vast as ours.

The United States, Ireland, France, Germany, Austria, Spain, Belgium, Italy, Canada, Switzerland, all contributed to form our hierarchy, and the bishops whose memory we are celebrating received a varied training in Rome, at St. Sulpice, in Paris, and in Baltimore, in Mount St. Mary's and elsewhere. Nine of the deceased bishops were members of religious orders; four were selected from the Lazarists, two were Jesuits, one a Sulpician, one an Augustinian, one a Trappist. Now this unavoidable variety was both a cause of danger; and, also, in God's providence, by which "all things work together unto good," an instrument of blessings.

It was a source of danger, for as each prelate was left largely to his own inspirations in mapping out his course and forming traditions for his diocese in harmony with local surroundings, as these surroundings varied in almost every case, so difference of discipline would naturally ensue, with deviations more or less permissible from the customs of the universal Church. In fact, even at this hour, considering the vast extent of the country and the cosmopolitan character of its inhabitants, it is almost as difficult to secure uniform ecclesiastical legislation for the United States alone as it would be for the whole of Europe. Nevertheless, it became necessary to provide, as far as practicable, for uniformity of discipline. With this view, in this historic cathedral, between 1810 and 1849, seven Provincial Councils were convened; while during the same period, with the exception of the Synod of Tuam in 1817, not a single Provincial Council had met in all Europe. In 1849 the late Sovereign Pontiff raised that apostolic voice which never goes forth in vain, exhorting the bishops of the Catholic world to revive the salutary discipline of assembling in Provincial Councils; and within the remaining years of his Pontificate, a larger number of such synods were assembled than the world had seen during the two preceding centuries. The bishops of France, England, Ireland, Germany, Austria, Italy, obeying the voice of Peter, held council after council, pouring forth those rich treasures of sacred erudition which come ordinarily of "opportunity of leisure." And now the bread cast on the waters by the American Church came back to the givers. The late Delegate Apostolic, observing the full and harmonious exposition of law and of discipline, with which these councils abound, conceived the design of preparing for this country also a body of law, complete in its kind and comprehensive—a body of law which would resume in itself all the legislative enactments of his predecessors—which would bring us all closer together in our customs and local usages by uniting us all more closely with the Holy Roman Church; which, foreseeing future growth and development, would introduce the normal life of the Church, intended to abide in perpetuity. The result was the second Plenary Council of Baltimore, embodying a code of national canon law, in which the spirit of moderation, of appropriateness to our peculiar condition, of practical good judgment, that breathes throughout, is made still more attractive and persuasive by the dignity, the grace and the elegance of expression, so that the reader knows not which most to admire, the wisdom of the decrees or the consummate beauty with which they are presented.

All subsequent legislation in this country has felt thus far, and will long continue to feel, the impress of the second Plenary Council. An advance has been made in Church polity and discipline from which we may no longer recede, even if we would. Hence, generations to come will have reason to bless the memory of Archbishop Spalding and the other prelates and divines who co-operated with him in accomplishing so beneficial a result. It sets the seal of perpetuity on their labors; for it would, after all, have been little to have achieved a vast material success, unless the result were to be enduring. "You have not chosen Me, but I have chosen you, and have appointed you, that you should go and bring forth fruit, and your fruit should remain."

And now, in conclusion, I cannot leave this pulpit—his pulpit, formerly—without an affectionate allusion to him, dear brethren, who consecrated your cathedral, and who—to employ the phrase used in his panegyric on this very spot—bequeathed you his best legacy in providing "so good a successor." Oh! my brethren, how noble, honest, and spotless was his soul! How genial, bright, and generous his character! How much grace and sunshine dwelt in all his ways, before that last, fatal malady fastened on him.

Your late archbishop, dear brethren, was always frank from childhood and outspoken, retaining through life that transparent sincerity, that unswerving loyalty to truth, that constant courage of his convictions which, under divine Providence, led him originally to the Church.

It is now about half a century since a handsome young student in Middletown, Conn., sat poring over the acts of the Council of Chalcedon, in the well-stored library of a distinguished Episcopalian divine. Suddenly a flash of light seemed to beam upon his mind, and he asked his preceptor the following question:

"Doctor, are the acts of this council authentic?" "Most assuredly," was the answer. The passage he had been reading was this: "The Fathers with one voice exclaimed: this is the faith of our Fathers! This is the faith of the Apostles! Peter has spoken by the mouth of Leo—*Petrus per Leonem locutus est.*" The quick inference and deduction came, that if Peter spoke through his successor then, in the fifth century, he ought also to speak through him now. This was the first gleam of light leading gradually to the aurora and to the perfect day. His sorrowing friends told him later in reply that Rome was corrupt, and if he would but go to Rome he would recognize the fact and relinquish his delusion. He went to Rome to examine honestly for himself, and there he was received into the Church, to become later your eighth archbishop.

He had large natural gifts, acute powers of observation, an unfailing fund of humor, a rare acquaintance with books, and a retentive memory. These qualities combined made him a delightful conversationalist and a great favorite in society. But back of all this was a deep, sincere and tender piety. Like St. Francis de Sales, his cherished patron, even while so well fitted to shine in the world, he longed for the peacefulness and privileges of a religious life. The week before he died, alluding to the subject, he said he was twice on the point of becoming a religious—first, in Rome on the occasion of his reception into the Church, and next, shortly before receiving episcopal consecration. In both cases it was thought best he should remain in the secular clergy, and there exercise the many gifts he possessed for the good of others. How well he used the talent confided to him, particularly that of organization, his labors in New York, New Jersey and Baltimore still bear testimony.

Seven years ago he died. I remember well his last conversation, a little before he lost consciousness. He had been talking of the dread responsibility that presses on the shoulders of a bishop—of the severe account to be rendered to the Supreme Judge, and the thought was suggested to him that God's mercy is above all his works.

"Yes," he replied, "this reflection has often encouraged me. For, after all, humanly speaking, I could have had no reason to expect the gift of faith, considering my early associations and surroundings. And that our Lord called me to His Church, and to His service, has always been to me a proof of His love and special mercy in my regard of His will to save me, because He brought me to the faith." And so the last conscious thought, as far as I know, of the dear archbishop, was kindred to that which supported the great St. Teresa in her agony, "After all, O Lord, I die a child of the Church."

As I began, so let me end, dear brethren, with the words of St. Augustine: "Nothing in this world is more difficult, more laborious, more perilous than the office of a bishop, yet nothing more blessed in God's sight, if discharged as our heavenly Leader desires."

The responsibility is terrible, the labor long and unceasing, and no day is exempt from anxiety. But the end is peace. The grace of God is with His own work. As the straining eyes look up to heaven, a voice of consolation comes to the faithful pastor as to the patriarch of old: "Fear not I am thy Protector, and thy Reward exceeding great."

Most Rev. Wm. Henry Elder, D.D.

The Priesthood.

SERMON OF MOST REV. W. H. ELDER, D.D.,

ARCHBISHOP OF CINCINNATI.

"Ego elegi vos, et posui vos ut eatis et fructum efferatis; et ut fructus vester maneat."—*St. John*, c. xv, v. 16.

IN the spectacle before our eyes we witness a part of the accomplishment of this mission. The Word of God is efficacious; what it declares it also effects. His Word said: "Let there be light: and there was light." "Young man, I say to thee: Arise. And he that was dead sat up and began to speak." So when our Lord commissioned His Apostles to produce fruit among men His efficacious Word went forth with them, and they did produce the fruit; and the fruit has remained, and this day's assembly is at once an evidence of its greatness, its extent and its endurance, and at the same time a provision under God that it shall continue and multiply in the future as it has done in the past. The gathering in this cathedral is a compendium of what is seen over the entire world—Christ living in those whom He has sent, and through them living in the civilized world and infusing life into the uncivilized. We see here spiritual teachers and rulers from all parts of our republic, itself constituted of descendants of all races and all nations; around these teachers, their faithful children in the Church, and mingled with these many not Catholics, not acknowledging these teachers as their own, and yet enlightened by the truths which He commissioned His Church to teach. Because these truths are diffused through the whole moral atmosphere of civilization; so that both within and without the Church they reach in various degrees the minds and hearts and daily lives of all.

And who are these spiritual teachers? Priests of God, holding the priesthood of Christ, the Son of God. It was through His priesthood that He redeemed man; and through that same priesthood He continues to give life in each successive generation till the end of time to those who are willing to receive it. He exercises His priesthood on earth through the mortal priest, to whom He gives His own power and in whom He lives. "All power is given to Me in heaven and on earth. As My Father sent Me, so I also send you. And behold, I am with you all days, even to the consummation of the world." What is this priesthood of Christ? What is the priesthood in the Church? What fruit has it produced and by what means? To what degree do we owe it to our civilization? These are questions which we shall dwell upon this morning; not to answer them fully, but to suggest some points of the answers—points for us all to meditate on, each one to produce in his own life his own portion of the fruits.

Among men Christ's priesthood is His mediation between sinful man and God outraged by man's sins. Our first parents rebelled against God, and thereby forfeited all claim to His favor for themselves and their children. And alas! his children have added their own sins to their parents', and thus sunk themselves still lower into misery, binding themselves in helpless slavery to their most hateful enemy. They needed a mediator. Even at the time when their crime was still fresh upon their souls, even before their punishment was all of it actually inflicted, already God's mercy was moved to promise them a mediator who should bring them pardon and reconciliation and triumph over the tyrant to whom they had so shamefully betrayed the precious gifts of their Creator. This was fulfilled when the ever Blessed Virgin Mary, by the power of the Holy Ghost, brought into this world our Lord Jesus Christ, giving to the Eternal Word a human nature—both soul and body. "And the Word was made flesh and dwelt among us."

With infinite condescension He came down to be our Brother on earth, that he might raise us up to be His brethren in the kingdom of His Father. And He did this by His priesthood.

"To as many as received Him He gave power to become the sons of God."

The highest act of the priesthood is sacrifice. All our Lord's earthly life was one continued sacrifice, consummated when He gave up that life for us upon the cross. By sacrifice we mean, in its perfect and divine character, an act or sign which fully and adequately expresses the acknowledgment by a creature of the supreme dominion and infinite majesty of God over all His creatures. And this is the highest worship, containing all other acts of worship. Men can, indeed, express an acknowledgment of this dominion by words and by various signs; but all these expressions are imperfect, and therefore not adequate; imperfect very often, because words do not prove the sincerity of the man who utters them; imperfect essentially, because all signs and all acts of creatures are finite. They can never, therefore, reach up to express adequately what is infinite in all perfection—the domain and majesty of God. It would seem, then, as if the Creator never could receive an adequate sacrifice or perfect worship from His creatures, since all creatures are infinitely beneath their Creator. Much less could He receive such an adequate acknowledgment from men sunk into sins and enslaved to God's hateful enemy. But God's goodness surpasses the conceptions of all His creatures, and His infinite wisdom and mercy, coming down to the help of creatures, even of His ungrateful creatures, the sons of man, devised a means by which the creature could offer this adequate acknowledgment in a perfect sacrifice; a sacrifice of infinite and divine value, by which man could render homage equal to all that God could ask; infinite and divine as God's divinity itself. This was through means of the adorable mystery of the Incarnation.

In this crowning mystery of God's love and wisdom, God the Son Himself, infinite, eternal God, having the one individual divine nature with the Father and the Holy Ghost, took to Himself likewise a human nature: so that He was at the same time divine and human—Creator and creature. Some illustration of this mystery we can see in the constitution of our own human being. Man is composed of body and soul—of spirit and matter each in its nature utterly and entirely distinct from the other. His body is matter, utterly incapable of thinking or willing or of any act of consciousness. The soul is spirit, having neither shape nor weight nor any other property belonging to matter. And yet so constituted man is one single human person. All our acts, whether done through the soul or through the body, are equally human acts. In like manner our divine Lord, being one divine Person with two natures, divine and human, all His acts were divine, whether done through His divine or His human nature. When, therefore, our Lord, God and man, made acknowledgment of the subjection of His human, created nature to Almighty God and declared the supreme dominion and majesty of God, His absolute right of life and death over Himself and all creatures—this confession and homage was a perfect and adequate act of sacrifice.

It was made by a creature, and yet it was perfect and adequate and infinite, because it was the act of God, a divine act, as the acts of our bodies are human acts.

But our Lord not only confessed this dominion; He submitted Himself to it in all the acts of His life. "I am come not to do My own will, but the will of Him that sent Me." He lived all His human life in obedience to it, and he filled up the measure of all possible obedience by suffering every pain of body, every anguish of soul that His human nature was capable of suffering; consummating His homage to His Father by laying down His life itself—the highest possible confession of God's dominion. "Christ became obedient for us unto death—even to the death of the cross." And while this suffering was endured in His human nature, yet since He was God who suffered, it, therefore, had a divine dignity and value. It was infinite, worthy of God Himself, and, therefore, an adequate, a perfect, an infinite sacrifice.

This was the completion, the filling up of the priesthood of Christ. But although it was the completion, it was not the termination either of His sacrifice or of His priesthood. They both endure for all eternity. "Thou art a priest forever."

Having risen from the dead and ascended to the right hand of God the Father, He did not cease to confess and declare the supreme dominion of the divine majesty over His own human nature as over all creatures. On the contrary, His very presence in heaven in His human nature, with his adorable body still marked with the sacred wounds He suffered in His obedience, is an authentic confession of that dominion, a perfect and divine praise, an eternal sacrifice. And thus Christ continues in heaven His eternal priesthood.

Let me relate a parable: A dutiful son, after years of toil endured for the love of his honored father and of his younger brothers, gathered means to purchase a valuable estate, and he conveyed this to his father as a testimony of honor and gratitude to him, and as a provision for the livelihood and education of his brothers. His gift was completed, when he duly executed the deed of conveyance. But this was not the end of his pious work. It was the beginning, rather. For after this his father continued, as long as he lived, to receive, year after year, the comforts and honors, accruing from the estate, and year after year the younger brothers continued to receive the livelihood, the education, the enjoyments, the society, which their brother's love had put within their reach.

The deed of conveyance was executed once, and never to be repeated; but the gift endured during the life-time of the family.

And so is it with the gift of our elder Brother—the Son of God made man. "Having died once, He dieth now no more." "He entered once into the holy place, having obtained eternal redemption." But His sacrifice, His confession of God's absolute dominion, His purchase of life and graces for His brothers in the flesh, as sinful men—this endured and shall continue to endure. "He hath an everlasting priesthood," says St. Paul, "whereby He is able to save forever them that come to God by Him, always having to make intercessions for us." (Heb. vii, 24.)

The eternal priesthood of Christ, then, may be said to be the ultimate end God had in view in the entire work of creation; for it is the perfection of the glory which He receives from all His creatures. We need not wonder, therefore, that His priesthood was declared from early ages, and confirmed by the solemnity of an oath from God in those mysterious words: "The Lord hath sworn, and it shall not repent Him: Thou art a priest forever." Such is the priesthood of Christ in its essence.

Now, what is the priesthood on earth—the priesthood exercised by mortal men—the priesthood we see in this assembly? It is the continuation of this essential priesthood of Christ through the ministry of men. The sacrifice which He is always offering before His Father in heaven, invisible there to us, that same sacrifice He is pleased to offer on our earth, made visible to our mortal eyes in the Holy Sacrifice of the Mass; and by this He gives us a perfect worship.

In this adorable mystery our Lord, in His own flesh and blood, under the appearance of bread and wine, truly and really comes upon our altar; and there before our eyes offers to His Father the same testimony of adoration, obedience and love—the same thanksgiving for all His gifts to creatures, the same atonement for the sins of men, the same supplication for new favors and renewed mercy—which He once sealed by His death, and which He is perpetually offering before the choirs of heaven. He wishes to make this offering visible and audible for our mortal senses. And, therefore, He has appointed visible mortal men to be His priests, and authorized them to utter His own words, with power to produce the same effect as when He uttered them with His mortal lips. The priest takes in his hands the bread and wine; he repeats the mysterious words of Christ; and on this utterance, the bread and wine are changed. Our Lord, in His real Body and Blood, descends upon the altar. By the hands of His priest He is elevated for the people's adoration; by the hands and the lips of His priests, He is offered to the Father in behalf of all the people; by His priest He gives Himself to His faithful disciples, to be the food of their souls, their strength and their life on earth and the pledge of their eternal life in heaven. "He that eateth Me, the same also shall live by Me." "Do this as a memory of Me." This is what we mean by the Christian priesthood; it is in this sense Christ's priesthood is communicated to mortal man. There is no other priesthood but the one, and that one is Christ's own. The mortal man is the agent of Christ, through whom He makes sensible on earth His perpetual sacrifice in heaven; through whom He exercises His one eternal priesthood.

"Sacrifice and priesthood," says the Council of Trent, "are so associated together by the ordinance of God that both have existed together under every law that God has given to men." (xxiii, 1.)

From the very beginning of the human race God appointed that there should be priests among men, and that these in the name of their brethren should offer sacrifice. Under the original law, given to our first parents and their children, commonly called the Law of the Patriarchs, it was ordinarily the first-born son, though others too were sometimes authorized, as we see in Abel. Under the law given to Moses on Mount Sinai, it was the sons of Aaron, himself the elder brother of Moses. So deeply rooted was this original tradition among men of God's requiring to be worshiped by sacrifice, and some men to be set aside who should offer sacrifice in the name of their brethren, so agreeable was this to the common sentiments of mankind in their dealings with God, that no people seem to have been ever ignorant of it. Pagans, idolators, and even savages who had lost the knowledge of almost everything else concerning God, still preserved this truth. They knew they must worship Him by sacrifice, and that the sacrifice must be offered by those who were constituted priests.

This was always the worship that God required from man—the offering of sacrifice. The appointed priest offered the victim in the name of all. The people stood around and united their prayers and praise with those of the priest. But it was the sacrifice that made their prayers agreeable to God, because the sacrifice united them with the future Great High Priest who was to offer the perfect sacrifice on Calvary.

And now in the Holy Mass the faithful gather around the altar where the divine victim offers Himself.

With Him they offer their adoration, their thanksgiving, their cries for mercy, their supplication for God's graces, and He receiving them from the lips and hearts of His brethren makes them all His own, and offers them to His eternal Father. Thus, in the Mass, each one of us can render a perfect and infinite worship through our Great High Priest.

Nay, more; as He gave Himself for us on the cross, so He gives Himself to each of us upon the altar. Each one of us can claim the Victim as our own, and thus, in the Mass, each one of the faithful present becomes himself in a secondary manner a priest, because each one of us offers the divine Victim. Each one of us can say with truth: Almighty and most Holy God—unworthy sinner as I am—I offer Thee a worship worthy of Thyself. "Look upon Me for the face of Thy Christ," and receive His homage and supplication as my own—since Thou delivered Him for us—and He gives Himself to us. Thus is fulfilled the declaration of St. Peter addressed to every Christian: "Ye are a holy people, a royal priesthood." (ii Peter.)

The old sacrifices appointed by God, such as the slaying of

victims, the immolating of fruits, and other articles that give life and service to man—all these were inadequate of themselves. They were appointed by God, and they had a value in His eyes as types of the future sacrifice of Christ. They all pointed to Mount Calvary; they were all acts of faith in the Messiah who was to come, and they had their value from His mysterious sacrifice upon the cross. When this was once offered, then the reality was accomplished. There was no more room for types, and all typical sacrifices were set aside by God. And now the one, true, perfect and divine sacrifice is offered every day all over the earth, by the one living divine priest, Jesus Christ, through the visible ministry of His mortal priests, and thus is fulfilled the prophecy of Malachy, "From the rising of the sun to the going down of the same in every place there is sacrifice, and there is offered to My name a clean oblation." (Mal. i, 2.)

But the priesthood of Christ was not only a homage to God, it was also an office of mediation to reconcile fallen man with God. Besides worshiping God, our Redeemer came to lift men up from their fallen state, and give them means to be children of God. "I, when I shall be lifted up, I shall draw all things to Myself."

He brought to men light and strength. He not only brought these, but He was Himself the light and the life. He was the very Word of God, by whom all things were made, from whom all things have their being, and, therefore, the light of our souls is to see Him, and the life of our souls is to live by Him. We see Him when we see what He did and said—when we listen to the Gospel. We live by Him when we eat of His Flesh and receive His graces. "I am the light of the world. He that followeth Me walketh not in darkness." "As I live by the Father, so he that eateth the same also shall live by Me."

This is the fruit to men of Christ's coming on earth: that men's souls be enlightened by His truth, and receive life from His own life, even as the branch has all its life from the sap of the vine which bears it. "I am the vine; ye are the branches; without Me you can do nothing"—nothing for your eternal life in heaven. This, then, is the fruit which our Lord commissioned His Apostles to bring forth—fruit that shall remain till the end of the world, and shall continue to ripen and to multiply, and give peace and joy on earth; and which, for all eternity, shall remain in the happiness of the saints and the glory they shall give to God in heaven; in the sanctification of souls enlightened and sanctified in various degrees, according to the measure in which they shall know Christ, and fill themselves with the spirit of Christ. And from this sanctification of souls arises the civilization of Christian society. For what is civilization, as our present illustrious holy Pontiff, Leo XIII, has said, but the development of man living in society? And what is the development of man but the unfolding of that which makes man to be man, and not a mere animal—that is, the image of God in his soul? "Let us make man after our own image and likeness;" and we develop this image in the measure in which we copy Christ and walk in His life.

This communication of the light of the life of Christ was the office of His priesthood. It was begun by Himself. It was spread through the world by the Apostles—the first whom He called and sent with the powers of His priesthood. "As the Father sent Me, so I also send you. Go teach all nations; baptize them in the name of the Father, and the Son, and the Holy Ghost; and lo! I am with you."

It has been spread wider and wider, and has been kept clear before men during these eighteen centuries by the preaching of those to whom that priesthood was handed down: the bishops, who hold it in all its fullness: and the priests of the second order, who hold not indeed its fullness, but its sublimest powers and those most needed for each individual soul—the power and grace to preach with authority and effect; the power to offer the Holy Sacrifice; the power to purify souls by loosing them from their sins; the power to sanctify them by blessing and by all the other means of grace.

It would have availed little to have these truths of salvation once proclaimed if they had not been preserved by living teachers. Many of them had been declared by God in the beginning. But they had been lost to men for want of priests devoted to their teaching. Because men's earthly inclinations, their sensuality, their pride and their passions led them to violate His laws; and soon the truths on which those laws are based became obscured and many of them entirely blotted out from their souls. Even the primary truth that underlies all others had been abandoned, and, instead of one personal God, Creator of all things, a loving Father yet jealous of His honor, a just Judge who renders to every one according to his works, they imagined to themselves a multitude of gods like unto men and with passions similar to their own. Even the most refined nations held gods as patrons of the coarsest vices. They had a god of drunkenness, a god of thieving, and gods of shameless indecencies.

All this, because they had not a living priesthood to keep the truth always before their minds, and to enforce its teachings in the practice of their lives. Some kind of priests, indeed, they had. For this need of priests, we have already seen, was a truth that survived, even when the truth of one God was lost. Yet they were not priests of God, they were self-made priests, or priests made by the civil power; priests given only to the pomp of outward worship; not caring to teach the truths of morals. Indeed, like the people, they had not those truths themselves.

Only the Jews preserved the original truths given to man, because only the Jews had a divine priesthood, with authority and command from God to teach. "The lips of the priest shall keep knowledge, and they shall seek the law from his mouth." "All things whatsoever they teach, observe and do." Even the Jewish priests, however, were such only in figure, since they had only a typical sacrifice, and consequently even their ministry was weak; the fruits of it were fast dying out when our Lord appeared on earth.

But the Christian priest has Christ living in him, speaking by his lips and giving divine efficacy to his words. "He that heareth you heareth Me." Hence it is by the priests His truths have been handed down to our day with the same clear sound, and the same certain meaning, and the same exactness, and the same intrinsic, living energy that they had from the mouths of the Apostles: because they are always the words of the same priest, Jesus Christ, having all the attributes which His divine priesthood gives to them.

Last Sunday you were shown how these truths have been steadfastly proclaimed to all the world by the great High Priest, the Sovereign Pontiff, and how they are reaffirmed to separate peoples by councils like our own. But to-day we are considering how they are brought home to every family, and impressed on every mind, and enforced in every life; to all who use their free will for the end for which God gave it to them. And this is done by the ministry of the priest.

If only these truths were kept commonly known among men in general, even this would be an advantage that paganism never had. But it is vastly more that they are drunk in by little children, so that men grow up with them from before the days of their earliest recollections; and as increasing years develop their mental powers and new relations in life give them need of more particular knowledge, so new knowledge is ever offered to them. And as new occupations tend to crowd out of sight these early teachings, they are ever renewed in their minds by continued repetitions and fresh explanations and illustrations. And who are God's instruments for thus keeping His truths fresh in each individual soul? They are the priests—the pastors of His Church—in their continued preaching and instructions.

For what men need—what all of us need—is not that the truth be once stated and received, but that it be kept before our eyes, so that we may never forget it, or once forgetting may soon be reminded of it again.

Let the most earnest Christian reflect what would be the state of his soul at this moment if, for the last ten or twenty years, he had never heard repeated the truths that he learned in childhood. If, with all his pressure of business, with all the daily solicitations of his evil passions, he had never heard the sacred admonitions of the priest—never had these truths renewed in his soul by the living words that Christ has addressed to him by the living priest. And still more: What would be the general condition of society if, for the last fifty or a hundred years, there had been no living priest to teach to the last three generations the truths of Christianity? We see it from time to time. We saw it most forcibly in the last century, when large masses of men, ignorant of many of these truths, or wilfully renouncing them, undertook to reform society, as in the excesses of the French Revolution, and in the outburst only fourteen years ago of the Communists and the petroleuses of Paris.

It was in the name not of Jesus Christ but of Christ's enemies (the new made religion of humanity), that the streets of Paris were drenched in the blood of her best citizens, that brothers denounced their own brothers, and children gave their fathers to the guillotine; that women and children were massacred as dangerous enemies. And even now, when in many places society is held in fear by the rumblings as of a threatened earthquake beneath their feet; who are those restless masses that are kept down only by the pressure of an armed government? They are those who know not or who reject the truths which our Lord commissioned His priests to teach: the fear of God; the obligations we all owe to our fellow-men, and the obligation to subdue our passions, to bear the evils that we cannot cure without doing wrong to others: and the great truth, deterring us from all evil and comforting us in all troubles, that man's only complete happiness is in the eternal joys of heaven, and that this life is given us to purchase these joys by our virtues and our patient bearing of the crosses that God lays on us. These are the men who hate God's priests.

Now, why has not the whole world run into those excesses and been buried under those miseries? Because the truths of Christianity and His life are preserved in man. They are kept before their minds, and kept not as abstract truths, but made living and practical in the model life of our Lord Himself on earth and of the saints of all ages, who have endeavored to copy His life and holiness in their own; in all good Christians, and in men who hold only a portion, but still a portion of them. And who are they that hold up this mirror of truth and holiness, but the priests whom He Himself has appointed; whom He has prepared under the training of His Church; to whom He has given the power and commission to teach these truths; to whom, in the Holy Sacrament of Orders, He has communicated the grace to preach them with fidelity; whom He strengthens every day with the divine food of His own adorable Body and Blood in the Holy Sacrament of the Mass?

It is they to whom the whole world is indebted for the preserving of these truths. Even when the sun is hidden from our eyes by clouds we still walk and work by the light of the sun. So men and even whole peoples who do not acknowledge the priests of God's Church, yet hold these truths from the traditions of society, and from public opinion; and these traditions are kept in vigor by the constant teaching of the Church. A great writer, learned in history and human nature has said that had not the Popes been unyielding in upholding the bond of marriage the sovereigns of Europe would come to live like the sultans of Constantinople.

But, dearly beloved, this is only a portion of what God gives us through His priests. When the Israelites were forty years journeying through the desert to reach the Promised Land; besides the multitude of lesser favors with which God blessed them, there were two continuous ones which overshadowed all the rest, and which indeed were the very means that enabled them to enjoy all the rest: the pillar of cloud that showed them the road by which God designed them to travel; and still more necessary, the manna which every morning fell from the clouds to be their food for each day's journey. Without these, with all their courage, they would soon have perished in the wilderness.

All these things, St. Paul tells us, were given in figure of the sublimer and richer realities that God was preparing for the world through the priesthood of His Son.

As we are journeying through the wilderness of this life, with all its fatigues and dangers, to the promised land of heaven, He has not only given His divine word as light to guide us, but He has likewise provided Food to strengthen us.

Alas! we know too well by our experience that it is not enough to know God and to know our duties. In spite of our knowledge the temptations around us are not always resisted; the passions within us are not always kept in due subjection; the enemies assailing us are often too strong to be repelled. And therefore has He furnished us with abundant Food, falling not from the clouds, but coming down from the highest heavens above. And this Food He has appointed should be furnished to us every day by His divine Son through those who continue His priesthood on earth.

This Food I need not tell you, in its perfection, is the adorable Eucharist of Our Lord's Body and Blood, brought down to the earth every morning in the Holy Sacrifice of the Mass. And while this is the perfection and the essence of that Food, He has furnished a number of other forms under which the virtue and the life of Christ is communicated to our souls, till we can say with St. Paul: "I live now; not I, but Christ liveth in me."

The richest of these forms are His holy Sacraments. They all derive their efficacy from the Body of Christ, which was delivered for us, and the Blood of Christ, the price of our redemption. And each of them brings with it a multitude of graces especially adapted to the needs of our soul in its journey.

And besides these again He has appointed, through His Church, another multitude in rich variety of blessings of sacred objects and sacred ceremonies, of forms of prayer and worship each one of which has its own peculiar efficacy, suited to all the multitude of our spiritual wants. They make vivid His truths; they defend us against our enemies; they heal our souls of their sins and infirmities; they console us in our trials; they encourage us in our difficulties; they enlighten us in our perplexities; they comfort us in our fears, and elevate us in our hopes. And all these again, as they are fruits of Christ's priesthood, so He continues as our priest to give them to us through those whom He has empowered to exercise that priesthood continually among us.

It was the priest who received us from our mother's arms—poor outcasts from paradise—children of the fallen Adam—nay, as St. Paul says, children of wrath—and in the waters of Baptism He gave us the new birth—to be called and to be the children of God. It was the priest who, when we were still too tender to listen to his own teachings, kept our mothers reminded of their duty, and enforced it on them, to give us the first knowledge of God, of the divine Child of Bethlehem, and of His Blessed Mother—our mother likewise. It was the priest who took up our mother's teachings, and led us to a deeper knowledge of the life and sufferings of our Blessed Redeemer, of the power of prayer, of the Commandments of God and of His Holy Church, and of all the means of sanctifying our souls. And when our souls had been wounded by sin—perhaps wounded unto death—it was the priest to whom we confided our weakness and our unhappy falls. It was he that set before us the motives of contrition and pointed out the ways to avoid future falls. It was he that encouraged us to trust in God's mercy, and he that applied that mercy to our souls in the pardon that he had power to issue to us in the name of God. And when we shall come to that dread moment when earthly friends can do nothing more for us, it is through the priest that God Himself will come to cleanse us once more from all the sins of our life, to feed us with the heavenly bread that shall strengthen us like Elias to complete our journey to the mountain of God; to anoint us for our last decisive struggle with the enemy of our souls; to purify our eyes, our ears and our lips, before they close on earth to open in heaven where we shall see and hear the things which no earthly eye hath seen, no ear hath heard, nor hath it entered into the mind of man to conceive. In a word, dearly beloved, all those things on earth which do make life well worth living, all come to us from our Great High Priest Jesus Christ through those whom He sends—as His Father sent Him—His earthly priests. The life that is worth living, is a Christian life, the life of the sons of God. This life, like the air we breathe, we are drinking in almost unconsciously daily and hourly in all the unnoticed means of grace which our High Priest provides. And as besides the air we breathe, our bodies are nourished (from time to time) with various kinds of food, and healed with medicines, and refreshed with delicacies, so our souls, from time to time, are nourished by some of the sacraments, or healed from sin by others: or they are led to higher perfection by the various devotions and religious exercises of the Church. And all these are ministered to us by men like ourselves, mortal and weak and liable to sin, yet strong and divine in the works they do through the ministry of the priesthood of Christ.

Such is the love of Jesus for your souls. Because it is for you He gives these blessings. For you He appoints His priests and gives them their wondrous powers not for their exultation and pride, but they may furnish your souls with light and life. You are the fruits He wishes to gather. God grant that you may never disappoint His loving heart. God grant that you may fill your minds with the knowledge of Him, and your hearts with the love of Him, so that united here in this sacrifice that you may join in His worship and share in His eternal priesthood.

And to you, venerable Fathers of the Episcopate, Reverend Brothers of the Priesthood, I will not presume to address any exhortation of my own. I speak to you rather in the words of one whose life of self-sacrifice so filled him with the spirit of our great High Priest, that for more than four hundred years this book has been teaching to both priest and laity the perfect Following of Christ.

"Oh! how great and honorable is the office of priests, to consecrate with sacred words the Lord of majesty, to bless Him with their lips, to hold Him with their hands, to receive Him with their mouth, and to administer Him to others. Oh! how clean ought those hands to be, how pure that mouth, how unspotted the heart of a priest, with whom the Lord of purity so often enters. When a priest celebrates he glorifies God, he rejoices the angels, he edifies the Church. He helps the living, he obtains rest for the dead, and makes himself partaker of all that is good."

Let thy grace, O Almighty God, assist us, that we who have undertaken the office of the priesthood may serve Thee worthily and devoutly in all purity and good conscience.

And if we cannot live in so great innocency as we ought, grant us at least to bewail the sins we have committed, and in the spirit of humility and the resolution of a good will, to serve Thee more fervently for the time to come.

Rt. Rev. P. Manogue, D.D.

Rt. Rev. J. J. Kain, D.D.

Rt. Rev. Wm. H. Gross, D.D.

Rt. Rev. J. F. Shanahan, D.D.

Rt. Rev. J. Hennessy, D.D.

Rt. Rev. B. J. McQuaid, D.D.

Rt. Rev. John Loughlin, D.D.

Rt. Rev. P. J. Baltes, D.D.

Rt. Rev. Tobias Mullen, D.D.

The Unity of the Church.

SERMON OF RIGHT REV. J. F. SHANAHAN, D.D.,

BISHOP OF HARRISBURG.

"God is faithful: by whom you are called unto the fellowship of His Son, Jesus Christ our Lord. Now, I beseech you, brethren, by the name of our Lord Jesus Christ, that you all speak the same thing, and that there be no schisms among you; but that you be perfect in the same mind, and in the same judgment."—*I. Cor., c. i, v. 9-10.*

YOU witnessed this morning, Fathers and brethren, the opening of this new Plenary Council, and you could hardly fail to be struck, as I was, with the solemnity of the occasion. You saw new evidence, if evidence were needed, of the wondrous spiritual organization that brings together at the call of authority such a body of prelates and clergy from every part of this vast country—from Canada to the Gulf, from the Atlantic to the Pacific—to confer together for a period, and enact such legislation as may seem most conducive to the spiritual welfare of the multitudes of the faithful committed to their keeping. You have seen before you men of many distant nationalities, men of many divergent opinions, doubtless, in secular matters—and it may be, too, in minor points of ecclesiastical discipline—and you know they have come together ready to sink individual preferences in the common good, because they have come as brethren of one household united in faith and charity.

This spirit of unity, calling us unto the fellowship of Jesus Christ, as the Apostle says, is a token of the mighty society of which those leaders are members, made compact with you in Christ, dearly beloved of the faithful. We are all of the one household of faith. And the Apostle exhorts us, like the Corinthians, to be perfect in one mind and one judgment.

God calls us unto the fellowship of Christ His Son; we obey His call; we are united in this supernatural fellowship; we stand within the hallowed circle of Christian unity; we are citizens of God's kingdom on earth; we are members of His holy and enduring Church. It has been thought well that after what has been said—and said so eloquently—to-day on "The Church in Her Councils," something should be presented to-night on "The Unity of the Church." Hence the text I have chosen and the words I have so far uttered, as intending to lead to a fuller development of the subject.

The Church, we say, is one. She must be one or she is no Church. What do we mean when we say that the Church is one—when we speak of the unity of the Church? How is the Church one?

"Because," says our catechism, the essence of theology, "all its members agree in one faith, are all in one communion and are all under one head."

Her members agree in one faith. Unity of faith is the common belief in all the articles of faith which have been revealed by Christ, and so declared by His Church. Her members agree in communion. Unity of communion is the union in one society of all who profess this faith, with participation in the same sacraments and the same prayers, under the guidance of their legitimate pastors, and all under the Roman Pontiff, who is their head upon earth. Unity of communion preserves the unity of faith. Union with and submission to the legitimate pastors preserve the unity of communion.

There can, in the nature of things, be but one true faith. Truth is one under every aspect. Its opposite is error. There are numberless errors, for there are numberless ways of opposing the truth. God gave man the true faith that he might embrace it and not fall into error. Why else should He have revealed it? He willed, then, that man should have unity of faith. To secure this unity among men scattered throughout the world and differing in language, habits and propensities, He established a unity of communion—that is, from such conflicting elements He formed a single spiritual society; and, leaving the members subject to their own governments, laws and institutions, He gained their willing adhesion to lofty religious precepts, and their loving allegiance to a settled ecclesiastical authority. He founded a society, in a word, of which all the members would agree in one faith, be all in the same communion, and be all under one head. This society, need I say, is the Church.

The Church being thus formed through unity of faith and unity of communion, there are two ways of separating from her: one by renouncing the faith—this is heresy; the other by withdrawing from the communion of her prayers and rites, and rejecting her authority—this is schism.

Men are scattered over the world. How is it possible to preserve this unity of faith and communion among them? God in His wisdom has provided a means. He has instituted a ministry for His Church commissioned and charged to teach the faith, to administer the Sacraments, officiate in divine worship and govern the Church. This ministry is made up of several orders called the hierarchy. You see the great body of priests discharging their sacred functions over broad areas under the jurisdiction of a minister of a higher order called a bishop. You see him again holding close communion with the other bishops of a province or nation.

But these bishops, numerous as they are, and often remote from each other, with their differences of race and habits of thought, might teach different doctrines and form conflicting societies or schools of opinion which they might set up as Churches. Without going so far, they might deviate widely in ceremonial and Church government. How are these dangers averted? Behold the wisdom of God! You see bishops coming together from afar, as during these days, in solemn council to confer with each other and with their brethren of the other orders of the clergy, in the light of the spirit of God, as to the best means of preserving uniformity of discipline and guarding against loss of unity of faith. But they come not together of themselves. Their enactments are not effective until ratified by higher authority. Christ has set one as bishop of bishops over all the rest whose office is to confirm his brethren, as Christ said to Peter—whose prerogative it is to keep the unity of the spirit in the bond of peace. On him Christ has conferred the primacy of honor and of jurisdiction, and placed him on high to look over and guard the whole Church and be her visible centre of unity.

"Thou art Peter and upon this rock will I build My Church," says our Lord. "I will give thee the keys of the Kingdom of Heaven." "Feed My sheep." "Confirm thy brethren." The primacy of Peter being destined to preserve the unity of the Church, it must have duration and permanence. His prerogative, like that of the other Apostles, has been given in the Church and for the Church. It is not personal merely, but through him for the Church, and therefore, cannot perish with his death. If the primacy of Peter is the rock on which the Church is built, it must last as long as the Church will last. Peter is the shepherd of the flock of Jesus Christ. His pastoral ministry then must extend to all times and all places. By the institution of the episcopacy, the particular Churches have a grand principle of unity. The universal Church has then greater need of a bishop of bishops to keep the body of the Lord from dismemberment. "Upon Peter," says St. Cyprian, "is founded the unity of the whole Church; he has transmitted his primacy to the Roman Church, which is the See of Peter with which all the other Churches must be in accord."

The primacy of the Pope is a necessary deduction from the very idea of the Church. It is the one, living, personal representation of the grand principles of authority, alone capable of preserving the unity of faith, and of directing with strong and sure hand towards the sovereign end, the activity and energy of all the orders and of all the members of this glorious organism which we know as the Church.

The supremacy of Rome in the Church is the arrangement of God. Why else should the Churches yield to her such free and willing obedience? And so you find in her a combination of admirable though seemingly opposite qualities: strictness with moderation; unshaken resolve with tenderest indulgence; ceaseless guard over the deposit of the faith with noblest encouragement to true temporal and material progress. Thus does she divinely rule the Church and uphold its essential unity.

According as the Church extended her limits and the nations flocked to her shelter, it was necessary that the central power should be stronger and stronger, and the unitive power of the Popes be exercised with ever increasing energy. And so, whenever the storms broke loose with more fury, threatening to engulf the bark of Peter; whenever pride above or revolt below made the danger of schism imminent, the nations turned towards Rome, eager to hear the voice of Peter, which was always the voice of truth and right. We wonder at the energy and tenacity of ancient Rome in establishing her dominion through the policy of her senate and the valor of her armies. Christian Rome affords us a grander spectacle. She surpasses pagan Rome in the heroism of her faith. She founds the universal Church on the supremacy of her ecclesiastical spirit and the spontaneous submission of the faithful. If Christianity has not confined itself in some obscure corner like a sect; if it has not crystalized in its forms like the religion of the Hindoos; if European energy has not sunk enervate in luxury and bondage as in the East; we owe it solely to that principle of life and unity; we owe it to this, that the Church forms one compact whole under the direction of a chief whose eye takes in the whole world, whose word all listen to with respect, who is the father and teacher of Christendom, to whom Jesus Christ has communicated his full powers in the person of St. Peter, to feed, to guide and govern the universal Church.

No kingdom, no government of the world has furnished the model of the glorious constitution of the Church or can attain its perfection. The Church is a monarchy, since it has a ruler who holds the plenitude of power, who commands all, and all obey. The Church is an aristocracy, for with the supreme ruler there is the episcopate, sharing with him the government of the Church and holding its place, too, by divine institution. The Church is a democracy, for in this kingdom all offices, even to the highest dignity, even to the triple diadem of the sovereign head, may be gained by the humblest born citizen. The Church, then, combines in her constitution the chief features of the three forms of civil society, hitherto best known in history. Through the primacy she possesses the strength and grandeur of that unity by which she embraces the nations of the earth, becoming thus, in truth and by exceptional privilege, the universal, the Catholic Church, as called for by the very notion of Christianity, which is the religion of mankind.

This wondrous constitution of the Church, received from Christ, it is that makes her strong—so strong that the gates of hell cannot prevail against her. Thus organized, she, and she alone, bears the recognized marks of her divinity. She is one, holy,

Catholic and Apostolic. We proclaim this in our creed. It is as one, indeed, that we are regarding her; but, what, in few words, are those four signs, but the essential qualities of revelation itself, made manifest always and everywhere—in every age, in every clime? What are they, tell me, but the prolonged action of Jesus Christ ever living in His Church and permeating it with His spirit? Whatever religious society wants any of these marks is wanting in a quality essential to the workings of Christ, and cannot therefore be the true Church.

Look at this more closely. The fundamental character of Christian revelations is the authority of the infallible Word of God, by means of which all men come by the shortest way to knowledge of the truth. Its object is the unity of the Church on the basis of unity of faith and ecclesiastical communion. For, the prototype of the Church, one God in three persons, is one. Christ is one with His Father: "The Father and I are one." The kingdom of the elect is one with Christ and the Father. Those regenerated in Him through the Church must be one, as by their corporeal birth they are one race in Adam. In the sight of the spirit of God mankind is also one, forming an organism whose characteristic is unity; a society of life and love in God, if its members are true to Him, the household of the chosen, who dwell in the new terrestrial paradise, the Church. The Lord is come to gather together those whom sin and error had dispersed. Unity was the object of the prayer He addressed to His Father just before His passion.

It is by her unity that the Church will be known by the world as the true spouse of Christ by being of one body and one spirit. The Apostle exhorts the faithful to unity: "I beseech you, brethren, by the name of our Lord Jesus Christ, that you all speak the same thing, and that there be no schisms among you." "The very derivation of the word Church," says St. Chrysostom, "means unity and unanimity. In that unity the Church is beautiful like unto God, the eternal beauty; like unto heaven, which knows not the deformity of sin—sin which alone is the cause of division. For *moral* division goes before national and sectional separation. Unity, while it is the beauty of the Church, is also her strength. Her unity it is that makes her invincible."

Why is there a Church at all? Is it not for the sanctification of man through the truth? Is it not to win him from sin to virtue? to lead him from earth to heaven? Then, holiness is a second characteristic of the Church, just as the sanctity of the doctrines of Christ is proof of His divine mission. But, He came on earth and died for all. He placed salvation within reach of all. His Church, then, must be Catholic or universal—no territorial limits—spread over the whole earth. But, furthermore, it must have come down through the ages by unbroken succession from the Apostles, and must be ever the same to the end of the world. It is, then, Apostolic. Reject one of these marks, and you reject the Church itself; you blot out Christianity, since you destroy one of its essential attributes.

Where, then, do you find this one, holy, Catholic and Apostolic Church? You see numbers who have gone out from her grouping themselves together and calling themselves Churches. But, the one grand, easily recognized mark of the true Church is, that it is always one and the same; while the others are always contradictory to her and at variance with each other. Their record is the record of their variations. None of the sects dares seriously to claim the title of Catholic; or if individuals here and there attempt it, they are put down as absurd even by their co-religionists. There is but one Church found all over the world, and embracing all classes in one faith, in one form of worship, with a stable hierarchy, and spoken of in tongues without number as the one, holy, Catholic Church.

She is Catholic solely because she is one, endowed with the principle of her unity, the ever-living authority of a teaching, infallible body, with its infallible head and living centre of unity, the Pope, the Vicar of Christ.

It is in her alone that is found the grand and incontestable seal of God and of His truth—unity, in which alone the human mind is satisfied in its aspirations, and by which the work of God is made manifest through the ages. The history of the Church is but the history of the struggles of the Church to preserve that unity in spite of the elements of discord and the spirit of nationality, and the forces of heresy and schism, ever trying to rend her asunder. And in this never-ending battle, sometimes the Church succeeds in winning back to herself the foes of her unity; sometimes she is compelled, when the disease is incurable, to cut off the gangrened parts to save the healthy members.

How different the course of civil societies! States would perish if they did not make compromises and modify their legislation under pressure of circumstances. But no peril, no disaster, can force the Church to modify a single dogma. It is not strange, says a philosopher, that one should save himself from ruin, by knowing how to give way on occasion, but that the Church should ever stand inflexible marks her divinity. Rome has never bowed before heresies, no matter how alarming. The emperors of the East proved recreant; the barbarian hordes that overran the empire became overwhelmingly Arian, and threatened the subversion of Rome; but Rome held fast to Catholic unity. She cut off the Greek Church from her communion, with sorrow indeed, yet undismayed by the fact that she was cutting off the half of the Christian world. Being one, she is the divine embodiment of Christianity, the body of the Lord who continues to become incarnate and take form in her, and yet is ever her life-giving principle. Being one, she must be exclusive. Outside of her pale she sees sects, professions, schools of active thought, earnest working associations, Churches with limiting designations; but not the one, Catholic Church. As she cannot lose nor deny her prerogative of Spouse of Christ, of the Body of the Lord, she cannot admit other bodies on an equality with her.

Take away unity, and Catholicity is impossible. Tired out with dividing and subdividing into sects, men will seek soon some kind of reunion, some shadow of compactness. Rulers see their opportunity, and so-called national Churches spring into ephemeral existence. This nationalizing of religion has ever been the anguish of the universal Church. Admit this principle, and you have, at best, but an aggregation of independent Churches with their inevitable and rapidly growing antagonisms. To neutralize such elements of dissolution, a sole, a central and unitive power must exist in the Church. Our modern creeds have followed the steps of the ancient national systems where the frontier of the State is the frontier of the religion.

And where government influences do not directly control them, as with us, yet do we not see a similar tendency to sectional or political division? Have we not seen a Church North and a Church South—a Church endorsing this or that candidate or party on mere political grounds? What wonder that members with opposite views on financial or industrial questions resent this pulpit antagonism to their honest opinions on secular matters, and class their Church with the other political agencies! What wonder that youth soon learn to covertly despise, and as they grow older, to scoff at all religion. What wonder, in the face of all these disentegrating causes, that faith dies out; that doubt prevails; that indifference to a future state is widespread; that reckless indulgence of every passion seems the creed of growing multitudes; that agnosticism is the fashion of the cultured, and God is a mere form of expression; while infidel blasphemy is applauded by the crowd.

The very expression, national or sectional Church, implies a contradiction in terms. In its very nature the Church rises above nationality. If the whole Church were parcelled out into national Churches, what would become of Christianity? It would soon be no more than the institutions of Greece and Rome, a matter of interest and speculation for the historian or archæologist. A territorial Church inspires no respect, no true devotion. Government power and national pride are its support. The government protects it for its supposed influence with the masses; but the masses, at heart, despise it in spite of the protection of power, or rather because of such protection. So much for the want of a bond of unity.

But if the Church would be free from the trammels of the State; if she would assert her freedom of action in her own sphere in the world, she is far from wrapping herself up in a cold and haughty disdain of the world. Her mission, on the contrary, is to penetrate the world with her spirit. She takes human nature as it is to ennoble and sanctify it. Man has not an idea in his mind, a desire in his heart, an aspiration in his soul to which the Church does not assign its proper end and assure its development and exercise and legitimate object. Within her pale genius finds room to spread its wings and take boldest flight towards the sublimest truth. The pious, humble soul, content to love and wait in peace and recollection, there finds the happiness he seeks. The Church has a place at her banquet-table for the man of the world and the recluse, for the scholar and the artist; for the monarch and the struggler for his daily bread. Well, then, may we say, with a profound observer, the Catholic regards the Church with deepest reverence and devotion. To rise up against her is abhorrent to his nature; to destroy unity is a heinous crime. The idea of community of prayer and feeling with his brethren of the faith satisfies his reason and imagination and coincides with his loftiest notions of duty. How grand, indeed, the thought, that those myriads scattered over the world, with free-will to indulge in any wild vagary of error, and with every peculiarity of race and character, yet make up one great brotherhood in Christ to promote each others spiritual welfare; becoming one day reconciled and united with each other in the faith, as mankind are reconciled with God through the incarnation and death of His Son.

As Christ is one and His work is one, as there is but one truth, and it is only truth that makes us free, so He can have intended but one Church—for the Church rests on Him, and her mission is simply to announce Him and His work. The human mind, on the other hand, is everywhere the same, created for the truth. Its essential spiritual wants, no matter what change of time or place, no matter what degree of culture and education, remain always the same. We all have sinned. We all stand in need of grace; and the faith of the simplest-minded toiler is the faith of the sublimest genius, even were he to possess the concentrated learning of all past generations. Thus, the oneness of the mind, as well as the oneness of truth, justifies the notion of the one true Church.

But, just because she is the one true Church, and the depository of the fulness of truth, she is the object of the attacks of those who reject the truth or have preserved but its fragments. Those who make everything of faith, and nothing of reason, accuse her of rationalism, because she grants reason its rights in connection with faith; while others declare her the enemy of reason, because she holds to the supernatural character of mysteries which are above reason. She refuses not her approval to the interior life, to peaceful contemplation, and she is accused of favoring fanaticism, mysticism and laziness. She lays down for the guidance of the Christian life laws, rules and fixed principles, and she is therefore accused by others of degenerating into outward and empty routine, or a dead formalism. She strives to secure Christian education for her children, and she is branded as a foe to liberty and the State. She exercises her well-established rights in the appointment of her ministers and the care of her faithful people, and she is driven into exile as thwarting the secular idea and as dangerous to the government. She suffers not Christ and His law to be the sport of a tyrant's caprice, of passing opinions, of intolerant passions; that is enough for her to be assailed and stricken down as obstinate, and not knowing how to conform to the spirit of the age. She gives the greatest sinner pardon if he repents, and she is reproached with laxity. Knowing she is Catholic, and therefore striving to embrace the world and penetrate into every condition of human life—it being her mission, as the salt of the earth, to preserve all from decay—she is set down as meddlesome and domineering. On the other hand, as she continues the preaching of the Apostles, and says: "Fear God and honor the king." Obey your rulers. Be true to your allegiance. Support lawful authority as the expression of the authority of God. As she condemns violence and the violation of rights, she is accused of sycophancy. When she admits development and progress, the Greek schism charges that she is destroying the foundations of faith; and when she guards the foundations of faith against the countless assaults of modern error, at once goes up the cry of fossilism and stagnation. What do these contradictory charges prove? Nothing, unless that the Church is above all contradictions, and is the living exponent of the one living truth.

And so, through unity, no matter what the obstacles, ever goes on the divine action of the Church. However limited her domain, the duty of the Church as the depository of revealed faith is ever the same. Need we wonder, then, that we find the same faith shared by the rich and the poor, the learned and the ignorant, the king and the peasant? Need we wonder that we find it the same in the days of persecution, in the days of toleration, in the days of security and peace? The same fountains of grace are flowing for all; everywhere the same waters of baptism, the same rite of confirmation, the same words of absolution, the same bread of life, the same nuptial blessing, the same unction for the dying, the same requiem for the dead. The world over the same Supreme Pastor is known and revered. Let sorrows overwhelm him as to-day; let him be robbed of his rights, and deprived of his freedom, and calamities fall on the Church; the same loving obedience is paid him as in the palmiest days of the papacy; the same loving prayers go up for him even with deeper fervor from all parts of the earth. For this unity of the head with the members is maintained under every condition, as Christ is one with the Church. We are one here below dearly beloved, as we hope to be one through eternity. How sweet the union, too, with the faithful who have gone before us. They have made their pilgrimage; they rest in the Lord; but even beyond the tomb they are sharers in our prayers. Are we not united with them in the communion of saints? Oh, indeed, how precious it is for brethren to dwell together in unity, not merely in the unity of natural affection, but in the supernatural unity of faith and communion. And why should we grow weary in our prayers to the one eternal God that the days of religious discord and dissension may be shortened; that the spirit of union and peace may overshadow the erring, and with sweet attraction win them from wanderings to the one true fold of Jesus Christ. Pray, dear brethren, for this happy consummation, especially now during this period of prayer and labor for the interests of God's Church in this land. With earnestness pour out your supplications that the work of this holy council may be efficacious, not only in keeping those within the Church from going astray, but in bringing back those who are wandering. Think of the solicitude of Jesus for souls; think of His touching prayer for unity on the very night when one of His Apostles went out and betrayed Him; and join with Him now in His pleadings to His eternal Father: "Holy Father, keep them in Thy name whom Thou hast given Me, that they may be one as We also are one. And not for them only do I pray, but for them also who through their word shall believe in Me; that they all may be one as Thou, Father, art in Me and I in Thee; that they also may be one in Us, that the world may believe that Thou hast sent Me; and the glory which Thou hast given Me I have given to them that they may be one, as We also are one."

The Missions for the Colored People.

SERMON OF RIGHT REV. W. H. GROSS, D.D.,
BISHOP OF SAVANNAH, GA.

THIS is a very grave and important question, because there are about eight millions of colored people living in our midst. There is hardly a town in the United States in which colored people are not more or less numerous. In some States and in some counties and towns they are in a majority over the whites.

We know the history of this people. In their native country, Africa, they were sunken from time immemorial in barbarism; and their religion, Fetichism, was the most depraved that the world has ever known. Africa has done great things for religion, as evidenced in Egypt, in the great monks of the desert—Anthony, Anthanasius, Cyril, Cyprian of Carthage, and others. Africa produced one of the greatest doctors of the Church in the person of St. Augustine, of Hippo. But our colored people came from that part of Africa where the light of Christianity has never penetrated. Here their condition was improved, though they were in a state of slavery. After two centuries of bondage they are suddenly set free. While slaves they could exercise no political influence; they had no equality with the whites before the law; they were excluded from all professions, and from a majority of the trades; they were the hewers of wood and the carriers of water for the whites. Now they will enter the professions, and with that wonderful power of the ballot select our rulers and lawgivers, and be themselves elected to such trusts. Therefore, in the highest sense of the word, they will wield an important influence, socially and politically, on the country.

We must remember that these eight millions of people are constantly increasing, as the last census shows. Consequently their power must increase for good or bad. The question arises, "What is to be done with them?" There is only one thing that will do any good, and that is to elevate them morally; make them honest men, chaste women, obedient, law-abiding citizens, having the real welfare of the State at heart. Morality is the basis of the true prosperity of every country. This can come only from the pure faith that is embraced in the Catholic doctrines that civilized in reality the barbarous Goths, Vandals and Huns, the forefathers of the present enlightened nationalities of Europe and America. We know as a fact that at present the colored people know very little if anything of these great truths of holy faith, whence all morality must grow. As a general thing, their ministers are poor colored men, the vast majority of them uneducated, and they only make a travesty of religion—"the blind leading the blind." Even the white ministers of Protestantism are so disunited and divided on doctrines and dogma that they could not teach these fundamental truths were they to go among them, which, as a general thing, they do not, especially in the South.

But besides dogma and doctrine there must be something else. Man has a fallen nature, and it is not necessary for me to state that the poor colored people do not stand very high in the scale of morality. The preaching of the Apostles in itself could not break the bond of bad passions and save the world, if they had not with their words God's grace. God's grace is absolutely necessary, and without it we can do nothing.

The Catholic Church, in her magnificent system of sacraments, possesses the grand channels of grace for the individual and for society. A child is sanctified by holy baptism. Matrimony is the foundation of the family and of all Christian society. It is not a mere contract between man and woman, but the great sacrament that brings the man and woman the grace to discharge properly the many duties towards themselves and their children.

Consider the influence the woman wields as wife, mother, and in society. The Catholic Church can alone give to the colored woman her proper elevation and make her influence widespread for good. By her great doctrines the Church holds up the Virgin Mary as the second Eve, and as the great model of woman—and of woman's greatest prize and charm—chastity. Outside of Christianity, women are degraded, as can be seen among the Turks and pagans, but she is elevated by Catholicity. The influence of women is but slightly appreciated. Take from the white race her influence, and there would be a lapse into barbarism.

Some sixty years ago, Mother Seton began in Baltimore her foundation of the Sisters of Charity. The work, so small in its commencement—a little grain of mustard seed—has become a mighty tree whose branches already fill the land. What services the Sisters of Charity have rendered in educating the young, in caring for the sick and poor, is well known. I am proud to think that Baltimore has witnessed the founding of another great work—the Oblate Sisters of Providence.

That the Catholic Church can elevate the colored women is evidenced by the fact, that here in Baltimore, exists this wonderful institution of the Oblate Sisters of Providence, a colored convent where women make vows of perpetual virginity and rival their white sisters by going among their race to educate the young, to take in the poor little orphan and help the sick and dying. Thus is it shown that the colored woman can be elevated to a place where she can bring blessings on her race equal to the beneficent influence which the white woman as a wife, mother, sister and holy nun has conferred upon the white race.

The great sacrament of confirmation gives the Holy Ghost in reality to the recipient, and fortifies him, like a soldier, to fight the battles of life. We have penance, where the soul, wounded by sin in the turmoil of life, may regain health and strength. Above all, we have that sacrament of the altar, where Jesus Christ is present in reality, and to Him those heavenly burdened can have recourse for help. We have the high act of religion possessed in the divine sacrifice of the Mass, wherein is represented the sacrifice of Calvary. What streams of grace will flow from this on those who devoutly assist at it the lives of the saints can testify. Even for poor man, when dying—that terrible moment, the most grievous and critical in our existence—we have the sacrament of extreme unction.

No wonder, therefore, that armed with this magnificent system of dogma and sacraments the Catholic Church has spread the flowers of religion in all the lands where she has been welcomed, and our colored people will not prove an exception to the rule. It is true that so long as slavery existed the Catholic priest, as a general rule, had no opportunity of coming in contact with the colored people. In Georgia and generally in the slave States, the slaveholders, with a few exceptions, were Protestants. But some works have already been started, and their success is gratifying in the highest degree.

I have spoken of the colored man to show his influence upon civil society, and that it is wise and patriotic for every citizen to wish for his elevation to the highest point of morality. I have shown the Catholic Church can do that, and has abundant means for it. But we Catholics must remember that the colored people should be dear to us from an even higher motive. They were created by the same God, are children of the same common father and mother—Adam and Eve—and were destined to see God and possess Him for all eternity. Remember that Jesus Christ shed His last drop of blood to redeem their souls, and that they are, therefore, inconceivably dear in His eyes.

Rt. Rev. J. L. Spalding, D.D.

Rt. Rev. T. F. Hendricken, D.D.

Rt. Rev. John Moore, D.D.

Rt. Rev. J. A. Watterson, D.D.

Rt. Rev. J. J. Keane, D.D.

Rt. Rev. John Tuigg, D.D.

Rt. Rev. Dennis M. Bradley, D.D.

Rt. Rev. J. P. Machebeuf, D.D.

Rt. Rev. P. T. O'Reilly, D.D.

University Education.

SERMON OF RIGHT REV. J. L. SPALDING, D.D.,

BISHOP OF PEORIA, ILL.

THE subject which I have been asked to treat is the higher education of priests, which, I suppose, is the highest education of man, since the ideal of the Christian priest is the most exalted, his vocation the most sublime, his office the most holy, his duties the most spiritual, and his mission, whether we consider its relation to morality which is the basis of individual and social welfare, or to religion which is the promise and the secret of immortal and godlike life, is the most important and the most sacred which can be assigned to a human being.

Religion and education like religion and morality are nearly related. Pure religion, indeed, is more than right education, and yet it may be said with truth that it is but a part of the best education, for it co-operates with other forces, with climate, custom, social conditions and political institutions, to develop and fashion the complete man, and the special instruction of teachers, which is the narrow meaning of the word, is modified, and to a great extent controlled, by these powers which work unseen, and are the vital agents that make possible all conscious educational efforts.

The faith we hold, the laws we obey, the domestic and social customs to which our thoughts and loves are harmonized, the climate we live in, mould our characters and give to our souls a deeper and more lasting tinge than any school, though it were the best.

My subject, however, does not demand that I consider these general and silent agencies by which life is influenced; but leads me to the discussion of the methods by which man, with conscious purpose, seeks to form and instruct his fellow-man; to the discussion of the special education which brings art to the aid of nature and becomes the auxiliary and guide of the forces which contribute to the development of our being.

In this age when all who think at all turn their thoughts to questions of education, it is needless to call attention to the interest of the subject, which, like hope, is immortal and fresh as the innocent face of laughing childhood.

Is not the school for all men a shrine to which their pilgrim thoughts return to catch again the glow of gladness of a world wherein they live by faith and hope and love, when round the morning sun of life the golden purple clouds were hanging and earth lay hidden in mist beneath which the soul created a new paradise? To the opening mind all things are young and fair, and to remember the delight that accompanied the gradual dawn of knowledge upon our mental vision, sweet and beautiful as the upglowing of day from the bosom of night, is to be forever thankful for the gracious power of education. And is there not in all hearts a deep and abiding yearning for great and noble men, and therefore an imperishable interest in the power by which they are moulded? When fathers and mothers look upon the fair blossoming children, that cling to them as the vine wraps its tendrils round the spreading bough, and when their great love fills them with ineffable longing to shield these tender souls from the blighting blasts of a cold and stormy world, and little by little to prepare them to stand alone and breast the gales of fortune, do they not instinctively put their trust in the power of education?

When at the beginning of the present century Germany lay prostrate at the feet of Napoleon, the wise and patriotic among her children yielded not to despondency, but turned with confidence to truer methods and systems of education, and assiduous teaching and patient waiting finally brought them to Sedan.

When in the sixteenth century heresy and schism seemed near to final victory over the Church, Pope Julius III declared that the evils and abuses of the times were the outgrowth of the shameful ignorance of the clergy, and that the chief hope of the dawning of a brighter day lay in general and thorough ecclesiastical education. And the Catholic leaders, who finally turned back the advancing power of Protestantism, re-established the Church in half the countries in which it had been overthown, and converted more souls in America and Asia than had been lost in Europe, belonged to the greatest educational body the world has ever seen. What is history but examples of success through knowledge and righteousness and of failure through lack of understanding and of virtue?

Wherein lies the superiority of civilized races over the barbarians if not in their greater knowledge and superior strength of character? And what but education has placed in the hands of man the thousand natural forces, which he holds as a charioteer his well-reined steeds, bidding the winds to carry him to distant lands, making steam his tireless ever-ready slave, and commanding the lightning to speak his words to the ends of the earth? What else than this has taught him to map the boundless heavens, to read the footprints of God in the crust of the earth ages before human beings lived, to measure the speed of light, to weigh the imperceptible atom, to split up all natural compounds, to create innumerable artificial products with which he transforms the world and with a grain of powder marches like a conquering god around the globe?

What converts the meaningless babbling of the child into the stately march of oratoric phrase or the rythmic flow of poetic language? What has developed the rude stone and bronze implements of savage and barbarous hordes into the miraculous machinery which we use? By what power has man been taught to carve the shapeless rock into an image of ideal beauty, or with it to build his thought into a temple of God, where the soul instinctively prostrates itself in adoration?

Is not all this, together with whatever else is excellent in human works, the result of education, which gives to man a second nature with more admirable endowments? And is not religion itself a kind of celestial education which trains the soul to godlike life?

No progress in things divine or human is made by man except through effort, and effort is the power and the law of education. The maxim of the spiritual writers that not to struggle upward and onward is to be drawn downward, applies to every phase of our life. Whence do we derive strength of soul but from the uplifting of the mind and heart to God which we call prayer? To pray is to think, to attend, to hold the mind lovingly to its object, and this is what we do when we study. Hence prayer, which is the voice of religion, is a part of education, nay, its very soul, breathing on all the chords of life, till their thousand dissonances meet in rythmic harmony. What is the pulpit but the holiest teacher's chair that has been placed upon the earth?

And as the presence of a noble character is a more potent influence than words, so sacramental communion with Christ is man's chief school of faith, of hope and love. There are worthy persons who turn, as from an unholy thought, from the emphatic announcement of the need of the best human qualities for the proper defence of the cause of God in the world. Such speech seems to them to be vain and unreal, for God is all in all, and man is nothing. But in our day it is easier to go astray in the direction of self-annihilation than in that of self-assertion; since the common tendency now of all false philosophies is pantheistic, and issues in unconscious contempt of individual life. If man is but a bubble merging forth and reabsorbed, without past or future, then, indeed, both he and what he seems to do sink into the eternal flow of matter and are undeserving of a thought. This certainly is not the Christian view, to which man is revealed as a lesser god and co-worker with the Eternal, whose thoughts can reach the Infinite and whose will can oppose that of the Omnipotent. In Christ, God co-operates with man for the salvation of the world, and in the Church man co-operates with God in the same end. The more complete the man, the more fit is he to work with God. Even bodily disfigurement is looked upon as an obstacle; how much more then shall lack of intelligence and want of heart render us unworthy of the divine office? I certainly shall never deny that love which the Apostle exalts above faith and hope, is higher also than knowledge. The light of the mind is as that of the moon— fair and soft and soothing, without heat, without the power to call forth and nourish life; but the light of the soul, which is love, is the sunlight, whose kiss, like a word of God, makes the dead to live and clothes the world in strength and beauty. Character is more than intellect, love is more than knowledge, religion is more than morality, and a great heart brings us closer to God, nearer to all goodness than a bright mind. Education is essentially moral, and the intellectual qualities themselves, which we seek to develop, derive their chief efficacy from underlying ethical qualities upon which they rest and from which they receive their energy and the power of self-control. Inequality of will is the great cause of inequality of mind, and the will is strengthened by the practice of virtue as the body by food and exercise. If this is a general truth, with what special force must it not apply to the ministers of a religion, the paramount and ceaseless aim of which is to make men holy, so that at times it has almost seemed as though the Church were indifferent as to whether they are learned or beautiful or strong? She pronounces no man a doctor, unless he be also a saint, and when I insist that the priest shall possess the best mental culture of his age, that, without this, he fights with broken weapons, speaks with harsh voice a language men will neither hear nor understand, teaches truths which, having not the freshness and the glow of truth, neither kindle the heart nor fire the imagination, I do not forget that without the moral earnestness which is born of faith and purity of life, mere cultivation of mind will not give him power to unseal the fountains of living waters which refresh the garden of God. The universal harmony is felt by a pure heart better than it can be perceived by a keen intellect. To a sinless soul the darker side even of life and nature is not wholly dark, and the mental difficulties which the existence of evil involves, in no way weaken the consciousness of the essential goodness that lies at the heart of all things. In the religious, as in the moral world, men trust to what we are rather than to what we say, and the teacher of spiritual truth is never strong, unless his life and character inspire a confidence which arguments alone do not create; for in questions that reach beyond the sphere of sensation, we feel that insight is better than reason, and hence we instinctively prefer the testimony of a godlike soul to the conclusions of a cultivated mind; and indeed our Blessed Lord ever assumes that the obstacle to the perception of divine truth is moral and not intellectual. The pure of heart see God: the evil-doer loves darkness and shuns the light. St. Paul goes even farther and associates mental cultivation with a tendency directly opposed to religious faith, which is humble. "Knowledge puffeth up." But the words of the Apostle should not be stretched beyond his purpose, which is to point to pride as a special danger of the intellectual as sensuality is a danger of the ignorant. For man to have aught is to run a risk and hence to do as little as possible is in the thought of the timid a mark of prudence. And indeed if fear be nearer to wisdom than courage, then should we fear everything, for danger is everywhere. A breath may sow the seed of death; a look may slay the soul. In knowledge, in ignorance, in strength, in weakness, in wealth, in poverty, in genius, in stupidity, in company, in solitude, in innocence itself danger lurks. But God does not abolish life that danger may cease to be, and they who put their trust in Him will not seek to darken the mind lest knowledge lead man astray, but will rather in a righteous cause make the venture of all things, as St. Ignatius preferred the hope of saving others to the certainty of his own salvation. And may we not maintain, since we hold that there is no inappeasable conflict between God and nature, between the soul and matter, between revelation and science, that the apparent antagonism lies in our apprehension and not in things themselves, and consequently that reconcilement is to be sought for through the help of thoroughly trained minds? The poet speaks the truth: "A little knowledge is a dangerous thing." They who know but little and imperfectly, see but their knowledge, if so it may be called, and walk in innocent unconsciousness of their infinite nescience. The narrower the range of our mental vision, the greater the obstinacy with which we cling to our opinions; and the half-educated, like the weak and the incompetent, are often contentious, but whosoever is able to do his work does it and finds no time for dispute. He who possesses a disciplined mind, and is familiar with the best thoughts that live in the great literatures, will be the last to attach undue importance to his own thinking. A sense of decency and a kind of holy shame will keep him far from angry and unprofitable controversy; nor will he mistake a crotchet for a panacea, nor imagine that irritation is enlighenment. The blessings of a cultivated mind are akin to those of religion. They are larger liberty, wider life, purer delights and a juster sense of the relative values of the means and ends which lie within our reach. Knowledge, like religion, leads us away from what appears to what is, from what passes to what remains, from what flatters the senses to that which speaks to the soul. Wisdom and religion converge, as love and knowledge meet in God; and to the wise as to the religious man, no great evil can happen. Into prison they both carry the sweet company of their thoughts, their faith and hope, and are freer in chains than the great in palaces. In death they are in the midst of life, for they see that what they know and love is imperishable, nor subject even to atomic disintegration. He who lives in the presence of truth yearns not for the company of men, but loves retirement as a saint loves solitude; and in times like ours, when men no longer choose the desert for a dwelling-place, the passionate desire of intellectual excellence co-operates with religious faith to guard them against dissipation and to lift them above the spirit of the age. The thinker is never lonely as he who lives with God is never unhappy. Is not the love of excellence, which is the scholar's love, a part of the love of goodness which makes the saint? And are not intellectual delights akin to those religion brings? They are pure, they elevate, they refine, time only increases their charm, and in the winter of age, when the body is but the agent of pain, contemplation still remains like the light of a higher world to tinge with beauty the clouds that gather around life's setting. How narrow and monotonous is sensation! how wide and various is thought! They who live in the senses are fettered and ill at ease; they who live in the soul are free and joyful. And since the priest, unless he be a saint, must have, like other men, some human joy, and since he dwells not in the sacred circle of the love of wife and children, in which the multitudes find repose and contentment, what solace, what refreshment, in the midst of cares and labors, shall we offer him? If there be aught for him, that is not unworthy or dangerous, except the pleasures of the mind, to me it is unknown, and though a well-trained intellect should do no more than to enable us to take delight in pure and noble objects, it would be a chief help to worthy life. And when the whole tendency of our social existence is to draw men out of themselves and to make them seek the good of life in what is external, as money, display, position, renown, is it not a gain, if while we open their minds to the charm of intellectual beauty, we make them see that this eager striving for wealth and place is a vulgar chase? And does not the spirit of refinement in thought, in speech, in manner, add worth and fairness to him whom it inspires, though the motive which preserves him from what is low or gross be no higher than a fastidious delicacy and self-respect?

To deny the moral influence of intellectual culture is as great an error as to affirm that it alone is a sufficient safeguard of morality. Its tendency unquestionably is to make men gentle, amiable, fair-minded, truthful, benevolent, modest, sober. It curbs ambition, teaches resignation; chastens the imagination and mitigates ferocity; dissuades from duelling because it is barbarious, and from war because it is cruel; and from persecution because it trusts in the prevalence of reason. It seeks to fit the mind and the character to the world, to all possible circumstances, so that whatever happens we remain ourselves—calm, clear-seeing, able to do and to suffer. At great heights, or in the presence of irresistible force, as of a mighty waterfall, we grow dizzy and in the same way, in the midst of multitudes, in the eagerness of strife, in the whirlwind of passion, equipoise is lost and we cease to be ourselves, to become part of an aggregate of forces that hurry us on whither we know not. To be able to stand in the presence of such power, and to feel its influence and yet not to lose self-possession, is to be strong, is, on proper occasion, to be great; and the aim of the best education is to teach us the secret and the method of this complete self-control; and in so far it is not only moral, but also religious; though religion walks in a more royal road, and bids us love God and trust so absolutely in Him that life and death become equal, and all the ways and workings of men as the storm to one who on lofty mountain peak, amid the blue heavens, with the sunlight around him and the quiet breathing of the winds, sees far below as in another world, the black clouds and lurid lightning flash and hears the roll of distant thunder.

It is far from my thought, it is needless to say, that mental cultivation can be made to take the place or do the work of religion even in the case of the very few for whom the best discipline of mind is possible. My aim is simply to show that the type of character which it tends to create is not necessarily at variance with religious principle and life, as is, for instance, that of the mere worldling, but that it conspires with Christian faith to produce, if not the same, at least similar virtues, though its ethical influence is comparatively superficial, and the moral qualities which it produces lack consistency and the power to withstand the fire of the passions. It is enough for my purpose to point out that if intellectualism is often the foe of religious truth, there is no good reason why it should not also be its ally.

No excellence, as I conceive, of whatever kind, is rejected by Catholic teaching, and the perfection of the mind is not less divine than the perfection of the heart. It is good to know as it is good to hope, to believe, to love. A cultivated intellect, an open mind, a rich imagination, with correctness of thought, flexibility of view, and eloquent expression, are among the noblest endowments of man, and though they should serve no other purpose than to embellish life, to make it fairer and freer, they would nevertheless be possessions without price, for the most nobly useful things are those which make life good and beautiful. Like virtue they are their own reward, and like mercy they bear a double blessing. It is the fashion with many to affect contempt for men of superior culture, because they look upon education as simply a means to tangible ends, and think knowledge valuable only when it can be made to serve practical purposes. This is a narrow and false view; for all men need the noble and the beautiful, and he who lives without an ideal is hardly a man. Our material wants are not the most real, for being the most sensible and pressing, and they who create or preserve for us models of spiritual and intellectual excellence are our greatest benefactors. Which were the greater loss for England, to be without Wellington and Nelson, or to be without Shakespeare and Milton? Whatever the answer be, in the one case England would suffer, in the other the whole world would feel the loss. Though a thoroughly trained intellect is less worthy of admiration than a noble character, its power is immeasurably greater; for, example can influence but a few and for a short time, but when a truth or a sentiment has once found its best expression, it becomes a part of literature and, like a proverb, is current for evermore, and so the kings of thought become immortal rulers, and without their help the godlike deeds of saints and heroes would be buried in oblivion. "Words pass," said Napoleon, "but deeds remain." The man of action exaggerates the worth of action, but the philosopher knows that to act is easy, to think, difficult; and that great deeds spring from great thoughts. There are words that never grow silent, there are words that have changed the face of the earth, and the warrior's wreath of victory is entwined by the muse's hand. The power of Athens is gone, her temples are in ruins, the Acropolis is discrowned, and from Mars' Hill no voice thunders now, but the words of Socrates, the great deliverer of the mind and the father of intellectual culture, still breathe in the thoughts of every cultivated man on earth. The glory of Jerusalem has departed, the broken stones of Solomon's Temple lie hard by the graves that line the brook of Kedron, and from the minaret of Mount Sion, the misbeliever's melancholy call sounds like a wail over a lost world, but the songs of David still rise from the whole earth in heavenly concert, upbearing to the throne of God the faith and hope and love of countless millions. And is not the Blessed Saviour the Eternal Word? And is not the Bible God's Word? And is not the Gospel the Word, which like an electric thrill runs to the ends of the world? "*Currit verbum*," says St. Paul, "man lives not on bread alone, but on every word that cometh from the mouth of God." Nay, there is life in all the true and noble thoughts that have blossomed in the mind of genius and filled the earth with fragrance and with fruit.

Shall I be told that the intellectual cultivation and discipline, which gives to man control of his knowledge, the perfect use of his faculties, justness of perception with ease and grace of expression, cannot bring serviceable advocacy or defence to the cause of divine truth? What does truth need but to be known? And since to reach the mind and heart of man it must be clothed in words, what is so necessary to it as the garb and vesture, the form and color, the warmth and life, which shall so mark it that to be loved it need but be seen? And who shall so clothe it if not he who has the freest, the most flexible, the clearest, the best disciplined mind? In the apostolic age, when the manifestations of miraculous power accompanied the announcement of Christian doctrine, the lack of persuasive words of human eloquence was not felt. Let him who can drink poison and touch scorpions, and not suffer harm, despise the aid of learning; but for us who are not so assisted, no cultivation of mind or preparation of heart can be too great, and to appear in the garb of a savage were less unseemly than to speak the holiest and the highest truths in the barbarous tongue of ignorance.

Our way here cannot be doubtful. Either we must hold with certain peculiar heretics that learning is a hindrance to the efficacious teachings of religious truths, or denying this, we must hold, since mental culture is serviceable, that the best is most serviceable.

May we not take this for a principle—to believe that God does everything, and then to act as though He left everything for us to do? Or this: since grace supposes nature, the growth and strength of the Church is not wholly independent of the natural endowments of her ministers?

As a matter of fact we Catholics are constantly speaking and acting upon principles of this kind. We maintain that without a proper education our children must lose the faith, and that without careful moral and mental training no man is likely to become a good priest, and all that I further insist upon is that if he is to do the best work, he must have the best intellectual discipline. In an intellectual age, at least, he cannot be the worthy minister of worship unless he is also the accomplished teacher of truth. In vain shall we clothe him in rich symbolic vestments, place him in majestic temples, before marble altars, in the midst of solemn music, in the dim sober-tinted light, with the great and noble looking out upon him, as from a spirit world—in vain shall all this be if when he himself speaks, his words are felt to be but the echo of a coarse and empty mind. And hence our enemies would gladly leave us to the poetry of our worship, would even enter our churches to be comforted, to be soothed, to seek the elevation and enlargement of thought and sentiment which comes upon us in the presence of what is vast, mysterious and sublime, if we would but confess that it is only poetry, good and beautiful only as art is good and beautiful. The spirit of the time, in fact, it seems to me, is more and more disposed to grant us everything except the possession of intellectual truth. That the Catholic Church is a marvelous power; that her triumphs have been so enduring and so unexpected that only the foolish or the ignorant will predict her downfall; that she overcame paganism; that she saved Christianity when Rome fell; that she restrained the ferocity of the barbarians, protected the weak, encouraged labor, preserved the classics, maintained the unity and sanctity of marriage, defended the purity and dignity of woman, espoused the cause of the oppressed, and in a lawless and ignorant age proclaimed the supremacy of right and the worth of learning—that to these signal services must be added her power to give ease and pleasantness to the social relations of men, keeping them equally remote from puritan severity and pagan license; her eye for beauty and grace, which has made her the foster-mother of all the arts; her love of the excellent and noble, which has enabled her to create types of character that are immortal; her practical wisdom, giving her the secret of dealing with every phase of life, so that her saints are doctors, apostles, mystics, philanthropists, artists, poets, kings, beggars, warriors, peasants, barbarians, philosophers—all this, if I mistake not, unbelievers even are more and more willing to concede. Nor are they slow to express their admiration of the strength and majesty of this single power amid Christian nations, which reaches back to the great civilizations that have perished, which has preserved its organic unity intact amid the social revolutions of two thousand years, and which is acknowledged still to be the greatest moral force in the world. But underlying all they say and think is the assumption that the foundations of this noble structure are crumbling, that the world of faith and thought in which it was upbuilt is become a desert where no flower blooms, no living soul is found; that the temple is beautiful only as a ruin is beautiful, where owls hoot and bats flit to and fro. "There is not a creed," we are told, "which is not shaken, nor an accredited dogma which is not shown to be questionable; not a received tradition which does not threaten to dissolve."

The conquests of the human mind in the realms of nature have produced a world-wide ferment of thought, an intellectual activity which is without a parallel: they have increased the power of man to an almost incredible degree, have given him control of the earth and the seas, have placed within his grasp undreamed-of forces, have opened to his view unsuspected mysteries; they have placed him on a new earth and under new heavens, and thrown a light never seen before upon the history of his race. As a part of this vast development new questions have risen, new theories have been broached, new doubts have suggested themselves; and because we have changed, all else seems to have changed also. And since, underlying all questions, there is found a question of religion, the discussion of religious and philosophic problems has in our day become a social necessity, and the science of criticism, together with the physical sciences, has driven the disputants upon new and difficult ground, where the battle must be fought, and where retreat is not possible.

As well imagine that society will again take on the form of feudalism, as that the human mind will return to the point of view from which our ancestors looked on nature.

And this world-view shapes and colors all our thinking, in theology as in other sciences, so that truths which were latent have come to light, and principles which have long been held find new and wider application.

Never has the defence of religion required so many and excellent qualities of intellect as in the present day. The early apologists who contrasted the sublimity and purity of Christian faith with a corrupt paganism had not a difficult task. In the Middle Ages the intellect of the world was on the side of Christ. The controversy which sprung up with the advent of Protestantism was Biblical and historical, and its criticism was superficial. The anti-Christian schools of thought of the eighteenth century were literary rather than philosophical, and the objections they urged were founded chiefly upon political and social considerations. In all these discussions the territory in dispute was well defined and relatively small. But into what a different world are not we thrown! These earlier explorers sailed upon rivers, whose banks were lined by firm-set rocky cliffs, by the overshadowing boughs of primeval forests, with here and there pleasant slopes of green where they might lie at rest amid the fragrance of wild flowers; but from our Peter's bark we look out upon the dark unfathomed seas toward an unknown world whose margin ever fades and recedes as we seem to draw near the haven of our desire.

As in the beginning of the twelfth century, the cry, "God wills it," rang through Europe, and from all her lands armies of mailed knights sprang into battle array and turned their faces towards the Holy City, resolved to wrench from infidel hands the Sacred Tomb of Christ, so now, from her thousand watch-towers, science sounds her clarion note with quite other intent, urging on to the attack of the citadel of God in the heart of man, renewing upon lower fields the war in which immortal spirits contended with the Almighty "in dubious battle on the plains of heaven and shook His throne." As he jests at scars that never felt a wound, so here the lesser knowledge makes the bolder man. Not that difficulties should create doubts, or that objections may not be answered, or that it is necessary to refute each hypothesis that appears and fades like a dissolving view, or to notice each unwarrantable inference from unquestioned facts, or that it is worth while to address ourselves to minds whose nebulous and shifting opinions make it impossible that they should receive correct impressions; but the field upon which attacks upon religion are made is so vast, the confusion of thought into which new discoveries and speculations have thrown the minds of even educated men is so bewildering, the methods for the ascertainment of truth are so tangled and misapplied, the rushing on of the multitudes to discuss problems which have hitherto been left to philosophers, and which they alone can ever rightly enunciate, is so stupefying, that those who have the clearest perception of the mental state of the modern world, and who are able to take the finest and the most comprehensive view of the religious, philosophic and scientific controversies of the day, seem loth to enter into a struggle where the ground continually changes, and where victory is only partial, and but leads to further contest. It is well to remember, also, that in the intellectual arena to attack is easier than to defend, and any shallow, incoherent talker or writer can propose difficulties which the keenest thinker will find great trouble to explain. Since we and our works fall to ruin and pass away, we seem instinctively to take the side of those who seek to undermine and overthrow systems of thought and belief which claim to be indestructible, and the human heart is half a traitor to the Church which declares that she is indefectible and infallible. Is there not, indeed, however we account for it, in all nature, a kind of dread and horror of the supernatural, such as one who hides within his bosom a secret of dark guilt, feels in the presence of the conscience of mankind? And does not this make the world lean to the side of those who would eliminate God from nature?

And yet, since man's heart is the home of contradictions, is it not also true to say that he is naturally religious? His faith in God is as deep and unwavering as his faith in the testimony of the senses, and if there are atheists there are also men who hold that all things are unreal and only appear to be; that the world is but a myriad-formed, a myriad-tinted idea—the dream of a substanceless dreamer. Not only do we believe in God and in the soul, but all that we love, all that we hope for, all that gives to life charm, dignity and sacredness, is interpenetrated, perfumed and illumined by this faith. If men could be persuaded that the unconscious is the beginning and the end of all things, what good would have been gained? The light of heaven would fade away and the soul's high faith be made a lie; the poor would have no friend and the rich no heart; the wicked would be without fear and the good without hope; success would be consecrated and death alone would remain as the refuge of the unfortunate. Even animal indulgence, in sinking out of the moral order, would lose its human charm. If then in our day there is widespread skepticism, a sort of vague feeling that science is undermining religion and that the most sacred beliefs are dissolving, the cause of this lies not so much in the natural tendencies of the mind and heart, as in social conditions, in passing phases of thought, in the shifting of the point of view from which men have hitherto been accustomed to look on nature, and the continuance and the progress of doubt, and consequently of indifference, is, to some extent at least, to be ascribed also to the fact, that the most earnest believers in God and in Christianity have for now more than a century, been less eager to acquire the best philosophic and literary cultivation of mind, than others who having lost faith in the supernatural seek for compensation in a wider and deeper knowledge of nature and in the mental culture which enables them to enjoy more keenly the high thoughts and fair images which live in literature and art. As a well-trained intellect, in argument with the unskillful, easily makes the worse appear the better cause, so in an age or a country where the best discipline of mind is found chiefly among those who are not Christians, or at least not Catholics, public opinion will drift away from the Church, until the view finally becomes general, that whatever she may have been in other times, her day is past. Nor will aught external, however fair or glorious, secure her against this danger. How often in the history of nations and of religions is not outward splendor the mark of inward decay? When Rome was free, a simple life sufficed, but when liberty fled, marble palaces arose: the monarch who built Versailles made the scaffold on which French royalty perished; and so a dying faith, like the setting sun, may drape itself in glory. The kingdom of God is within; there is the source of life and strength, without which nor numbers, nor wealth, nor stately edifices, nor solemn rites avail. Nor can we be certain of men's love when we cease to have influence over their thoughts. The proper appeal is to the heart through the mind, and even a mother loses half her power when she ceases to be the intellectual superior of her children. How then shall the heavenly Mother of the soul keep her place in the world, if those who speak in her name, mar by imperfect and ignorant utterance the celestial harmony of her doctrines?

Ah! let us learn to see things as they are. In face of the modern world, that which the Catholic priest most needs, after virtue, is the best cultivation of mind, which issues in comprehensiveness of view, in exactness of perception, in the clear discernment of the relations of truths and of the limitations of scientific knowledge, in fairness and flexibility of thought, in ease and grace of expression, in candor, in reasonableness; the intellectual culture which brings the mind into form, gives it the control of its faculties, creates the habit of attention and develops firmness of grasp. The education of which I speak is expansion and discipline of mind rather than learning; and its tendency is not so much to form profound dogmatists, or erudite canonists, or acute casuists, as to cultivate a habit of mind, which, for want of a better word, may be called philosophical, to enlarge the intellect, to strengthen and supple its faculties, to enable it to take connected views of things and their relations, and to see clear amid the mazes of human error and through the mists of human passion. I speak of that perfection of the intellect, which, to use the words of Cardinal Newman, "is the clear, calm, accurate vision and comprehension of all things as far as the finite mind can embrace them, each in its place and with its own characteristics upon it. It is almost prophetic from its knowledge of history; it is almost heart-searching from its knowledge of human nature; it has almost supernatural charity from its freedom from littleness and prejudice; it has almost the repose of faith because nothing can startle it; it has almost the beauty and harmony of heavenly contemplation, so intimate is it with the eternal order of things and the music of the spheres." This is, indeed, ideal, but they who believe not in ideals were not born to know the real worth of things:

> Spite of proudest boast
> Reason, best reason is to imperfect man,
> An effort only and a noble aim—
> A crown—an attribute of sovereign power,
> Still to be courted—never to be won.

It is plain that education of this kind aims at something quite different from the mere imparting of useful knowledge. It takes the view that it is good to know, even though knowledge should not be a means to wealth or power or any other common aim of life. It regards the mind as the organ of truth and trains it for its own sake without reference to the exercise of a profession. Hence its distinguishing characteristic is that it is liberal and not professional. It holds cultivated faculties in higher esteem than learning, and it makes use of knowledge to improve the intellect, rather than of the intellect to acquire knowledge. Hence, one may be a skillful physician, a judicious lawyer, a learned theologian, and yet be greatly lacking in mental culture. It is a common experience to find that professional men are apt to be narrow and one-sided. Their mind, like the dyer's hand, is subdued to what it works in. They want comprehensiveness of view, flexibility of thought, openness to light and freedom of mental play. They think in grooves, make the rules of their art the measure of truth, and their own methods of inquiry the only valid laws of reasoning. These same defects may be observed in those who are given exclusively to the study of physical science. When they sweep the heavens with the telescope and do not find God, they conclude that there is no God. When the soul does not reveal itself under the microscope, they argue it does not exist; and since there is no thought without nervous movement, they claim the brain thinks.

Now, if it is desirable that those who are charged with the teaching and defence of divine truth, should be free from this narrowness and one-sidedness, this lack of openness to light and freedom of mental play, the education of the priest must be more than a professional education; and he must be sent to a school higher and broader than the ecclesiastical seminary, which is simply a training college for the practical work of the ministry. The purpose for which it was instituted is to prepare young men for the worthy exercise of the general functions of the priestly office, and the good it has done is soo great and too manifest to need commendation. But the ecclesiastical seminary is not a school of intellectual culture, either here in America or elsewhere, and to imagine that it can become the instrument of intellectual culture is to cherish a delusion. It must impart a certain amount of professional knowledge, fit its students to become more or less expert catechists, rubricists and casuists, and its aim is to do this, and whatever mental improvement, if any, thence results, is accidental. Hence its methods are not such as one would choose who desires to open the mind, to give it breadth, flexibility, strength, refinement and grace. Its text-books are written often in a barbarous style, the subjects are discussed in a dry and mechanical way and the professor wholly intent upon giving instruction, is frequently indifferent as to the manner in which it is imparted, or else not possessing himself a really cultivated intellect, he holds in slight esteem expansion and refinement of mind, looking upon it as at best a mere ornament. I am not offering a criticism upon the ecclesiastical seminary, but am simply pointing to the plain fact that it is not a school of intellectual culture, and consequently, if its course were lengthened to five, to six, to eight, to ten years, its students would go forth to their work with a more thorough professional training, but not with more really cultivated minds.

The test of intellect is not so much what we know as the manner in which it is known; just as in the moral world, the important consideration is not what virtues we possess, but the completeness with which they are ours. He who really believes in God, serves Him, loves Him, is a hero, a saint; whereas he who half believes may have a thousand good qualities, but not a great character. Knowledge is not education any more than food is nutrition; and as one may eat voraciously, and yet remain without bodily health or strength, so one may have great learning and yet be wholly lacking in intellectual cultivation. His learning may only oppress and confuse him, be felt as a load, and not as a vital principle, which upraises, illumines and beautifies the mind; mentally he may still be a boy, in whom memory predominates, and whose intellect is only a receptacle of facts.

Memory is the least noble of the intellectual faculties, and the nearest to animal intelligence, and to know well is, in the eyes of a true educator, of quite other importance than to know much. But a memory, more or less well-stored, is nearly all a youth carries with him from the college to the seminary, and here he enters, as I have already pointed out, upon a course not of intellectual discipline, but of professional studies, whose object is not "to open the mind, to correct it, to refine it, to enable it to know, and to digest, master, rule and use its knowledge, to give it power over its own faculties, application, flexibility, method, critical exactness, sagacity, resource, eloquent expression," but simply to impart the requisite skill for the ordinary exercise of the holy ministry. Hence it is not surprising that priests, who are zealous, earnest, self-sacrificing, who to piety join discretion and good sense, rarely possess the intellectual culture of which I am speaking, for the simple reason that a university and not a seminary is the school in which this kind of education is received. That the absence of such trained intellects is a most serious obstacle to the progress of the Catholic faith, no thoughtful man will doubt or deny.

Since the mind is a power, in religion as in every sphere of thought and life, the discipline which best develops and perfects its faculties will fit it to do its work, whatever it may be, in the most effective manner. Hence, though the education of which I speak does not directly aim at being useful, it is in fact the most useful, and prepares better than any other for the business of life. It enables a man to master a subject with ease, to fill an office with honor, and whatever he does, the mark of completeness and finish will be found upon his work. He sees more clearly, judges more calmly, reasons more pertinently, speaks more seasonably, than other men. The free and full possession of his faculties gives him power to turn himself to whatever may be demanded of him, whether it be to govern wisely, or to counsel judiciously, or to write gracefully, or to plead eloquently. Whatever course in life he may take, whatever line of thought or investigation he may pursue, his intellectual culture will give him superiority over men who, with equal or greater talents, lack his education. And he possesses withal resources within himself, which in a measure make him independent of fortune, and which, when failure comes and the world abandons him, remain, like faith, or hope, or a friend, to make him forget his misfortunes.

Of the English universities, with all their shortcomings, Cardinal Newman says: "At least they can boast of a succession of heroes and statesmen, of literary men and philosophers, of men conspicuous for great natural virtues, for habits of business, for knowledge of life, for practical judgment, for cultivated tastes, for accomplishments, who have made England what it is—able to subdue the earth, able to domineer over Catholics." It is only in a university that all the sciences are brought together, their relations adjusted, their provinces assigned. There natural science is limited by metaphysics, morality is studied in the light of history, language and literature are viewed from the standpoint of ethnology, the criticism, which seeks beauty and not deformity, which in the gardens of the mind takes the honey and leaves the poison, is applied to the study of eloquence and poetry; and over all religion throws the warmth and life of faith and hope, like a ray from heaven. The mind thus lives in an atmosphere in which the comparison of ideas and truths with one another is inevitable, and so it grows, is strengthened, enlarged, refined, made pliant, candid, open, equitable.

When numbers of priests will be able to bring this cultivation of intellect to the treatment of religious subjects, then will Catholic theology again come forth from its isolation in the modern world; then will Catholic truth again irradiate and perfume the thoughts and opinions of men; then will Catholic doctrines again sink into their hearts, and not remain loosely in the mind to be thrown aside, as one casts away the outworn vesture of the body; then will it be felt that the fascination of Christian faith is still fresh, supreme, as far above the charm of science, as the joy of a poet's soul is above the pleasures of sense. The religious view of life must forever remain the true view, since no other explains our longings and aspirations, or justifies hope and enthusiasm; and the worship of God in spirit and in truth, which Christ has revealed to the world, the religion not of an age or a people, but of all times and of the human race, must eternally prevail when brought home to us in a language which we understand; for we place the testimony of reason above that of the senses. To the eye the sun rises and sets; to the mind it is stationary, and we accept, not what is seen, but what is known. Is there need of, stronger evidence, that the power within, which is our real self, is spiritual? And is it not enough to see clearly to perceive that in the struggle of mind with matter, which is the essential form of the conflict of spiritualism with materialism, of religion with science, the soul, in the end, will be victorious and rest in the real world of faith and intuition and not in the pictured world of the senses?

Religion, indeed, like morality, is in the nature of things, and Catholic faith is Una's Red Cross Knight, on whose shield are old dints of deep wounds and cruel marks of many a bloody field, who is assailed by all the powers of earth and of the nether world, armed with whatever weapons may hurt the mind or corrupt the heart, but whom heavenly providence rescues from the jaws of monsters and leads on to victory.

But what true believer thinks himself excused from effort, because Christ has declared the gates of hell shall not prevail against His Church? Does he not know that though, when we consider her whole course through the world, she has triumphed, so as to have become the miracle of history, yet has she at many points suffered disastrous defeat? Hence, those who love her must be vigilant and stand prepared for battle. And in an age when persecution has either died away or lost its harshness, when crying abuses have disappeared, when heresy has run its course, and the struggle of the world with the Church has become almost wholly intellectual, it is not possible, assuredly, that her ministers should have too great power of intellect. And consequently it is not possible that the bishops, in whose hands the education of priests is placed, should have too great a care that they receive the best mental culture. And if this be a general truth, with what pertinency does it not come home to us here in America, who are the descendants of men who, on account of their faith, have for centuries been oppressed and thrust back from opportunities of education, and who, when persecution and robbery had reduced them to ignorance and poverty, were forced to hear their religion reproached with the crimes of her foes? And now, when at length a fairer day has dawned for us in this new world, what can be more natural than our eager desire to move out from the valleys of darkness towards the hills and mountain tops that are bathed in sunlight? What more praiseworthy than the fixed resolve to prove that not our faith, but our misfortunes made and kept us inferior? And, since we live in the midst of millions who have indeed good will towards us, but who still bear the yoke of inherited prejudices, and who, because for three hundred years real cultivation of mind was denied to Catholics who spoke English, conclude that Protestantism is the source of enlightenment, and the Church, the mother of ignorance, do not all generous impulses urge us to make this reproach henceforth meaningless? And in what way shall we best accomplish this task? Surely not by writing or speaking about what the influence of the Church is, or by pointing to what she has done in other ages, but by becoming what we claim her spirit tends to make us. Here, if anywhere, the proverb is applicable — *verba movent, exempla trahunt*. As the devotion of American Catholics to this country and its free institutions, as shown not on battlefields alone, but in our whole bearing and conduct, convinces all but the unreasonable of the depth and sincerity of our patriotism, so when our zeal for intellectual excellence shall have raised up men who will take place among the first writers and thinkers of their day, their very presence will become the most persuasive of arguments to teach the world that no best gift is at war with the spirit of Catholic faith, and that, while the humblest mind may feel its force, the lofty genius of Augustine, of Dante and of Bossuet, is upborne and strengthened by the splendor of its truth. But if we are to be intellectually the equals of others, we must have with them equal advantages of education, and so long as we look rather to the multiplying of schools and seminaries than to the creation of a real university, our progress will be slow and uncertain, because a university is the great ordinary means to the best cultivation of mind. The fact that the growth of the Church here, like that of the country itself, is chiefly external, a growth in wealth and in numbers, makes it the more necessary that we bring the most strenuous efforts to improve the gifts of the soul. The whole tendency of our social life insures the increase of churches, convents, schools, hospitals and asylums; our advance in population and in wealth will be counted, from decade to decade, by millions, and our worship will approach more and more to the pomp and splendor of the full ritual; but this very growth makes such demands upon our energies, that we are in danger of forgetting higher things, or at least of thinking them less urgent. Few men are at once thoughtful and active. The man of deeds dwells in the world around him; the thinker lives within his mind. Contemplation, in widening the view, makes us feel that what even the strongest can do, is lost in the limitless expanse of space and time, and the soul is tempted to fall back upon itself and to gaze passively upon the course of the world, as though the general stream of human events were as little subject to man's control as the procession of the seasons. Busy workers, on the other hand, having little taste or time for reflection, see but the present and what lies close to them, and the energy of their doing circumscribes their thinking.

But the Church needs both the men who act and the men who think, and since with us everything pushes to action, wisdom demands that we cultivate rather the powers of reflection. And this is the duty alike of true patriots and of faithful Catholics. All are working to develop our boundless material resources; let a few at least labor to develop man. The millions are building cities, reclaiming wildernesses, and bringing forth from the earth its buried treasures; let at least a remnant cherish the ideal, cultivate the beautiful, and seek to inspire the love of moral and intellectual excellence. And since we believe that the Church which points to heaven is able also to lead the nations in the way of civilization and of progress, why should we not desire to see her become a beneficent and ennobling influence in the public life of our country? She can have no higher temporal mission than to be the friend of this great republic, which is God's best earthly gift to His children. If, as English critics complain, our style is inflated, it is because we feel the promise of a destiny which transcends our powers of expression. Whatever fault men may find with us, let them not doubt the world-wide significance of our life. If we keep ourselves strong and pure, all the peoples of the earth shall yet be free; if we fulfill our providential mission, national hatred shall give place to the spirit of generous rivalry, the people shall become wiser and stronger, society shall grow more merciful and just, and the cry of distress shall be felt, like the throb of a brother's heart, to the ends of the world. Where is the man who does not feel a kind of religious gratitude as he looks upon the rise and progress of this nation? Above all, where is the

Catholic whose heart is not enlarged by such contemplation? Here, almost for the first time in her history, the Church is really free. Her worldly position does not overshadow her spiritual office, and the State recognizes her autonomy. The monuments of her past glory, wrenched from her control, stand not here to point, like mocking fingers, to what she has lost. She renews her youth and lifts her brow, as one who not unmindful of the solemn mighty past, yet looks with undimmed eye and unfaltering heart to a still more glorious future. Who, in such a presence, can abate hope, or give heed to despondent counsel, or send regretful thoughts to other days and lands? Whoever at any time, in any place, might have been sage, saint or hero, may be so here and now; and though he had the heart of Francis, and the mind of Augustine, and the courage of Hildebrand, here is work for him to do.

In whatsoever direction we turn our thoughts, arguments rush in to show the pressing need for us of a centre of life and light such as a Catholic university would be. Without this we can have no hope of entering as a determining force into the living controversies of the age; without this it must be an accident if we are represented at all in the literature of our country; without this we shall lack a point of union to gather up, haromonize and intensify our scattered forces; without this our bishops must remain separated and continue to work in random ways; without this the noblest souls will look in vain for something larger and broader than a local charity to make appeal to their generous hearts; without this we shall be able to offer but feeble resistance to the false theories and systems of education which deny to the Church a place in the school; without this the sons of wealthy Catholics will, in ever increasing numbers, be sent to institutions where their faith is undermined; without this we shall vainly hope for such treatment of religious questions and their relations to the issues and needs of the day, as shall arrest public attention and induce Catholics themselves to take at least some little notice of the writings of Catholics; without this in struggles for reform and contests for rights we shall lack the wisdom of best counsel and the courage which skillful leaders inspire. We are a small minority in the presence of a vast majority; we still bear the disfigurements and weaknesses of centuries of persecution and suffering;

we cling to an ancient faith in an age when new sciences, discoveries and theories fascinate the minds of men and turn their thoughts away from the past to the future; we preach a spiritual religion to a people whose prodigious wealth and rapid triumphs over nature have caused them to exaggerate the value of material progress; we teach the duty of self-denial to a refined and intellectual generation, who regard whatever is painful as evil, whatever is difficult as omissible; we insist upon religious obedience to the Church in face of a society where children are ceasing to reverence and obey even their parents; if in spite of all this we are to hold our own, not to speak of larger hopes, it is plain that we may neglect nothing which will help us to put forth our full strength.

I do not, of course, pretend that this higher education is all that we need, or that, of itself, it is sufficient, but what I claim is that it would be a source of strength for us who are in want of help. God works, in many ways, through many agencies, and I bow in homage to the humblest effort in a righteous cause of the lowliest human being. There are diversities of graces, but the same spirit; diversities of ministries, but the same Lord. *Numquid omnes doctores?* asks St. Paul. But since he places teachers by the side of apostles and prophets, surely they will teach to best purpose who to the humility of faith add the luminousness of knowledge. To those who reject the idea of human co-operation in things divine I speak not; but we who believe that we are co-operators with Christ cannot think that it is possible to bring to this god-like work either too great preparation of heart or too great cultivation of mind. Nor must we think lightly even of refinement of thought, and speech and behavior, for we know that manners come of morals, and that morals in turn are born of manners, as the ocean breathes forth the clouds, and the clouds fill the ocean.

Let there be then an American Catholic university, where our young men, in the atmosphere of faith and purity, of high thinking and plain living, shall become more intimately conscious of the truth of their religion and of the genius of their country, where they shall learn the repose and dignity which belong to their ancient Catholic descent, and yet not lose the fire which glows in the blood of a new people; to which from every part of the land our eyes may turn for guidance and encouragement, seeking light and self-confidence from men in whom intellectual power is not separate from moral purpose; who look to God and His universe from bending knees of prayer; who uphold

> The cause of Christ and civil liberty
> As one and moving to one glorious end.

Should such an intellectual centre serve no other purpose than to bring together a number of eager-hearted, truth-loving youths, what light and heat would not leap forth from the shock of mind with mind; what generous rivalries would not spring up; what intellectual sympathies, resting on the breast of faith, would not become manifest, grouping souls like atoms, to form the substance and beauty of a world.

O solemn groves that lie close to Louvain and to Freiburg, whose air is balm and whose murmuring winds sound like the voices of saints and sages whispering down the galleries of time, what words have ye not heard bursting forth from the strong hearts of keen-witted youths, who, Titan-like, believed they might storm the citadel of God's truth! How many a one, heavy and despondent, in the narrow, lonesome path of duty, has remembered you, and moved again in unseen worlds, upheld by faith and hope! Who has listened to the words of your teachers and not felt the truth of the saying of Pope Pius II—that the world holds nothing more precious or more beautiful than a cultivated intellect? The presence of such men invigorates like mountain air, and their speech is as refreshing as clear-flowing fountains. To know them is to be forever their debtor. The company of a saint is the school of saints; a strong character develops strength in others, and a noble mind makes all around him luminous.

Why may not eight million Catholics upbuild a home for great teachers, for men who, to real learning and cultivation of mind, shall add the persuasiveness of easy and eloquent diction, whose manifest and indisputable superiority shall put to shame the self-conceit of American young men, our most familiar intellectual bane and an insuperable obstacle to all improvement—self-conceit, which is the beatitude of vulgar characters and shallow minds? If our students should find in such an institution but one man, who, like Socrates, with ironic questioning, might make for them the discovery of the new world of their own ignorance, the gain would be great enough.

Why may we not have a centre of light and truth which will raise up before us standards of intellectual excellence which will enable us to see that our so-called educated men are as far from being scholars as the makers of our horrible show-bills are from being artists, which will teach us that it is not only false, but vulgar to call things by pretentious names; as, for instance, to call a politician a statesman, a declaimer an orator, or a Latin school a university?

Ah! surely as to whether an American Catholic university is desirable there cannot be two opinions among enlightened men. But is it feasible? A true university is one of the noblest foundations of the great Catholic ages when faith rose almost to the height of creative power, and it were folly in me to maintain that such an undertaking is not surrounded by many and great difficulties. To begin with the material for foundation, money is necessary, and this, I am persuaded, we may have. A noble cause will find or make generous hearts. Men above all we need, for every kind of existence propagates itself only by itself. But let us bear in mind that the best teacher is not necessarily or often he who knows the most, but he who has most power to determine the student to self-activity; for in the end the mind educates itself. As distrust is the mark of a narrow intellect or a bad heart, so a readiness to believe in the ability of others is not only a characteristic of able men, but it is also the secret charm which calls around them helpers and followers. Hence, a strong man, who loves his work, is a better educator than a half-hearted professor who carries whole libraries in his head.

To bring together in familiar and daily life a number of young men, chosen for the brightness of their minds and an eager yearning for knowledge, is to create an atmosphere of intellectual warmth and light, which invigorates and inspires the master, while it stimulates his disciples. In such company it will not be difficult to form teachers. But will it be possible to find young men, who will consent when after years of study they have finally reached the priesthood, to continue in a higher institution the arduous and confining labors to the end of which they have looked as to the beginning of a new life? In other lands such students are found and if with us there is a tendency to rush with precipitancy and insufficient preparation to whatever work we may have chosen, this is but a proof of the need of special efforts to restrain an ardor which springs from weakness and not from strength. Haste is a mark of immaturity. He who is certain of himself and master of his tools, knows that he is able, and neither hurries nor worries but works and waits. The rank weed shoots up in a day and as quickly dies, but the long-growing olive tree stands from century to century and drops from its gently waving boughs ripe fruit through the quiet autumn air. The Church endures forever, and we American Catholics, in the midst of our rapidly-moving and ever-changing society, should be the first to learn to temper energy with the patient strength which gives the courage to toil and wait through a long life, if so we make ourselves worthy to speak some fit word or do some needful deed. And to whom shall this lesson first be taught if not to the clerics whose natural endowments single them out as future leaders of Catholic thought and enterprise, and where can this lesson so well be learned as in a school whose standard of intellectual excellence shall be the highest?

While we look, therefore, to the founding of a true university, we will begin, as the University of Paris began in the twelfth century, and as the present University of Louvain began fifty years ago, with a national school of philosophy and theology, which will form the central faculty of a complete educational organism. Around this the other faculties will take their places, in due course of time, and so the beginning which we make will grow, until like the seed planted in the earth, it shall wear the bloomy crown of its own development.

And though the event be less than our hope, though even failure be the outcome, is it not better to fail than not to attempt a worthy work which might be ours? Only they who do nothing derive comfort from the mistakes of others, and the saying that a blunder is worse than a crime is doubtless true for those who have no other measure of worth and success than the conventional standards of a superficial public opinion. We at least know:

> There lives a Judge
> To whose all-pondering mind, a noble aim
> Faithfully kept is as a noble deed:
> In whose pure sight all virtue doth succeed.

Rt. Rev. Wm. Quinn.

Rt. Rev. Thos. S. Preston.

Rev. Michael Kelly.

Very Rev. J. M. Farley.

Rev. P. M. Abbelen.

Rt. Rev. Geo. H. Doane.

Rev. J. P. O'Connell, D.D.

Very Rev. Henry Cluver, D.D.

Very Rev. John T. Sullivan.

The Necessity of Revelation.

SERMON OF RIGHT REV. R. GILMOUR, D.D.,

BISHOP OF CLEVELAND.

IN discussing the problems of the age there are two or three currents of thought tolerably well marked. Among these are a sharply defined attack upon authority, and a pretty well accepted determination to make man the beginning and end of himself. In the sixteenth century reason was made the judge of faith. What *it* accepted it held to be true; what *it* rejected it held to be false.

The results of thought are not the products of a day, so when reason was made its own master, and society was committed to its guidance, it required time, not only to accept the new, but to get rid of the old. The united and uniform teaching of the Church for sixteen hundred years had so moulded and formed public thought that time alone could change or destroy its work. But thought once started and fairly accepted will in time work its logical results. The human mind is fairly logical, and principles once accepted are in time pushed to their legitimate conclusions.

The actors of the French Revolution attempted to push to its legitimate conclusion the doctrine of the sixteenth century that "Reason was its own guide," but society was not then sufficiently advanced to deify reason, or to accept the horrors of unbridled passion. But since that the work has been steadily, and of late rapidly, going on, giving as legitimate results, the Communist and Nihilist as the advance guard of our Freethinkers, Agnostics, and Rationalists, to whom is to be added that vast army of No-Churchmen, steadily but imperatively coming up to fill the swelling ranks of the advance guard, who boastingly proclaim themselves *the* thinkers of the age, and the true exponents of what is known as "Modern Thought."

The phrase "Modern Thought" expresses two forms of progress—one material, the other spiritual. That the present age has made rapid and successful progress in the development of natural science and material comfort is undeniable. The press and the railroad are rapidly breaking down the lines between nations, and steadily moulding the human race into a homogeneous whole. As long as "Modern Thought" confines itself to the development of the natural, it is to be commended and encouraged. But more than mere material progress is needed for the safety of society and the well-being of man. There is needed the cultivation of the soul and the maintenance of the moral law. "Thought," whether ancient or modern, that neglects the soul, must not only be condemned, but rejected, let it be modern or no modern.

Now what is "Modern Thought?" What is its drift?

"Modern Thought" is not of modern origin, nor is it a single thought. It is the resume of the thoughts of the last three hundred years, and has for its basal thought: "Reason is supreme, and physical science is the sole test of truth?"

In the discussions of the day we hear much of science and discovery, progress and liberty; but little of God and the soul. "Modern Thought" seems centered on man and nature. God and the supernatural are either denied or but grudgingly tolerated. Dogma and creed are passing away. Heresy has attacked every cardinal doctrine of Christianity and been defeated. The controversy of the age, stripped of its verbiage and reduced to its simple form is, the Natural *versus* the Supernatural. In other words, does God exist in society? Has He any rights that man is bound to recognize?

I know quite well that the great mass of society has not yet reached this advanced position, but I do also know that thought never rests, and that once the human mind has fairly accepted a thought, it will in time push it to its logical conclusion. When the Reformation made reason the judge of God's law, it had no intention of pushing the consequences to their present position; nor did the authors of the French Revolution intend to end in the deification of a prostitute. But both came, and the signs of the times are that it is but a matter of time when the non-Catholic world will have abandoned Christian faith and dogma. As it is, the non-Catholic Churches are rapidly losing their hold on the masses, and society is seeking in man and nature what must be got in God. Under the cry of "science" revelation is being rejected; and under the cry of "progress" the supernatural is scouted. To such length is this going that now the question is no longer, "Which of the Christian Churches is the true Church?" but, "Is there a Supernatural?" "Is there Revelation?"

The man, or Church that to-day boldly declares, "God reigns," requires both courage and vigor. Courage, to assert the doctrine; vigor, to maintain it. "All power comes from the people," says the modern statesman: "All knowledge comes from nature," says the modern teacher. These two propositions cover the whole ground. In the first, man is made the beginning and end of himself; in the latter, nature is made the limit of man's hopes and ambitions. By them the Supernatural is denied, Revelation rejected, and God dethroned. For the supernatural is substituted, nature; for revelation, reason; for God, man.

Is there then a Supernatural? Is there a Revelation?

Nature in its widest sense means the entire collection of things created: hence the distinguishing mark of the term Nature is, that it is contingent, finite, limited. Nature from this point of view includes every species of creature from the invisible atom to the noblest of the angelic host. By this definition we also see that Nature is the creature of an eternal, self-existing being, who *in se* is above Nature. With the naturalist pure, who makes nature its own creator, we have, and can have no controversy, for the simplest of reasons that Nature can not be its own Creator. Nor will we contend with the pantheist, who would make all nature God. The controversy of the day is with those who admit a God, but deny that man has a supernatural end, and with this, deny revelation as given us in the Old and New Testament.

The assumption of these Naturalists, who admit a God Creator is, that God having created man, left him with the powers that He had given him to work out his own destiny; and further, that man has no supernatural end. These Naturalists, who are so glib and ready to tell us all about Nature and God, also assume that when God created the world He imposed upon Nature laws, that even He could not change, and on this assumption they deny the possibility of miracles, sneer at the idea of prophecy, and the power of prayer.

You will please notice, all this is pure assumption and assertion, for which these Naturalists offer not a single particle of proof. Their whole mode of reasoning is, to assume certain conclusions and from them build up a system of laws. So they assume, Reason is its own beginning and its own end, and hence that all truth is subjective, and is only truth so far as Reason accepts it. It was on this principle that Protestantism adopted "Private Interpretation of the Bible" as its foundation stone, a principle that has led to the melancholy spectacle of the present age, in which we see society seeking in Nature, and Science, and human power, what alone can be found in God,—the true and only supernatural.

I think truth is entirely too delicate with error. It is the duty of "Modern Thought" to prove its assumptions and verify its assertions. These modern theorists assume that God having created Nature lost all further control over it, and has no further interest in it. Now this assumption knowingly and brazenly ignores the fact, that cannot be denied or disproved, "that God precedes creation and from Him creation gets all it has." It is therefore the clear duty of these modern assumptionists to prove their assumption ere they attempt to rob God of what is clearly His. God is in possession, and it must be shown that He has lost possession ere "Modern Thought" can be permitted to assert its conclusions.

God is supernatural, and though He could have created man as He now is—the effects of the Fall excepted—and left him to the enjoyment of a natural happiness, yet as a matter of fact He did not; on the contrary, from the beginning God destined man for a supernatural end, and coeval with man's creation God revealed Himself to man and added grace to nature, so that from the first moment of man's existence he had, and knew he had a supernatural end.

Theoretically we can consider man at the moment of creation, with all his powers of nature in a state of perfection. Considered in this state of pure nature it is permissible to teach that man had within himself all the power needed to reach his natural beatitude. But as a matter of fact, man was at no moment of his existence in a state of pure nature, nor is he now. Before the fall man had what theologians call integral nature, that is, pure nature elevated to the supernatural by grace and revelation. The Fall did not destroy nature, though it weakened it by depriving man of grace by which, without other help, he would have reached the supernatural. Man in his present state cannot be discussed as if he were in the condition he was before the Fall. Then he was with the powers of nature unimpaired, and in the fullness of grace; now he is with grace lost and nature weakened, and passion impelling him on to evil. We must then take man as he is, not as he was, nor as he can be conceived. Now it is a fact of individual and universal experience, that man in his present state cannot, with his present powers, unaided by grace, reach a state of natural perfection, far less supernatural. On the contrary, it is certain man, as he now is, cannot of himself keep the natural law. This inability comes not from the insufficiency of pure nature for itself, but from the inefficiency of pure nature for the end above pure nature to which man has been graciously called by God. Besides man's inability, in his present state, to keep the whole law of nature, it is a demonstrated fact that at no time and under no form of human existence has man been able, without the aid of revelation, to formulate a system of religion capable of sustaining him, or keeping him within the law of nature. At his worst, in the savage state, man is little less than brute. At his best, in Greek and Roman society, passion was deified and man without hope. Here and there may be seen a glimpse of higher thought and purer morality, as in Socrates and Plato, and Cicero and Seneca, but this was either a remnant of the primitive revelation, which was never entirely lost, or it came from the Jewish law, which was tolerably well known throughout the East. Yet a Christian child, taught the first rudiments of his religion, knows more of God and creation; of man and his powers and destiny, than the wisest of pagan philosophers.

If then man in his present state, and as we now find him, is unable of his own power to keep the whole law of nature; and, further, if man of his own powers is unable to create a system of religion fit to govern and purify society, then we are forced either to admit the existence of revelation, or to charge God with having created man and then left him without the means of reaching reasonable perfection here and ultimate perfection hereafter. But such assumption is impossible, as God is not only just, but generous, and hence could not and did not leave man without the means of reaching his end. It is therefore imperative to conclude, that as man cannot, by the powers of nature keep nature's law, nor devise a system of religion fit to govern society, then God hath given grace and revelation, that by them man may be saved and society directed, and this is entirely in conformity with man's nature and with the whole history of the human race.

The tradition of a primitive revelation is a permanent, continuous fact of history. It permeates its every page and forms the basal thought of every tribe and people. Everywhere there is the memory of the creation and the fall: a heaven, a hell, a Redeemer, a God supreme. The wail of the human race is and has been for a beatitude once possessed, but now lost. The cravings of the human heart are for happiness beyond the grave, all proving not that a revelation is necessary, but that a revelation has already been made.

The history of the world is explicable only on the assumption of a supernatural revelation. The Jews are a proof of this; the Church is a proof of this; the traditions of every race and people, even in their rudest condition, is a proof of this. It is *the* fact of history, and is found in every form and phase of detail in the Gentile, Jewish and Christian world. Any attempt to explain the history of the Jews, or the rise and continuance of Christianity without the existence of a supernatural Providence is a failure. Gibbon tried to explain the rise of the Church, excluding God and revelation, and failed; Voltaire tried it, and failed; Macaulay tried it, and failed; our modern infidels and rationalists have tried it, and failed.

Admit the fact of revelation and all history is not only explainable, but the aspirations of the soul and the cravings of the heart are explainable. Admit the fact of revelation and the object of human existence and rational life is explainable. Admit that man has a soul and at once you bring him into relation with God and the supernatural, and give a reason for immortality and the complement of his being. History is an undeniable fact, and in it is found written on every page thereof the clear permanent evidence of a primitive revelation that has never been entirely lost, and is the underlying and enlightening element of all Gentile thought. The creation, the fall, a Redeemer, a heaven, a hell, a supreme God, are found in multiplied variety amid every tongue and people past and present. The force of this testimony cannot be ignored nor overlooked; on the contrary it is a most powerful and overwhelming argument in proof of the existence of a supernatural revelation.

Man is composed of body and soul. The body is mortal, the soul immortal. From the first moment of man's existence he was conscious of the spirituality and immortality of his soul. Down through the ages of history, amid civilized and savage, man's immortality has ever, and everywhere been accepted and taught, corrupted if you please, but the doctrine simple has always been accepted as the faith of mankind. As a part of this immortality, the soul has certain inherent longings for a higher and nobler end than life here can give. This longing is not confined to the enlightened, the sage or philosopher. It is felt by the lowest, it is proclaimed by the highest. The feticism of the savage, as well as the poetic creations of the polished Greek and Roman are founded on it. Another world where the soul will dwell, blessed for the good, or punished for the evil done in life, has been and is a doctrine co-extensive with the human race. This longing reaches beyond any created good, and will be satisfied with nothing less than God, the supreme good. Even God as attainable by nature will not suffice, nothing less than God in the supernatural completely satisfies these cravings of the soul. Whether these longings and cravings were inherent in man's heart as a part of pure nature matters not, as at no moment of man's existence was he limited to a state of pure nature. These longings exist. They enter into all man's acts and thoughts. Reason admits there is an unknown reality beyond the limits of rational knowledge. Now whence comes this universal longing, this universal belief? The longing comes from the nature of the soul, the belief comes from the primitive tradition given to man at the moment of creation. This longing, and this tradition are not denied even by the incredulous. Philosophy leads to faith, faith to the beatific vision.

Science, says the modern teacher, destroys faith, because it lays bare and exhibits to reason and the senses what faith teaches, forgetting that science ends in nature, while faith begins in super-nature, that is, science ends where faith begins. But faith is revelation, and revelation is an exterior manifestation of a supernatural truth made by God to man, which may, or may not, be discoverable by human reason. If, like the existence of God and the immortality of the soul, the doctrine revealed can be discovered by reason, then revelation but confirms reason; but if the revelation cannot be discovered by reason, then the truth of the revelation will depend upon the credibility of the witness.

If God in person makes the revelation directly to man, as he did to Adam, He first proves that He is God. If He makes the revelation through others, as He did through Moses and the prophets, then He proves by miracles that He speaks through them. The miracles attest the witness, and the witness attests the revelation.

Miracles and prophecy are infallible evidence that God speaks, as none but God can work a miracle, and none but God can foretell the future. Magicians and soothsayers may by the power of the devil work wonders and for a moment deceive; so may diviners make happy guesses. But a miracle or prophecy in its true meaning can only be by the power and knowledge of God.

When Moses appeared before Pharaoh and the Israelites, he proved by miracles that he was sent by God. When the prophets came, they not only proved their mission by miracles, but the fulfillment of their prophecies hundreds of years after proved the revelations made were of God. When Christ came He proved by miracles that He was God, *then* He made His revelations and proclaimed His law. The miracle proves the veracity of the witness, and the fulfillment proves the truth of the prophecy. And the miracle and the prophecy prove the revelation. Now, has God wrought miracles? Has God given prophecies?

The infidel denies both, but the testimony of the whole Jewish people proclaims the miracles of Moses, and Josue and the prophets. The Apostles and the multitude saw the miracles of Christ, and they were so clearly the works of God that even the ignorant exclaimed, "God hath visited His people." The prophecies of the patriarchs and prophets read like a page of past history, so complete are they in their fulfillment and minute in every detail of time, and place, and person. If human testimony is evidence of fact, then the existence of miracles and prophecy is not only beyond doubt, but beyond the possibility of rational discussion. But miracle and prophecy are the evidence that God hath spoken, and the word of God is direct revelation from God to man, giving us the supernatural and all that is embraced in the word, religion.

But if God hath spoken and given man divine revelation, as undoubtedly He has, then revelation must be accepted. God's word is not an empty sound. God is the beginning and the end, the creator and preserver of all there is or can be. From Him and by Him nature gets her laws and man his being, and without Him there is and can be nothing. Man is but a breath, and creation but the fiat of His will. He is supreme. His law is supreme. What we have is His. What we can do is by Him. Of ourselves we can not add a hair to our head, nor an hour to our lives. He made us as we are, the effects of sin excepted. We have therefore no rights as against God, and therefore no right to gainsay His word, or discuss His law. When He speaks there remains but obedience, but obedience founded on reason, which tells us God is truth and can not deceive.

But says the man of "Modern Thought" this is the doctrine of master and slave, and I am a freeman and must act according to reason. But in obeying God you do act according to reason, nay, exercise the highest powers of reason, because reason teaches us to give to every one his due. Now we owe to God all we are, have, or can do. We are absolutely His, body and soul. He is therefore our Sovereign Lord and Proprietor with the absolute right, as absolute owner, to do what He will with us. When therefore God reveals Himself to man, there remains for man but to accept the revelation, but it is the duty of God to prove that it is God who speaks, and not till God has proved to reason that it is God who speaks, has God a right to demand from reason obedience and acceptance.

Catholic doctrine teaches that reason precedes faith and that faith confirms reason. It farther teaches that faith is above reason but never contradicts reason. When therefore God comes before reason it is the duty of God to prove that He is God. But when by miracles He has proved that He is God then reason is bound to accept Him and all He says or does. When God appeared to Adam, He proved He was God; when He appeared to the patriarchs and prophets, He proved He was God; when Christ appeared upon earth He proved He was God; in each case by such signs and works as left no possible doubt that it was God who spoke. When God thus speaks by signs and miracles reason is bound to accept what God says, if reason will act according to reason.

Now, when God created man, He not only endowed him with the powers of nature, but at the same moment He made Himself known to man and proposed to him a supernatural end. In the course of time when God would add to the primitive revelation, He called to himself patriarchs and prophets and sent them forth with signs and miracles to speak the words which He placed in their mouths. So marked were these miracles and so clear and minute the prophecies, that only the malicious unbeliever can disbelieve or doubt.

It is easy to doubt. It is easy to pretend to disbelieve, scout prophecy, and pretend that miracle is impossible, but it is impossible to ignore the fact, that from the day of creation down to the present time revelation is, and has been the cardinal fact of history, just as Christ has been the cardinal fact of revelation. It cannot be ignored nor denied. It will not down, and though at times individuals, or large portions of society may deny it, or in part reject it, yet revelation ever returns to stare the world in the face and demand a hearing and acceptance. At the present moment "Thought" has started in a current of exaggerated humanity, by which man is pitted against God, and under the cry of liberty, progress and the rights of man, God and religion are assailed—in Europe by open hostility to the Catholic Church, in America by widespread indifference to religion. The basal thought of the present non-Catholic world is, that religious forms and beliefs are matters of indifference, if the heart is right. To such extent has this gone that outside the Catholic Church religion is banished from the school; and our youth are reared without God or religion.

The sky looks dark indeed. Morality is on the wane, and the standard of truth and justice steadily sinks. Our public men are no longer chosen for their honesty and ability, but for their availability.

The unity of marriage has ended in divorce and polygamy. Our youth are irreverent, blasphemy stalks the land, and drunkenness and lust are a stench in the nostrils. Material progress has replaced religion, the temporal is preferred to the eternal, the body to the soul, man to God.

In such state of things it behooves us not only to defend revelation, but to insist upon its acceptance. It is the heresy of the day that man is not bound to accept religion. It is true man is not bound to accept religion from man, and therefore as man against man, we can assert religious freedom, but as man against God, man is bound to accept religion; nay more than that, he is bound to accept pure and simple the religion God gives him.

It is true, by the gift of free will man has the power to disobey God and reject his law, but there is a vast difference between the power to disobey and the right to disobey. Man has no right to disobey God, or to reject his law. But revelation is the law of God to man, hence man has no right to reject revelation, or to substitute man's word for God's word. God's word must be accepted. Revelation must be accepted. Religion must be accepted. The Church must be accepted, because she is the voice of God to man. It behooves us as Catholics, it behooves the non-Catholic Christian world to rally round the standard of God, and to say to infidelity and irreligion: "Thus far and no farther." If we will save our country, we must build on religion. If we will save our youth, we must build on morality. If we will save our laws and institutions, we must build on truth and justice. Our youth must be taught reverence, passion must be bridled, drunkenness suppressed, marriage sanctified, and lust subdued.

We must cease permitting sentiment to rule, teach religion and replace God in society. The State must take from the Church, as the Church takes from God, and both must work for a common end. It is folly to assert that the State can prosper without the Church, or society exist without religion. God must rule, man must obey. Religion must be accepted and revelation maintained.

Indian Missions.

SERMON OF MOST REV. C. J. SEGHERS, D.D.,

ARCHBISHOP OF OREGON CITY.

"She reacheth therefore from end to end mightily and ordereth all things sweetly." —*Wisdom, c. viii, v. 1.*

CHRISTOPHER COLUMBUS fitted out his ship to sail in search of a western route to India; European monarchs sent their viceroys to take possession of newly discovered tracts of land and to add them to their domains; adventurers left Europe in quest of gold; merchants dispatched their vessels to supply the markets of the Old World with the produce of the new continent; but over all that bustle and that feverish activity there was, in the designs of God and in the mind of our Lord Jesus Christ, a lofty object kept in view, to which these actions of men were made subservient, as means are used to reach an end; and that was to call to the true faith numerous tribes seated in darkness and in the shadow of death, to make known to them the glad tidings of the Gospel, to throw open to them the portals of the Church and to point out to them the road towards heaven.

Ask me not why Divine Wisdom deferred till the fifteenth century to communicate the treasures of the new law to the inhabitants of the New World. When we view the vicissitudes of things and the fluctuation of events to which the preaching of the Gospel and the professions of the true faith have been subject in both parts of this continent, we may thank God for the existence and the vitality of the Church here in these days. Other countries in the Old World received the true faith much earlier than this continent,

Rev. F. Goller.

Rev. C. P. Grannan, D.D.

Very Rev. F. Wayrich, C.SS.R.

Very Rev. D. E. Lyman, V.F.

Rev. T. P. Thorpe.

Most Rev. J. J. Lynch, D.D.

Rt. Rev. J. V. Cleary, D.D.

Rt. Rev. John Walsh, D.D.

Rt. Rev. J. J. Carbery, D.D.

but they lost it completely long ago. Perhaps America received the true faith later to keep it forever.

Alas! for the wickedness of man. The antecedent will of God and the desires of the Sacred Heart of Jesus are often frustrated by our evil actions. Devoted men, apostolic priests, zealous missionaries were not wanted in the past to undertake the work of the conversion of the aborgines of America. And when the Dominican Las Casas, the Jesuits Marquette, Brebœuf and Goupil, the Franciscan Junipero Serra, and a host of others crossed the ocean, mountains, lakes and rivers to penetrate into the forest in search of the erring sheep, the angels looked down upon these apostles of the cross with joy and admiration and exclaimed: "How beautiful upon the mountains are the feet of them that bring good tidings and that preach peace." (Isaias, ii, 2.) For if there is joy in heaven at the sight of one sinner that does penance, what must have been the rejoicings of the angels and saints at the prospect of millions about to be converted and made holy?

But when we review the work of the last three centuries in both the northern and southern part of this continent, we are prone to ask "Has the white race done justice to the red man? We hear, indeed, of flourishing Christian communities of Indians, in Canada, in Mexico, in California, in Paraguay, recorded by historians with terms of admiration; but the rapacity of the adventurer, the tyranny of the ruler, the evil passions of the profligate, the anti-Christian spirit of certain secret organizations and other causes beyond the reach of my research have prevented the spread of Christianity in some places, and rooted up the Church in others. St. Paul speaks of an interchange of spiritual and temporal things between those that impart the Christian doctrine and those that receive it; the latter receive spiritual, the former receive temporal things. (Gal., vi, 6.) We are in possession of the red man's country, we occupy his hunting ground, we are masters of the soil where his wigwam stood; have we communicated to him the light of the Gospel that is in us? Daniel speaks of the angel of the Persians and of the angel of the Greeks. (Dan., x, 20.) We infer therefrom that every nation is placed by Almighty God under the guidance and protection of an angel. Behold the angel of the Indian race: his countenance is not lit up with gladness, his eyes do not beam with joy, his lips bear not the graceful curve of a pleasing smile; he points to the soil of this continent, bleached with the bones, red with the blood and black with the ruins of a destroyed race of men. Let us draw a veil over this gloomy picture.

The Apostle of the Gentiles when deploring the reprobation of his countrymen, exclaims with the prophet Isaias, (Rom. ix. 27), "Reliquiæ salva fient—a remnant shall be saved;" let us say the same, in our age, of the remnant of the Indian race. If vast numbers of them have disappeared from the earth, if instead of bringing to them the olive branch of civilization, we have followed towards them a policy of extermination, let at least those that remain be an object of our charity. Arise, zealous missionaries, apostles of the cross, and continue the work begun by holy men! Your mission is a noble one. When our Lord was requested by St. John to give proof of the divine origin of His work, He did not say, "The rich are evangelized," but He answered, "Pauperes evangelizautur." "The poor have the Gospel preached to them." What better proof do we wish that the work of the Gospel among the aborigines is a continuation of the work of Christ? Blessed therefore be the memory of Norbert Blanchet, Modeste Demey and Father De Smet, who like Abraham went out of their country and of their kindred, to cross the lofty range of the Rocky Mountains and proceeded as far as the shores of the Pacific, because they could go no further. Blessed those that walk in their footsteps. Blessed also those that continue the good work in the Indian Territory, in Dakota, Nebraska, Montana, Wisconsin and other States and Territories. I say they are blessed, for do you not remember, beloved brethren, that our Lord pronounced His curse on the man who scandalizes the little ones and "through whom evil cometh?" If, therefore, the one who gives scandal and does spiritual evil to his neighbor is anathematized by our Lord Jesus Christ, is it not evident that he is blessed that does good to and edifies and sanctifies and saves the little ones? Who are those whom Christ, in another place, calls the least of His brethren? Are not the Indians the least of the brethren of Christ? The least—yes, the poorest, the most ignored and the most despised. Blessed, I repeat it, those who contribute to the work of their edification and sanctification.

In the address I am making to you this evening, beloved

brethren, I have for object to secure your favor, to enlist your sympathy in behalf of this good, great and meritorious work of christianization and civilization of the aborigines. I say christianization and civilization, for, say what they will, the people of this country will never convert and civilize the Indians by schools, unless the latter be based upon the Christian faith and permeated with a Christian atmosphere. Religion and civilization go hand in hand; discard religion and you prepare the condition of the barbarian or the savage.

But how shall I succeed in making you feel interested in this work? It seems to me that I cannot find a more successful way than by giving a description of our missionary work among the Indians, and this I will do by dwelling on the difficulties we met with, or the obstacles we have to overcome. Let me premise two remarks: 1. I desire chiefly to speak of the work of the conversion of the Indians as we find them in their primitive, untutored and savage condition. 2. I wish to dwell chiefly on facts that have come within my own knowledge and personal observation. I trust, therefore, you will excuse and pardon me if I refer often to myself, if I often speak of myself. Not wishing to state things which I know from hearsay, I will speak of things I saw with my own eyes and heard with my own ears.

The diocese about to be confided to my care consists of two parts—Vancouver Island and Alaska, formerly known as Russian America, and now a part of this republic. Originally these territories formed part of an immense vicariate apostolic, embracing the whole western part of North America, from California to the Arctic Ocean, but that immense vicariate was subsequently divided into dioceses, and Vancouver Island welcomed her first bishop, the late Modeste Demers, in 1851.

Vancouver Island is nearly three hundred miles in length, and the population consists partly of whites, who dwell chiefly in the towns of Victoria, Nanaimo and Esquimalt, and in the settlements of Saanich, Cowichan and Comox, and of Indian tribes numbering about 11,000. There are but eleven priests in the whole island to minister to all these people, and the absence of pecuniary resources places an obstacle in the way of increasing the number of the faithful.

An Indian tribe numbering 4,000, and occupying the western

shore of the island, was seated in the darkness of error and in the shadow of death until 1874, when, being then Bishop of Vancouver Island, and accompanied by one priest, I visited the twenty-one villages into which that tribe is divided, preaching to them the holy faith; and we succeeded in the course of that year in teaching all those Indians all the Catholic prayers in their own language, besides several religious canticles, and in baptizing 960 of their children under seven years of age. And there, where before my first visit in 1869 no priest had ever set foot, are now three churches and four priests laboring to evangelize and Christianize those poor people. Alaska, formerly Russian America, which is larger than all the New England States together, contains 60,000 Indians as yet unconverted to the faith. In 1879 I built a church and stationed a priest at Wrangel, a small town in the southern part of that territory, but he was later on recalled to Vancouver Island, where his services were indispensable, so that in this immense country, and among that multitude of souls, there is now not a single Catholic priest. After the father's departure an Indian woman was seen Sunday after Sunday kneeling before the closed door of the church, beseeching our Lord to send a priest again to that mission. Who can refuse aid, so that this poor woman's prayer may be heard, and the door of the church opened once more?

In 1879 I left the Diocese of Vancouver Island to become Archbishop of Oregon, and I was called to Rome last year with the other Archbishops of the United States to assist in preparing for the next Council in Baltimore. And when in November last the Cardinal Prefect of the Propaganda expressed his grave apprehensions for the future of Catholicity in the Diocese of Vancouver Island, which was vacant, and which there was no prospect of providing with a bishop, I volunteered to leave Oregon and to return to my former Diocese of Vancouver Island. My offer was both gladly accepted by the Propaganda and approved by the Holy See.

More priests are needed to establish new missions both on the island and in Alaska, for the harvest indeed is great, but the laborers few. Brothers, too, are needed to educate the Indian children. Then the necessary vestments and sacred vessels for the suitable celebration of divine worship are wanting. Furthermore, a new church and a new house for the clergy are urgently needed in Victoria, the bishop's place of residence in Vancouver Island. The present cathedral is a wooden structure, 75 feet long, and can last but a few years longer. The bishop's house, also of wood, is fast decaying, and its unhealthiness exposes the clergy to serious danger. Such are, in brief, the reasons that have determined me to travel from country to country, from town to town, yes, from house to house, to solicit the aid of my brethren in the faith.

Christian Marriage.

SERMON OF RIGHT REV. M. J. O'FARRELL, D.D.,

BISHOP OF TRENTON, N. J.

TEXT:—*St. Paul to the Ephesians, c. v, v. 22-31.*

DURING the past week you listened to some admirable discourses upon the Christian Church, her constitution, her mission and her characteristic marks. You also heard a most eloquent lecture on Christian education, its necessity, its extent and its advantages. But there is another great truth underlying them both. They describe the magnificent building, rising lofty and beautiful, challenging the attention and exciting the admiration of thoughtful observers. But beneath there must be a solid basis to support the weight. To bear up this mighty structure, whose beauty and majestic proportions have so arrested our gaze, there must be broad and strong foundations. So whilst we admire the strength and durability of the Christian Church, whilst we exalt the merits and advantages of Christian education, let us remember that underlying all is the Christian family. All Christian society, the whole edifice of Christian civilization, rest upon it. There is no Christian society without the Christian family, and no Christian family without Christian marriage. Thus we are naturally led to the subject of this evening's discourse.

Again, on the other hand, when we cast our eyes around and see the many evils that afflict our modern society—family ties loosened and family honor so frequently stained; paternal authority losing its force and treated with disrespect; filial obedience constantly declining; domestic quarrels and discords so often darkening our social life· the

Very Rev. M. Aldarick.

Very Rev. Joseph M. Losen, O.M.C.

Rt. Rev. Wm. O'Hara, D.D.

Very Rev. Edward McColgan, V.G.

Very Rev. E. Serin, C.S.C.

Very Rev. P. A. Stanton, O.S.A.

Very Rev. Thomas Steffanini, C.P.

Rt. Rev. I. Robot, O.S.B.

Very Rev. Leo Da Sarracena, O.S.F.

sacred obligations of wife and mother cast aside in so many instances, as too irksome to be borne; shameful crimes and horrible excesses, that should not even be mentioned amongst Christians, so well known and in some places so common; the very laws of nature wantonly and unblushingly trampled under foot—when we see these and many other evils we naturally ask what can have given rise to them and whence do they spring? If we make the examination seriously we shall find that, for the greater part, they arise from ignorance or contempt of the true nature of Christian marriage or violation of its laws. Through false teaching and the lawless tyranny of unrestrained passions many have lost the true notion of the institution of marriage, such as God and nature has established.

It becomes then our duty, particularly at a season like this, when the representatives of the entire Catholic Church in this great country are gathered together in this Plenary Council, to announce the full truth concerning the nature and obligations of Christian marriage. We owe it to you, dear brethren, faithful children of holy Church, in order to warn you and fortify you against the false and corrupt maxims of the age; and we owe it also to our fellow-countrymen, to whatever religious denomination they may belong—"for we are debtors to all"—that they too may learn these important truths and all society be blessed through the knowledge.

Marriage was instituted by God Himself for the propagation and preservation of the human race. It differs from all other contracts made by men, which derive their binding force from the will of the contracting parties and from human laws which sanction them. They depend entirely on the conditions affixed to them. They are limited both in duration and force by the terms of the agreement. Men can place their conditions upon every other contract; they buy or sell, lend or borrow, as they may agree, and human laws will ratify the compact, unless it should be considered injurious to the public good.

But in marriage it is not so; for marriage is of divine institution and can exist only on the conditions fixed by God Himself. Christian marriage, in its essence, can be governed only by the laws of the divine legislator of the Christian Church. Society did not institute marriage, for marriage was established before all society.

Without it society could not have existed. The same God who established society and communicated to it the powers necessary for its preservation, instituted marriage as the foundation upon which all society rests. We must then first examine the manner of its establishment and the conditions and laws assigned to it, and accept them as coming from God. No human laws can avail against divine ones. Society cannot legislate against the eternal Law Giver. The fundamental and primordial law of marriage and the absolute condition of Christian marriage is its unity and indissolubility. Marriage is the union of one man with one woman for purposes intended by the Creator, and this union must be forever. Such was marriage at the beginning of the world. Such did it become again when our divine Saviour restored it to its primitive state, and even raised it higher still, making its unity and indissolubility more perfect by appointing it one of the sacraments of His law and the type of the perfect union existing between Himself and His Church.

The words of Christ laying down the doctrine of marriage are found both in His Sermon on the Mount, in St. Matthew, 5th chapter, 31st verse, but still more at length in the 19th chapter of the same Evangelist, 4th and following verses, to which I shall more particularly refer.

The circumstances which led to this declaration deserve our consideration. There were amongst the Jews at that time two factions which held different opinions with regard to the causes which would justify divorce, as the Jewish law permitted it. One party maintained that divorce was lawful for any cause, no matter how trivial. The other faction held that for no cause, except for adultery on the part of the wife, could the marriage tie be dissolved. The Pharisees hoped to ensnare the Saviour, and by obliging Him to give a decision that He would certainly displease either one of the factions and make new enemies for Himself. "They therefore asked Him," says the Scripture, "tempting Him: Is it lawful for a man to put away his wife for any cause?" How admirably Jesus avoids the snare, and yet still makes known His will and doctrine about marriage. "Have you not read," says He with gentle irony—"you learned men, so profoundly skilled in the Sacred Scriptures—have you not read that He who made man in the beginning, made them male and female?" And He said: "For this cause shall man leave father and mother and shall cleave unto his wife, and they two shall be in one flesh. Wherefore they are no more two, but one flesh. What, therefore, God has joined together let no man put asunder." (St. Mat., xix, 4-6.)

In those clear words the Saviour takes them back to the original institution of marriage, to the beginning of all things. When God created man He made only two persons, only one man and one woman, not one man and several women. He thus indicated by the very fact of their creation the unity of the marriage tie.

Not only by facts and the mode of creation did God manifest the unity of marriage, but also by His words: "Wherefore shall man leave his father and his mother and shall cleave to his wife, and they who were two shall be one." Our Lord here attributes to God Himself these words, which, as we learn from Genesis, were uttered by Adam; because it was God's inspiration and in the spirit of prophecy that he pronounced them. "For this cause," that is, as the woman had been created from the side of man, and thus formed part of his being, that she was bone of his bone and flesh of his flesh; as the man and the woman had been one before the separation, so they must become one again when God unites them; *propter hoc*, for this cause, shall man give up all else, his nearest and dearest affections, even father and mother, and shall cleave to his wife with the deepest love, and be united to her in the closest of all relations; so intimate, so sacred that "now these two are but one flesh." And to make this point still clearer, our Lord Himself draws the conclusion from all that preceded—"therefore they are no more two, but one flesh." See how He insists upon this; therefore they are after marriage only one, where they had been two before. Finally He lays down the supreme principle and the final conclusion— "what therefore God hath joined together let no man put asunder." Remark how He does not even say "*whom* God has joined," but "*what* God has joined"—the contract which God has thus formed, the one person thus constituted out of two by God Himself, no man can put asunder. No human power can break this bond. This union is the work of the Omnipotent Creator; let not man dare to meddle with it.

The Pharisees, disconcerted at this reply, so entirely unexpected, urge strongly an objection. If that be as you state, if marriage be naturally indissoluble, "why, then, did *Moses* command to give a bill of divorce and to put away?" Our Lord gently corrects their exaggeration. "Moses, because of the hardness of your hearts, *permitted* you to put away your wives." Moses did not command the divorce, he only tolerated it on account of your stubborn dispositions, to avoid greater evils. "But from the beginning it was not so." Before Moses granted the permission, from the very foundation of the world, marriage was indissoluble. And now I, greater than Moses, I who have come to give a more perfect law than that of Moses, I withdraw this toleration, I restore marriage to its primitive purity and unity—"I say to you, whosoever shall put away his wife, except it be for fornication, and shall marry another, committeth adultery; and he who shall marry her that is put away committeth adultery." The whole Catholic Church firmly holds that the apparent exception stated by our Lord does not destroy the marriage tie; that the guilty wife may be dismissed from her home, but the marriage remains unbroken. This is not the place to enter fully into all the reasons which justify this doctrine. It is sufficient here to indicate that the whole context and tenor of Christ's discourse, and the entire purpose of His argument, absolutely requires this sense; that the greatest of the Fathers of the Church asserted it; that the entire Latin Church for fifteen hundred years before the Reformation, and the whole Catholic Church since, has always maintained it. The arguments to prove these different points would be out of place in a plain discourse like this to-night, and would require it to be prolonged beyond all reasonable limits. I will simply refer to this reasoning which you can all follow. When the other Evangelists, St. Mark and St. Luke, relate this scene and quote the words of the Saviour they affirm absolutely the law and make no mention of the supposed exception. Thus, in St. Mark, x, 11, it is stated that when the disciples asked their Master to explain His words, He thus replied in the most general terms: "Whosoever shall put away his wife and marry another committeth adultery against her. And if the wife shall put away her husband and be married to another, she committeth adultery." Again, in St. Luke, xvi, 18: "Every one that putteth away his wife and marrieth another committeth adultery: and he that marries her that is put away from her husband committeth adultery." Here there is no exception to the law, nor any excuse for making an exception. "Whoever marries the woman that is put away by her husband, no matter on what ground or pretext she was put away, commits adultery." Therefore, the first marriage is never broken, for if it were, the woman put away would be free to marry again, and he who should marry her could not be guilty of adultery in so doing. Therefore, the words of the Saviour must be taken in their plain, literal sense as the only one that the early Christians who might have only the Gospel of St. Mark or that of St. Luke could possibly attach to them.

Again let us see how the Apostles understood the law. St. Paul, the great Apostle of the Gentiles, will serve as interpreter for all. Here is what he declares in his Epistle to the Romans, viii, 2, 3: "For the woman that hath a husband, whilst her husband liveth, is bound to the law; but if the husband be dead, she is loosed from the law of her husband. Wherefore, whilst her husband liveth, she shall be called an adulteress, if she be with another man: but if her husband be dead, she is free from the law of her husband; so that she is not an adulteress if she be with another man." Again, 1 Cor., vii, 10, 11: "To them that are married, not I, but the Lord commandeth, that the wife depart not from her husband, and if she depart, that she remain unmarried." And in the same chapter, v. 39: "A woman is bound by the law as long as her husband liveth; but if her husband die, she is at liberty, let her marry whom she will." Thus it is clearly stated by St. Paul that marriage is indissoluble,—that the woman is bound to her husband as long as he lives, and that nothing but death, no human enactment, no State or earthly power, can loose the bonds which bind them together. Finally the same doctrine is placed upon even higher grounds in the beautiful words of my text—Epistle to the Ephesians, v. 22, where he declares that the union of man and wife is typical of the union between Christ and His Church, and must last forever, for as Christ shall never be separated from His Spouse, the Church, which He loved and for which He delivered Himself up, that He might sanctify it, so also men ought to love their wives as their own bodies. "He that loveth his wife, loveth himself." Hence he can no more be separated from his wife than he can from himself, or than Christ from His Church.

Such was the doctrine laid down by the Apostle of nations; such was the doctrine taught the entire world by the Christian Church: and it was by virtue of this law and this divine institution of marriage that she undertook to regenerate corrupt and dissolute peoples.

It is impossible to describe the degraded condition into which the world had fallen when the Christian Church began her mission. Society was rotten to the core. The true notion of the family had disappeared,—and woman was little better than a slave in the household, entirely dependent on the caprices or tyranny of the husband,—at one time his plaything,—at another his victim. Home—home as we understand it, with all its sweet memories and hallowing associations—was entirely unknown. The Christian Church renewed all. She reconstructed the family and made it the firm basis of the new Christian society. She raised up woman from her social degradation. She gave the wife an assured position that no tyranny could deprive her of. She made her the queen of the domestic circle,—the guardian angel of the home, the partner of her husband, his true helpmate and companion,—increasing his joy, sharing in his sorrows, ever associated with him in the responsibilities of the family. The Christian mother was invested with a sacred dignity such as paganism never recognized. Her children looked up to her with the most loving reverence and called her and made her truly blessed. With this elevation of woman in the family circle by the assured certainty of her position in her home, the Church laid the foundation of a new society. Christendom was formed by the Christian family,—as the family itself by Christian marriage. To this was Christendom indebted for the higher civilization which it attained above the rest of the world. The noblest energies of man were developed, and the most heroic qualities manifested. Christian marriage elevated the nations of Europe to the highest degree of true civilization, whilst polygamy corrupted and degraded the peoples of Asia. Had the Church not fought bravely and unremittingly the battle for the indissolubility of marriage, Europe would have sunk into the same degradation as the Mahometan nations. But the Catholic Church never faltered. Against the fierce passions of the half-barbaric tribes,—against the unbridled lusts of despotic rulers, she constantly asserted the divine rights of marriage. The

Sovereign Pontiffs, the faithful defenders of truth and morality, were ever foremost in the struggle. Again and again throughout the Middle Ages did this voice proclaim to the world, with no doubtful sound, the unity and indissolubility of marriage. In vain did haughty kings and powerful emperors seek to make their own passions the sole standard of right, by trampling upon God's law; to them, as to the humblest of their subjects did the Pope reply: *Non licet*,—you cannot break the bond which God has tied,—you cannot dismiss your lawful wife. For the sake of helpless women,—a betrayed or forsaken wife, the Popes of Rome braved the anger of the most despotic tyrants, and exposed themselves to the terrible vengeance of their disappointed passions. Witness the struggle of the Pope against Philip Augustus, when all France was laid under an interdict until the king consented to receive his lawful wife and abandon his second sacrilegious marriage. History tells of the heroic contest of Gregory VII against the emperor, Henry IV of Germany, in defence of a wronged and banished wife. And do you not all know how Clement VII refused to abandon the rights of Catherine of Aragon, whom the lustful passions of Henry VIII wished to discard, even though by his refusal all England should be lost to the Church? But the divine principle of the unity of marriage could not be sacrificed, no matter what the consequences might be. During all those ages the Roman Pontiffs sedulously guarded and bravely defended this fundamental principle.

How differently the Reformers proceeded. In England the new Church was built upon the broken marriage vows and adulterous passions of a most brutal king. In Germany it sprang from the broken religious vows of disorderly monks, and was fostered by the greed and lust of princes. Scarcely had the German Reformation begun when by an act unexampled amongst Christians the very leaders of the movement, Luther and Melancthon, allowed in writing to Philip of Hesse that he might have two wives at the same time without even pretending to divorce the first. If the Popes had thus acted Europe would most certainly have lost Christian civilization, and would have descended to the level of the barbarous nations of Asia, degraded and demoralized by the practice of polygamy. If now the Christian woman enjoys so much consideration; if the name of wife and mother be so holy and venerable; if the memories of home be so dear to the heart of every true man, it is due to the blessed influence of Christian marriage.

But there are agencies at work around us that threaten to sap and destroy this holy institution. The system of divorce and the laws establishing it in the various States are certainly a fearful danger to the welfare of society; and all who believe in God's law as supreme above all the laws of men, and all who wish to preserve our country from moral ruin should seriously consider the consequences that will necessarily follow if the sacredness of the marriage tie be destroyed or even tampered with.

For divorce destroys the unity of marriage and introduces virtual polygamy with many of its worst consequences. The people of this great country, whose instincts are so generally Christian, hold in detestation the doctrines of Mormonism and consider them a disgrace and a curse to the nation. Yet in what does Mormonism really differ from the system of divorce? Mormonism allows men to have several wives at the same time, while divorce permits them one after the other. Divorce allows a man to be married twice, three times, etc., no limit fixed, while the first wife is still living. In what does that really differ from Mormonism? It is just as much opposed to the real ends of marriage, to the mutual love of the married couple, and the proper education of children; and it is much more adapted to gratify the basest passions, as it offers a greater freedom from the embarrassments of open polygamy. With whatever disgust then we view the shameful doctrines of Mormonism, with even greater dislike should we treat the question of divorce. For, as I have just said, it is opposed to the natural ends of marriage and disturbs the laws established by the Creator. It destroys the mutual love which should unite the husband and wife, it develops all the causes which can lead to their unhappiness, it stimulates the worst passions of our nature and leads often to the foulest crimes. When married persons know that they are united for good or ill until death, they will naturally cultivate mutual love and mutual forbearance; they will support each other's defects and overlook many imperfections. For their own sake they feel that they must overcome many petty dislikes and make the most of the good qualities of their companions. Divorce encourages these quarrels and fosters them. It leads even to the worst evils. For if a married person know that by personal quarrels or by crimes the marriage can be broken, what an inducement to foster dissension or to fall into foul sins! Nay, even snares and pitfalls are thus often prepared by one of the parties to entrap the unwary steps of the other, in order to have a pretext for the dissolution of marriage. It is not a very rare thing that the husband should agree beforehand with the seducer to secure the proofs of his wife's unfaithfulness in order to have the right to divorce her. I pass over in silence many things; the shocking revelations of the divorce courts cannot even be alluded to. You can judge from what I have said if divorce be not injurious to the ends of marriage. The woman becomes degraded by such a law. She is no longer certain of her position in the household; for under one pretext or another she can be driven from her home.

It is no longer even for crime that divorce is granted. The most frivolous charges, the most futile reasons are considered sufficient in many places. Nay, even without the knowledge of one of the parties it can be obtained by the other. These causes are so multiplied that in some of our States nothing is more easily granted. Hence we see the rapid and fearful increase in the number of broken marriages,—and the horrible fact that in many places divorces come as high as one in every twelve or ten or even nine marriages. Divorce then is simply a legalized prostitution; and marriage itself no better than a temporary cohabitation, stigmatized as a very foul crime in all Christian lands. But even this is not the whole malice of divorce. It prevents the proper training and education of children, which is one of the essential ends of marriage. The true education of the child requires both father and mother to bring it to completion—the strong authority of the father, and the loving affection of the mother. But where can we get this necessary co-operation on the part of the parents, if divorce be permitted? To whom will the child belong? Who shall take charge of him when father and mother are torn asunder? If he be sufficiently advanced in years, he must decide for himself. Cruel alternative, unhappy decision, when he has to reject one or the other parent. If he be very young, how heart-rending this separation becomes. Shall the young child be torn from the frantic grasp of a broken-hearted, wretched mother, driven from her home and her little ones? Ah! you can recall many such scenes; our daily papers often give us the harrowing details. And there, too, we read of the desperate efforts of the father to recover possession of his children. But what shall become of the miserable children themselves, thus parted from their natural guardians? Shall they grow up in the principles of honor and integrity, or rather shall they not become indifferent to all virtue? And how shall they regard in after years the parents who brought such shame and ruin upon them?

I have said enough, I trust, to convince you of the many evil consequences which necessarily flow from divorce; yet I have not enumerated more than a part. When men break down the barriers which God Himself has raised up to curb the passions, no one can adequately foresee the fearful havoc and widespread ruin produced when the full torrent of these passions finds an outlet for their fury. The exceptions allowed may at first seem without danger, but they soon create the necessity for granting others. The little rills soon swell into a mighty torrent that sweeps away everything in its resistless force. Just as in some countries dykes and banks have been erected to prevent the waters of the ocean from covering the land; the country is safe while the dykes remain uninjured. But let a little rift be made in them; let the slightest break occur, and little by little, through the incessant action of the sea, the fissure is widened, the breach is gradually enlarged, until at length the full fury of the angry waters bursts through all bounds, and then widespread ruin and devastation follow, and the land, with all its riches and beauty, its cultivated plains and smiling gardens, is entirely submerged. So around society, for its preservation, the Almighty erected the strong barriers of holy marriage with its unity and indissolubility, as the powerful safeguards of our best interests. Let but a slight break be made in its binding force, let but even one exception be admitted, and very soon through the fierce surging of human passion,—through the constant cravings of the ever restless heart of man, the whole structure will be overturned and society be flooded with countless evils.

Let us then, dear brethren, firmly hold that Christian marriage is one and indissoluble; that it is the union of one man with one woman and forever. Let us firmly believe that this is God's ordinance from the beginning of the world, and that this is the law of Jesus Christ, the Legislator of the new Covenant. For us Catholics there can be no hesitation. It is the doctrine of our Church. No matter then what human enactments may be framed,—no matter what laws of divorce may be published,—no matter how few or many—whether one or twenty,—causes of divorce be admitted in the government of our States,—our duty is plain,—we cannot accept them nor profit by them to break a lawful marriage sanctioned by the Church of God. Our duty is to honor ourselves this great sacrament, and to teach others to prize it by our words and examples. Our duty is to prepare ourselves worthily for its reception and to live worthily in it after its reception: to understand its sacredness and its inviolability when we receive it, and ever after by Christian lives manifest all the true, blessed fruits of Christian marriage: thus fulfilling the words of St. Paul cited in my text. (Eph. v, 22, 23.)

The Observation of Feasts.

SERMON OF RIGHT REV. S. V. RYAN, D.D.,

BISHOP OF BUFFALO, N. Y.

"And a voice came out of the cloud, saying: This is my beloved Son in whom I am well pleased."—*St. Luke, c. ix, v. 35.*

THE ineffable mystery of the Incarnation opens to the eyes of faith fathomless depths of love and mercy. "God so loved the world as to give His only begotten Son." (John, iii, 16.)

We love to gaze in spirit at the ravishing beauty of that divine countenance. We love to contemplate Jesus, the God Man, coming forth from the throne of His eternity, clothed with all the splendor of divinity, "the splendor of His Father's glory, the figure of His substance," and we stand enraptured with the three privileged disciples on Mount Tabor, where we see Him transfigured, His countenance as bright as the sun, His garments white as the driven snow; and yet, my brethren, it is in His character of Master, Teacher and Legislator that the Eternal Father presents Him to our view. "Behold my beloved Son in whom I am well pleased, *hear* ye Him."

In this character, then, we must consider Him. Jesus came to be our Saviour, to teach to us the truths of faith, to make known to us the ways of eternal life. "I am the way," He says of Himself, "the truth and the life." (John, xiv, 6.) "I am come that ye may have life, and may have it more abundantly." (John, x, 10.) "This is eternal life, that they know Thee, the only true God, and Jesus Christ whom Thou hast sent." (John, xvii, 3.) "If thou wouldst enter into life, keep the Commandments." (Mat., xix, 17.) Thus Jesus spoke, thus the well-beloved Son of the Father

Rt. Rev. S. V. Ryan, D.D.

Rt. Rev. K. C. Flasch, D.D.

Rt. Rev. E. P. Wadhams, D.D.

Rt. Rev. L. S. McMahon, D.D.

Rt. Rev. Francis McNeirny, D.D.

Rt. Rev. James A. Healy, D.D.

Rt. Rev. John Verlin, D.D.

Rt. Rev. J. Rademacher, D.D.

Rt. Rev. Thomas A. Becker, D.D.

taught all through His public ministry, after His glorious resurrection, and even to the day "when, giving commandments by the Holy Ghost to the Apostles whom he had chosen, He was taken up." (Acts, i, 2.) The mission of Jesus was not to close with His mortal life. His office of Teacher, Master and Law-giver was to be perpetuated down through the ages. He came to save all men, and "there is no other name under heaven whereby we can be saved but the name of Jesus." Belief in His revealed truths and obedience to His laws are made the essential conditions of salvation. "He that believeth not shall be condemned." "If thou wouldst enter into life keep the Commandments." These truths must then be taught, these Commandments made known and enforced, and hence Jesus bequeaths His powers with His divine mission to the Apostles. "As the Father sent Me, I also send you. Going, teach all nations, teaching them to observe all things whatsoever I have commanded you." And thus Jesus is to-day, in this nineteenth century, as truly and as certainly our Teacher, Master and Legislator as when from that bright overhanging cloud the Father's voice proclaimed, "This is My beloved Son, hear ye Him." The Church of God was thus to continue His mission; and as her mission was not to invent new doctrines, nor to reveal new articles of faith, but sacredly and jealously to guard the deposit of faith, unerringly to explain and interpret revealed truth, and infallibly to define faith and morals; so, in like manner, her office is not to make new commandments, though invested with all needful authority to legislate for her children; her office is not to impose new burdens on the consciences of her children, but rather to expound and interpret and enforce the divine law; and hence the precepts of the Church are generally only determinations of God's commandments, more explicit, full and detailed reiterations of what God's holy law commands. This is obviously the case in regard to the commandments of the Church, to which I have been requested this evening to direct your thoughts, and to which, because of its vital importance, its vast far-reaching influence on society, on the religious and moral character of the people, I would most respectfully ask your serious attention. The first commandment of the Church is, then, the sanctification of the Lord's day and religious festivals—to hear Mass, and rest from servile work on Sundays and holydays of obligation.

In order not to trespass too much on your kind indulgence, I will try this evening to confine myself to the consideration of the obligation incumbent on all Christians of keeping the first commandment of God's Church and the means of observing it, the grounds on which it rests, and the duties which it imposes. Besides the observance of the Sabbath, under the Jewish dispensation, other festivals were by God's own command to be kept holy, religious rites and other holy sacrifices were prescribed on other days besides the Sabbath. So, also, from the earliest ages, the Christian Church instituted and religiously solemnized various feasts, differing in different countries, and varying according to times and circumstances, principally intended to keep in grateful and loving memory the chief mysteries of our blessed Saviour's life, the glories and prerogatives of His immaculate Mother, the example and heroic sanctity of the saints. These religious festivals are often epochs in our lives, hallowed by sweetest memories, to which we look forward with pleasing anticipation; to which we look back with unmingled pleasure. Blessed festivals, they are green, refreshing oases in the desert of our dreary, plodding life, and not a doubt, but they tend materially to keep alive the spirit of piety, to impress more deeply on Christian souls the great mysteries of religion, to serve as outposts to guard the citadel of faith; and hence we should ever cherish these festivals of our Church, and although I may not stop now to dwell upon the wisdom of the Church in instituting festivals, more or less directly connected with the leading mysteries of faith, or to urge the many pressing motives that should impel dutiful children to be faithful in the observance of these religious holydays, it will suffice to say that we are bound under pain of mortal sin to observe them as the Church commands, in virtue of the ecclesiastical precept, by hearing Mass, and resting from all unnecessary servile works, unless when compliance with the precept would entail a grievous inconvenience, amounting to a physical or moral impossibility.

Apart from the strict obligation of obedience to the precepts of the Church, the pious Catholic will never fail on them to assist at the offices of the Church, to renew his fervor and rekindle devotion, and reap for himself the rich harvest of grace and spiritual blessings attached to their religious observance. We must ever remember with St. Augustine, "that no man can have God for his Father who has not the Church for his mother." Obedience to the Church is identical with obedience to God; "He that hears you, hears Me."

The observance of the precepts of the Church will be the criterion of our fidelity to the divine law, and this in turn will be the true test and measure of our love of God. "If you love Me keep My Commandments."

But, my dear brethren, we are principally concerned with the observance of the Sunday, the Christian Sabbath—only premising that the general observance of the Sunday throughout the Christian world is a glorious testimony to the authority and traditions of the Church of God—for only to her authority and her venerable traditions can the Christian appeal in justification of the law abrogating the Jewish Sabbath and substituting the Christian Sunday. This substitution implies not only the abrogation of the Jewish Sabbath day, but it implies that the ancient provisional dispensation has been replaced by the new and more perfect law of grace, that the Church has supplanted the Synagogue, that Christ, who came not to destroy the law but to fulfill it, having entered into His rest, has become the Mediator of a better testament, the High Priest of the new alliance, and that the priesthood of Aaron has been succeeded by the everlasting priesthood of Christ; that the sacrifices of the old law have been superseded by that "one oblation of the body of Christ by which He hath perfected forever them that are sanctified," by that one pure and holy sacrifice, which, according to the prophet, "from the rising of the sun to the going down thereof shall be offered to the name of the God of Hosts."

The Christian Church, prescribing for Christians the observance of the Christian Sabbath without trenching on the substance of the divine law, has made it obligatory upon us to hear Mass and rest from servile work. Though the observance of the particular day and the ceremonial rites has been altered and abrogated, the law itself of keeping the Sabbath holy substantially remains. The obligation of observing this divine law in substance and in spirit has not been and could not be abolished; resting on the imprescriptible law of nature itself, it goes back to a higher source than any mere positive enactments.

Learned doctors, and among them the Angel of the Schools,

regard the duty of observing a certain fixed day, recurring at regular intervals of about seven days, as appertaining to the moral law, imprinted by the Creator's hand upon the human soul. The antiquity, universality and unanimity of its observance by all nations and peoples and tribes and tongues, from the cradle of the human race to our own day, prove it rooted in our very being, flowing from the first principles of reason, born of primitive instincts, and consequently the obligation of observing it we can neither ignore nor repudiate. To this law of nature was superadded a positive command of God even before the written tablets were given on Sinai's Mount. Even anterior to the patriarchal times the Sabbath was kept holy. From creation's dawn, when the morning stars sang together and the sons of God made joyful melody in praise of their Maker, the voice of man was attuned to the music of the spheres, praising the Eternal in thanksgiving for the great benefit of creation, commemorating the Maker's rest from His work.

This divine ordinance thus imprinted on the heart of man, thus universally recognized and observed, received an additional sanction, a new promulgation amid the thunders of Mount Sinai, and became, as it were, divinely and indestructibly stereotyped when the finger of God sculptured in stone the command, "Remember thou keep holy the Sabbath day."

Thus this divine Commandment comes to us with holiest sanctions, and this law of God our Maker, our Master, our Sovereign Lord, who can claim the homage of our whole lives, and to whom all our days and years belong on the title of creation, so undeniably sacred in its origin, so variously promulgated, so divinely sanctioned, it were surely a grievous sin to disobey.

To this law the Church of God has added a new consecration. In the Christian dispensation the Christian Sabbath commemorates a work infinitely transcending the material creation—the work of redemption consummated and crowned by the resurrection of Jesus, sealed by the pentecostal advent of the divine Spirit; and therefore the Church adds her sanction to the law inaugurating her work of saving souls made in the image of God, redeemed by Christ, sanctified by His Holy Spirit, and thus consecrating to the ever adorable Trinity a day already on so many titles sacred. Whether, then, we consider the authority which commands it or the glorious mysteries clustering around and hallowing it, we cannot fail to realize the sacredness of the day therein blessed and the obligation of keeping it holy.

Well, then, may we repeat that this law of sanctifying the Sunday comes to us with the very highest and holiest sanctions— the law of nature dictates it, primordial revelation enjoins it, the positive law of God prescribes it, the ecclesiastical law commands it. But this obligation is incumbent on society as well as on individuals. That is, man, not only as an individual person, but as a member of society, must pay homage to God. It does not suffice to praise God in private; we must worship God in public. Deists as well as Christian doctors teach that the obligation of public worship, of worshiping God in public, and not merely in private, is of the very essence of the law of nature. Hence we find that this unalterable law of consecrating one day in the week to the public worship of God, Christian society has everywhere recognized and enforced, and so from earliest Apostolic times the observance of the Sunday became of civil as well as ecclesiastical precept.

Civil rulers in all Christian lands, following the lead of the first Christian emperor, have accepted, sanctioned and enforced the universal ordinance of God's Church, and, therefore, besides all this solemn sanction already mentioned, the sanctification of the Sunday has the sanction of the civil law.

This brings us at length to the second most important, because most practical, consideration: How are we as Christians bound to sanctify the Christian Sabbath? The authority that has transferred to the Sunday its binding obligation is unquestionably the best qualified to determine the nature, conditions and extent of the obligation imposed, and therefore, though ours is not a Jewish or a Puritan Sabbath, it were a great mistake, it were indeed a pernicious error to suppose that the Catholic Church could sanction, connive at, or in any way be made responsible for the sinful desecration of the Sunday by those who set at defiance the law of God and her own solemn injunction, declaring the Sunday holy, prescribing for its due observance not only rest from servile work, but attendance at divine worship—the holy Mass.

Whilst we can have no sympathy with the gloomy, cheerless and fanatical spirit that would take all the sunshine and joyousness out of a day commemorating events that make every Christian soul thrill with religious joy, a day gladdened by the glory and triumph of the risen Saviour, a day made bright by the advent of the spirit of light and life coming to irradiate the Christian world, and to inflame all Christian hearts, yet we must say that we rejoice exceedingly to see the general observance of the Sunday in our cherished land, and we congratulate our fellow-citizens of all religious denominations at this evidence of Chrisianity and this glorious tribute to Christian faith.

We devoutly hope and we fervently pray that our fellow-citizens of all religious denominations may ever jealously guard this point of revealed faith, and that the spirit and the law of our land may ever be in harmony, as it is now, with the spirit of the Church and the law of God. Catholics, surely, who recognize the Church as the spouse of Jesus Christ, the organ of the Holy Spirit, the divinely commissioned interpreter of God's holy law, the infallible teacher of faith and morals, can have no excuse for the profanation of a day which she commands her children to keep holy. To spend in dissipation, riotous excesses, debauchery or sinful indulgence the day consecrated to God and claimed by Him, on so many titles, were indeed a crime, a sacrilege, and an outrage on public morality. No wonder, then, that zealous pastors, holy Popes, Provincial and Plenary Councils should most earnestly exhort the faithful to fidelity in the observance of the Sunday; no wonder that they should raise their voices, and, in sharp, clear and ringing tones, denounce abuses by which the Sunday is profaned, God robbed of the homage due Him, faith, "that cometh by hearing," imperiled, the Word of God neglected, the public conscience debauched and society demoralized. Religion reprobates these scandalous abuses, and all good men, irrespective of religious creed or political affinity, should frown down the attempt to change the religious Sabbath rest of the Lord's day into public carousing by the unrestricted sale and excessive use of intoxicating drink, by promiscuous excursions, picnics and other similar demoralizing public nuisances.

Whilst, then, we would enter a solemn protest against the growing tendency of assimilating the Sunday to the ordinary week days, and thus forcing the laboring classes, the poor but noble sons of toil, to forego on the Sunday needed rest of mind and body, robbing them of needed relaxation, which the law of nature and nature's God, as well as the law of God's holy Church, legitimatizes and approves—to fulfill a duty of conscience in the interest of religion and morality, and for the honor of our holy mother Church, we must raise our voice against a still more crying evil, and abuse more to be deprecated, that of making an exception in favor of Sunday commerce in intoxicating drink, thus making this a privileged traffic, and those engaged in it a favored class, while imposing restrictions on and prohibiting on the Sunday all other honest trades, all other honorable avocations by which men gain their livelihood. This, we fear, would be to invite the profanation of the Lord's day, to expose our good people, and especially the young, to dangerous occasions; in a word, to open such places of business on the Sunday, just as on the ordinary week day, is to put a premium on the sale of liquor, to encourage the vice of intemperance, and open an avenue to licentious excesses of all kinds on the Sunday. This no Christian community could tolerate; this no man who loves his country or his kind will sanction; this the Catholic, who has the honor of his Church and the salvation of souls at heart, must reprobate. Catholics, distinguished, as they confessedly are, for the religious observance of the Sunday, should tolerate nothing that has even the appearance of evil, or that might appear to bring a stain on the fair name of their holy Church. And think not, dear brethren, that in thus enforcing the sanctification of the Sunday we are innovating; think not that it is only the pastors and the Popes and the councils of to-day that insist on the strict religious observance of the Sunday; believe not that this is an invention of narrow-minded fanaticism or bigoted Puritanism. Such legislation is thoroughly Catholic, it breathes the very spirit of Christianity, and the Church from the earliest ages has insisted upon the stringent and religious observance of the Sunday. From the earliest ages pastors of the Church and civil magistrates were at one, acted in concert in enforcing the observance of the Christian Sabbath. At the solicitation of bishops of the Church laws were enacted by the Roman emperors protecting the faithful against scandalous and criminal diversions on the Lord's day, and in the year 425 the Council of Carthage petitioned the Emperor Theodosius to protect the people against similar abuses. The great St. Charles Borromeo, the ter-centennial of whose blessed death, in unison with the whole Christian world, we celebrated but a few days before the opening of our council, in at least two of his famous Councils of Milan, positively declares that sotting in taverns and ale-houses on Sundays and festivals is a most criminal and scandalous sin. A Council of Cologne in 1536 orders taverns to be closed, and no riotous or excessive drinking on Sunday to be tolerated. In 1557 a Council of Paris ordained the same in almost identical terms. Thus we find that the Church of God, from the very commencement, has insisted most urgently on the avoidance of those things that are calculated to scandalize others, or may become a source of danger and of sin to her own children, and in doing so she has but interpreted and enforced the divine law, "Remember thou keep holy the Sabbath day," and faithfully expressed the mind and will and law of Jesus Christ, who declares that "He came not to destroy the law but to fulfill it," to perfect it, to Christianize it.

For the unsought and unexpected honor of being able during this great Plenary Council of ours to raise my humble voice to plead for the strict observance of a law of our holy Church, which we hold to be of the last importance, for the preservation of the faith, for the growth of the Church and the prosperity of religion in these United States, I am most thankful. To spend the Sunday in sinful dissipation and scandalous profanation is a sacrilege, an insult to God, on a day by Himself called holy; it is, too, an outrage on Christian morals, whose tendency is to blunt the moral sense of the community and destroy the last remaining vestige of respect for revealed religion and Christian faith. It begets a spirit of lawlessless and contempt for all authority—civil, ecclesiastical and divine—enjoining the observance of the Sunday, and hence it is a loosening of the very foundation of society; and, therefore, it behooves all good men who have the interest of society and religion at heart, to pause and reflect whither this growing disregard for the sacredness of the Christian Sabbath is leading us. For Catholics, however, it is not enough that the Sunday should not be a day of sin and sacrilege and a Sabbath of Satan; it must not be a day of idleness and sloth and a Sabbath of the brute irrational beasts; it must in reality be a holy day, sanctified by the holy observance which the Church commands, and did time permit I would fain dwell a few moments upon that holy Mass which we are bound to hear, and which the Church prescribes in order to sanctify the Sunday. I can, my dear brethren, only call your attention to the fact that this holy Mass gives to God true divine homage, fulfills all the ends of sacrifice, enables man to discharge the obligations of adoration, thanksgiving, propitiation and supplication which he owes to God, and thus the pure oblation, foretold by the prophet, supersedes all the ancient sacrifices, and becomes the source of blessing and of heavenly grace to the Christian world.

Let us then, my dear brethren, faithfully keep the Sunday holy; it is truly the Lord's day; let us then consecrate the day, and not simply a half hour of it but the whole day, as far as possible, to Him to whom it belongs, in the spirit of Christian faith and Catholic piety, according to the prescriptions of the Church of God, and thereby give glory to God, edification to our neighbor, and bring grace and salvation to our own souls.

Faith and Reason.

SERMON OF RIGHT REV. J. A. WATTERSON, D.D.,

BISHOP OF COLUMBUS

THE subject assigned to me by the Most Rev. Apostolic Delegate, "The Education of the Laity," was a very congenial one to me; but, as much of my ground was covered by his Lordship of Peoria in the discourse you listened to last night, it has been suggested to me to change my theme. I trust, that what I will therefore say to you this evening on another topic will be neither uninteresting nor uninstructive, especially in these days of rationalism and naturalism, in which religion seems to consist in giving as much as possible to man, and as little as possible to Almighty God.

A great number of persons, particularly young persons, are governed by fashion in the formation of their opinions. Some, without any pains to form opinions for themselves at all, allow their language and outward actions to take their form and coloring from those with whom they associate. Many a young man has been fool enough to say, not in his heart, but with his lips, "there is no truth in revelation," because he hoped to gain eclat by the bold impiety of his language. Many another, without knowledge, without examination, without reflection, has scoffed at all belief in miracles and mysteries, in order to win the name of thinking for himself and bowing to no authority, but that of his own individual reason. Irreligion is fashionable, and therefore contagious. Incredulity is tempting, as the shortest way to a very pitiful kind of Ingersollian distinction. This evil, the bad legacy of three hundred and fifty years of disputation, doubt and denial

Rt. Rev. Wm. Geo. McCloskey, D.D.

Rt. Rev. F. Janssens, D.D.

Rt. Rev. W. M. Wigger, D.D.

Rt. Rev. John C. Neraz, D.D.

Rt. Rev. Henry Cosgrove, D.D.

Rt. Rev. N. A. Gallagher, D.D.

Rt. Rev. H. P. Northrop, D.D.

Rt. Rev. D. Manucy, D.D.

Rt. Rev. C. P. Maes, D.D.

in religious matters, is not yet completely exorcised. This anti-Christian spirit, though often rebuked, is not yet banished. A long period must elapse, before the world will see again what has been briefly, but happily, described as an age of faith, an age in which all the civilized nations of the earth will form a Christendom once more; when all will be united in the belief of the same religious truths and in the bonds of a common Christian charity and a common Christian brotherhood. We may salute that blessed epoch from afar; we may long for its advent, and each one in his own way and measure do something to hasten its return; but no one of us may reasonably hope to witness its arrival, and then sink to rest in peace with the *nunc dimittis* on his lips: "Now dost Thou dismiss Thy servant, O Lord, in peace, because mine eyes have seen Thy salvation." But it seems to me, that we are advancing towards it. The spirit of doubt and denial has nearly run its course; and it is time for the human mind, worn and desolate with its long and weary flight over the ocean of uncertainty, to return to the ark of salvation, which is its only resting-place. The idolatry of reason, of man's individual reason, must succumb at last, like the old pagan idolatries, to the divine authority of faith.

Attempting to show you this evening the utter inadequacy of reason, whether as a substitute for faith, or as the judge and arbiter of faith, I have not the slightest fear, that I will lay myself open to the charge of being an enemy of reason. To the right use of reason I am not opposed. To reason herself I can have no hostility. In fact I am going to appeal to reason throughout the course of my observations. It is the abuse of a good thing, it is the idolatry of reason, that I oppose; and it is a most criminal abuse of reason to attempt to substitute her teachings for the revelation of Almighty God, or to make her the judge of Him and of His infallible declarations.

There is a philosophy, which, fixing itself on the firm basis of revelation, so far as religion and morals are concerned, is content with hunting arguments and illustrations from history, analogy and experience, in favor of the truths which it reveres. It knows full well that the supernatural is far above the sphere of its contracted powers; that its true province is the wide field of nature, in which it has room enough to expatiate and employ in fruitful research its principles of natural science, which would only be misapplied, if brought to bear upon the supernatural. It is no irreverent scrutinizer of majesty; it does not strive, with rash and impious hand, to lift the veil of mystery, but, approaching the sanctuary of God, the Holy of Holies, it bows in humble adoration before His throne, and acknowledges His supreme authority. This is the right use of reason; this is true philosophy.

But there is another philosophy, which, professing not only ignorance, but also disbelief of all revealed truth, undertakes to give us the speculations of pure, unaided reason, as all-sufficient to guide us through this life and prepare us for the next; and this is the substitute which is kindly offered us for that religion, which has civilized and reformed, enlightened and blessed mankind. Now, my dear brethren, it cannot be wrong to examine what titles to our respect and confidence are possessed by this bold pretender; what certain truths requiring our belief, what lessons of wisdom to be reduced to practice, have been taught or can be taught by this mere philosophy of reason.

The most important and deeply interesting questions to the human mind are those which concern the nature, attributes and providence of God, our relations with Him and our duty towards Him, our origin, the purpose of our present existence, our future destiny and the causes of the evils which surround us. These are the great problems which reason has tried to solve from the very dawn of history to the present day. Now, what progress had she made towards a right solution of any one of them? Can it be shown that of herself she ever discovered one single, solitary truth regarding even one of them? On the contrary, is it not certain to a demonstration, that she has fallen into the most serious errors on each and every one of them? Every scholar will admit, that the wisest and best of the philosophers of pagan antiquity did but little credit to reason by their researches into these matters. Their ignorance and blindness surprise us; their degrading errors seem to us almost inconceivable. Yet it must be observed, that while the mistakes and absurdities, which abound in their speculations, are their own, whatever fragments of truth may be found amid their masses of error are just as certainly not their own, are not discoveries of reason, but vestiges of revelation. It is one thing for reason to discover a truth, and quite another thing to recognize the form and lineaments of truth in that which is proposed to her as such. We would laugh at the silly arrogance of the man who would pretend to have discovered the propositions of Euclid or the theory of Newton, merely because he believed in them and could repeat their demonstrations.

Reason herself, though unenlightened by revelation, cannot deny, on the contrary, must admit as a probability at least, that our Creator, at the very origin of our race, may have manifested something of His wisdom, power and goodness to His rational and therefore responsible creatures, may have prescribed their duties to Him and to each other by imposing laws upon them; may have held out to them the hope of rewards and the fear of punishments hereafter. Now, this is precisely what we know to have been done on the testimony of the inspired writings, which give us an authentic account of the facts, and are corroborated by all the monuments and traditions of our race. I read a book some time ago, called "*La Bible sans la Bible*," ("The Bible without the Bible,") written by the Abbe Gainet, in which he shows that, even though the records of the ancient Testament had perished, all the salient facts that are chronicled in the book of Genesis regarding the general welfare of our race, would be substantially known to us from the monumental and traditionary history of the various nations of the globe. The dogmas of the existence of the Creator and Ruler of the universe, the necessity of sacrifice, priesthood and religious worship generally, the immortality of the soul, future rewards and punishments, and the fall and promised restoration of our race, were not the fruits of philosophic inquiry. Revealed by the Almighty to our first parents, to be transmitted to all their descendants, found among the most rude and barbarous as well as the most civilized and refined nations of the ancient world, they were the common inheritance of the human race, the traditionary religion of mankind. In the course of time, however, that same neglect and indifference, which are still exhibited by so many, and to which every man is liable, if he is not faithful to the grace of God, the power of passion and vice to darken the mind, and the pride of reason exercised about things entirely above her sphere of comprehension, gradually so dimmed and weakened the remembrance of these great truths of primitive revelation, blended with them so many errors and absurdities, and engrafted so many superstitions on them, that the fair image of truth was barely to be recognized in the monstrous systems of polytheism and idolatry, which prevailed in every nation but one of the ancient world, and which still prevail, wherever the Christian revelation is not yet received. Look, for example, at China and Japan. It is the boast, that their books and public schools antedate Christianity itself. They are intellectually cultivated and commercially prosperous, and have been so for centuries and centuries. Their philosophy has been studied with interest by keen observers, and yet with all their enterprise and culture, they are still groping in the darkness and groveling in the filth of the most abominable idolatry.

The philosophers of the Grecian States and of the Roman Empire were certainly men of the highest genius and ability. While the world lasts, the monuments they have left us will bear witness to their herculean and collossal powers of mind. Indeed it is claimed, that the human intellect, in point of natural reason, attained its highest excellence in the old pagan days. The heathen philosophers were acute, subtle, earnest, eager, energetic, persevering in their search for truth. They devoted themselves, body and soul, heart and mind, to moral, metaphysical and theological investigations. In their ardent inquiries they could discern absurdity and folly in the religion which they practiced; and by visiting in person, or collecting the reports of travellers who had visited the East, they occasionally caught some echoes of the faith of a chosen and separate people, who worshiped one only God in spirit and in truth. And yet, with all their advantages, they were only groping in the dark; and their own conclusions were so far from satisfying their minds, from appeasing the mighty hunger of their souls, that we find them all confessing their doubts, uncertainty and ignorance, and some of them openly declaring that reason had utterly failed, that philosophy could not enlighten them, that there was no hope for man but in a revelation from above. They never dreamed of reforming the popular religions of their respective countries. They might as well have attempted to command the tempest, chain the winds or check the tides; for, supposing them to have had what they unquestionably had not, the will to sacrifice themselves in such a cause, and the power to force unpalatable truths upon unwilling multitudes, who were ready to stone or burn them for their pains, they had no truths to teach, no doctrines which they firmly believed, even on the first and what are sometimes called the fundamental points. They had done what man, left to himself in this dark world, could do to arrive at truth. We know the state of their minds, the extent of their knowledge and their ignorance; for their opinions are recorded in their writings; and we confidently summon them as witnesses to prove the utter insufficiency of reason to guide us through this life or prepare us for the next.

Let us select one or two of the questions, which are obviously most important and would necessarily claim the first attention; for example, the doctrine of God, Creator of all things. This tenet was originally revealed, and was always believed by those who retained that pristine revelation. By arguing from effect to cause they were able to reason out the existence of God with the natural power of intellect alone; but the proper attribute of creative power was too great, too vast for the comprehension of unaided reason; and that pure, simple and sublime idea of omnipotence, which the Israelite and Christian acquire in childhood, never entered the minds of the wisest sages of antiquity. To create is to make out of nothing, to draw into being from no being, from a state of possibility to actual existence without any pre-existing materials whatsoever. Now, reason by herself could not conceive how anything could be created in the proper sense of that term. Matter exists; therefore it must have existed from all eternity. It might be shaped or fashioned into different forms, differently combined, variously modified, as it is on a small scale by the hand of man, or the machinery of man's invention; but drawn from nothing! called into being by the fiat of Almighty will! reason by her own efforts never reached this sublime, but now familiar belief. This may seem to some a purely speculative question; but there are practical consequences of the highest moment, resulting from the utter failure of reason to realize the truth of a God Creator. For, according to any system of philosophy or to any religion, save that revealed to us, God was not regarded as the Creator of man in the proper sense of that term; and man, therefore, did not look upon himself as the creature of God. He did not owe his existence to God, but at most his form and mode of being. This is evident from the old pagan fables concerning the origin of man. He could not, therefore, call God his Father. He knew not whether the Deity cared for him or not. He might fear His superior power, but he could not love Him. The idea of loving Him never entered his mind. Having read a good many of the pagan writings, I confidently assert to-night, that, in the whole range of the Greek and Latin classics, there is not a phrase to show that the first and greatest Commandment, "Thou shalt love the Lord, thy God, with thy whole heart, and with thy whole soul, and with all thy strength, and all thy mind," was ever thought of by them. And looking at the evils, to which he was subject, the miseries of that condition, in which the Deity had placed him, and the apparent moral disorder of the world, man could scarcely feel that he owed either gratitude or love to a Supreme Being, whom he did not know as his Creator and his Father. No, my dear brethren, in all the loftiest flights that philosophy ever took, she was never able to reach the sublime simplicity of that wondrous prayer, which we learn from the lips of our blessed Saviour on the Mount: "Our Father, who art in Heaven, hallowed be Thy name, Thy kingdom come, Thy will be done on earth as it is in heaven." Another practical consequence of the utter failure of reason was an almost total ignorance of the second great command, which is like unto the first: "Thou shalt love thy neighbor as thyself, for God's sake." Hence, that heartless indifference to human suffering, that cruel barbarity, that bloodthirstiness, which disgraced every pagan nation, exhibited by them in peace as well as in war, in the heroism of Horatius, in the patriotism of Brutus, in the cruel treatment of prisoners and slaves, in their inhumanity to women and children, in their human sacrifices, in their bloody gladiatorial shows, and in the practice which universally prevailed, as it still does in China and every nation not enlightened by divine revelation, the practice of exposing infants to death as soon as they were born, which both law and philosophy sanctioned among Greeks and Romans in the days of their greatest refinement, and which was never declared illegal, until the first Christian emperor, Constantine the Great, ascended the throne in the beginning of the fourth century of the Christian era. Looking at the frequency of feticide, infanticide and abortion, seeing how shamefully and almost barefacedly they are practiced in our large towns and cities at the present day, may we not rationally fear that with all our boasted progress and enlightenment, we are going back to paganism instead of advancing towards the perfection of our race? We have all sympathized with the pagan audience that rose in the great Roman theatre one day to applaud this sentiment of an actor: "*Homo sum; humani nihil a me alienum puto*—I am a man, and feel an interest in all that concerns my fellow-men." Why is it never noted that the whole plot of this play of Terence turns on the fact, that the father, who utters this noble sentiment, discovers his child, supposed to be lost, because exposed to death in its infancy according to a custom, which was so well regulated, legalized and sanctioned, that when the new-born child was presented to its father, if he did not take it in his arms, if he turned his back upon it, it was to die as a matter of course? We hear men in our own days repeating the ancient sentiment: "We are men and think nothing foreign to us that concerns the human race." Humanitarianism is fast becoming a substitute for religion; and yet, with all our pretended philanthropy, men, ignoring the fatherhood of God, are fast forgetting the common brotherhood of men, as is evident from the conflicts between rich and poor, capital and labor, authority and obedience, the strikes and riots and revolutions that have so often convulsed society during the present century.

The idea of creative power being totally lost, all religion might have perished with it, but that the imperfect remains of traditionary truth, the feeling sense, that religion after all is the first great want of humanity, the hunger and thirst of the soul for some object of supreme veneration and worship, the idea of Divinity originally and indelibly stamped on the mind of the whole human race drew men back from the dark gulf of atheism, at least practical atheism, towards which reason was hurrying them by her restless efforts to measure with her feeble powers the infinite and incomprehensible.

Let us interrogate philosophy as to the fruits of her researches on another point of importance and vital interest to all mankind. Divine Providence, a superintending care of the moral and physical universe, was merely a question, on both sides of which reason had much to say. Fate, blind, inexorable destiny, a power superior to gods as well as men, was commonly supposed to be the ruler of the universe. Moreover, the question of a Providence was complicated by the want of a clear and firm belief in the unity of God. The philosophers, who listened to the voice of tradition, and thus received an intimation of this important truth, still fell short of any just conception of the relative or moral attributes of the Supreme Being, whose existence and absolute attributes they indistinctly knew. Some regarded Him as the soul of the universe, animating the whole frame of nature; others as an inert being, indifferent to the affairs of men, or committing their government to inferior gods. Whether He could be propitiated by man, whether prayer, sacrifice, or any other religious act was necessary or could aught avail, they professed themselves utterly unable to determine. The Epicureans released all their gods from every sort of care, and to that extent there are thousands of Epicureans also at the present day. The Stoics thought that man was all-sufficient for himself; and accordingly they pronounced it weakness to pray for bodily blessings, and waste of time and folly to petition heaven for the goods of the mind; and in that sense there are plenty of Stoics also in our own times. The Peripatetics were doubtful and contradictory, and the Academicians ready on this, as on every other point, to maintain either side of the question. In fact there was more of truth in the popular superstitions than in the speculations of philosophy. The people prayed to their false deities; they called on gods that could neither hear nor help them; they offered their petitions to beings more vicious than themselves, and oftentimes for objects most unholy. But still they recognized the sacred duty, the principle of prayer. The philosopher, on the contrary, guided by pure reason, scoffed at this divine instinct of our nature; this in-born tendency of our being; this universal sentiment of our race. He proposed to rob poor human nature of its last defence of prayer, the language of faith, the voice of hope, the cry of weakness and of want, the only refuge from despair—prayer, the bond of union between man and his Creator, the homage which we offer Him in concert with the heavenly hosts that minister round His everlasting throne, the one of all our acts and occupations which immediately and of itself prepares and practices and fits us for heaven. And if he, who at the pressent day acknowledges no higher philosophy than that of reason, does sometimes bend the knee in supplication to his Maker, it is not from any certainty that his philosophy gives him of the necessity or efficacy of prayer; for how can reason assure him that the Deity wishes to be invoked, or that He who has foreseen, predetermined and predestined all things, will hearken to the petitions of weak and erring mortals? When, therefore, he prays, he is obeying a higher voice than that of reason—the voice of conscience, enlightened by some rays of Divine revelation.

On the question of the immortality of the soul, reason may be expected to speak a more confident language. It is emphatically the faith of the human race. It was clearly revealed from the beginning. The soul, whose immortality is in question, is our own; and through consciousness we have some natural knowledge of it as the substance which thinks, remembers, wills, and differs in all its ascertained properties from body or matter. It might then be inferred, without the help of revelation, that the soul is not subject to the decay or dissolution to which the body is liable; and could only be destroyed by the same Omnipotence which called it into being. Yet human philosophy, by its ceaseless questionings, has been able to overshadow even this subject with its gloomy doubts. The wisest and best men of antiquity affirmed that the soul was immaterial, and therefore indestructible. They shrunk with instinctive horror from the prospect of annihilation; they fondly hoped to live beyond the grave; they thought that the universal traditionary belief must be right. At all events they would rather err on this side, if err they must; they would cherish the delusion, if it were a delusion; they would cling to the belief in a hereafter, as the only adequate motive and recompense of virtue, the solace of adversity, the support of wronged and suffering innocence, the last hope of trembling humanity.

Those who are versed in Greek and Roman lore will recognize the argument, while at the same time they will sympathize with the feelings of these ancient advocates of the immortality of the soul; but, after all, what is the character of this argument? It is mainly not an appeal to reason, but to the instincts and sentiments of our race. How different, too, is this opinion or persuasion of theirs from the firm, immovable and unwavering confidence which revelation gives! How unlike the Christian's "*Credo in resurrectionem mortuorum et vitam æternam. Amen*—I believe in the resurrection of the body and life everlasting. Amen." But philosophy never did and never will produce a *Credo*. It never did and never will construct a creed. On this subject it held not so much the language of certainty, as of hope and desire blended with fears and haunted with doubts, which philosophy had not the power to exorcise. For then as now there were those who, vindicating the rights of reason, claimed some firmer foundation for their faith and would not believe what did not present to their minds the character of evident and indisputable truth. "We want proofs," these philosophers exclaimed: "we want proofs from reason; we want conclusive arguments addressed to reason; and you offer us hopes and fears, instinctive feelings, a natural dread of annihilation; you offer us vulgar superstitions, and your crude notions of the substance of the soul, which we do not feel bound to admit, which you cannot prove true, and which science may hereafter refute."

Pressed by such difficulties, the nobler spirits among the old philosophers felt, that reason alone was but a treacherous guide, and turning reproachful looks upon her, and uttering a cry of distress, a prayer for help, took refuge, so to speak, in the temple of hope, resolved to wait there, until their ignorance should be enlightened by some messenger from above. In truth, the strongest testimonies of the absolute insufficiency of reason to determine this and similar questions, abound in the writings of Cicero and Plato, and may be found in the declarations of other philosophers. On this very subject, and after a full discussion of it, Cicero, though persuaded of the immortality of the soul, says in his Tusculan questions: "It would require a God to decide which of the opinions is true: as for ourselves, we cannot even determine which is the more probable." Plato, in his work called Phaedo, had previously put into the mouth of Socrates the following language, speaking also of the immortality of the soul: "The clear knowledge of these things is in this life impossible, or at least very difficult. The philosopher, therefore, should hold to that which appears more probable, unless he has some surer light, or the *word of God Himself* to guide him." This is remarkable language from a pagan; but stranger still that rationalists of the present day have not risen even to its height.

Now, we ask whether reason, which could not rise to anything higher than a mere probability, a cherished though possibly a delusive persuasion on a matter so clearly proposed to it by the belief of mankind, could ever have discovered this truth, if it had not been primitively revealed to our race? It is very easy for a man at the present day to say: "My reason teaches me to know and adore God; my reason teaches me to believe in a Providence; my reason teaches me to expect an immortal life hereafter; my reason teaches me this, that and the other thing." He stands on the vantage ground, to which Christianity, not philosophy, has raised him. He lives in the light of divine revelation, though, like some African tribes that we read of, he may curse and blaspheme the luminary that vivifies and irradiates his mind. Had he not been reared in a Christian land, under the influence of Christian ideas, Christian traditions and Christian faith, he might, with that same boastful reason for his guide, be to-day a groveling and superstitious idolator, or at best a doubting and bewildered inquirer after unknown truth.

Reason, then, is not that pillar of light which is to guide us safely through the desert of this life to the promised land that lies beyond. We needed a revelation, and a revelation has been given us. Knowing how the wisest and the best of the philosophers of antiquity longed for the dawning of this heavenly light, we would suppose that its appearance was hailed with universal joy. But history tells us quite a different story; and the erring reason, the proud, rebellious reason of man, was not the least potent and conspicuous among the formidable antagonists of early Christianity, just as it is not the least powerful of the adversaries of Christianity at the present day. The Cross of Christ was indeed a stumbling-block to the Jews, but to the Greeks, the educated, refined, the æsthetic and philosophic Greeks and Romans, it was downright folly, as it is downright folly to the æsthetic and philosophic pagans of our modern times. It happened then, as it often happens now, that reason was ready with her line and plummet, her compass and her square, to sound the depths and take all the dimensions of truths, which reached from the highest heavens even to the lowest abyss of hell; and when her line was out, she was sure that she had fathomed the fathomless, and when her compass was stretched to its very utmost, she was quite sure that she had measured Infinitude itself. It is a great question, no doubt, whether the doctrines of revelation are to be implicitly believed, or subjected to the examination of reason.

But to state the question is to solve it. It is the most presumptuous folly that can possibly be conceived, for man, with the powers of unaided reason, to undertake to determine what God must say, when He speaks to His rational and responsible creatures. It is a most blasphemous inversion of order for the creature to attempt to give laws to the Creator.

> To seize the balance and the rod,
> Rejudge His justice, be the God of God.

It is the finite measuring the infinite; weak, puny, human reason declaring herself the judge and arbiter of divine, eternal reason. When, therefore, anything is proposed to me with the seal of revelation on it, if my reason cannot fathom it, if it surpass my powers of comprehension, am I, therefore, to pronounce it false and reject it as unreasonable? Would not such a rule as this be destructive of revelation itself? Would it not throw us back into the condition of the old pagan philosophers, lost like them, but without their excuse, in the mazes of human opinion? What doctrine of revelation could stand such a foolish test? It has been applied to all of them successively, and as a consequence of its application, all of them have been successively rejected. If it enable you to-day to reject some article of my faith, will it not enable some other man to-morrow to overturn your peculiar belief? And descending step by step through all the grades and forms of religious opinion, must it not inevitably lead to naked deism? And since there is nothing so incomprehensible as Almighty God Himself, nothing so incredible to reason as creation out of nothing, nothing more difficult to understand than a Being self-existent, infinite, independent, eternal, omnipresent in all space and in every minutest point of space, must it not end by denying Him entirely? What other limit has it than downright atheism? Reason then is not, in this sense, the judge of revelation. No one is authorized to reject a doctrine simply because he cannot comprehend it. I speak as a Christian philosopher, not in the interest of my own creed alone, or of any peculiar dogma now, but as the advocate of a common Christianity; and I solemnly denounce a principle, which is not only false, but subversive of human reason as well as divine revelation. Reason herself then, if truly enlightened, will direct us to believe what we cannot comprehend, when its truth is duly attested. While, therefore, not the judge of revelation, she may be the judge of the evidences of revelation. They who do not comprehend the truths of geometry would exhibit little wisdom in pronouncing them false. The immense majority of men who understand nothing of the calculation of an eclipse or the return of a comet, or the nature and velocity of wind currents, should not therefore refuse all credence to the predictions of astronomical and meteorological science. The tribes that live within the tropics are not admired for their extensive knowledge and profound philosophy, when they will not believe that water can become solid, so that men may walk on it, and the huge elephant move securely over its stony surface, though they do not and cannot understand how this may be. The true position evidently is, that our inability to comprehend a fact or doctrine does not by itself authorize us either to affirm it or deny it; but when we have satisfactory evidence of its truth, then we are bound to believe it, whether we comprehend it or not. Now, the dogmas of revealed religion must surpass our comprehension, because they relate to God and to the future life, which to us are subjects essentially mysterious and incomprehensible. The believer is the first to proclaim that such is their nature. He knows that, if you strip them of their character of mystery, you take away one of the most evident marks of their divine origin. He knows, too, that mysteries are not confined to revelation. The most familiar facts in nature are often the most incomprehensible. The union of soul and body, and their mutual action and reaction on each other, the principle of intelligence and affection in brutes, gravitation, electricity, galvanism, magnetism, all the so-called known laws of the physical universe, are so many mysteries, in regard to which we believe the facts that have been ascertained, though we do not and cannot satisfactorily account for them. You all, I trust, hear me to-night. If you do, you know the fact; you know that my voice puts certain waves of air in motion, and these striking the drum of your ears convey the sounds to your outward sense of hearing and my thoughts to the inward intelligence of your souls. You know the fact of this, but how it happens, neither reason nor science is able to explain. There is not a blade of grass, or flower of the field, or dew-drop sparkling on its leaves, or tiniest insect nestling in its chalice, that may not present to the reflecting beholder a multitude of questions, which reason cannot answer. And shall the intellect, which at every turn and every glance is so forcibly reminded of its ignorance and impotence, presume to require of Almighty God a full and perfect explanation of every truth, which He in His wisdom declares to us, before it will condescend to believe His divine attestation?

There is another point of view in which enlightened reason must admit her perfect incompetency to deal with revelation any otherwise than by submissive assent and lowly adoration. I refer to that most extravagant of all the extravagancies of the human mind, its pretended right to improve or amend, in any manner whatsoever, the doctrines and institutions, the system of faith and practice, once declared to us on the part of the Most High. To believe in Christianity, because its Author was the incarnate Son of God, and its promulgators His inspired Apostles, and then to maintain that what was divine at the origin of our faith must change and undergo revision and correction, that it may keep pace with the pretended march of intellect, the progress of human knowledge, the material improvement of our race; to imagine, in a word, that we of the present day can manufacture a better Christianity than the Son of God has made for us and entrusted to our hands is indeed to verify the expressions of the poet, that

> Fools rush in,
> Where angels fear to tread;

And

> Man, weak man,
> Plays such fantastic tricks before high heaven,
> As make the angels weep.

It would be just as rational to pronounce the sun an obsolete and antiquated luminary, quite good enough to give light and warmth and gladness to the world some two or three thousand years ago, but now totally behind the times, utterly unsuited to the increased knowledge, enlarged philosophy and higher wants of this grand and glorious nineteenth century. We might as well cry out: "Down with the sun, and up with Edison and his electric light!" though he has not yet succeeded in making it a respectable substitute for even the smallest star that twinkles its steady twinkle in the quiet midnight sky. Why, if one of the Apostles, rising from the grave, or if an angel from heaven (we are but repeating the energetic language of him who was wrapped to the third heavens), if an angel from heaven were to offer us a new Gospel, a pretended revelation, differing but in one iota from that which the Son of God has given us, our only salutation to the rash innovator must be anathema.

Resting on this firm foundation, the believer is delighted with every effort to enlarge the boundaries of science, and hails with joy every new discovery of truth. He never dreams that Christianity can be endangered by the progress of science. He knows that every tenet of Christian faith is an infallible truth, based on the sure authority of Him who has revealed it. How can that which is true ever be proved false? Or how can any one truth ever be at war with any other truth? Truth is truth eternally. The believer may sometimes hesitate to accept the mere theories of science. He may question, for a while, the arguments on which they rest; but as soon as they work themselves out of the region of scientific theory, and work themselves into the region of demonstrated scientific fact, they become scientific truths, and no believer in revelation can have a moment's fear that religion will in any way be injured by them. Thus the Church hesitated for a time, to abandon even a mere traditional interpretation of a Scriptural text at the demand of Galileo. The Copernican system was afterwards demonstrated to be objectively true; but in its theoretic stage it was subjectively uncertain. Some of the arguments, which Galileo urged in support of it, were false and had to be rejected; and so the Church, always cautious and conservative, hesitated, until the false was separated from the true and the system stood on the solid basis of scientific fact; and then she readily accepted it in its bearing upon Holy Writ. Had Galileo been content to teach the system merely as a theory and to leave the issue to such scientific tests, as would eliminate all uncertainty and doubt, history to-day would be without one of its notable sensations. Again, geology has been urged as contradicting the revealed history of the creation of the world. Some geologists have presumed, that the six days of Genesis must be taken as days of twenty-four hours each. The Church, however, the guardian and interpreter of revelation, has never so defined them; but from the beginning, as is evident from the opinions of many of the early Fathers, she has left us free to accept them either as natural days or as indefinite periods of time; and, waiving the question of the possibility of creation in six days of twenty-four hours each, she leaves the fact entirely to science. Faith is in no wise involved; and geology itself has not yet emerged from its theoretic period. Who imagines that the demonstrations of mathematical science will ever be refuted? Who is afraid that any of the conclusions of geometry will be disturbed by the progress of discovery? Yet no Christian philosopher will pretend that mathematical certainty is higher than the certainty of divine revelation. If this comparison appear bold and hazardous to any one, it can only be because he does not understand the very meaning of the term revelation. He who holds a system of doctrines which he thinks may have been revealed, while he is not perfectly, that is, infallibly certain, that they have been revealed, cannot venture on such a comparison. The reason is obvious. He does not believe truths divinely revealed; he entertains opinions about what has been revealed, and these opinions may be partly true and partly false, or wholly true or wholly false. Such a man is or should be an inquirer, a seeker after the sure and perfect and infallible truths that God has revealed. A believer, a man of Christian faith, he is not and cannot be, as long as a shadow of doubt or uncertainty rests upon his mind.

But reason still claims to be the judge of revelation, so far at least as to feel authorized to choose among revealed dogmas, to give a decided preference to some, and a cold, if not a contemptuous, look to others. According to this notion, some doctrines are essential and must therefore be believed. Others are unimportant, and you may believe them, if you choose, or deny them, dispute about them, proclaim them false, or treat them as altogether unworthy of consideration. The first class of doctrines are fundamental. This is the favorite phrase. They must be retained, because they are supposed to be the foundation, on which the whole edifice of Christianity is based. Admitting the distinction only for the sake of argument, still I would ask, what are the foundations without the superstructure? Surely the foundations of a building will be of very little service when the walls and roof and all the other parts are forcibly taken away. But we are also compelled to ask, how is reason to determine which doctrines are fundamental and which are not? What appears so to the mind of one man may seem very unimportant to another; and experience proves this to be an insuperable difficulty; for they who have assumed the principle in question have never yet been able to designate precisely the fundamental dogmas of Christianity, or to give such a definition or description of them as may enable us to recognize and identify them when we see them. But the principle is a bad one, not only false and impious, but also clearly irrational; for it presumes a revelation only to destroy what it presumes. A revelation supposes that God has spoken to His rational creatures; that He has made known certain things to them which are above their natural comprehension; that He has declared certain truths, given us certain laws and established certain institutions, to enable us to know and attain the end for which we are created. And is it not blasphemy to say that any truths which He in His wisdom has declared to us are of so little consequence, that they may be disputed, denied, spurned with contempt? Is it not a bold defiance of the Omnipotent for man to disregard, to set aside as trivial and useless, to nullify on any pretext whatever any law that God has given him? Is it not ingratitude and insult, combined in the highest degree, to make light of and reject any institution, whether the Church in general or the sacramental system in particular, which He, through infinite mercy and condescension, has established for our sanctification in this life and our eternal happiness in the next? There is wisdom in the homely saying that "beggars should not be choosers." There is a good deal of rugged truth in the old Shakspearean adage: "Put a beggar on horseback and he is sure to ride to the devil." Only mount the beggar man upon the balky steed of human reason, and it is not hard to tell in what direction he will gallop; for he has been going in but one direction ever since he cast off the authority of faith. For if it be reason's privilege to play the lord and master with the Word of God, to canvass the merits and demerits of divine truths, to discuss their comparative value and worthlessness, to sift the supposed wheat from the supposed chaff, to treat them as a pile of rubbish containing some hidden gems, or as a decayed and ruinous and rotten fabric, which must be cleared away to the very foundations before we can get any good out of it, then I say to you to-night, my dear brethren, welcome deism, welcome atheism, welcome anything else, which will only be consistent with itself and not give the lie to its own silly pretensions!

If then we are asked, what is the province of reason in relation to revealed religion, we answer, to seek the light of revelation, if it has not been found, and to follow its guidance, if it has been found. If the farther question is put, how shall reason distinguish and recognize revealed truth; without attempting to give a complete answer to the inquiry now, we will simply say that she must weigh the evidences of revealed religion, but weigh them with prayer as well as study and investigation; and God, who has said: "Ask and you shall receive, seek and you shall find, knock and it shall be open unto you," will grant the needed gift of faith. Reason has the undoubted right to question and reject whatever comes to her in the guise of mere human opinion. She cannot fairly be required to admit as revealed what does not purport to be such. All the truths of revelation are unchangeable, infallible, divine. Doctrines which have these characters stamped upon them claim the assent and submission of human reason. With anything else she may deal as she pleases. But the unchangeable, infallible, divine truths of revelation are given us from heaven to be accepted and believed, not to be the themes of philosophic criticism or theological speculation. We may indeed examine them so as to be able to "give a reason for the faith that is in us:" but the investigation must be carried on in the spirit of faith and humble adoration.

Rev. B. J. McManus.   Rev. D. J. O'Connell, D.D.   Very Rev. H. Gabriels, D.D.

The Catholic Church in the United States.

SERMON OF RIGHT REV. BERNARD J. McQUAID, D.D.,

BISHOP OF ROCHESTER.

THE growth of the United States within the century of their existence as an independent sovereignty, in population, in commerce and manufactures, in extension and development of territory, in literature and fine arts, in diffusion of elementary knowledge among the masses of the people, in successful trial of government of the people by the people, is unparalleled in the history of the world.

Scarcely had peace between the mother-country and the thirteen revolted colonies been declared, after a trying and bloody struggle of seven years, than the emancipated colonists resolutely set to work to construct a form of government that should keep in view the best and largest interest of the people while strongly upholding law and order. These colonies threw wide open their vast domain and invited the oppressed and down-trodden of European countries to enter into possession. There were forests to be felled and fields to be broken up and cultivated. There was no room for the idler, the drone or the dreamer. It was a new country of immense resources for the hardy sons of toil. It offered the freedom and dignity of self-respecting manhood to lovers of liberty and independence.

The readiness with which the invitation was accepted is known to all. From every country and from every class of life the bravest and most venturesome, longing for escape from the thraldom of the old countries of Europe, flocked to the shores of the young Republic. The narrow strip of seaboard running from Massachusetts to Georgia rapidly widened westward to the Mississippi, and then, without more than a temporary break, reached to the Pacific. It is a mighty empire bounded by the two oceans, the great lakes on the north and the gulf on the south. The three millions of revolutionary days have increased to the fifty-five millions of to-day. The thirteen colonies are replaced by thirty-eight States. The experiment of government by the people has withstood successfully rude shocks, serious defeats, conflicts of material interests, even a civil war. All avenues of advancement to wealth and honor have been thronged with the children of intellect and industry. The home, the freedom and the prosperity promised in the invitation have been found by millions. The dire forebodings of eventual disruption and ruin have come to naught. The predictions of anarchy to befall a government so largely entrusted to the people have not been verified. The old country first pitied us, then fought us, and again defeated, feared us. It is now compelled, most reluctantly, it is true, to learn from us the advantage and necessity of entrusting to the people a larger share in the direction and control of political affairs. Ours is a government of the people by the people, in the largest sense consistent with the maintenance of good order and the equal rights of its citizens.

It is assigned to me to speak of the growth of the Catholic Church in a country such as the one here described.

In no better way can I place before you the growth of the Church than by grouping the statistics of Church work, such as we have them, at three periods of the century just ended.

1. The condition of the Catholic Church in 1784.
2. Her progress after fifty years, in 1834.
3. The Church as she is to-day, in 1884.

In 1783 the number of Catholics, according to Bishop Carroll's calculation, as quoted by Shea, might amount in Maryland to sixteen thousand souls; in Pennsylvania, to seven thousand; and in the other States, to fifteen hundred; not as many all told as may be counted to-day in a single parish in some of our large cities. Mass was commonly celebrated in private houses. There were few or no churches. There was no bishop, and in the judgment of the eighteen or twenty missionaries who ministered to the spiritual wants of these scattered members, as expressed in a letter to Rome, there was no need of a bishop, inasmuch as a vicar apostolic, *in spiritualibus*, would suffice. There was no college, school, asylum or hospital. Of religious communities of men or women there was not one. It is a bare picture on a large canvass that is here presented to our view.

The See of Baltimore was erected by Pius VI on the 6th day of November, 1789, and in 1790 its first Bishop, Rev. John Carroll, was consecrated. The establishment of a hierarchy placed the Church in America in line with her sister Churches in other parts of the world, and gave her officials a rule to work by. In a diocese the bishop is the recognized conservator of Catholic faith and morals, in unity and harmony with the head Bishop of the Universal Church. With this first bishop began the regulation of discipline and the founding of institutions needed for the growth and stability of the Church as an organized body.

Bishop Carroll, and others after him, planned to place bishops in every extended geographical district. It was rightly judged that these bishops would give a start and direction to the Church's work from the beginning. In this sense Bishop Connolly, of New York, wrote to the Cardinal Prefect of the Propaganda on the 28th of February, 1818: "Bishops ought to be granted to whatever State here is willing to build a cathedral, and petition for a bishop as Norfolk has done." On the 31st of October, 1818, he wrote to Archbishop Maréchal: "I approve of erecting Charleston into a bishopric, and wish that every one of the seventeen United States had each a bishop." Indeed there was no delay in carving up the country with episcopal sees; bishops sometimes preceded the priests. There were only four priests in New York when Bishop Connolly came to his diocese; two in that of Charleston, comprising the States of North and South Carolina and Georgia, when Bishop England took possession of his allotted district; the same number preceded Bishop Bruté's arrival at Vincennes. At a later date, Bishops Loras and Miles prepared the way for the coming of the first priest into the Dioceses of Dubuque and Nashville.

Vast territory, slow and tedious modes of traveling, few helpers in the work, the poverty of the Gospel fell to the lot of our American pioneer-bishops. That they were apostolic men of God no one can doubt. They were eminently far-seeing and hopeful laborers in an unbroken and rough field—in a wilderness of spiritual destitution.

Six prelates met for the holding of the first Provincial Council of Baltimore in 1829, and ten for the second in October, 1833. Their work, as seen in the decrees of these councils, gave evidence of wisdom, prudence and learning, in adapting discipline to the peculiar circumstances in which they, their priests and the faithful under their care were placed. From the first their thoughts and efforts were directed towards the education of the young. Colleges and academies sprang into existence; Christian free schools, such as are known to-day, for want of religious communities, devoted to the education of the people's children, languished when set agoing and were few in number. The duty of providing churches, ever so small and poor—mere shanties and log-cabins oftentimes—engrossed the time and means of bishops.

From the beginning of the century until 1834, Catholics who had known suffering and persecution in Maryland and Europe, moved among their fellow-citizens quietly and with exceeding humility and meekness. They were specially careful not to offend their separated brethren, and received in return becoming pity and tolerance. No one feared them; they were so few in number, so inconsequential and so anxious not to offend. The condition of tolerance was accepted as a boon rather than demand the right of equality before the law to which they were born.

About this time, however, the steady influx of immigrants from all the countries of Europe, but chiefly of Catholics from Ireland, the building of large and costly churches in important cities, as here in Baltimore and in New York, the opening of colleges and convents, the multiplying of bishops and priests, turned pity into fear. The Fathers of the second Council refer to this change of feeling and treatment in their pastoral letter. "We notice with regret," they write, "a spirit exhibited by some of the conductors of the press engaged in the interests of those brethren separated from our communion which has within a few years become more unkind and unjust in our regard. Not only do they assail us and our institutions in a style of vituperation and offence, misrepresent our tenets, vilify our practices, repeat the hundred-times-refuted calumnies of days of angry and bitter contention in other lands, but they have even denounced you and us as enemies to the republic, and have openly proclaimed the fancied necessity of not only obstructing our progress, but of using their best efforts to extirpate our religion." This is a mild arraignment of an exhibition of fanatical bigotry that suddenly burst on the Church. Secular and religious press alike, and all the pulpits from Maine to Louisiana, weekly and oftener poured out torrents of rancorous abuse and calumny, and left unused no art or device with which to fan the flame of religious hate and passion in the minds and hearts of their readers and hearers. In the August of 1834 the answer to this temperate rebuke of the bishops was the setting fire to the convent of the Ursuline Nuns of Charlestown by citizens of Boston town and vicinity. Gallant men burned over the heads of defenceless women and school-girls their rightful home, even as less than a century before savage Indians, wrought to rage by many wrongs, had set ablaze the huts and cabins of the early settlers in Massachusetts.

While noting this phase of intolerance as a hindrance to the growth of the Church within the first half of the century, it will not be out of place to refer to the continuance of the same spirit of opposition, amounting to persecution, which furiously manifested itself in 1844 and in 1854. This malevolent spirit deepened and grew bolder among our non-Catholic fellow-citizens as soon as our numbers, wealth and activity arrested attention by the building of churches, convents and schools. These outbursts of malignant hate and fear were like to the upheavings of volcanoes; slumbering for years, suddenly masses of fire and burning stones shoot into the air, and, falling, roll in hot streams down the side of the mountain, carrying devastation in their path.

The angry passions engendered by persistent onslaughts in press and pulpit, outrageous calumnies, unmanly insinuations, fearful forebodings and warnings of evil to come upon the country at a time when it was struggling into existence, prepared the minds of bigots for barbarous deeds. Maria Monk's "Disclosures," as the utterances of an abandoned woman were called, the stock in trade of venal book-publishers and fanatical parsons, deceived and led astray many who honestly desired to live at peace with their neighbors. The riots and burnings of 1834 were the outcome of years of guilty misrepresentation. In 1844 politicians, always dragging their nets in foul waters, thought they saw political capital in the still seething religious ignorance and prejudice prevalent among the people. The bad elements already existing among our own population had been considerably augmented by recent arrivals from Europe, too ready to revive in America the religious wars in which they had been engaged at home. The Philadelphia riots, church burnings and murders followed as a consequence. Disturbances in other parts of the country broke out at the same time and from similar causes. The riots and murders of 1854 were akin in character and cause to those of 1844; they had their source in religious rancor and political scheming trading on the passions of ignorant bigots. There were no riots in 1864. The civil war, just ending, had put a stop to the diabolical machinations of bigots and politicians. Men who had stood shoulder to shoulder in the hour of danger, who had rested side by side under the shelter-tent, had learned forbearance and mutual respect, and to treat with contempt the old-time calumnies and all who uttered them. The politician's objection to Catholics because they were foreigners was valid as against Columbus in the mind of the aboriginal natives, and will end only when America forgets the hospitality she owes to the down-trodden of the world, and which the progenitors of her citizens of to-day had received in their turn. The reign of insults and wrongs that lasted from 1830 to 1860 proved a formidable hindrance to the advance of the Church. The timid, the ill-instructed, the ambitious, the vain, feared to belong to a body of so little esteem in the world's eye, and fell away. Fanaticism and proselytism worked hand in hand. Money was lavishly spent in perverting the minds of the young. The spenders of it thought that they were doing God's work. Because the enemies of the Church are not working on the same lines to-day, it is not to be inferred that the battle is over, and that all danger has passed.

But the main cause of defections must be looked for in the years from 1784 to 1834, and be attributed to the scarcity of priests and churches. Bishop England, of Charleston, in a letter to the Society of the Propagation of the Faith in France, estimated these losses at three millions and a-half at the time of his writing, in 1839. He gives, however, no trustworthy data on which to base such a conclusion, and I cannot but consider it as greatly exaggerated. Yet it must be confessed that the number of those that lost the faith, or, that having no means of hearing the Word of God and of receiving the helping graces of the sacraments, lapsed into indifference, is startlingly great. Even when parents never apostatized, their children succumbed to the influence of their surroundings, and learned to despise and deny the belief and practices of their parent's religion through the adverse and malignant pressure of companionship and daily intercourse with revilers of Catholic doctrines. Social seductions and fashions overmaster the young and lead them captive. When mixed marriages in such conditions of society intervened to increase the danger, the children had no hope and were invariably lost. Without Catholic lessons at home, with neither Church nor priest to teach and support them, they fell an easy prey to the vigilant and zealous labors of the enemies of the Catholic Church. In spite of all disadvantages and losses from peculiar and unavoidable evils, the Church made headway. The French emigrant priests driven to our shores by the revolution of 1789 were men of learning and piety. They had passed through the fires that try men's souls. Their zeal was unbounded, and their success was marked in holding many Catholics to the practice of religion and in winning the esteem and good will of non-Catholics whose antagonism they disarmed. Chevereux and Matignon, Dubois and Bruté, Flaget and his companions in the West, Dubourg in the South, and the Sulpicians who chose Baltimore for their field of labor, performed noble work and laid broad and solid foundations. Nor should we forget to speak a word of praise of the Society of the Propagation of the Faith, established in Lyons, whose generous and unfailing pecuniary help came to the assistance of the American Church in her days of struggling infancy. It was this help which set a-going dioceses and institutions and enabled bishops and priests to live while seeking after the wandering sheep of a widely scattered flock.

By 1834, after fifty years of faithful perseverance under most trying difficulties, the Church of the United States was able to show an archbishop, eleven bishops, two hundred and fifty priests, about thirty colleges and academies, but not a dozen parochial schools for the half million Catholics who comprised our population at that time. This exhibit may not strike one as very remarkable, but its merits should be judged by the greatness of the sacrifices, the zeal of the laborers, their small number and limited resources.

Between 1830 and 1850 the tide of immigration began to set

in strongly. Poverty, famine and revolutions swelled the crowds of fleeing emigrants. Disasters at sea and long voyages could not hold back men and women whose hearts were turned toward the promised land. The first immigrants coming in large numbers were from Ireland. Of all the peoples of Europe they were the best fitted to open the way for religion in a new country. Brave by nature, inured to poverty and hardship, just released from a struggle unto death for the faith, accustomed to the practice of religion in its simplest forms, cherishing dearly their priests whom they had learned to support directly, actively engaged in building humble chapels on the sites of ruined churches and in replacing altars, they were not appalled by the wretchedness of religious equipments and surroundings in their new homes on this side of the Atlantic. The priest was always the priest, no matter where they found him, or from what country he had come; the Mass was always the Mass, no matter where it was offered up. They had lived among the bitterest of foes and had never quailed or flinched; misrepresentations and calumnies, sneers and scorn, made no impression on their faithful hearts. Men who prefer death to denial of Christ are not cowards or traitors. In such a school of discipline they had been trained to do missionary work. They and their descendants have not in a new hemisphere unlearned the lessons taught at home.

Quickly following the Irish came the Germans from all parts of the fatherland. They, too, were a sturdy race, able to hold their own. Many of them had also known persecution for religion's sake; most of them remembered the stories of bloody times which had come down to them among the traditions of their hearths. They were prompt to rival their Irish brethren in building up the Church. At home they had their old parish churches, with the chants and ceremonial, which lend to religion much that is consoling and instructive. The religious traditions and glories of the old land they have sought to emulate in this. Better than all, they have stood fast by the duty of maintaining Christian schools for Christian children. There is much that they can copy from the Irish, and much that the Irish can learn from the Germans. Both have bravely led the way in the Church's march. All the other nationalities of Europe can kneel at their feet and imbibe salutary and profitable lessons.

Before proceeding to account for losses to the Church, even during this favorable period from 1834 to 1884, a brief summary of statistics, as found in Sadlier's Directory, will show at a glance what has been accomplished in church work.

A Cardinal of the Holy Roman Church, the Most Eminent and Illustrious Archbishop of New York; an Apostolic Delegate, the Most Reverend and Illustrious Metropolitan of this See of Baltimore; thirteen other archbishops, and coadjutor archbishops, and sixty-one bishops and vicars apostolic rule over God's Church in this republic; 6,835 priests, under the leadership of these successors of the Apostles, in 7,763 churches and chapels, feed their flocks with the bread of life and devotedly care for their souls. In 708 seminaries, colleges and academies, the higher education of clerics and of the youth of both sexes is carried forward by learned professors and accomplished nuns. Many thousands of brothers and sisters, of all the teaching orders and communities, assist these priests and perform a part that, without their services, would be left undone. Our orphans, the aged, the abandoned, are sheltered in 294 asylums, and our sick are nursed in 139 hospitals. The crowning glory of the Church's work, however, is derived from her success in providing, not for the exceptional members of her household, the few who are bereaved, sick and helpless, but for the many who constitute her army of able, active and self-maintaining members. For the children of the Catholic community, for the offspring of the parents who build churches, asylums and hospitals, she has within these fifty years built and she now sustains 2,532 Christian schools, in which secular learning is imparted without sacrificing instruction in the belief and observances which the Lord commanded His Apostles and their successors to preach to the end of time. During the year 1883, 481,834 pupils frequented these Christian schools, built, fostered lovingly and supported for the people's children without aid from the State. The charity which comes to the relief of the sick and the fatherless is beautiful indeed, and the blessing of heaven falls hourly on those who tend and those who help; but the duty of instructing the many, the hope of the future, cannot be omitted without punishment in this world and the next.

The Directory estimates the Catholic population at 6,623,176. It is easy to see that these figures are not based on correct information. The editor fulfills his task in accurately counting up the numbers sent to him. But estimates of population, year after year the same, in rapidly growing dioceses, must be at fault, for they are clearly wide of the mark. An estimate that would place our Catholic population at eight millions, would, in my judgment, not be far from the truth. A few years hence, with priests in abundance, having parishes restricted within territorial limits, so that a pastor may be able to know his parishioners, and when baptisms, marriages and deaths are faithfully recorded and reported, it may be possible to reckon our numbers without guessing.

The dry figures here submitted for consideration give no adequate idea of the amount of work performed during these fifty years. They do not tell of the sacrifices of the poor people who furnished the money, often drawing out of purses all but empty; they do not tell that the stone church of to-day, monumental in size and beauty of architecture, replaced an humbler one of brick, which in its turn had displaced the first modest wooden structure; they do not tell that driven by State monopoly in school teaching, upheld by unlimited expenditures of money from the public treasury, Catholics are forced to make their school buildings and furniture unnecessarily expensive and grand; that needless costliness is forced upon them to maintain the honor and good name of their schools in the face of State extravagance; they do not tell that the burden and the cost of these churches and schools have for the most part fallen on poor people and poor priests; they do not tell of the many priests that, broken in health and spirit, sank into untimely graves, victims to toil of body and anxiety of mind more than nature could endure.

Again, the bald figures summing up the number of cathedrals, churches, colleges, convents, etc., do not convey an idea of the character of these edifices. There are among them edifices which Europe of modern days cannot equal in size, grandeur and completeness. What has Europe to place by the side of the New York cathedral as her contribution to church building in the nineteenth century? Look at the seminary buidings at Overbrook, Baltimore, Boston; at our collegiate buildings in the East and in the West; at convents and monasteries innumerable; at our charitable institutions. These are not State buildings erected with money from the

State treasury. The people's pence and the personal sacrifices and savings of priests, brothers and nuns have built them. Not much help has come from our rich members. They testify what can be accomplished by a believing flock when untrammeled by governmental interference. Free and unhampered, upheld by the fidelity and generosity of the masses of her children in Christ, growth and prosperity have marked the course of the Church along every line of work—in every agency and force. If material and intellectual America can point with exultation of soul to its marvellous accomplishments, so can spiritual and intellectual Catholic America hold up its head as not unworthy of its predecessors in the faith in any country and in any age. If non-Catholic America can with just pride call attention to its colleges and universities, the noblest of modern times in wealth of endowments, the gifts to learning of its millionaire friends and patrons, so can Catholic America bespeak consideration for what zeal, devotion and the generosity of the poor have brought into existence. In this study of successful work we must ever keep in mind who were the workers and what was the treasury from which the required millions were drawn.

With the proof here presented of large and substantial growth, giving well-founded hope of continuance and permanence, the Catholics of the United States can face their brethren in any quarter of the world and bid those whose surroundings are at all like ours to compare work with work, success with success, loss with loss. We frankly admit that we have not always held our own. But we in America do not take reproof from our brethren in Europe with amiability and good grace. Many of the Christians they have turned out on our shores have not been models of piety and holiness; nor does the light of faith burn brightly in their souls. They accept the services of religion as a compliment to the priest rather than as a necessary fulfillment of duty. They must be helped rather than be a help. Thousands already perverted by the soul-destroying influences of secret societies and the demoralizing notions of socialism, so prevalent in Europe, impede our onward course. Our humble Catholics are amazed at the looseness of principles in the hearts of many who come to us, and are disedified. We cannot but ask: Are there no losses to the Church on the other side of the ocean? Corrupted in faith and morals before they leave home, they bring corruption with them.

The hindrances to our growth in the first half of the century were not unknown in the second half. The one which came from the low social standing of Catholics in most parts of the country, little by little yielded to claims that could not be ignored. Wealth, education and refinement asserted their rights. Political, commercial and professional pre-eminence, in many quarters, told in our favor. Members of our Church were of marked distinction in every walk of life—on the bench, at the bar, in the medical profession, in the army and navy—wherever brightness of intellect and capacity for work are needed they are to be found. Even in the political arena, while their religious connection does not advance their interests, it is ceasing to be an actual impediment, and it is discovered that political punishment for religious belief is becoming a dangerous experiment.

While all admit that the social status of our numbers has changed for the better in cities and towns, it is highly satisfactory to know that in rural and agricultural districts, where so many of our body are found to-day and where their homes will be greatly multiplied in the future, our farmers and their families win the respect due to their worth and useful citizenship. They cannot be, nor are they, despised. When known, they advance in the esteem of their neighbors.

Misrepresentations and evil reports still are heard, but newspapers that care for their reputation do not repeat false charges that will not be believed by their readers. Fair play and a love for the truth on the part of non-Catholics have put a stop to low abuse of their neighbors and associates in business, whom they know to be honorable and upright men, and whose wives and daughters they know are pure, gentle and amiable. The people's good sense reformed pulpits and newspapers.

Church contentions and squabbles, having their origin in a faulty understanding of the rights and duties of the clergy and laity in the management of temporalities and money transactions, have led to heavy losses. When the century began men's minds were warped by non-Catholic ideas with regard to the tenure of ecclesiastical property. It was thought that the freedom and independence in political affairs, common in the country, should extend to church matters. Good Christians were easily led astray by one or two cunning and infidel minds in a congregation. An occasional mistake or blunder on the part of an ecclesiastic served as an excuse for fault-finding. But in what other profession or in what other line of commercial and monetary transactions have the mistakes been so few and the failures so infrequent? And when ecclesiastics have blundered in business concerns, has it not been because other responsibilities than those rightly within the sphere of their work have been assumed by them? The better to understand the cogency of this argument, it is no more than just to remember that hundreds of millions have passed under the control and use of priests within the half century. It is simply a marvel that in the handling and disbursing of these large sums of money so little has been lost and so seldom have pastors forfeited the confidence of their flocks. Pastors can do nothing without the co-operation of their parishioners, and soon learn that a wise appreciation of the rights of those who freely open their purses at the call of religion or charity best secures a generous response. Both then work hand in hand for God's glory; the frictions incidental to human nature are little noted, and the few in a congregation who are ill-disposed find no encouragement from the majority. This well-ordered and happy condition of church management, based on the proper consideration of the rights and duties of priests and people, is a gratifying note of stable growth.

It is often remarked that a country which does not furnish a supply of priests for its altars will lose the faith. This saying cannot be predicated of a new land into which thousands and hundreds of thousands are year by year flowing. These immigrants must bring their priests with them. But when the newly arrived families have had time to settle down in their new homes the developing of vocation begins. No one fosters piety and zeal for God's honor in a child's soul like a devout, God-fearing mother. You cannot have homes in which the Christian virtues are cultivated without vocations to the priesthood and the religious life. In our young republic vocations abound. Our preparatory and theological seminaries are filled with promising aspirants to the work of the sanctuary; our convents are thronged with holy virgins bringing to the service of religion whatever of bodily strength, intellectual capacity and devotion of soul they have to offer and that can be used. Our schools would be empty buildings but for the armies of teaching Brothers and Sisters who fill so well the office of instructors. Here, too, is evidence of faith and stability.

Christian families demand Christian schools. The father and mother most exact in the religious education of their children are the most earnest in providing Christian schools. Their own efforts to teach their young ones convinces them of the necessity of the every-day school to supplement and enforce their words and lessons. Parents who rarely give a lesson to their children are the loudest in protesting against schools strictly Catholic. They do not know the value of a child's soul, often as they may have heard that Christ died to save it.

Scarcely had the work of building churches for our rapidly increasing population been taken in hand by priests and people than a yet heavier task was imposed on them. Churches might suffice for the elders of the flock, who, trained to religion in a Catholic atmosphere at home, could neither be cajoled nor deterred from its practices; but what was to become of children growing up in an atmosphere not simply innocuous, but positively dangerous and hurtful. Bishops and priests were most unwilling to add to the burden already weighing down their congregations. They sought, as well in justice they might, that a portion of their own money paid to the State might come back to them. Unkindly, rudely, contemptuously, their reasonable request was spurned. Politicians and parsons were our fiercest antagonists. When passions are aroused it is useless to argue. The passions of a nation cool slowly. There were some Catholics who hoped that an education purely secular might be made to answer. No doubt it will give to the children of secularists the husks of education—all they ask. They wonder that Catholics seek for more. They cannot comprehend our doctrine that the school for the child is as necessary as the church for the parent. Without further argument or dispute, but, nevertheless, grieving and groaning under the wrong put upon us by process of law and the vote of the majority, Catholics gathered their children into their own schools, that therein they might breathe a Catholic atmosphere while acquiring secular knowledge. Without these schools, in a few generations our magnificent cathedrals and churches would remain as samples of monumental folly—of the unwisdom of a capitalist who consumes his fortune year by year without putting it out at interest or allowing it to increase. The Church has lost more in the past from the want of Catholic schools than from any other cause named by me this evening. The 2,500 schools, with a half million of scholars, which now bless our country, tell Catholics and non-Catholics that the question of religious education is settled, so far as we are concerned. The good work so well advanced will not halt until all over the land the children of the Church are sheltered under her protecting care. The establishment of these schools and their improvement in management and instruction is our surest guarantee of future growth and fixedness.

The gross exaggerations of writers who substitute imaginings for facts, in asserting that millions upon millions of our Catholic people have lost their faith, are not deserving of much notice. The immigrant who landed on our shores faced two dangers which affrighted him. If, in the early days of our history, he sought a home out in the agricultural districts, there was neither church nor priest; if, deterred by dangers to his faith from settling on farm-land, he clung to cities and factory towns, he lived without a home and his children perished in infancy, victims to the miseries of tenement-life. The immigrants of to-day can find healthful homes in all parts of the United States near to churches, schools and priests. They have no excuse for settling far from a church or from a neighborhood that will soon be blessed with one.

I bring to a close my allotted task. No one more than myself feels how inadequately it has been executed. Compressing so extensive a subject into a small compass has been difficult. Memory goes back to early days in our history. My first lessons in religion came from some who were among the pioneers of the Church in our country. My first years of priesthood were spent as a missionary in New Jersey. While journeying through this district, hunting up the stray sheep of the fold, the experience was acquired that without churches and schools our children, and especially those of mixed marriages, would be lost. No doubt every missionary's experience has been the same.

But what a change since those days! There were among the first bishops and priests men who conceived and planned great things for the Church's welfare; their plans when enunciated seemed visionary, the speculations of dreamers, of impracticable workers. A few years demonstrated that their plans were insufficient and too restricted for the wants of the country. We plan to-day with the light of the past to guide us. Another generation may smile at our narrowness of vision and weakness of heart.

A noble duty, worthy of a man's labor and life, the building up of Christ's Church in a great, growing and free republic, falls to our lot. God and country, most dear to us, claim love and service. It is for us to help say to the world that government of a free people by the people, whose conceptions of morality are based on God's law, can safely be entrusted to the people, and that this largeness of trust gives ample scope to the Christian's ambition in furthering a sacred cause. No man's help is beneath consideration. The humblest layman, the very child in the school, their capable and devoted teachers, they who pray in cloisters, missionaries who live in the saddle, priests who minister in crowded cities, professors in our seminaries, bishops who rule, have each and every one a part to take. What glowing words of praise may justly be spoken in commendation of our predecessors! They fought the good fight, they laid a solid foundation, they showed the way, they illustrated their teachings by their lives. Let us not prove unworthy of them and their examples.

Rt. Rev. L. M. Fink, D.D.

Rt. Rev. John B. Brondel, D.D.

Most Rev. J. B. Salpointe, D.D.

Rt. Rev. Edward Fitzgerald, D.D.

Rt. Rev. R. Seidenbush, D.D.

Rt. Rev. T. L. Grace, D.D.

Rt. Rev. M. Marty, D.D.

Rt. Rev. James O'Connor, D.D.

Rt. Rev. J. J. Hogan, D.D.

The Sacrifice of the Mass.

SERMON OF RIGHT REV. E. FITZGERALD, D.D.,

BISHOP OF LITTLE ROCK, ARK.

"For Christ, being present a High Priest of the good things to come, by a greater and more perfect tabernacle not made with hands, that is, not of this creation; neither by the blood of goats nor of calves, but by His own blood, entered once into the sanctuary, having obtained eternal redemption."—*Heb.*, c. ix, v. 11-12.

BEHOLD I am with you all days even to the consummation of the world." The abiding presence of Christ in His Church, my brethren, may be considered from two points of view. We may regard it as the Mind enlightening her and guiding her unto all truth; or as the Heart giving her life, strength, courage. Of Christ regarded as the Light of His Church, you have heard several times these days past from this pulpit; for, if the Church teaches with infallible authority and if we are bound to listen to her voice it is because He is with her, and "whosoever hears her hears Him." Of Christ, the Life of His Church, ever present with her in the sacraments, but more especially in the Sacrifice of the Eucharist, which is the Heart of Catholic worship and action, I shall offer you a brief consideration this morning; for, as the heart receives and again distributes the vital current throughout the bodily frame, so from the Holy Sacrifice of the Mass, which is one with the cross, do we receive all grace and strength, and through it do we pay back to God that worship of adoration, praise, thanksgiving, prayer and expiation which we owe to Him. The Mass, the highest act of our worship, is most sacred in the eyes of the Catholic for what it is in itself; and for the venerable ceremonies with which the Church has environed it as a gem in its setting. Even to the non-Catholic it will be a subject of great interest if he reflects that it is the public worship of 400,000,000 of civilized people on the face of the globe to-day; and that for 1500 years it was the public worship of his forefathers, no less than of ours.

I will go farther and lay down a proposition which may be a little startling at first, but which I hope to make clearer as we proceed: that while the Mass is eminently the Christian sacrifice, it is also in a certain sense the sacrifice of all ages, and has been offered up to God from the "constitution of the world."

There is a modern view of God and of His relations with mankind—one high in favor with certain modern physicists—that God (if there be a God) when He created this universe (if the universe was created) gave to nature certain fixed and unchangeable laws, which He Himself cannot transgress. The Creator thus becomes the slave of His own laws; He has no freedom of action in the creation which is the work of His hands; and everything is reduced to the law of inflexible, mechanical necessity. Such a God is not the God of humanity. The instincts of the human race are more philosophical. They tell us of a God who has not renounced His freedom of action in the creation; who manifests Himself to man in a manner suited to man's own free will and rational nature; who is more *human*, as it were; and whom, therefore, we may approach; move by prayer and oblation; and when offended, propitiate by sacrifice. This view of God's relations with His rational creatures—and who shall say that it is not more reasonable?—lets in at once the supernatural, if that can be called supernatural, which is after all only natural in man's present and actual condition. For the Church teaches—the traditions and instincts of humanity bear her out—that man never existed on this earth in a purely natural condition; that from the very beginning he was elevated to the supernatural state; a supernatural destiny was set before him, and the means given him to attain it. Man fell; but even in his fall retained a dim perception of his first estate:

> For even in savage bosoms
> There are longings, yearnings, strivings,
> In the good they comprehend not.

He is a prodigal from his Father's house, who has dissipated his goodly inheritance, and fallen so low as to contend with swine for the husks of existence; but who in his uttermost degradation still retains a consciousness of what he has lost; feels that somehow the Great Father's heart goes out to him as to none of His insensible or irrational creatures; and he longs to return, and, throwing himself at his Father's feet, win back his forgiveness. Only on this principle does the universal custom of prayer become intelligible—for who would pray to a God who could not be moved?—of oblation, which is the outward embodiment of prayer; of sacrifice, which is the expression of the need of expiation; and of the universal belief, though often expressed in the most grotesque forms, in an incarnation of the Deity. Christianity tells us the meaning of the half-utterances of the pagan world. They are the attempt of the human soul, "naturally Christian," to grasp and give expression to the great truths of the primitive revelation: and in this broad sense we may say that all religions are one: for the "unknown God whom you worship without knowing is what I preach to you," says the Apostle, "God, who made the world and all things that are in it, ... who giveth life and breath, and all things, ... hath made of one, all mankind to dwell upon the whole face of the earth." (Acts, xvii, 23, et seq.)

Yes, my brethren, in all ages mankind prayed and "sought God, if haply they may feel after Him: although He be not far from any of us." (Acts, xvii, 23.) But man also felt the need of giving outward body and expression to the spirit of prayer. Hence the act of oblation, or the offering to heaven of the elements of food and drink (usually bread and wine), by which life is sustained, as symbolizing the belief that we owe our life to the sustaining hand of our Creator. Hence, also, the universal practice of sacrifice. Man felt he had sinned; the traditions of the Fall are found everywhere. Therefore the need of expiation, and of expiating through the awful rite of the shedding of blood. This was always and everywhere regarded as the highest act of worship. The idea of it appears to be this: that life is a direct emanation from the Deity. (I do not mean, of course, from His substance, but from His power or virtue; though undoubtedly many of the pagans believed the former). The body is subject to the ordinary laws of matter, and of itself tends to dissolution. A more direct recognition of God's power over life and death is made therefore when the blood of the victim is shed before the altar, and the gift of life is again given back to heaven by the sacrificial act. And if we go back to the beginnings of the human race, we may gather the necessity of sacrifice from the pages of the inspired volume. Cain and Abel offered victims, the one of the first fruits of the earth, the other of the firstlings of his flock. The patriarchs Abraham, Isaac, Jacob, Melchisedech, worshiped in this manner, and their worship was accepted by heaven. The pagan nations, as has been said, enlightened by primeval traditions, or obeying that law written on the fleshly tablets of their hearts, sacrificed to their idols, which they took for the true God. Everywhere in ancient times, and no less in modern times, even among the heathen tribes do you find the altar, and the priest, and the knife, and the smoke of the sacrifice; nay, in some nations, so strangely had the light of nature been dimmed, the awful rites of human victims offered in sacrifice were the only ones supposed to be capable of appeasing the anger of an offended deity.

In like manner when we come to the history of the chosen people we find God Himself carefully and zealously prescribing the quality, manner, number and place of the various sacrifices which He would be pleased to accept from their hands, as may be seen from Leviticus and Deuteronomy, and indeed from their whole history up to the time of Christ. We may, therefore, conclude, as it has always been observed, that sacrifice belongs to the essentials of religion; and therefore that we Christians to-day must "have an altar of which they cannot eat who serve the tabernacle."

For, my brethren, as the old dispensation in its entirety was only provisional and a promise of "better things to come," we must conclude that the chiefest part of its worship, sacrifice, gave way to a greater and higher act of worship, which should give meaning to what was only prefigured by the ancient rites. The ancient rites were temporary, shadows of coming events, symbols which had no meaning of themselves, and apart from the things which they symbolized. They had no virtue or efficacy in themselves, except as referring to another and completing sacrifice. "For it is impossible that with the blood of goats and of oxen sins should be taken away," says the Apostle, "for if," he says again, "the blood of goats and of oxen and the ashes of a heifer being sprinkled can sanctify such as are defiled, how much more shall not the blood of Christ clean our conscience to serve the living God?" (Heb., ix, 13.) As though he should say, God is pleased to accept the sacrifices which you offer, all nothing as they are, because they symbolize the shedding of the blood of the great Victim through whom we are saved. Being, therefore, in their own nature temporary, the sacrifices of the Old Law were to cease; which is further shown by the destruction of the temple or place of sacrifice. With the abolition of the old sacrifices, therefore, the world would be left without "an offering for sin," except we have a Christian sacrifice, which the Catholic Church believes and teaches to be the Mass.

This was also clearly foretold by the prophet Malachias. In this well-known passage (Mal., i,) the prophet foretells: 1. That the ancient sacrifices would cease to exist. 2. That for the many of of the Old Law, one would be substituted. 3. That this would be offered not in the temple, but everywhere. 4. That it would be offered by people, not of Jewish lineage only, but of Gentile blood as well. Where is the prophecy fulfilled if not in the Mass?

Again, our Lord is styled by St. Paul a priest according to the order of Melchisedech, which has no meaning except we admit the Mass, which, under the forms of bread and wine, Melchisedech's oblation, contains the victim of salvation. And in the Acts, the Apostles are described as "serving the Lord," a word being used which signifies sacrifice; and again St. Paul, contrasting the Christian altar with the Jewish, plainly shows that we have a Christian sacrifice, which were not true if we have not the sacrifice of the Mass. This, therefore, is the culmination of the figures of the Old Law, the fulfillment of the prophecies, as the Church teaches, and as has been held by her from the beginning. Here is one High Priest; here one Victim; here the altar of propitiation for the sins of the living and the dead.

But, how? Or, in other words, what is the Mass? I do not know that I can answer in better language than that of the little catechism: "The sacrifice of the Body and Blood of Christ which are really present upon our altars, and are offered to God for the living and the dead. The *sacrifice*, because it is an oblation of a victim to God by a lawful priest, to represent by the act of oblation and the slaying or other destruction of the victim," His supreme dominion over life and death. The essence of sacrifice does not, however, cease in oblation, otherwise every oblation would be a sacrifice, which is not true. Neither in the slaying of the victim, otherwise every killing would be a sacrifice. It consists rather in the symbolism of the act, by separating the blood, "which is the life," from the body of the victim, and laying it on the altar. In what more expressive way can the sacrificing priest show forth the utter dependence of man upon God for his life and everything in life which he possesses?

"Of the Body and Blood of Christ, which are really present on our altars, and are offered up to God for the living and the dead." Our faith teaches us that by a wonderful condescension Christ gave to the priests of His Church the power of drawing Him down from heaven and placing Him on our altars; or, if transforming the Bread and Wine of the Sacred Mysteries into His adorable Body and Blood, God obeys the voice of a man, and at his call, He who annihilated Himself in taking our human nature and in bearing the ignominy of the cross, again conceals the majesty of His Divinity under the appearance of a morsel of bread and a few drops of wine. I am not arguing the question of the Real Presence this morning, my brethren. I will but say that Christianity were not Christianity if it had no mysteries; that He who changed water into wine at Cana of Galilee can change bread and wine into His Body and Blood; that it is not harder to believe the Mystery of the Real Presence than that of the Incarnation or adorable Trinity; indeed, I might go farther, and say, than many of the mysteries of nature with which we are surrounded.

The Body and Blood of Christ, who was broken for us, who was nailed to the cross, are present on our Christian altars; and the priest sacrifices them, that is, makes an offering or presentation of them to God the Father for the living and the dead. The Mass is therefore identical with the sacrifice of Calvary. It is the same Victim, offered by the same High Priest, Jesus Christ, through the ministration of His visible priesthood, to the same God and for the same purposes of sacrifice. But while Calvary was a bloody sacrifice, this is an unbloody one; while the former was an absolute sacrifice, this is representative. That is, while Christ really died for us on Calvary, and with that "one act of oblation perfected forever them who were to be saved," this presents anew His death as symbolized by the separate consecration of the elements of bread and wine, and His atonement through death; while on Calvary He offered Himself, here He is offered through His minister. Perhaps our meaning will be more clear if we compare the Mass with the Old Law sacrifices. They had no virtue or efficacy of themselves, as St. Paul declares, (Heb., ix, 13), "for it is impossible that the blood of goats and oxen should take away sin." Yet they *were* efficacious, because they related to Calvary; they were the preliminary steps to Calvary; they *were* Calvary, in a word, being all integral parts of the one supreme act of which Calvary was the completion and perfection. As therefore the ancient sacrifices availed as representative of and a part of Calvary *yet to come*, so the Mass, but in a much higher sense, avails as representative and part of Calvary's sacrifice, *made eighteen hundred years ago;* and in a higher sense, for in the ancient sacrifices you had only shadows, figures, symbols—"weak elements." Here you have the reality, the thing symbolized, the very Victim Himself, the very Body that was broken and the very Blood which was shed for us!

But in all this, my brethren, we are using human language and speaking of things as they present themselves to our human vision and apprehension. We speak of eighteen hundred years ago; of Calvary, of other places. To God there is no time nor place; no succession of minutes, and hours, and days, and years, and centuries; no distance of place from place, but one simple, single act; and one ever presence everywhere. In His eyes, therefore, the Mass is not a repetition or re-presentation of Calvary, as we have called it in our human way. To Him Calvary is everywhere and always present. We cannot understand this; but even modern science may be used to give us an insight into the mysteries of heaven. Distance has been annihilated in respect to sound by the telephone, and in respect to time by the phonograph, so that with the aid of these two instruments one can hear the identical voice of another though hundreds of miles and hundreds of years may separate them. It is said, with what truth I do not know, that an instrument has been invented which will do for light what the instruments mentioned do for sound, and that the identical rays of light proceeding from a given body may be transmitted to a distance of, say, one thousand miles. If this be so, and I would not say it is impossible in this age of marvels, time and distance are annihilated; and I may be heard and seen in hundreds of places and at the same moment hundreds of miles apart! Truly a marvel of human invention! What must it be, then, with the mysteries of heaven? And while we shall never fully comprehend it, we may see, as it were in a glass darkly, how the one act of sacrifice on Calvary in the eyes of God is not yet a thing of the past, or of distant Judea, but one, everlasting and ever-present offering up of the "Lamb that was slain from the constitution of the world."

Therefore we have in the Mass a sacrifice which not only completes the figures of the ancient sacrifices of the people of God, but also enables us to understand the struggles of the Gentile world to give expression to the hereditary religious feelings of the race, all overlaid as they were by the errors and impurities of the pagan worship and superstition. It is Christ, the expectation of the Gentiles, and the hope of the people of Israel, again and again pleading His wounds, sufferings and blood for us; once indeed, and once only, shed, but ever bleeding, an open fountain for the redemption of the sinner, and "making peace through the blood of His cross, both as to the things that are on earth, and are in heaven," (Col. i, 20); and the Lamb whom we offer here below, is the same Christ who, sitting at the right hand of the Father, makes continual intercession for us. The Mass here below is the counterpart of the heavenly Jerusalem. The sacred ministers, the lights, the incense are but the reflection of the supernal glory, and a visible representation of that majesty of God which no man may look on and live. And now lift up your eyes higher—sursum corda: "I saw a new heaven," says the inspired Apostle; "I saw the holy city, the new Jerusalem, coming down from God out of heaven." Perhaps this very church is heaven! Heaven is not a place. It is wherever God and His blessed spirits are. Oh, I see this church in which we are assembled filled with the brightness of the heavenly Jerusalem, for the Lamb that was slain from the foundations of the world is the light thereof. I see here His throne, and under the throne the bodies of the martyrs, which are the prayers of the saints; and in the attendants of the altar I see the four-and-twenty ancients who minister unto Him; and in the sheen of the sacred vestments I see the radiance of the celestial hosts; and in the chant I hear the song of the angels; and in this throng of devout worshipers I see the twelve thousand sealers of each of the twelve tribes of Israel, and that immense multitude whom no man could number of all nations, and tribes, and peoples and tongues, standing before the throne, and in the sight of the Lamb clothed with white robes, and palms in their hands, and saying: "Amen, benediction and glory, and wisdom, and thanksgiving, honor, power and strength to one God for ever and ever. Amen." (Ap. vii.)

Brethren, I am not drawing on imagination; I am stating the sober facts. The heavenly spirits are not visible to our mortal eyes; but they are here, and encircling this altar which God has made His throne and are visible to the eye of faith. Can we believe this, believe that we so nearly touch God, and yet go on in our old ways? Believe that the drama of Calvary is re-enacted in this place, and before our very eyes, and yet come so cold, and undevout, and perhaps with the burden of our irrepentance on our hearts? Believe this to be the "Mountain of the Lord," and His holy place, and yet presume to come whither only the "innocent of hand, pure of heart may ascend?" "Can man see God and live?" Can anything defiled enter heaven? Oh, pray God we may be cleansed. Sprinkle me, O Lord, with hyssop and I shall be cleansed; wash me, and I shall be made whiter than snow. And thus cleansed and free from every defilement, "we may go with confidence to the throne of grace; that we may obtain mercy, and find grace in seasonable aid." (Heb., iv, 16.)

Thanksgiving Day.

SERMON OF RIGHT REV. J. L. SPALDING, D.D.,

BISHOP OF PEORIA, ILL.

THE practice, which, with us, has now grown to be national, of appointing one day in the year for general thanksgiving to God, the Creator and Giver of all good, has seemed to the Fathers of the Third Plenary Council of Baltimore consonant with the principles of faith and with the promptings of the heart of a Christian people, and they have, therefore, determined to recognize and commend, in a public and solemn way, a custom which declares our dependence upon God, both as a nation and as individuals, while it tends to strengthen the spirit of gratitude and to increase our confidence in His all-wise and Fatherly Providence. The appeal made by the civil authorities of our country, requesting all citizens to cease from work and business on this day, and to raise their thoughts to God, while they bring to mind the great and numberless blessings which He continues to shower upon them and their country, is a call to which we gladly hearken. The duty of religious thankfulness is constantly urged by the Church, and in this age, when many call in question the good of life, even when most fortunate, we should more than ever cherish the spirit of gratitude, which springs from the faith and feeling that God is all good and merciful, and that life is a blessing even to the most wretched, if they look to Him and walk in the ways of His Commandments. Surely we, whether as Catholics or as Americans, can never lack reasons for thankfulness.

In common with all other Americans, we have here a home

and a country, in which we enjoy the rights of freemen, and opportunities to use the powers which God has given us in a way never before granted to men, nor offered to them now even, except in America. Whatever fills the hearts of our fellow-countrymen with joy and pride when they contemplate the marvelous growth and ever-increasing prosperity of our common country, sends also a thrill of gladness through our Catholic hearts. We join with them in looking with delight upon this noblest experiment in self-government ever made by men. We feel a common joy in the thought that we have grown, within a century, from three millions to fifty-five millions of people, from an obscure and almost unknown people, to one of the most powerful and influential nations of the earth. Our prodigious wealth, our unrivalled success in developing the almost inexhaustible resources of our country, our popular cities which, by tens and twenties, have sprang up as by the enchanter's wand, our numberless happy homes, where men of every race and every tongue enjoy the blessings of liberty and peace, under the sway of wise and just laws, are to us sources of gratitude and joy, not less than to other Americans. When we reflect that we, the freest of peoples, have probably the most stable government in the world, that the terrible conflict, the seeds of which were planted like an inherited taint in our blood, and which arrayed in fierce battle half the States against the other half, has only served to strengthen the bonds of national unity, and to bring the whole people into fuller harmony with the great principles which underlie our civil constitution; our belief in the sublime destiny of our country is strengthened, and we look with higher hopes and serener confidence to the future. We are, in a word, a part of this great people, and whatever is good for our country is good for us. This New World was discovered by a great and deeply religious Catholic hero. Catholics were the first to proclaim and put in practice here the principles of religious toleration, and they will be the last to renounce or to violate the Christian chart of freedom of conscience. American Catholics shed their blood for our independence, and the aid which we received from Catholics of other lands was the Providential means which enabled us to come forth victorious from the struggle and to establish ourselves as a free and separate people.

Catholics, who bore a chief part in the founding of this great republic, must ever feel that it is their duty to labor to make it perpetual. The Church holds the fulness of God's supernatural bounties, and the republic His richest earthly gift to His children. Both have a world-wide mission to purify, elevate, ennoble and enlighten men, to free them from slavery, whether of soul or body, of heart or mind. The republic gives liberty to the Church, the Church strengthens the spirit of obedience and devotion to the republic, and both co-operate to make prevail the will of God, which is justice, righteousness, peace, goodness. There is a natural harmony between the Catholic religion, which is wide, strong and enduring, and the character of a great and free people. Among a narrow or enslaved race its action is narrowed; but amid half a world of freemen the vigor of its godlike life expands and pushes forth in every direction. Hence it is in the nature of things that Catholic faith should make headway in a country like our own.

What cause for thankfulness have we not when we recall the progress of the Church in America during the last hundred years? From a few thousand we have grown to be eight millions. Then we were without organization. Now this solemn council, more numerous and more free than any which could be assembled elsewhere, is the most striking evidence of our perfect organization. Then we had no schools; now nearly half a million children receive instruction in Catholic schools. Then churches were few and poor; now they are counted by thousands, and many of them are monuments to the taste and generosity of their builders. But I may not stop to tell the story of the rise and spread of the Church in the United States. Like the growth of the country, progress has been so rapid and so manifest that words but enfeeble the impression stamped upon all minds by the facts themselves.

But while we recall the blessings and privileges which God grants us as Catholics and as Americans, let us bear in mind that what we most need is not wealth or numbers, but virtue, which alone can prevent the bountiful gifts of the Creator from becoming dangerous and hurtful to us. Only they are truly grateful who seek to render themselves worthy of the good they receive, and only in this way can we have the well-founded hope that the blessings we enjoy shall continue. Morality is the basis both of religion and of civil liberty, and if the Church and the country are to remain strong and free, the cause of virtue and of public morality must find in us earnest defenders. Let American Catholics, therefore, ever uphold and show forth in their lives the great principles which underlie free government. Let them, in the spirit of religion and of self respect, lend a willing obedience to law and stand on the side of those who seek to correct abuses and maintain intact the practices and institutions which are the outgrowth of Christian faith, and which have been the great instruments in elevating and purifying human conduct. Let them be sober, honest, peaceful and true to all the obligations which bind them as members of the Church and as citizens of a free country. So shall they become less unworthy of God's blessings and the sense of gratitude growing from year to year and lifting them to higher and nobler life will make them more able to defend both the cause of religion and the cause of patriotism which both work to one end.

Catholic Societies.

SERMON OF RIGHT REV. J. J. KEANE, D.D.,

BISHOP OF RICHMOND.

"As the body is one, and hath many members," etc.—*I. Cor., c. xii, v. 12-27.*

IN the discourses addressed to us since the opening of this council, we have been contemplating, in its various phases, the beauty of the Church of God. Reminded this evening by St. Paul that the Church is the Body of Christ, and knowing that the beauty of the Body of Christ is the beauty of our Incarnate God, we understand how truly it was said, in the opening discourse, that God hath put upon the Church His own beauty. And this, too, is the sublime thought of the Prophet Isaias, who, foretelling the splendors of the kingdom of Christ, says of it: "They shall see the glory of the Lord and the beauty of our God." (Is., xxxv, 2.)

In the preceding discourses we have meditated on the most glorious and exalted constituents of the Church. We have contemplated its divine Head, our Lord and Saviour, Jesus Christ, from whom the whole body receives its growth and its life. We have reflected on its divine Spirit, the Holy Ghost, who proceeds from the Father and the Son, and who has been bestowed by the Father and the Son to be the soul of the Church, the source of its unity, its infallibility, its holiness and its perpetuity. We have considered its heart and arteries and life-blood—namely, the eternal priesthood of our Lord, poured forth through the priesthood of the New Law, and sending through them, by its own divine pulsations, the graces of His redemption to every soul that receives their ministrations. We have gazed upon the majestic symmetry

Very Rev. J. N. Reinbolt, S.F.M.

Very Rev. E. F. Schauer, C.SS.R.

Very Rev. M. D. Lilly, O.P.

Very Rev. A. Magnien, S.S.

Very Rev. C. Fournier, C.S.V.

Very Rev. L. Bushart, S.J.

Very Rev. John B. Hogan, S.S.

Very Rev. C. A. McEvoy, O.S.A.

Very Rev. A. M. Geoble, S.J.

of its well-knit frame, the perpetual apostolic hierarchy, which Christ our Lord formed with such divine art and endowed with such divine strength, that it stands erect with the vigor of perpetual youth in the midst of a changing and crumbling world. And we have seen the energy which it puts forth to turn the lives of men heavenward, to "renew the face of the earth," to pour abroad to the ends of the world the glorious sonship of the children of God.

This evening the words of the holy Apostle invite us to the consideration of an humbler theme, but not, therefore, less important, nor, I trust, less interesting. He tells us of the eye and the ear and the foot and the hand, of the parts of the body which may be in themselves less comely or less honorable, but which all share, nevertheless, in the dignity and comeliness of the one same body of which they are members, and whose functions, though humbler, may yet be very important and even essential to the well-being of the body. It is in this light that I deem it best to treat the subject which has been assigned to me by the Most Reverend Apostolic Delegate, namely, "Catholic Societies." There is too often a tendency to view societies from a merely or principally utilitarian stand-point. But the data in a utilitarian problem are very fluctuating and its conclusions uncertain. I prefer to view the subject in the light of principles, and these the principles given us in Holy Writ. I invite you, therefore, beloved brethren, to reflect with me on the life of the laity, the action and work of the laity, and their combination in associations for the better realization of their work—but to reflect upon it all in the light of this divine fact, that the laity are members of the Body of Christ, that their legitimate action and work as Christians is a participation in the life and work of our divine Head. First, therefore, let us see what is this life of the Body of Christ.

"Christ came," says St. Paul "to be the second Adam, to give life to a dead world." "In Him was life," says St. John; and He says Himself, "I have come that they may have life, and that they may have it more abundantly." This life which he came to bestow—His own divine life—to use his own comparison, He communicated to His members, as the vine communicates its life to its branches: "I am the vine; ye are the branches;" or, to use the figure of St. Paul, as the members live by the life of the body. It is the life of God poured forth on His creatures through the mystery of the Incarnation.

By that bestowal of the life of God He renews in us the image and likeness of God. In the beginning that image and likeness was bestowed on man through the divine Word, who is declared to be the perfect image of the Father; and, therefore, when that image was disfigured in man by sin, it was the same divine Word who came to renew it in us. But, now think what it is to be in the image and likeness of God. God's life is essentially one of action. He is called by the great theologians "*actus purissimus*"—that is, "most pure act." This means that in God there is nothing inert, nothing inactive. Inertia is the imperfection of finite things. Therefore, to be in the image and likeness of God, is to have the action of all the powers of our nature made like to the action which is the life of God. Let us, then, look further, and see how this can be and what it means.

We can view the action, the life of God, in two ways—either in His own being, or in the external works which His act produces. To see that action, that life, that beauty of God in Himself, and in its full clearness, is the beatitude of heaven. "Here," says St. Paul, "we see through a glass darkly; but there, face to face. Here I know in part; but there I shall know even as I am known." And then adds St. John: "We know that we shall be like unto Him, because we shall see Him as He is." The image and likeness of God shall, then, be made perfect in us in the full presence of the adorable Original; and, filled with the overwhelming beatitude of that vision and that likeness, our whole being shall eternally breathe forth the song of ecstacy, "Holy, holy, holy." Here below we see that life of God in Himself, although obscurely and imperfectly, through divine revelation, through the grace of faith, through the embrace of divine love, in contemplative prayer; and, though obscure and imperfect, yet so far is even this sight of the life of God in Himself above all the sweetness and beauty of earthly things, that the soul is forced to cry out, like St. Augustine, "Too late have I known Thee, too late have I loved Thee, O Beauty ever ancient and ever new!"

The second way of viewing God's action is in the external works which it has produced. Freely, and of his own bounteous love, God gave existence to the universe of created things. Everything that He has made bears the stamp of God, and tells of the infinite power, the infinite wisdom and the infinite love which gave it being. St. Augustine exclaims: "God hath made the mighty angels in heaven and the little worms in the earth; and He is not more wonderful in the angels, not less wonderful in the little worms." It is only stunted and darkened minds that do not thus see God in His works. Let me illustrate this by a comparison. We all know how beautifully round and symmetrical an orange is, notwithstanding the little furrows which cover its surface. Now, imagine one of those tiny animalcules, which are so small that they can be discerned only by the aid of the most powerful microscopes, trying to make its way over an orange. The poor little thing would find itself surrounded with mountains which it could not scale and abysses which it could not bridge over, and it would seem lost in a chaos of confusion. In like manner, to minds that have been dwarfed and blinded by losing or shutting out the light which beams from the face of God, the universe is a puzzle, over which they may wail like poor John Stewart Mill, or curse like the pessimists of our day. But, to him who views things, as holy David did, in the light of Him from whom they come, the universe is a mirror which shows forth the beauty of God; all things declare His glory, and even the shades introduced by the sin and folly of the creature only serve to enhance the glorious light of the picture, and blend into the beauteous harmony of the Creator's wisdom, justice and love.

As it is with the life and action and beauty of God, so it is with the life and action and beauty of our divine Saviour. We can consider them either in Himself or in His works. We can contemplate them in Himself, pondering with adoring gratitude the wonders which constitute the mystery of the Incarnation; or we can meditate on the mighty power that goes forth from Him, on the beauty and grandeur of the kingdom of God which He has established on earth.

So, again, it is with the Church. We may view her life and action and beauty in her own organism, in which the divine action of our Lord and the Holy Ghost is so wondrously united with the human action of her ministry and her members, even as the divine nature and the human nature are united in Christ, her divine Head; or we may dwell upon the admirable work which she accomplishes externally, enlightening the world's darkness, purifying the world's corruption and covering the earth with the fruits of civilization, learning and holiness.

And so, in fine, we may consider the divine life bestowed on each Christian soul. We may study its interior silent growth in the beauty of faith, hope, charity and religion; the more and more perfect development of that "kingdom of God which is within us;" the higher and higher advance, as on the ladder of Jacob's vision, from earth and earthiness up towards the bosom of God, and the greater and greater perfection of its likeness to Him as it draws nearer to Him. Or we may view the divine life within it reaching out in good works—as it does in God and in Christ and in the Church—in godlike works, that is, works done in the grace of God, and for the love of God, and by the promptings of the Spirit of God, and after the example of Jesus, the Man-God.

Philosophy tells us that it is through created things that reason comes to the knowledge of the Creator. Thus, too, it is by our external godlike works that the life of God within us is made manifest; for it is the good tree which must bring forth good fruit, and which is known by its fruit. Therefore does St. John lay down the principle and the test: "If you love not your brother, whom you see, how can you say that you love God, whom you see not?" Hence, also, the test which, our divine Lord has told us, shall be applied in the judgment—the presence or absence of the divine life in the soul, and its consequent fitness or unfitness for heaven, shall be decided by its having done, or not done, the godlike works of faith and charity. For, again, life is action, and action must show itself in works.

Thus, beloved brethren, we are led to understand clearly that, in the divine plan of creation, the image and likeness of God, which was bestowed on man, was to consist in his being like to God, not only in the spirituality and immortality of his soul, but also in the noble, holy and useful external works in which his being was meant to exert itself. Thus, also, we understand why, in the plan of divine Providence for the carrying on of the world's life, while the Almighty could easily supply all the wants of all His creatures by His own power and action alone, He has left much of the work to man; has made human action an integral part in the economy of His Providence; has ordained that the welfare of His creatures and the harmony of the world should largely depend on the right or wrong action of men towards one another, in order that man might be a sharer in the glorious work of Providence, in the action and life of his Creator. And hence we likewise understand the two ends for the realization of which our divine Lord established His Church. The first is the advancement of souls in interior holiness and perfection. The second is, the direction of human action in the channels which will be the most useful to mankind and give the greatest glory to God. She is the mother of the contemplatives, whose sublime vocation it is to spend their lives in closest communion with God, and to breathe the atmosphere of heaven around them in this cold earthly world. But she is also the mother of the myriads of holy toilers, whose labors have transformed the face of the earth; and the great bulk of her saints have been the most active and hardworked of men.

I remember reading, not long since, of the daring project of some one who wished to turn the momentum of Niagara and the other cataracts of the country into electric force. He saw in the tremendous rush of the great waterfall a mighty power that was only wasting itself in churning and grinding away its bed, and he asked why it should not be transformed into a force that could be used for lighting and heating our homes and moving our machinery. In like manner, the Church beholds the vast amount of human activity which, all the world over, is lying dormant, or wasted on trifles, or spent on purposes which do not rise above the earth; and her desire is to rouse all inertness into action, and to turn all action towards God—to purify it, to energize it, to direct it to the noblest ends, after the model of the divine Master, who "hath given us an example, that as He hath done, so we also may do;" in a word, to deify it by transforming it into the life and action of the Body of Christ.

Now, one of the chief characteristics of God and of His works, is unity. As, in the adorable Trinity, the Father, the Son, and the Holy Ghost, while distinct in Personality, meet in the unity of the divine Being, so in all God's works the endless multitude of things is everywhere rounded by harmonious order into the unity of the divine plan. From the glorious hierarchy of the angels, down to the shaping of a crystal or the organism of the tiniest insect that floats in the sunbeam, all action is orderly, symmetrical, the tendency everywhere being from isolated force to combined action, and to shapely organisms, and to regular classes, and to the grand order of the universe. So it is likewise with the Church, the Body of Christ, both in her interior life and in her external action. Her interior life of faith, hope, charity and prayer takes shape in her majestic liturgy, culminating in the adorable Sacrifice of the altar, in which all the homage and supplications of all creatures meet in the one masterful homage and supplication of the Immaculate Lamb, through whom all find acceptance before the throne of God. And the outpouring of that interior life in the external works of faith, charity and zeal of all her countless members obeys the same divine law and shapes itself into united and orderly action in thousands of associations. Let us glance at these associations in detail.

First, the craving for Christian perfection, for entire consecration to God's love and His holy service, moulds itself into the Church's religious orders. Obedient to the breathing of the Holy Spirit, to the drawing of His grace, to the impulse of the divine life within them, thousands upon thousands of chosen souls in all ages leave all earthly cares and ambitions, to have God for their only portion and His work for their only occupation. The influence of the Holy Spirit gathers and unites their action, under the control of wise rulers and holy superiors, and the garden of God blooms with the harmonious beauty of monastic perfection. The Carmelites and Carthusians make the solitudes of earth melodious with their chants of adoration to God and of tender love to the Virgin Mother. The Benedictines swarm forth from their convents like a mighty army of zeal and love to conquer a barbarous and heathen world to civilization and to God. The Franciscans cluster around the Seraph of Assisi, and, set on fire by him with love of Jesus Crucified, they carry the sweet example and the irresistible power of our Lord's poverty, humility and sufferings unto the ends of the earth. The Dominicans band together, a great phalanx of sacerdotal learning and zeal, to win a heedless world to Christ by the attraction of the brilliancy and the fervor symbolized by the torch of their illustrious founder. The sons of Ignatius rally around the chair of Peter like a rampart impregnable to all the attacks of error, and from the centre of religious life they carry to every land the light of the Gospel and the blessings of a true Christian education. And so, as the ages roll on and the needs of the world vary and multiply, we see a St. Charles Borromeo, a St. Philip Neri, a St. Vincent de Paul, a St. Francis de Sales, a St. John of God, a St. Alphonsus, a St. Paul of the Cross, a Father Olier and other such giants of ability, holiness and zeal, become centres of attraction for chosen souls and mainsprings of concerted action for great and noble ends. And we see thousands upon thousands of holy men and women filled with cravings and aspirations which nothing but God could satisfy, rejoicing to leave all things for the divine Master's work, and gathering according to the direction of the divine impulse, around one or another of these providential leaders, shaped for united and systematic effort by wise constitutions and rules, consecrated to God and their work by holiest vows, toiling at their allotted tasks in the earnest fervor of that consecration, and pouring the healing, comforting, saving ministrations of Christ and of His Church into millions and millions of grateful hearts.

Then we see the same divine action and life pervading all the ranks of the laity, moving every member and tissue and fibre of the Body of Christ, rousing them to holy desires and efforts, combining them for concerted and efficient action, and making the world teem with organized Christian endeavor for good. First we see the laity combining for distinctively religious ends in confraternities and sodalities, each animated by some special prompting of divine love, all the members striving to increase their own fervor by their united devotion and to kindle the sacred fire, as our Lord desires, in all the hearts around them. Thus the devotion of the faithful increased towards the loving heart of our dear Lord, towards His adorable Sacrament, towards His Immaculate Mother; and by the example of saintly patrons, by the guidance of wise rules and pious directors, the members are moulded to habits of prayer, to the frequentation of the Sacraments and to the practice of Christian virtues. In every place where these holy associations are carefully and zealously directed, they are centres of piety, from which the spirit of devotion is breathed forth into every home and almost into every heart in the parish. There are few parishes, if any, that do not need them; there are none that are not the better for them. And the same may be said of individual souls. There are very few that are not greatly helped in the spiritual life by membership of some well-conducted sodality or confraternity, and there are surely not many who can honestly say that they have no need of such spiritual aids. We live in a world that is full of distractions to lead our minds and hearts from God, full of influences that chill devotion and breed distaste for prayer and piety. If we appreciate this fact, and if we recognize that such a chilling and drying up of the soul is a misfortune to be dreaded and guarded against, then we must recognize too that it is a wise thing to seek spiritual help in these pious confraternities, nay, that it should require very good reasons to excuse one from using them, and that spiritual laziness is certainly not such a reason, but the very contrary.

It would be a most interesting study, did time permit, to see how the Providence of God has, in successive ages, caused the Church's interior piety to take external shape in one or another predominant form of popular devotion. Thus, in our own age, when the rush after material interests makes it so difficult for men to find time and heart for God, it has been the divine Will that the great popular devotion should be that to the Sacred Heart of Jesus, the adorable furnace of holiest love for God and tenderest love for men, whose contemplation must surely suffice, if anything can, to keep our hearts warm and tender and faithful towards our Saviour and God. And now the Providence of God is unlocking that Sacred Heart, that we may understand whence its flames proceed, that we may see that its love is the Holy Ghost, the love eternally proceeding from the Father and the Son, and finding in the Sacred Heart of Jesus our Mediator the channel through which its sweet and blessed flames are poured forth upon mankind. Thus we are given a clearer insight into the mysteries of the Incarnation and the Redemption, and are animated to a more intelligent, a more interior, a more truly spiritual piety. Hence in our days of universal aspiration after popular enlightenment, filled with so many dangers from mistaken science, unspiritual aims and mere externality of life, even among good people, it has pleased God to breathe forth the first beginnings of a special devotion to the Holy Ghost, and to give it form in the Confraternity of the Servants of the Holy Ghost. I am convinced that the time is not far distant when the devotion to the Paraclete, the Spirit of light and love, will be the predominant devotion of the Church. Happy are they who have the grace of tasting and appreciating its first fruits.

Next in dignity and importance to the associations which are the embodiment of popular devotion, come those whose object is to co-operate with the clergy in spreading throughout the world the Gospel of Jesus Christ, and in establishing, maintaining and perfecting every appliance of the kingdom of God for the enlightenment and salvation of men. Throughout the whole Body of Christ, we behold the same zeal which sends the missionaries to the ends of the earth, banding together the multitudes of the faithful in associations for supplying the means which will carry the missionaries to their destination, support them in their arduous labors, and erect the churches and schools which their missions need. Such are the world-wide associations of the Propagation of the Faith and the Holy Childhood; such the kindred associations for supporting the missions among the Indians and the colored people of our country; such the mission unions to aid poor dioceses in building up the Church within their borders; such the admirable societies for supplying poor churches with decent vestments and proper ornaments for the altar and the tabernacle; such the associations for supporting Catholic education, like the noble Young Catholics' Friend Society, which is such an honor to this archdiocese; such the various Catholic publication societies for supporting the Catholic press and for the diffusion of Catholic books and periodicals; such too, the Catholic academies, like the Academy of St. Thomas and the Academy of History, established in Rome by Leo XIII, the Catholic academy founded in London by Cardinal Wiseman, and other similar associations, in which bodies of learned men come together to study science, philosophy and history in the glare of light which modern thought and research have thrown upon them, and to demonstrate the glorious accord between reason and revelation, between science and religion, between the Church and civilization; such, in fine, the great national and international combinations which have taken shape in the Catholic congresses of Europe, and which in faithful Germany have banded together the Catholics of the country as a rampart of adamant for the protection of the inalienable rights of conscience against injustice and tyranny. In all these various ways the members of the Body of Christ labor directly for the glory of God, for the salvation of souls, for the building up of the Church of Christ; and whoever loves God ought to be anxious to have a hand in the work. Nor is it a matter of supererogation, of merely superfluous zeal, that God's creatures should thus seek to take a part in God's work. On the contrary, we have seen that this exercise of human activity, this co-operation of the creatures in the designs of the Creator, is an integral part in the plan of divine Providence; and whoever shirks his part in the toil wrongs both God and his fellow-creatures, and becomes a rusty, broken wheel in the great machine of humanity— a hindrance rather than a help. "He that is not with Me, is against Me," says our Lord, "and he that gathereth not with Me, scattereth." If we have time and strength, we owe them to His work; and if we have not time or strength, we must help with our pecuniary means; and if we have neither time nor strength, nor money, then we must do our best with our prayers, our sympathy, our encouragement, our moral assistance. No one can be selfish, or indifferent, or negligent, and stand excused before the divine Master. There must be no dead, inert members in the Body of Christ.

Closely allied to these associations for the spread and maintenance of the work of Christ, are those whose aim is the suppression of immoral influences which resist the cause of Christ. The ministry of the Church strive for the suppression of immorality by their labors in the pulpit, in the confessional, in their daily contact with the people; but all the faithful must co-operate with them. As all the nerves and forces of the human system co-operate for the expulsion of noxious humors, so must all the members of the Body of Christ work together for the expulsion of evil. "If one member suffer anything," says St. Paul, "all the members suffer with it." As our divine Lord deigned to suffer in His mortal body weariness, hunger, pain and outrage, while His Divinity was almighty, glorious and impassible, so is it the providence of God that His mystical body should be afflicted with the ailments of poor sinful human nature, even while its Head is Christ the Son of God, and its vivifying Spirit God the Holy Ghost. But ah! what a grief to the heart of our Lord are the sinfulness and defilements of His unworthy members! And, as love prompted Veronica to burst through the mocking crowd and wipe away the defilements which marred the beauty of His sacred face, and Magdalen to kiss and soothe His pierced feet, so does the love of Christ prompt generous hearts to labor for the removal from His mystical body of the disfigurements that are unworthy of it.

Now the evils which beset the poor frail members of the Body of Christ are of two classes. Some of them shun the light, and do their wretched work in the hidden secrecy of individual souls; and the Spirit of Christ combats these hiddenly, by the silent influences brought to bear on the individual conscience in the confessional, or in the sanctuary of a good home, or by friendly fraternal correction. Others, on the contrary, are public and aggressive, and strive openly to build up the kingdom of the Evil One on earth; and these have to be resisted openly, publicly, by concerted action. It is needless for me to inform any one who knows the state of society that chief among these open, public and aggressive immoral influences, is the vice of intemperance. It fights against God in the noonday; it plants its batteries of destruction along all our thoroughfares; it seizes on innumerable victims in every class of society, and drags them down to temporal and eternal ruin; it wrecks lives, blasts homes, undermines society, and brings disgrace on the Church of God; it bands its leaders and their minions into a mighty host to control politics and to sway legislation.

Therefore does the Spirit of God rouse thousands upon thousands of earnest souls to a holy indignation against this monstrous evil, and band them together in societies to oppose it, to check its ravages, and, if possible, to banish it, if not from the whole social body, at least from the Church, the Body of Christ. This is the providential origin of our Catholic temperance societies; this their spirit and their aim. Who that has in his heart any love for humanity, any love for Christ, but must sympathize heartily and practically with their endeavor? Who that loves his brethren but must long to save them from this curse? Who that loves Christ but must yearn to wipe this foul stain from His mystical body, as Veronica wiped the defilements from His blessed face? Into our temperance societies, therefore, flock those who have felt the curse and flung it off, and those who have experienced the danger and escaped it; but their main strength lies in the great number of good and zealous men who have never felt the pollution of the monster's touch, but who hate it and combat it, because they love Christ and His Church, and the souls He died to save. They know from the sad experience which is to be found too abundantly around us, that for those who once have been poisoned by the tempter's fang total abstinence is their only safety. Therefore, these lovers of their brethren not only go among the fallen and the tempted ones to reason with them, but add to their words the stronger influence of example, and cheerfully take upon themselves the self-denial of total abstinence, that they may the better save the souls for whom Christ denied Himself all things. They who love sinful indulgence, or they who derive profit from it, may scoff and sneer; honest but mistaken men may hesitate and doubt; but the work is prompted by the Spirit of God, and it must go on. So long as the Church of Christ mourns over the scandalous and devastating work of intemperance, so long must her loving and earnest and self-sacrificing children labor for the abatement of the evil and, if possible, for its cure. Brethren, look at this matter in its true light, and if, as I am confident, you are worthy to be members of the Body of Christ, then will you be sure to give to this great moral movement your practical co-operation, or, at least, your heartfelt sympathy and encouragement. God bless our Catholic temperance societies; God bless our Catholic Total Abstinence Union; and God bless the good and zealous men—bishops, priests and laymen—who are leading and directing them. Our Holy Father, the Pope, has repeatedly blessed them; and to his blessing may that of every bishop and priest and Catholic in the land be added. They are doing a most important work, yea, considering our circumstances, a most essential work in the Church. May their success be glorious, and their reward great and everlasting.

Thus is the Church, like her divine Head, ever intent on "saving her people from their sins." But, besides saving them by delivering them from sin, she longs to save them by preserving them from it. Her fondest desire is to take her members while they are sinless, and keep them sinless. Hence, with true maternal instinct her heart goes out especially towards the young, and her arms encircle them with especial care. She strains every nerve to provide for them the most important of all the blessings of their life—a good Christian education. But education is not confined to school and school-days. School-days are the spring-time, the seed-time of education. The growth and the harvest must develop under the scorching summer sun of subsequent life in the world. The time after school days is the critical period of life, when it is decided whether the carefully-planted seed shall be cultivated and brought to fruit, or allowed to wither away and rot. Besides, the young are naturally gregarious. The old may love solitude, but the young crave companionship; and on the nature of their companionship will largely depend the fortune of their lives. Therefore does the life-force of the Body of Christ naturally put itself forth in the formation of associations for the guidance and improvement of youth, and especially of young men, with whom the danger and the need are greatest. From the day they leave school they are prone to give up all care for their intellectual improvement; therefore they are to be surrounded with incentives to the acquisition of sound knowledge and of a taste for good reading. They are beset with allurements to dangerous amusements and ruinous companionships; therefore are they to be supplied with means of innocent recreation with good companions of their own faith. They are apt to fall into neglect of their religious duties; hence the need of inducements to their approaching the Sacraments regularly.

These are the objects aimed at in our Catholic young men's associations—whether sodalities, lyceums or institutes. To any one who appreciates the dangers to which our young men are exposed, no arguments can be needed to demonstrate the importance of providing them with these safeguards. They are the natural outgrowth of the Church's maternal solicitude and practical good sense. Pastors, above all, who are so well acquainted with the propensities and perils of young men, must recognize the absolute necessity of making special provision for their welfare; and if they desire, as of course they must desire, to mould into true Christian men the youth on whom the future hopes of their congregations depend, they cannot fail to see that the assiduous paternal direction of young men's societies must form an integral and most important part in their pastoral solicitude. This has been again and again urged on the attention of the pastors of the Church by our Holy Father Leo XIII. And our young men must remember that on their seeking, and cheerfully accepting, and dutifully abiding by this guidance, the usefulness and success of their societies must almost entirely depend. If united with the clergy, and heartily in sympathy with their guidance, then their society draws its life directly from the channels of the Church's life, and will be a powerful means for making them intelligent, energetic and thoroughly practical Catholic men.

But should a mistaken spirit of false independence creep in and alienate them from the clergy; should they begin to prefer their own way of thinking and acting rather than the Church's way; should they begin to take the attitude of "we are a society of Catholics, not a Catholic society;" then they may rest assured that their society will not only be no comfort to their pastor, and no blessing to the parish, but it will be an injury rather than a benefit to themselves. It will breed a set of half-hearted Catholics, in little or no sympathy with their Mother, the Church, and they will be only a drag on the wheels of her progress, a hindrance to the extension of the kingdom of Christ. There is great truth in the old saying: "*Corruptio optimi pessima*"—that is, "the very best, when corrupted, becomes the very worst;" and this is pre-eminently true of societies. It behooves both our young men and their pastors to see, therefore, that they avoid the two evils of neglecting to use so powerful a means of vigorous Catholic life as the young men's societies are, and of permitting the societies to languish and go to ruin for want of proper direction. But let the priests and the young men stand together and work together, and then we may rest assured that we are forming a generation of thorough Christians, of loyal Catholics, of devoted soldiers of the Cross of Christ.

Next to the various associations for the spread and preservation of Catholic faith and virtue, we may well place those whose aim is the exercise of Catholic charity. How tender was the heart of Jesus! He never saw a tear but He longed to wipe it away; He never met a bruised heart but He longed to heal and soothe it. These charitable societies are channels through which the tenderness of the heart of Jesus is poured out upon the suffering and the sorrowful. Among them all we may mention as worthy of special honor the St. Vincent de Paul Society, whose conferences are fountains of benediction to the poor in nearly every country of the world. They prove themselves worthy to bear the name of the Apostle of charity under whose patronage they labor. Gladly would I, if time permitted, speak of the thousand contrivances through which the Church exercises that loving care for the poor, which is one of the chief characteristics of Christian civilization. Gladly would I do honor to the myriads of noble hearts who devote their hours of leisure, and many their whole lives, to the sweet task of binding up the wounds of suffering humanity. Gladly would I enumerate the almost countless associations who take charge of destitute little children or of helpless old age; of the poor in their homes and the poor who are homeless; of the working woman's little ones while she is at her work, and of poor servants who can find no work; of the lonely girl who is tottering amid dangers, or the poor neglected bootblack or newsboy; of the needy sick and the friendless dead. Their name is legion, and not one is missing from the Book of Life. We bless and praise them now, and one day they will hear the Master say: "As often as ye did it to these My least ones, ye have done it unto Me." Oh! let them remember that it is upon Him they bestow their charity, and let them do it with all the tenderness and thoughtful considerateness which He deserves. Let them give not merely food and clothing to the body, but sympathy and affection to the suffering heart. Let them pray as they approach the poor man's door, that they may see Jesus there, and deal with Him reverently and lovingly; and, if they find some whom misfortune has discouraged, and hardship has hardened, and whom temptation has led astray from God, let them here see their highest and best work, and cease not till the sweet influences of genuine charity have melted the hardness and brought the wanderer back to the Good Shepherd. Let them, after the example of St. Vincent and of our divine Lord, aim at making the poor really better and happier, that they may be worthy of the glorious position which they hold as the dispensers of the tender charity of Christ and of His Church.

There is another class of societies which, though they may not be considered to flow directly from the Spirit of Christ, so as to be functions of His mystical Body, are in perfect harmony with it and deserving of our commendation. These are the societies which are formed for the promotion of social union among Catholics, or to secure their pecuniary assistance to one another in times of sickness and death. These objects are the natural dictates of practical good sense; and there is always sure to be found a close relationship between practical good sense and the religion of Christ. It is unquestionably the will of God that we should associate fraternally with one another, and aid one another in times of need; and as the Church loves to see her people industrious and thrifty, so does she love to see them band together for the better securing of even their temporal comfort and prosperity.

But these societies have another great advantage. They are a strong safeguard against the allurements of societies which conceal evil or dangerous designs under the attractive cloak of benevolence and mutual assistance. A great writer has well said that the devil is the ape of Almighty God, always counterfeiting the ways of divine Providence, in order to lure men astray by the glitter of his false coin. We all know how cunningly and how successfully he is now using for that purpose the specious but delusive and pernicious brotherhood of secret societies. It is not my province to enter into any detailed examination of their nature. The Vicar of Christ has lately given to the world a summing up of the Church's long experience in dealing with them. He has shown that in many countries they stand arrayed in open hostility to the religion and the Church of Jesus Christ, and that elsewhere they contain the same evil tendencies, at least in germ. We have all heard expressions like these: "I will be a good enough man if I am as good as my society would make me," "If I can live up to the spirit of my society, that will be religion enough for me," and other declarations of a similar sort. Now, no matter how good a thing may be in itself, if it put itself forward as a substitute for the religion and Church of Jesus Christ it becomes a counterfeit, a delusion and a snare. Natural religion or natural benevolence is good, as far as it goes, as a vestibule to supernatural religion and Christian charity; but should it wish to make itself the religion of the world, and thus virtually supplant Christ our Lord, then it is "Satan clothed as an angel of light." The Church is convinced, from her long and world-wide experience, that such is the tendency and the aim of the secret societies, whose ramifications now cover the earth. Therefore she warns her children against them, and forbids membership in them under penalty of exclusion from her communion and Sacraments. And she rejoices at the multiplication of thoroughly Catholic benevolent and beneficial associations, in which the natural virtues are brought into their proper relation with supernatural religion, and in which Catholics are guarded against the inducements held out by bad or dangerous societies.

And now, beloved brethren, let us glance back and conclude. We have studied, although very briefly and imperfectly, the providential work of the laity in the Church of God. We have glanced at the various associations in which they are banded together by the instincts of nature and the guidance of grace for holy and admirable purposes—for increasing popular piety, for extending and establishing the kingdom of Christ, for resisting the destructive influence of an aggressive and scandalous vice, for moulding our youth into sterling Christian men, for bringing comfort and relief to the suffering poor, for promoting fraternal union and co-operation among Catholics, and thus rendering harmless the attractions of dangerous societies. We have seen how naturally their activity in all these good works flows from their being members of the Body of Christ, living by its life and moved by its action. We have seen how, by zealous activity in the prosecution of these noble ends, they are made worthy of our divine Head, and are perfected in the image and likeness of our heavenly Father, the ever active and infinitely loving God. And we have seen how naturally and how profitably individual zeal is combined and shaped for concerted action by Catholic associations.

In the light of these facts, no one surely can question whether Catholic societies are advisable or not. As well might one question whether the members of the Body of Christ should act, and should act harmoniously and efficiently. If, in any particular instance, Catholic societies are found not to work satisfactorily, it must be that they are not acting in harmony with the spirit of the Church, because they are not acting in union with her. They must have in some manner drifted away from the paternal direction of the clergy; they have got outside of the Church's guidance; they are not moved by her life. It is a great misfortune when zeal and energy are thus wanted and perhaps misused for want of being rightly directed; and it behooves both societies and pastors to see to it that no such drifting loose, no such waste or misdirection of energy be allowed. Catholic activity is not so abundant that we can afford to let any of it go to loss. Let priests and people, therefore, be careful to keep united, that all their action may be harmonious and useful, as becomes the Body of Christ.

Nor again can any one, with all these facts before him, question whether it is advisable or not for every individual Catholic to take an active interest in the work of Catholic societies. As well ask whether it is allowable to a Catholic to feel indifferent about the advance of religion, the spread of the Church, the temporal and eternal welfare of his brethren; or, whether he might not confine his interest in them to a mere sentimental sympathy, without active co-operation. The notion carries with it its own condemnation, and is repugnant to the instincts of every truly Catholic heart. There must be no cold, inert, sluggish members in the Body of Christ. Above all, there must be no carping, sneering members, who try to palliate their own inaction by decrying the activity of others. If the spirit of God is in us, let us show it by the untiringness of our Catholic action, and let our hearts, like that of our dear Lord, be eaten up with zeal for the honor and beauty of the Church of God. Let time, and strength, and money, and loving encouragement be all employed assiduously and to the utmost, in pushing on the work of God and in strengthening every organization that is engaged in it. Let the motto of every Catholic society and of every individual member of the Church be that of the illustrious founder of the Society of Jesus: "*Omnia ad majorem Dei gloriam*—All for the greater glory of God."

The Church and Science.

SERMON OF RIGHT REV. THOMAS A. BECKER, D.D.,

BISHOP OF WILMINGTON, DEL.

"The house of God, which is the Church of the living God, the pillar and ground of truth."—*St. Paul's First Epistle to Timothy, c. iii, v. 15.*

WHETHER we consider the actual existence of the Catholic Church presenting herself before the world, and claiming to be the mother Church of Christianity, or examine her history in the records of Holy Scripture and the chronicle of every age, one fact must necessarily challenge our admiration—namely, she is the only constant quantity in the midst of evanescent variables. This peculiarity, certainly not communicated to any other moral organization, has caused thinking minds, accustomed to and fond of change, to give an almost scientific classification to the Catholic Church as something apart, and they deem her at least a wonderful fossil, the precise nature of which, perhaps, even as a conservative power, they can hardly imagine. It is our duty to point out as concisely as we can what are some of the claims and essential characteristics of the Church, of which "the Maker and Founder is God," for it is of her that our Lord and Redeemer speaks when He says emphatically, "I will build My Church," (Matt., xvi, 18,) and of her St. Paul uses the remarkable words of the text, describing to his beloved disciple in the faith how he was to conduct himself as a bishop in the "House of God, which is the Church of the living God, the pillar and ground of truth." (I. Timothy, iii, 15.)

By the Church in the Old Law was clearly meant that society which God had chosen and called forth from among all other nations to be the recipient of His gracious promises, and to be the chosen people when the Redeemer should come as the Ruler of the whole world. That society had a divine protection, since through it the glory of God was to be made known by the salvation of men. More definite words cannot be found than those used by the Apostle of the nations, St. Paul, when writing to the Romans in the 9th chapter, 4th and 5th verses, he describes the claim of the Church in the Old Law: "To whom belongeth the adoption of children, and the glory, and the covenant, and the giving of the law, and the service of God, and the promises: whose also are the fathers, and of whom is Christ, according to the flesh, who is over all things God blessed forever. Amen." In this Church, which was indubitably a divine institution, Almighty God set forth His power in the most distinctively evident manner. Not only did He appear to the patriarchs, but by his wonders left that permanent impression upon the Hebrews which to this day they retain as the best corroborative testimony of their records. They cannot be understood, as a people, without a knowledge of their religion. Their religion is maimed, and inexplicable unless by the Church, which bore the promise of a Redeemer. This promise was fulfilled in Him who was born according to the prophecy of Isaias. All, therefore, which had preceded the coming of Christ was simply the promise; here is the fulfillment, for He came not to destroy, but to fulfill. (St. Matt., v, 17.) To one of His disciples He makes ampler declarations, almost appalling in their wondrous extent. He speaks of that one chosen to be the head over his brethren, that he should be a rock on which Christ would build His Church and the gates of hell should not prevail against it; that to him should be given the keys of heaven, and that his loosing and binding on earth should be ratified in heaven. (St. Matt., xvi, 19.) And to the same person, carefully mentioned by name and surname, the Lord, risen from the dead, gives triple faculties beyond his brethren; after having exacted from him a triple attestation of fealty, to feed His lambs, feed His sheep, to feed His whole flock, (St. John, xxi, 15, 16, 17,) in order that it might be a fold in unity, indivisible. Christ was therefore, when on earth, *the whole teaching Church*. He possessed all truth, complete authority, and permanently infallible magistracy. He promised to give all that He possessed to His Church, that which He had as the Redeemer and the Teacher of mankind. He promised this to His society, which is the Church.

But this teaching was for the benefit of men to the end of time. The permanency of Christ's teaching was to be provided by Himself. He would send the Holy Ghost to lead His Church into all truth. (St. John, xiv, 26.) "But the Paraclete, the Holy Ghost, whom the Father will send in My name, He will teach you all things, and bring all things to your mind, whatsoever I shall have said to you." And, finally, as the last blessing He says, "Go ye, therefore, and teach all nations, baptizing them in the name of the Father, and of the Son, and of the Holy Ghost; teaching them to observe all things whatsoever I have commanded you, and behold I am with you all days, even to the consummation of the world." (Matt., xxviii, 19-20.) This, then, is the theory; this, also, is the practice of the Church of God, which is the House of the living God, the pillar and ground of truth. She claims to be, and she is, the sole possessor of all the rich heritage of authority from her divine Founder, and, like all absolute truth, she is intolerant of rivals. She would be untrue to her divine Founder were she to abate one jot or one tittle of that deposit which belongs to her as the "pillar and ground of truth."

Nor is it possible to have the full consciousness of Catholic truth until we have entirely grasped the idea of authority with which the Church teaches. It is exactly the same teaching authority as is that of Christ. It was especially in this that the teaching of Christ differed from that of the doctors of the law, since it is most distinctly asserted of Him that "He taught with authority, and not as the scribes." (St. Mark, i, 22.) When, therefore, it is thoroughly understood by thinking men the Church Catholic is simply, truly and really Christ continuing his mission, living in the world, according to His gracious promises, "even to the consummation of ages," (St. Matt., xxviii, 20,) and teaching all men "who wish to come to a knowledge of the truth" the entire system of revelation, they feel the vigor of St. Paul's admirably graphic description of that perennial society, concerning which he says that she is "the House of God, the pillar and ground of the truth."

Thus we have by anticipation a universal solvent of all difficulties, however plausible they may be presented against the Church; for she is made out to be the very voice of the living Saviour, guiding our footsteps in all that belongs to the supernatural life. We have an impregnable position, since the promise is divine, that the gates of hell shall not prevail against that house which is built upon a rock. It was chiefly for the higher manifestation of His Godhead that He performed miracles, since these were, in their nature, transient; but His teachings were enduring. The truths which He revealed were such as reason could not have known, and they belonged to a sphere as much beyond mere worldly interests and favor as the soul is above the body. It would, therefore, be insulting to right reason to suppose a conflict possible, since parallel lines cannot meet. It is only science falsely so called which by the malice of men is perverted to seem antagonistic to the Church. Systems from this source have often presented a bold front. Chiefly remarkable for their newness of expression, they have had their little day, and the unchangeable Church saw them born, and calmly watched their funeral.

On the other hand, while the Church logically insists on the great truth, "what does it profit a man to gain the whole world and lose his soul," (St. Matt., xvi, 26), yet she can appeal with equal truthfulness to the facts of history concerning her developments of science and learning. She has, like a vestal virgin, fed the earthly flock in arts and sciences with celestial nutriment, and can count among her faithful children the best intellects and first discoverers in every branch of knowledge. Are examples of philosophy required? Who can compare with St. Thomas, the Angel of the Schools? Do we desire to take up an indefinite amount of time recounting the Fathers and doctors of the Church? In architecture, we point to those glorious cathedrals, which, like permanent prayers, proclaim in stone the glory of that sublime religion which produced them and gave them life and voice. In painting, the theme was furnished by her history, and the execution faithfully performed through the inspiration of her genius, while life was breathed into the marble by those who, at her bidding, caused the virtues of the saints to take enduring form in the stead of the apotheosis of vices, or earthly praise of mere human prowess. In music, who can compare with those transcendent intellects born of the Catholic Church, who blended the harmonies of the angels with the human voice in honor of Him "whose kingdom shall have no end?" (St. Luke, 1.) Not an art exists but she has chained in loving obedience to her triumphal chariot, not a science can exist but is at once made subservient to her sway.

It is true, she weighs well her conclusions, and being eternal, she can afford to wait until the sober thought of matured judgment shall have corrected hastily drawn inferences. The Sacred Scriptures, for instance, under her protection—where alone they can be properly understood—have undergone innumerable attacks on the part of intellects so keen and indwelt by a hatred so far beyond expression that no future reinforcements can arise to equal either their ability or audacity, when battling against the Word of God and His Church. Yet, the Scriptures, defended by the invulnerable panoply of the Church, stand forth unchanged and unscathed, and both remain sublimely calm and beautiful after the battles of centuries, as the rainbow which smiles upon the earth after the tempest. It is right and logical to draw an inference from the past, and since no antagonism has hitherto been able to be proved between divine revelation and true human science, we may unhesitatingly assert that no contradiction can ever be conceived. Their objects or aims are different, but by no means contradictory; they are diverse, yet never opposite. Revelation has in its very nature to give us a knowledge of the invisible world, the superior, nay, even the immortal part; science must treat of the empirical, the material, the transient. The former is fixed truth, which depends on the veracity of God; the latter must be tried or experimented upon—is subject to progress or even neglect. Experimental evidence is the ultimate barrier beyond which it dares not go.

Here the Church steps in, and, using the highest formula of science as her lowest stepping stone, claims within her own ambit the power and potency of all things. She gives to an intelligent Cause the first act of creation, which atheists unintelligibly ascribe to senseless matter, which they should logically fall down and worship as the author of their highest and most perfect realizations. We prefer to rise from effect to cause; from the visible to the invisible; from thought to the Author of mind; from the creature endowed with noble intellect to the Creator. In this the Church fears no examination; she dreads no investigation. Unthinking and superficial views she fears. She beseeches men to lay aside the prejudices by which they have been enwrapped, and pleads with all to consider her claims as the constant guide; her works as the fruits of her teachings; her history as the constant quantity which can no more diminish than that truth, of which she is the pillar and foundation, and which is for men the voice of the living God.

The Catholicity of the Church.

SERMON OF RIGHT REV. JAMES O'CONNOR, D.D.,

VICAR APOSTOLIC OF NEBRASKA.

Going, therefore, teach ye all nations.—*Matt., c. xxviii, v. 19.*

THE subject on which I have been asked to address you this evening, dear brethren, is "The Catholicity of the Church." Catholicity, or universality, is an essential attribute of the Church of Christ. She is necessarily Catholic, and she alone is or can be such. Her mission, the object for which she was established, is Catholic, and she must needs be Catholic. She was instituted to lead men to a knowledge of the true God, to train them to the practice of the Christian virtues, and, by so doing, to prepare them for eternal happiness. This she was to do, not by writing, but by teaching and by administering to every individual visible sacraments. Faith was "to come from hearing." No one could enter into the kingdom of heaven except by baptism. No one could have life in him who did not "eat the flesh of the Son of Man, and drink His blood."

But the Church could not do this sort of work, could not teach and administer sacraments, where she did not exist. Hence our Lord commissioned and positively commanded His Apostles to put themselves in a position to perform it in the very natural manner in which He had prescribed it should be done. "All power," He said to them, "is given to Me in heaven and on earth. Going, therefore, teach ye all nations, baptizing them in the name of the Father, and of the Son, and of the Holy Ghost. Teaching them to observe all things whatsoever I have commanded you. And behold I am with you all days even to the consummation of the world."

He had previously restricted their teaching to the Jewish people. "Go not," He said, "into the way of the Gentiles, and into the city of the Samaritans enter ye not." The Law was for the Jews. "In Judea," said the Psalmist, "God is known." This restriction He now removes, and throws open the whole world to their preaching. Now the kingdom of God is to be taken from the Jews, "and given to a nation yielding the fruits thereof." "And I will say to that which was not My people, thou art My people."

The diffusion of the Church over the world was to take place without fail. It was not left to depend on the unaided efforts of the Apostles. Our Lord Himself guaranteed its success, when He said: "I am with you all days, even to the consummation of the world." But for this assurance the Apostles would have shrank appalled from the task assigned them. When the Lord commanded Moses to free his people from the bondage of the Pharoes, the Patriarch exclaimed in very natural surprise: "Who am I that I should go to Pharoe, and bring forth the people of Israel out of Egypt?" But when he heard that "I will be with thee," and received power to work miracles in proof of his mission, he hesitated no longer, well knowing that what was impossible to him would, with the divine aid, be not only possible but easy.

But the voice of the Apostles, or their teaching, was not to reach every individual beyond the confines of Judea. Many would be found unworthy of such a favor. Their culpable idolatry and infidelity, their violations of the natural law written on their hearts, the shameful vices to which the majority of them were addicted, would keep from them the apostolic message. They would, indeed, always have sufficient grace to merit it, but, not corresponding with this grace, the message would not be delivered to them.

And we know that, in point of fact, many who heard it, did not heed it. They "loved darkness rather than the light," for the light led to the narrow way in which only the few care to walk. Or, "they neglected, going their way, one to his farm, and another to his merchandise;" or, they laid hands on the servants of the King, and, having treated them contumeliously, put them to death.

These two classes, they who do not deserve the grace of faith, and they who reject it, have constituted the great majority of men, in every age, and will continue to do so to the end of time.

For, "many are called, and few are chosen." And wide is the gate, and broad is the way that leadeth to destruction, and many there are who go in thereat. How narrow is the gate and straight the way that leadeth to life, and few there are that find it.

The Catholicity of the Church, then, was to be not physical, but moral. She was to be morally, not physically, Catholic. She was not to include all men within her fold, or even the majority of them, but a sufficient number, nevertheless, to show that she had fulfilled the commission of her divine Founder, to "teach all nations." These words, "all nations," in this text and other texts quoted in this connection cannot, from what has been said, be taken in a physical sense. They cannot mean absolutely all men. They must, then, be taken in, at least, a moral sense. The Church was to be so diffused as that she could be said with truth to be world-wide, Catholic, universal, though actually embracing only a minority of those in the world.

Again, the Catholicity of the Church was not to be simply a material Catholicity, a Catholicity of mere numbers, the Catholicity of a crowd, or of a vast number of crowds scattered over the face of the earth. No; it was to be a formal, organic Catholicity, a Catholicity in unity. The Church was to grow as the vine grows. She was to grow as the grain of mustard seed, "which is the least of all seeds, but which, when it is grown up, is greater than any herbs, and becometh a tree, so that the birds of the air come and dwell in the branches thereof." She was, in a word, to be a growth, not an aggregation, and, in growing, she was, by the very law of growth, to preserve her identity. Spread and increase as she might, she was always to remain that same Church on which the Holy Ghost had descended on the day of Pentecost. Then the Church was a society, an independent, perfect society, and she must needs grow as a society grows, by bringing her newly acquired members under obedience to a common authority, directing them by general laws, and the same means, to the attainment of a common end, and thus assimilating them to and incorporating them in herself.

Her mission, the work she had to do, required her to be Catholic, and to be Catholic always. Her very nature and her constitution made her Catholicity formal and organic. She was to become Catholic by teaching and baptizing, and her teaching and governing authority was to preserve and perpetuate her Catholicity. It was well calculated to do so. It was an external, visible, speaking authority, capable of explaining itself, so that no one could possibly mistake its meaning. It was a divine authority, which all were bound to obey under pain of eternal death, for He who gave it had said: "He that hears you, hears Me;" "those that do not believe shall be condemned."

Men, indeed, were to be physically free to recognize that authority or not, or having submitted to it, to again reject it. Those who were invited to the marriage feast would not come; and the Apostle tells us, "there must be also heresies." But this was not to hinder or destroy the Catholicity of the Church. If some would refuse the Gospel, others would accept it. If, in the lapse of ages, many would fall away from Catholic unity, others would take their places, and thus, "the wedding would be filled with guests."

From what has been said, it is, I think, evident that Catholicity is an essential quality or attribute of the Church of Christ. Let me now endeavor to show you that it does not and cannot belong to any of those Christian societies not in communion with the Church of Rome.

If we consider those societies singly and apart, there is not one of them that can claim even material Catholicity. Each is restricted to a particular country; or, if we find societies of the same name in two or more countries, we shall find that they differ more or less in doctrine, and are wholly independent of each other in government. They are different organizations, different societies, and therefore different Churches. Some of them, indeed, have insignificant make-believe missionary stations in pagan lands, but these exercise no appreciable religious influence on the people amongst whom they have been established.

And if we take those societies collectively, whatever may be said of their material Catholicity, they certainly have not formal Catholicity. Yet without this formal Catholicity, though they might count their adherents by hundreds of millions, they would have no claim whatever to be regarded as the Church of Christ. They are not one but many Churches, differing as widely from each other as do the civil governments under which they live, and to which several of them belong. Such of them as are State Churches, are organized on national, not Catholic lines, and these as well as those that are not State institutions, make it a standing objection to us, that we recognize a supreme authority outside the countries where we are. They thus, implicitly at least, deny the Catholicity of the Church of Christ, for how could she be Catholic without a supreme general authority such as we acknowledge in the Bishop of Rome?

"The Church," says St. Augustine, "is everywhere, and heresy is everywhere. But the Church is everywhere one and the same; heresies are not the same, but most different. They do not recognize each other, and are not, therefore, Catholic." Nor is there anything in any of those societies that would give hope of their formal Catholicity in the future. Quite the contrary. In each and every one of them, private judgment is the fundamental rule of faith, and private judgment sooner or later reduces religious life to individualism, and makes authority, which is the formal bond of every society, civil and religious, a usurpation and a contradiction. If every one of those societies is not what Macaulay calls the Church of England, "a hundred sects battling within one Church," and that, let me add, a Church which nowadays teaches no doctrine and condemns no heresy, and which, as Dr. Pusey said, "has made England a numerous nation of heathen," it is always in a fair way to become such.

Then Protestantism, it should be borne in mind, was not diffused by teaching the nations, but by detaching men from the Church, and that chiefly by misrepresenting her doctrines, by appeals in the first instance to the grosser passions, and by brute force. Nor has it acquired any new territory since the Reformation, except by colonization. On the contrary, it has everywhere lost ground, and nowhere more than in its former strongholds. Germany and Switzerland are now dominated by infidelity. The Protestant theologian Claude Harms, said of Germany, that "he could write on his thumb nail, all the doctrines of the reformers, still universally held there," and another Protestant writer quoted by the *Catholic World* for last June, compares its condition to "that of pagan Rome, just before the advent of Christ, when the people had ceased to bring sacrifices, and cared no more for their idols, yet had nothing to put in their place." Let it suffice to add, in this connection, that the poor remnant of orthodox Protestantism in Prussia, is now fighting for its life in the Catholic

Centre of the Reichstag, under the leadership of the eloquent Windthorst. For more than a century, Protestants did not even dream of evangelizing the heathen. The Synod of Dort declared that, for any one to expose himself to the danger of doing so, without a special mission from on high, would be to tempt God. Not thus thought St. Paul, the "vessel of election" that had been chosen to carry the name of Christ before the Gentiles. "A necessity lieth upon me," said he, "for woe is unto me if I preach not the Gospel." He, indeed, and the other Apostles had a special mission to teach the Gentiles, but to restrict that mission to the Gentiles of apostolic times would be simply absurd, and would be to blame the action of even modern Protestants, who at least attempt the conversion of the heathen. Nor did Protestants undertake anything of importance in this matter, till the beginning of the present century. Since then they have spent millions yearly on foreign missions, but with no other result than to show the utter barrenness of such enterprises. Protestant missioners have succeeded as traders; they have in some places succeeded as school teachers,—there is no reason why they should not have done so—but they have made no converts to speak of. They have been able to convince many of their pupils of the folly of idolatry and polytheism,—any mere deist might have done this,—but the scholars as a rule became infidels, not Christians. Why, it is enough to say, that a table compiled by the writer in the *Catholic World* already referred to from the latest edition of "Christian Missions," gives but eight hundred and fifty converts, such as they were, for all the Protestant missions in Asia, Africa and Australasia!

How could it be otherwise? "If any one," says Christ, "abide not in Me, he shall be cast forth as a branch, and shall wither."

And, now, if we turn our thoughts to the Church in communion with Rome, what a different state of things do we not find! From immemorial time she has had material Catholicity. At the very beginning of the second century the Proconsul Pliny wrote to the Emperor Trajan that Christianity had spread so widely in Bithynia that "the temples were nearly deserted and the sacrifices suspended." "There is," says St. Justin Martyr, in the same century, "no people, whether Greek or barbarian, among whom prayers and thanksgiving are not offered to the Father and Creator of the world, in the name of Christ crucified." "We are of yesterday," says

Tertullian, "and we fill all places, leaving to you only the temples." "Everywhere," says the same Father, "are to be found the disciples of the Crucified, among the Parthians and Medes, the Elamites and Mesopotamians, in Armenia and Phrygia, Cappadocia and Pontus, Asia Minor, Egypt and Cyrene, mingled with the various tribes of the Getuli and Moors in Gaul, in Spain, in Britain and Germany."

This was in the days of persecution. This was in times when to profess Christianity exposed men to the danger of losing all that is most precious in life, and life itself even, under tortures the most appalling. After the conversion of Constantine, when the Church was able to walk in the light of day, we see her lines extending across all known lands—in Europe, Africa and Asia—till they lose themselves in the wastes and forests of the outside barbarians. Indeed, so completely has she filled the world since that time that, looking back through the centuries, we see little else but her. Her history since then may be said to be the history of the civilized world.

Heresies and schisms, formidable by their numbers and their influence, went out from her from time to time, but her conquests more than compensated her for the losses thus sustained. The empire fell, but she survived it, tamed and softened its fierce destroyers, and formed them into the Christendom of the Middle Ages.

She increased steadily from age to age, and her growth has been most rapid during the last four centuries, when defections from her ranks were most numerous and the opposition of her enemies was most formidable. A table showing the gradual growth of the Church from the first century to the present time was published recently in Germany by some non-Catholic statisticians. According to it, she had in the first century five hundred thousand members, in the second two millions, in the third five millions, in the fourth ten, and so on to the nineteenth, when, in 1876, she could count two hundred and sixty millions.

There can then be no doubt as to her material Catholicity. But her formal Catholicity is equally beyond question. St. Ireneus says of the Roman Church: "For with this Church, on account of her more powerful principality, it is necessary that every Church, that is, the faithful who are on all sides, should agree." This saint was a Greek, a disciple of St. Polycarp, who was a disciple of St. John the Evangelist, and carried with him into Gaul, in the second century, the apostolic traditions of the East. The Bishops of Rome have ever insisted on this agreement, and defined its limits. They have always claimed a primacy of honor and jurisdiction over all the Churches of Christendom, or, as St. Chrysostom expresses it, "the presidency of the universal Church," which Christ committed to Peter after his fall, and the claim has been acknowledged everywhere and always. This is simply matter of fact, but of fact that can be established by whole volumes of evidence, and which, I doubt not, will be satisfactorily established in the course of these evening sermons.

"In virtue of his office," says Archbishop Kenrick, "the Pontiff teaches with authority, and directs his teaching to all the children of the Church, wherever they may be found, pastors and people; he pronounces judgment on all whose faith is suspected, to whatever rank they belong; he condemns heresy wherever it may have originated, or by whomsoever it may be supported; he calls on his colleagues, the bishops, to concur in the condemnation; he assembles them in council to investigate and judge with him the controversies that are raised, or to concur, by their harmonious judgment and action, in rooting out condemned errors; he promulgates their definitions of faith, and incessantly guards the sacred deposit of divine doctrine. All these acts have been performed in all ages of the Church by the Bishop of Rome, as successor of St. Peter, and have been universally acknowledged to be the prerogatives and duties of his office."

Whoever is anxious to see the proofs of these general statements of your late illustrious archbishop, will find them in his work on "The Primacy," published in this city in 1857.

And, I need not tell you, that this authority of the Pope over the universal Church is exercised more fully and more freely to-day than at any former time. A writer in a recent number of the *Contemporary Review* says of the reigning Pontiff, Leo XIII, in this connection: "On May 28, 1878, he creates the Diocese of Chicontrini in Canada; on June 21, the Apostolic Vicariate of Kansuh in China; on July 31, he converts the Apostolic Vicariate of Montevideo into a bishopric; on September 13, he cuts off a tract of territory from the See of Canstantineh and annexes it to that of Algiers; on December 20, he divides the Diocese of Beverly to make a new Diocese of Leeds; and, in September of the next year, makes the Church of St. Anne its Cathedral; on January 20, 1880, he raises the Vicariate of Cracow into an episcopate, and gives it a new territorial definition; on May 25, he halves the Diocese of Yucatan, in Mexico, and forms that of Sabasco; on July 29, he divides, in the same way, the Archiepiscopal See of Santa Fe de Bogola, in New Granada, and forms the Diocese of Sunza; on July 5, 1881, he constitutes an episcopal hierarchy in Bosnia and Herzigovina; on September 30, he reduces the number of the Portuguese bishoprics, and remodels their territorial distribution."

"Every thought of the pontifical heart," observes the same writer farther on, "dilates and broadens to embrace the world. He is the only power in existence whose inherent and essential obligation it is to go on incessantly acquiring and extending over all civilized, and even all barbarous, nations, an intellectual and moral ascendency."

Yet it should be borne in mind that these are only a very few acts of the universal jurisdiction exercised by the present Pope since his elevation to the Chair of Peter.

It is then evident that the Churches in communion with Rome, whilst having each her own local government, have ever been integral parts of one great Church, under one supreme head, and that this Church, and this alone, has been always Catholic in numbers, in doctrine, in government, in unity, and has had in the teaching and governing authority of her chief bishop a principle preservative of her unity and her Catholicity. She alone, then, is the Church of Christ. For a church that is not Catholic cannot teach all nations, cannot do the work, to do which Christ established His Church. In her, too, and in her alone, are fulfilled the prophecies in regard to the Catholicity of Christ's Church.

She is that "city of God" of which "glorious things are said." She is that Church promised by the eternal Father to His only begotten Son, when He said: "Ask of Me, and I will give Thee the Gentiles for Thy inheritance, and the utmost parts of the earth for Thy possession."

In her all nations praise the Lord. She speaks to-day as she spoke on the day of Pentecost, "in diverse tongues, as the Holy Ghost gives her to speak."

They were her children in whose name the ancients sang: "Thou hast redeemed us to God, in Thy blood, out of every tribe, and tongue, and people, and nation, and hast made us to our God a kingdom and priests, and we shall reign on the earth."

She, in fine, is the Church which, her struggles and her sufferings in this world at an end, will form "that multitude which no man can number, of all nations, and tribes, and peoples, and tongues, that will stand before the throne, in sight of the Lamb, and sing His praises for ever and ever."

The Sanctity of the Church.

SERMON OF RIGHT REV. JOHN HENNESSY, D.D.,

BISHOP OF DUBUQUE.

"Husbands, love your wives as Christ also loved the Church and delivered Himself up for it, that He might sanctify it, cleansing it by the laver of water in the word of life, that He might present it to Himself a glorious Church, not having spot or wrinkle, or any such thing, but that it should be holy and without blemish."—*Ephesians*, c. 5, v. 25–27."

IN the verses just read, St. Paul sets before us two stages in the life of the Church, one in time and the other in eternity, one a stage of preparation and the other of perfection; one of sanctification and the other of glory, in which she shall appear without spot or wrinkle or any such thing. She is at present on the way to what she will be. Our Lord delivered Himself up to sanctify her by the laver of water in the word of life; that is, by faith and baptism, or by teaching and the dispensation of mysteries. That His sacrifice was not without fruit of sanctity is declared implicitly by the Apostle when he speaks of Christ's love for His Church, and proposes it as a model to every Christian husband. Knowing the relations between husband and wife and the indissoluble love by which they are united, the Apostle surely wished and desired that the love of the husband for his wife be constant and unremitting. To make good His argument, the model love should not be less perfect than its imitation. He could never have proposed to a Christian husband as His model a love which could be interrupted, which could degenerate into hate; therefore, the love of Christ for His Church must be permanent—perpetual. "No man ever hated his own flesh, but nourisheth and cherisheth it as also Christ doth the Church." Between Christ and the Church

Very Rev. A. Leeson, S.St.J

Very Rev. L. Gollbehœde, O.S.F.

Very Rev. Henry Drees, C.P.P.S.

Very Rev. Theobald Butler, S.J.

Very Rev. Robert Fulton, S.J.

Very Rev. R. Phelan, V.G., D.D.

Very Rev. James Strub, C.S.Sp.

Very Rev. John N. Lemmens, D.D.

Very Rev. A. J. Smits, O.C.C.

there never can be hate. As the object of Christ's love in the Church is her sanctity, it follows that it also must ever remain continuous, unbroken, without interruption of any kind. It must be as lasting as the laver of water and the word of life that produce it. This has been the faith of the ages. It is the teaching of the Apostles and of the Fathers of Nice in the creeds they have left us. It is found unmistakably in the noble epithets so often applied to the Church throughout the New Testament, such as, "Kingdom of Heaven," "City of God," "Temple of the Holy Ghost," "Body of Christ." It is the crowning attribute of God's Church. All her other properties are subservient to it; all her agencies and activities conspire to produce it. It is the life of all and the end here below of their existence and energies.

Of this heavenly property of the visible society which Christ instituted; of this undying life of the Church of God called sanctity, it is my privilege to speak this morning. I shall endeavor to show you in what it consists, how it is produced fundamentally, and where it is found among men.

The word holy has various significations. It is applied to things as well as to persons. Churches, altars, chalices and other sacred vessels are called holy because they are consecrated to the service of God. Doctrine, Sacraments and laws are called holy also because they serve to produce holiness in the individual and to protect it. Personal sanctity is moral rectitude before God, implying a resemblance to Him and union with Him. It is a cleanliness of soul from the defilement of sin which in the present state of nature is produced by the infusion of sanctifying grace and supernatural virtues. Sanctity under this twofold aspect is a property of the Church, which as a whole is dedicated to the service of God as each of its members is consecrated thereto in the Sacrament of Baptism. It has a holy doctrine and Holy Sacraments, and always has and must have holy members.

Doctrine and Sacraments are called holy not alone because they come from God, but because they are given to produce personal sanctity and are capable of doing so. Nor is it necessary that they should produce that effect in every instance, since sanctity in the adult is the result of two factors, one of which is the co-operation of the free will of man. As this co-operation varies in different persons, and as it may be wholly denied, it follows that the consequences, spiritual death or weakness, are not attributable to the Church which has no part whatever in their production, for they occur in spite of her, but are to be set down wholly and solely to the malice of the individual or to his imperfect dispositions.

By the sanctity of the Church is not meant that all its members are holy. That they are not is a fact declared by our Lord in parables which He has Himself explained. According to these the Church is like a field in which good grain and cockle grow up together till the harvest time, when the angels come to separate them. It is like a net in which there are good and bad fishes; in other words, it is a society composed of good and bad members, of sinners and saints, and it will continue to be such to the end of time. Nor does the sanctity of the Church require that the saints outnumber the sinners, though no doubt this is always the fact; it is enough that the Church is able to produce saints, and always does produce them in notable numbers. As nations are called prosperous where prosperity is within the reach of all, and the possession of many in a remarkable degree, while others through their own fault are poor and miserable; so the Church is called holy since all her members may be holy, though many through weakness or malice are pitiable sinners. Hence, to find fault with the Church because there are sinners in her communion; to reproach her with scandals which exist in spite of her, and which like the cockle in the field are the work of the wicked one; to deny on this account her divine institution, and reject her, is to betray ignorance of our Lord's description of her or to act dishonestly. The misdeeds of sinners belong to themselves; the Church has no share in them; they have no force as objections to her sanctity.

As the measure of grace, which is according to the giving of Christ, is different for different persons, and as co-operation therewith varies with the dispositions of those receiving it, it follows that in those who are holy there will be always found different degrees of sanctity. There are usually reckoned three such degrees. The first or lowest is that of those who keep out of mortal sin, but are not solicitous to avoid venial faults. The second degree aims at avoiding deliberate venial sins and employs means adapted to that end. This is said to include also the observance of the counsels in the religious state. Each of these degrees has different grades. The third degree is that of those whose virtue is heroic, who uniting to extraordinary grace the most intense fervor, and soaring on the wings of charity to the very presence of God, so far surpass the saints of their day in the practice of every virtue as to seem like to the God-man Himself. These degrees and grades and countless shades of sanctity, differing from one another as "star doth from star in brightness," form the heavenly vesture of the bride of Christ. They are the golden robes decked with every variety of ornament, in which the Royal Prophet saw the spouse of Christ clothed when he said to the king, "The queen stood on thy right hand in gilded clothing surrounded with variety." Her robes reveal the queen; sanctity marks the spouse of Christ and proclaims to the world her heavenly origin.

To sanctify His Church and prepare it for that stage in which it should appear without spot or wrinkle, our Lord established therein a ministry. This ministry was to take up His work and continue it forever. It was to apply the merits of His passion to those for whom He died. He made it perpetual. He gave it the whole world as its field of labor and all time as the duration of its mission. He gave it a vitality that could not know death, a principle of growth and a power of attraction and assimilation to meet all its wants. He rooted it in His own priesthood. He took it by the hand to walk with it and work with it through the ages, and the nations bless its labors and make them fruitful. He sent His Holy Spirit to dwell in it and abide with it forever.

To these ministers He gave all His doctrine, the whole Gospel, and secured to them its possession. He gave them a Sacrifice and Sacraments for the sake of His people. He made them priests, dispensers of the mysteries of God, and rulers of His Church.

The Apostles were the first members of this ministry. They were sent to teach all nations, baptizing them, etc. They did as they were commanded. They taught by the grace of God, they produced faith and thereby brought the proud intellect of man to the feet of God. They baptized. By baptism they cleansed the soul from all defilement of sin, and made the human will subject to the law of God. They brought the whole man to the foot of God's throne. They established God's sovereignty over man and secured his obedience. They harmonized all the powers of the soul, set it at peace with God, made it holy and thereby fitted it for heaven. "He that believes and is baptized shall be saved." They who were baptized were born again of water and the Holy Ghost; they received a new birth; in the strong language of the Apostle they were made new creatures, with new powers and a new destiny; they were lifted into the supernatural order, where they could lead lives meritorious of heaven.

The life given in baptism, like every other life, comes from God. Like every other life, vegetable, animal, human, it depends for its continuance and preservation on secondary causes. Like these, it has a nutriment and safe-guard of its own order. In the economy of God, it was to be nourished by the blessed Eucharist, true bread from heaven, developed, strengthened and perfected by the Holy Ghost and His gifts and graces in the Sacrament of Confirmation. It was to be restored by penance when lost by sin, and was to be preserved in a trying hour against the final and fierce assaults of principalities and powers by the mysterious influence of the last anointing. To give and preserve this life was the work of Christ's ministers. They were to carry it to the nations that were given to Him as an inheritance and to the ends of the earth which were to be His possession. The power of working miracles was to be a means to this end. It was promised to them by our Lord. It is numbered by the Apostle among the gifts of the Holy Ghost. They exercised this power as the spirit prompted for the sake of the infidel, on whose account it was given. Like our Lord Himself, they proved to him thereby the divinity of their mission, established their undoubted claim to his reasonable service, and if not converted, left him without excuse in his unbelief. As commanded, they taught those whom they baptized *to observe all things* whatsoever Christ commanded or delivered to them, ("quocumque mandavi vobis"), to observe the whole Gospel which they were to preach to every creature, counsels as well as precepts, poverty, chastity and obedience as well as justice and brotherly love. As the commission to teach, thus rooted in Omnipotence—"All power is given to Me in heaven and on earth," etc.—aided efficaciously by our Lord all days even to the consummation of the world, brooded over and blessed by the Holy Ghost, could not fail of effect, could not prove barren; as it must succeed and prove fruitful, it follows that the observance of the whole Gospel counsels as well as commands must ever characterize the life of God's Church and be inseparable from her sanctity. The whole Gospel, as a living fact in the hearts of her children, is the sanctity of the Church, and this fruit of a divine ministry can never be dissevered from fecundity and the gift of miracles.

How this sanctity embracing all the virtues of the Gospel with the gifts of fruitfulness and miracles is produced, will be better understood by a further analysis of the constitution of the Church. The supernatural society instituted and organized by Christ has two elements, a divine and human, so united and so related that the Church is thereby a striking image of the mystery of the Incarnation. As the mystery of the Incarnation is the ineffable and indissoluble union of God and man in the person of Jesus Christ, so is the Church the marvellous and indissoluble union of humanity and divinity. To regard the Church as composed of men only, even admitting its divine institution, is an error similar to that which would declare Christ to be a mere man. As a correct conception of our Lord and Redeemer embraces two natures, a divine and human united forever, so does a correct conception of the Church require two elements, a divine and human united indissolubly. Any error regarding either element, the nature of their union and mutual relations, is fundamental and must prove the fruitful source of many others.

The Church is frequently compared in the Sacred Scriptures with the human body, living and active. As the soul is in the body, the Holy Ghost is in the Church. He was promised at the Last Supper. He was given to her at Pentecost to be in her and to abide with her forever. Numerous texts of Scripture confirm this truth; tradition in a variety of forms repeats it. St. Paul, in his letter to the Corinthians, says that the Holy Ghost distributes graces in the Church: "There are diversities of graces but the same Spirit." (I. Cor., c. xii, v. 4.) Among these graces he names that of miracles, and concludes by saying: "All these things one and the same spirit worketh, dividing to every one according as he will." And St. Irenæus says: "Where the Church is, there is the Spirit of God. And where the Spirit of God is, there is the Church and every grace." The Church, the Holy Ghost and every grace, that is all the virtues, the observance of the whole Gospel, counsels and commandments are inseparable forever. Find one and you have the others. The union of the Holy Ghost with the Church is perpetual, indissoluble. It is not like the union of the soul and body which is severed by death; nor like that of the soul with God by grace which is destroyed by grievous sin; it is attended with no conditions, it depends on the will of no man or set of men, it is an absolute fact made so by an act of the omnipotent will of God. As He placed the sun in the heavens to rule the day, and the moon and stars to rule the night, and no man can interfere with these ordinances, so did He place the Holy Ghost in His Church to do His work therein and abide there forever.

Not only is the Holy Ghost in the Church as the soul in the body, but every member of the Church is, as it were, formed by Him, passes, so to speak, through His hands. "Unless a man be born again of water and the Holy Ghost he cannot enter into the kingdom of God." As He formed the human body of God's eternal Son, by the will of heaven, in the chaste womb of the Virgin Mary, out of her virginal flesh and blood, and made it a temple in which He has never since ceased, and never will cease, to dwell, so in like manner, the formation of the second body, the mystic Body of Christ in every member out of the great mass of humanity, is His work and His dwelling place forever. His special work in the Church is its sanctification. It is the proper object of His temporal mission. This is the idea the Apostles meant to convey by the words of the Creed: "I believe in the Holy Ghost, the holy Catholic Church." They not only believed in the Holy Ghost as one of the persons of the most adorable Trinity, but expressed their belief in Him as an agent here below doing a visible work, that is, operating in the Catholic Church and making her holy. As they professed their faith in God the Father as the Creator of heaven and earth, and in God the Son as the Redeemer of the world, so did they in God the Holy Ghost as the spirit by whom the Church is sanctified. With good reason therefore did St. Irenæus say: "Where the spirit of God is there is the Church and every grace, that is the sum of all the virtues."

The Holy Ghost is the vivifying principle of the Church, because Christ, whose spirit He is, is its divine Head. In speaking of the

Church, St. Paul very frequently compares it with the human body. It is a living body, of which Christ is the Head, as the Holy Ghost is the soul. The relations between the Church and Christ, its Head as described by the Apostle, throw a flood of light on the question of her sanctity. Employing his favorite comparison, St. Paul writes to the Romans: "For as in one body we have many members, but all the members have not the same office, so we being many, are one body in Christ, and every one members of another." (Rom., c. xii, v. 4.) That is, no matter how numerous are the members of the Church, be they counted by millions or by billions, no matter how varied their offices, they all are one body in Christ and by reason of their union with Him, they are members one of another. To the Corinthians he writes: "For as the body is one, and hath many members, and all the members of the body, whereas they are many, yet are one body, so also is Christ; that is, as the human body is one, though it has many members, so is the Body of Christ or the Church one, though it has many members." (I. Cor., c. xii, v. 12, 13.) But instead of saying Church, which he compares to the human body, he says Christ, as if Church and Christ were synonyms. Again he says: "For in one spirit were we all baptized into one body, now you are the Body of Christ and members of member." (Cor., c. xii, v. 13–27.) Speaking to the Ephesians of the love of Christ for His bride, the Church, he says: "No one ever hated his own flesh, but nourisheth and cherisheth it as also Christ doth the Church. For we"—that is, all true Christians as well as St. Paul and the Ephesians—"are members of His body, of His flesh and of His bones." (Eph., c. v, v. 29–30.) We are members of His humanity, for the Church is the second Eve taken from the side of the second Adam as He slept on Calvary. And as Adam said of Eve when presented to him by God: "This is bone of my bones and flesh of my flesh," (Gen., c. ii, v. 23,) so does Christ say of His Church by the lips of His inspired Apostle: "We are members of His body, of His flesh and of His bones." He took our nature by becoming man; became bone of our bone and flesh of our flesh. He made that nature His own; He made it the nature of our Head. And this He gives back to us in baptism—not to speak of the Blessed Eucharist—purified, elevated, all but deified.

Discoursing on the power and pre-eminence of Christ, the Apostle says: "And He (the Father) hath subjected all things under His feet, and hath made Him Head over all the Church, which is His body, and the fulness of Him who is filled all in all." (Eph., c. i., v. 22–23.) "And He is the head of the body . . . . because in Him it hath well pleased the Father that all fulness should dwell." (Colos., c. i, v. 18–19.) That is, the fulness of the body comes from the head, and all the members according to their place or office, thus filled, furnish the head with a body suitable to it, a body which is the fulness of Him who is filled all in all.

In the fourth chapter of his letter to the Ephesians he says: "And He gave some Apostles and some Prophets and other some Evangelists and other some pastors and doctors for the perfecting of the saints, for the work of the ministry, for the edifying of the Body of Christ." . . . . "By doing the truth in charity we may in all things grow up in Him, who is the Head, even Christ; from whom the whole body being compacted and fitly joined together, by what every joint supplieth, according to the operation in the measure of every part, maketh increase of the body unto the edifying of itself in charity." (Eph., c. iv, v. 11–16.) To the Collossians he writes of heretics: "And not holding the Head, from which the whole body, by joints and bands being supplied with nourishment and compacted, groweth unto the increase of God." (Colos. c. ii, v. 19.) These grand and sublime passages of St. Paul regarding the union of Christ and His Church, the relations between them and the mysterious operation by which she lives and grows, set before us boldly and vividly the economy by which her sanctity is produced and made permanent. The teaching of the Apostle in the texts cited may be briefly summed up as follows: That all the faithful united to Christ the Head, and through Him to each other, form one body, and this body, the Church, is called Christ by the Apostle, as if Church and Christ were one. That all Christians are so united by baptism to the humanity of Christ, and so formed from it that they are bone of His bone and flesh of His flesh, or, as the Apostle more boldly puts it, members of His body, of His flesh and of His bones. That in Christ the Head, by the gift of the Father, dwells permanently and absolutely the plenitude of grace and truth and all virtue, and from this fulness diffused throughout all the members comes the fulness of the body which completes, so to speak, the Head by its adaptation to it. That this Head, when glorified on the right hand of the Father, after having led captivity captive, gave gifts to men, even His own Spirit; that these gifts were made to a ministry composed of Apostles, Prophets, Evangelists, pastors and doctors; that this ministry, by the use of these gifts, build up the Body of Christ unto the perfecting of the saints, that is, unto perfect sanctity; that by these ministrations each member of the body, according to its office, dispositions and the measure of grace vouchsafed to it, grows up in the head Christ, and that this increase in all the members, collectively considered, which is the growth of the body in charity, is also called by the Apostle in his letter to the Collossians, with his wonted vigor, the growth of God. This growth of the body, this growth of God and the life that underlies it, is the sanctity of the Church which externally manifested as it must be, being the life and growth of a visible society, distinguishes that society from all others, and marks it clearly as the dwelling place of God with men.

Unless you realize that the Holy Ghost is in the Church as the soul is in the Body, preserving doctrine, distributing gifts and graces, building up the Body of Christ and working unceasingly for its sanctification; unless you realize that Jesus Christ is the head of the Church which He loves as His own Body, as His bride to whom He is indissolubly united by a mystic marriage, with a love stronger than death, for He died to sanctify her; unless you realize that all her fulness, all her truth and grace and beauty are from Him, communicated by a most mysterious operation through the appointed channels; unless you realize the existence of two elements in the Church, the divine and the human, their union and relations, how the divine acts on the human as the soul on the body, how the human responds to such action and co-operates with it as the brain and nerves and senses do to the action of the soul; unless you realize all this and more, you can have no correct conception of the Church of God, and consequently none of the great and incommunicable attribute of her sanctity.

These two elements are as essential to the Church as two natures are to Jesus Christ. As Christ was not God only nor a mere man, but God and man at once, so the Church is not a divine society or a human society only, but is a union of both, a society at once divine and human. As the human will of Christ, though free, was so controlled by the divine nature that it could neither sin nor be for an instant out of harmony with the divine will; so the Church, the Body of Christ, though composed of those whose wills are free, and intellects weak, and passions strong, is so governed, directed and influenced by her divine Head, that she can never for an instant betray the truth confided to her by God for the sake of His people, or lose the charity with which the Holy Ghost filled her on the glorious feast of Pentecost. The divine nature of Christ so filled His humanity with heavenly gifts through their mysterious union, that there is between both an interchange of attributes, so that God is man and man is God. So true is this of the elements of the Church, of the Church and her Head, that the Apostle calls the Church Christ, and that they who hear the Church hear Christ, and they who persecute the Church persecute Christ. As the only begotten Son of God took a human body by the power and operation of the Holy Ghost to redeem man and reinstate him in God's friendship; as it was in that body He dwelt among men, commencing by it the fulfillment of an eternal plan; as it was in it and by it He taught them, blessed them, healed their infirmities, offered sacrifice for them, and enriched them with gifts; so, according to the same eternal plan, it is in a human body, a human society, formed also by the Holy Ghost, that He continues the work of teaching, ruling, blessing, offering sacrifice and dispensing mysteries in order to sanctify His Church and make to Himself a spouse without spot or wrinkle. As the divine nature of Christ acting on the human, to which it was united, filled the soul to overflowing with grace and truth, vested the body with the glory of the transfiguration, made the members thereof instruments of miraculous powers, communicating this virtue even to the hem of its garment; so the same God-Man, Head of the Church, by His Holy Spirit, in His own way, through appointed channels, fills the soul of His beloved spouse with grace and truth, producing in her thereby faith and hope and charity, clothes her with all the virtues of the Gospel as with a precious robe of peerless beauty, makes her members instruments of divine power, and imparts that gift not alone to their relics or to the hem of their garment, but even to their very shadow as they walked along the streets in the days of their probation. Nearly nineteen hundred years ago a man revealed to men on the hills and in the valleys, by lake and river in Judea the presence of the eternal Son of God as their Redeemer, and proved that presence not alone by signs and wonders, but by a life of superhuman perfection; ever since, a society of men organized by God as His body and filling the earth, found everywhere, reveals to the world the abiding presence of Jesus Christ and His Spirit, and proves it by the same line of argument, by the same powers, and the same virtues. The biography of Christ is complete only in two chapters or volumes, to wit: the Gospels and Church history. The life of the Church is the second chapter; it is the life of Christ and His Holy Spirit in society, and that life, like His life in the flesh, is and ever must be holy, wonderful, fruitful, and visible. It is our great argument that God is with us. Now you can understand why the Church is called in the New Testament "the Kingdom of God, the Kingdom of Christ, the Kingdom of Heaven, the Holy City, the New Jerusalem, the House of God, the House of Christ, the Great House, the Temple of God, the Holy Temple of God, the Temple of the Living God, the Temple of the Holy Ghost, one Body, and that the Body of Christ;" why the holy Fathers apply to it half a hundred epithets of similar import; why the Royal Prophet, as he gazed on it in spirit, called it the holy mountain, as if sanctity were its chief or sole attribute; why the Prophet Isaias said of the Church that her stones would be laid in order and her foundations laid with sapphires, that her bulwarks would be of jasper, her gates of graven stones, and all her borders of lovely stones—that she should be as a crown of glory in the hand of the Lord, and a royal diadem in the hand of her God—that her children should be taught of God, and that great should be their peace—that is, sanctity—a peace or sanctity which the Psalmist declared should abound and flow over and last till the moon be taken away, that is, forever.

Sanctity such as I have endeavored to describe it is an attribute of the Church. Its external manifestation is a mark of it. It is essential to the Church and incommunicable, that is, only the Church of God can possess it, and being visible it is before the world, and may be seen by all. Whatever Christian society possesses it, that and only that is the Church of God. What Christian society does possess it is the question now before us. Or to put this question more fully and pointedly, what society of Christians instituted by Jesus Christ, and therefore existing since His time, organized and compacted into one body, His own Body, all whose members are knitted together like those of the human body, having teachers, rulers, dispensers of mysteries in the successors of the Apostles to build up that body to perfection, can justly lay claim to all the virtues that constitute sanctity, to all the virtues of the Gospel, point to the means that have produced them and to the miraculous gifts that have accompanied them? Can Protestantism do this? Even if it represented a society, or a body, or a temple, or a kingdom, which it does not even in the remotest manner; even if it were not a motley multitude of warring sects, each of which may become the fruitful parent of many others, it would be debarred by its youth from claiming with any show of plausibility the essential and incommunicable attribute of a society fifteeen centuries older.

The visible society on which God set this mark, that all may know it to be His, and which, as a property, is the very object of its existence, has been laboring among men eighteen hundred years openly in all parts of the earth. This settles the question of the Protestant claim when such happens to be made, for you will be surprised to learn that the Church of England is said to deny (has denied, in fact, according to Dr. Murray) that sanctity is an essential attribute of the Church of God. To enquire further into the grounds of such a claim on the part of Protestants is a superfluous work. Nor is it an agreeable one. Did not such a question manifestly come within the scope of this instruction, did it not form its chief aim in a certain sense? I should for obvious reasons gladly pass it over, but as I cannot do so altogether without a notable void, I shall touch it as lightly as possible and in a half-hearted fashion, leaving those who feel so disposed to compare Protestantism and its principle with the picture I have endeavored to give of the Church and her sanctity. I have no inclination whatever to examine the lives of the leaders of that religious rebellion of the sixteenth century which brought so many and varied disorders in its train; of those men who set themselves up as reformers of the bride of Christ, the object of His undying love, and ended by discarding her, though such an enquiry would be very much to the point. To speak of Martin Luther, a Roman Catholic priest, an Augustinian monk, bound to religion and to God by the sacred vows of poverty, chastity and obedience, who, by a farcical marriage, became the reputed husband of a nun who had contracted before God similar obligations—to speak of his sottish habits, his boorish manners, his vulgar, obscene conversation, his ungovernable temper, his rabid fury when contradicted, his scurrilities, his blasphemies—to speak of his associates and imitators, Zwingli, Calvin, Beza, Henry VIII, etc., who, in a certain sense, even improved on his work—is not at all to my taste, however much my subject should require it. Let them pass. They are too well known. Who that has any idea of the religion of Christ could think of them in connection with an apostleship? I shall only say, then, and have done with this point when I do so, that whoever reads the history of Protestantism in Germany, Switzerland, France, Holland, Denmark, Sweden, England, Scotland, throughout Northern Europe, calmly, critically, honestly, at the best sources of information, will find that virtue and intelligence had nothing to do with its production; that pride and lust and rapine rocked its cradle; that persecution, plunder, confiscation, violence, sacrilege, the horrid desecration of everything sacred, tracked its blighting course and chiefly fostered its rank, rapid, but short-lived progress.

Have the sects, as they swarm, any earthly resemblance to the Body of Christ as described by St. Paul? Have their teachings, like the tongues around Babel, any resemblance whatever to the utterings of the Spirit of Truth? Has Protestantism means to produce holiness? Has it a holy doctrine? It has no doctrine. It has only conflicting, contradictory opinions, and even these are as changeable as the winds or the fashions, and this, not by accident, but as the result of its boasted principle, private judgment, which, nevertheless, it takes up and lays down according to circumstances and to suit its convenience. It has nothing certain; nothing that can beget an act of divine faith without which it is impossible to please God, and without which there can be neither hope nor charity nor any other virtue, for it is the very root of every virtue in the soul.

Justification by faith, even though an act of faith on Protestant principles, is impossible; that is, no matter what a man does if he believes he is justified. Good works are not necessary. The grossest sins do not hurt the elect. God is the author of sin, and at the same time the avenger of it. Once in grace one is always in grace, how grievous soever the sins he may commit. There is no free will in man; God sees no sin in believers; no sin, unbelief excepted, can cause damnation. These are samples of the teachings of Protestantism. Are these teachings holy? Do they lead to holiness; or rather, do they not remove every check that God has put to the grovelling propensities of a fallen nature? Do they not remove every restraint, awaken every passion, arouse and excite every vicious inclination, whet their appetite for indulgence, since their gratification has no influence whatever, unless it be a favorable one, on man's eternal destiny?

I know that all these propositions are not now held by Protestants. I suppose they never were by any one sect. I am sure that many of them, I hope most of them, reject and reprobate them from their hearts; but Protestantism, of which I am speaking, has held them and taught them, and is responsible for them. They hold, however, the principle that gave them birth, private judgment in opposition to divine authority, the mother of the sects and the isms and all their progeny yet to come, the principle that has unsettled the human mind, severed it from God, shut out from it the light of heaven, and made it in matters of religion the sport of every whim. They hold the principle that has blighted the human heart, dried up the springs that would irrigate and enrich it, sapped the foundation of the social edifice by desecrating the great sacrament of marriage and undoing its tie in the face of God's prohibition, broken up families and scattered them to the four winds of heaven, destroying in them charity and creating for them misery. This is the principle that has brought man down from his high estate in the supernatural order, where the light of heaven was around him and in him, where the bread of life was on his tongue and the blood of the Lamb on his soul, making it fair as the angels, where heaven was his home and God his Father and the saints his friends and brethren—down to that depth of darkness and destitution in which, blind to the future, seeing nothing to live for beyond time, all his energies seem absorbed in the pursuit of wealth and pleasure, as if in them, and in them only, human happiness, whatever there is of it, is to be found.

It is at the root of the evils that darken our day and infect our atmosphere, that fester in the social body, waste it like a cancer and make it loathsome and offensive, growing evils which good men see and deplore, but which they try in vain to remedy from their unfortunate standpoint.

Protestantism has no sacraments or channels of grace. The Lord's Supper is not one, and as to baptism, their claim to it is no better than would be that of a literary club, since any man or woman may administer it.

Is it fruitful? It has never made any heathen nation, or any notable part of one, Christian. It never thought of attempting such a thing before the end of the seventeenth century. On the result of its efforts since, read Marshall's "Christian Missions," the most exhaustive work ever written on the subject, and you will find on the testimony of Protestant writers, eye-witnesses of what they relate, that it has only made the heathen worse and Christianity a laughing stock. Though some missionaries were good men, learned, eloquent and earnest, though all the elements of success that men could give them were placed at their service, though they had Bibles by the shipload and money by the million, and all the influence that social position and the prestige of a dominant race could give them, yet was there a blight on their work and death in the atmosphere they breathed. Distributing Bibles, bribing the heathen, perverting Catholics, manufacturing false reports for home societies in view of further aid, keeping out of the way of danger, living genteelly, watching for an opportunity to better his fortune is a mild presentment of the ordinary occupation of the average Protestant missionary in pagan lands.

As to miracles, they only laugh at them, as if it were ridiculous to connect them with the Body of Christ, or absurd to attribute to it or Him such power. They scoff at them, they reject them—not because they are unsustained by evidence, but in the face of the strongest, most varied, irrefragable testimony ever adduced in a human court; they reject them for the sole reason, as Middleton ingeniously confesses, that if they admit the testimony they must accept the facts and with them the institution they so luminously illustrate. Originating in insubordination to the established and recognized authority of God, without doctrine, or sacraments, without men or means to make anyone or anything holy, without divine faith or the virtues that spring from it, or any element of the supernatural life, without the blessing of God or any testimony of His favor, Protestantism, as a religion, is a barren fig-tree; it bears no fruit of life, it never will bear any. It is to the sanctity of the Church of God what a pale, cold corpse is to the fire, and flush, and healthy glow of manhood's blooming prime.

Does the Catholic Church bear the mark of sanctity? She is a society that goes back to the days of Christ. Her history commences with the acts of the Apostles. Look at her to-day. Her children throughout the world of every clime and color number over two hundred millions. Divided into parishes or missions, they are governed by some two hundred thousand priests, who also teach them in the name of God and dispense mysteries to them by His authority. People and priests divided into dioceses or districts are governed by one thousand bishops. All are governed by the Bishop of Rome. They have the same faith, and sacrifice, and sacraments in China and in the United States, in Australia and in Italy. Look at that society again, view it closely, search it thoroughly, examine its constitution, its doctrine, its practice. Is it not one, is it not compact and closely jointed? Viewed even from a human standpoint, do you know any government that can be compared with it? Well, as you see it to-day, such it has been since the days of St. Peter. The chain of rulers that binds Leo XIII to Peter in this great society is as real and substantial and visible as that which binds Chester Arthur to George Washington in the government of our own great republic. Throw out the ages like a map, unfold the scroll, put the Pontiffs between Leo and Peter in line, two hundred and fifty-eight in number, and seven or eight years apart on an average. Around each of these Pontiffs sweep a circle whose circumference will reach to the ends of the earth. These circles will intersect and grasp and bind each other fast as the links of a triple chain. Place within each of these circles around the Sovereign Pontiff the hundreds of bishops, the tens of thousands of priests, the millions of every tribe and tongue and nation that in his day he governed. Look at these two hundred and fifty-eight circles that have Rome as centre and the uttermost bounds of the earth as circumference; look at the bishops, priests and people along the whole line; listen to their teaching, proceeding as if from one mouth; listen to their act of faith as it sweeps through the years and rings through the earth; look at their ministrations, their dispensation of mysteries, and tell me, has the world ever seen a government or a society such as that? Is there anything in all history to be even remotely compared with it? Now, if the Father and Son sent the Holy Ghost on that glorious Pentecost Sunday, eighteen hundred years ago, to animate the society which Christ had formed to be its soul, its internal teacher; to distribute gifts and work therein for its sanctification and abide with it forever, as we are taught to believe through several chapters of the Gospel of St. John; if before St. Paul wrote to the Romans, Corinthians, Ephesians or Collossians, Jesus Christ was the head of a society which was to last forever, to which He was bound indissolubly as to a bride by a mystic marriage tie, which He was ever to love and cherish as His own body, bone of His bones, and flesh of His flesh; if this be so—and if not, you may fling Gospels and Epistles, and even the facts of history, to the winds—if this be so, does not history compel you to admit that such a society is the Roman Catholic Church, for there is no other; and you must remember that the society in which these divine persons dwell is like a mountain on the top of the hills, like a city on the mountain top lighted up from heaven, brighter than the moon at night or the sun in his noonday splendor.

The history of heresies confirms this fact. They have tracked the course of the Roman Catholic Church throughout her history. With the sword of the spirit she cut the rebels from her communion. Severed from her, they began at once to show signs of decay, of death, of corruption. In being separated from her they were evidently cut off from the living Body and Christ and from all the fountains of supernatural life. From that day forward neither learning, nor eloquence, nor wealth, nor the support of kings, nor the strength of armies, nor any other force from earth or beneath it, could galvanize them into anything like a semblance of the holy Church of the living God. In spite of everything that man could do for them, there they lie before the world's gaze like sapless branches or amputated limbs, scattered here and there along the highways of history.

Has the Roman Catholic Church means of sanctification? Has

she a holy doctrine and holy institutions? I cannot examine these points in detail now. I shall only say that they are to-day and always have been such as they came from the lips of the divine Founder of the Church. The Catholic Church claims infallibility. Surely the body of Christ and the temple of the Holy Ghost ought to be infallible. The Catholic Church not only claims infallibility but proves the justice of her claim, and with her history of nineteen centuries before the world, she boldy, confidently defies the lights of this, as of every other age, to name a single doctine that she has ever changed one iota, the time and place and circumstances and history of the change, to name a doctrine of the past that she does not teach still, or any doctrine of the present time that she did not teach in all the past, every day during the centuries of her existence, explicitly or implicitly. The endowment of infallibility is the equivalent of sanctity in the matter of doctrine. To say that the Church is infallible and to prove it, is to prove that her doctrine is the primitive teaching in all its details, and therefore as holy as when it came from the lips of God as a means of sanctification.

Has her mission been fruitful? She had converted all Europe before the birth of Protestanism, and her labors since in every pagan land, in China, in India, in Japan, in Africa, have encountered no such obstacle as the scandal given by the sects which, by their numbers and contradictions, made the heathen think that Christianity had more Christs than paganism had gods.

As to her miracles throughout her long, long history, they are like the stars in the heavens, as countless and as brilliant.

Has she had always holy members? The myriads of martyrs of the early ages of every age and sex and condition, who, in the coliseum or other amphitheatres of the Roman empire, surrounded by every instrument of torture that human barbarity could employ, face to face with death under his most terrific aspect, dared, in the very teeth of tyranny, as they writhed in agony, to profess Christ and Him crucified, were, whether bishops, priests or people, members of the Roman Catholic Church. So were the anchorites, these holy men of old, who, fleeing from the corruption of the great cities, retired to the desert that they might be more with God, who, in an age of sensuality, lived as if they were out of the body, and who, by prayer, meditation, study of the Sacred Scriptures and conferences after sun-down, while they were still fasting, did more perhaps to counteract the evil influences of the false teaching and bad principles of the Eastern schools than any other body of men then living. The names of the Popes for eight hundred years, with three or four exceptions, emblazon the catalogue of the saints of God. The apostles of the nations and the missionaries who accompanied them, who, by their indomitable zeal and heroic virtue, extended the stakes and multiplied the tents of the Christian conquest, were bishops and priests of the Roman Catholic Church. The sixty tomes of the lives of the saints by the Bollandists give us but a mere fraction of the multitudes of her sainted children. The Benedictines, the Augustinians, the Trappists, the Dominicans, the Franciscans, the Jesuits, the Redemptorists, all the orders and communities of religious men and women scattered all over the ages and the nations, who have consecrated their lives on the altar of religion to the service of God and their neighbor by the holy vows of poverty, chastity and obedience, who cannot call anything on this earth their own, who have stripped themselves of everything to give no hold to the enemy, who have lived the whole Gospel, the counsels as well as the precepts, in their effort to be perfect as their Father in heaven is perfect—these angels in the flesh, these holocausts of charity are not only Catholics, the pride and flower, and crown, and glory of the Catholic Church, but they are the precious stones spoken of by the prophet—the jasper, the sapphire, the emerald, the topaz, the beryl, the amethyst, that blaze in beauty in the golden vesture of the bride of Christ.

The widow, the orphan, the blind, the lame, the deaf, the dumb, the victims of yellow fever and cholera deserted by their nearest friends, the dying soldier on battle's bloody field nursed and comforted by the Sister of Mercy or Sister of Charity, all the children of misfortune lift their eyes and hearts to heaven invoking blessings on the sons and daughters of the Catholic Church for their godlike charity.

The Catholic Church is now and ever has been the altar of every sacrifice, the home of every charity, the asylum of every misery, for she is the body of Him who died to save us, who is still our Sacrifice, our Priest and Victim. Of all the societies ever seen on this earth, she alone can say with her divine Founder to her enemies: "Who can convict me of sin? If I had not done among them works that no other society hath done, they would not have sin. They hated me without cause." And pointing to her teaching, to her sacrifice, to her sacraments, to her altars, to her pulpits, to her confessionals, to her hospitals and asylums, for every misery to which fallen nature is heir, she can say to all who doubt or deny her mission and her character what our Lord said to the vacillating messengers of the imprisoned Baptist: "The blind see, the lame walk, the lepers are cleansed, the deaf hear, the dead rise again, the poor have the Gospel preached to them, and blessed is he that shall not be scandalized in Me." Her works and virtues proclaim the sanctity and make manifest the divinity of the Catholic Church, and the voice of God thundering through the ages and the nations in the unmistakable language of signs and wonders confirms with the great seal of heaven the incommunicable holiness of the bride of Christ.

The Work of the Council.

SERMON OF RIGHT REV. J. L. SPALDING, D.D.,

BISHOP OF PEORIA.

"I believe in the Holy Ghost, and in one, holy, Catholic and Apostolic Church."

AT this closing session of the largest and most important council of Catholic bishops ever held in America it is altogether befitting that some expression be given to the thoughts which so august an assembly suggests. Even a casual observer can hardly fail to perceive in this venerable body something of the marks which stamp the Church with the impress of God's hand. Here are men, born in many lands, speaking many tongues, and bringing with them from distant parts of the earth the thousand varying shades of thought and sentiment, which spring from difference of climates, customs and laws. They show forth in their bearing and characters the action of the forces which diversify human life and throw nations and individuals into rivalry and antagonism. But when they meet in council these differences and oppositions of opinion and feeling are merged in the unity of faith; and the harmony which reigns in the Universal Church, in spite of the divergent and conflicting influences that work in its members, breathes also in the deliberations of this venerable body, and moves all minds and hearts to the enactment of wise and just laws. Thus we have here a type of the Unity and of the Catholicity of the Church. At the call of the Vicar of Christ this council has assembled under the presidency and guidance of the Apostolic Delegate, whose authority is derived from Pope Leo XIII, who succeeds through Pius IX, Gregory XVI, Leo XII and a line of Pontiffs, stretching through eighteen centuries to Peter, to whom Christ said: "Thou art Peter, and upon this rock I will build My Church, and the gates of hell shall not prevail against it;" and so the Apostolicity of the Church is visible in this body, which professes the faith first delivered to the saints and proclaimed at Jerusalem, at Nice and in all the councils since held throughout the Catholic world, and handed down from Pope to Pope, who each in his day taught the whole Church in the name of Him who said to Peter: "Feed My sheep, feed My lambs;" and again: "I have prayed for thee that thy faith fail not, and thou once converted, confirm thy brethren."

And the mark of holiness too,—the essential mark of true religion—is not absent from this reverend body. I may not indeed speak of the lives of the venerable men who are here assembled, of the sacrifices they have made, of their zeal, their trials and labors; of the generous devotion with which they have given their whole strength to the service of their fellow-men, preaching the Gospel to the Indian and the African with the same love with which they announce its glad tidings to those who are bound to them by ties of race and country. But, apart from this let me ask what motive has led them hither from distant parts of this vast continent, from the towns and cities of this great and prosperous land? To this question I can find but one answer:—the desire to work with God in uplifting men to higher, purer and freer life. No one could listen to their long and earnest discussions, or witness the reverent thought and patient care with which they examined each subject as it came up for debate, without being convinced of the truth of what I affirm. The various subjects which have been the matter of our deliberations during the four weeks of the council's sittings, have all a direct bearing upon the welfare, religious, moral, intellectual and social, of the people with whose spiritual care we are charged, and therefore upon the welfare and prosperity of our country itself. Our sessions have been private, but the only secrecy which need be observed, is that necessary to the free and untrameled action of the Sovereign Pontiff to whose final judgment whatever we have done must be submitted. The expression of opinion upon all points which have come up for discussion has been full and frank; no restraint has been felt or exercised; and the spirit of fairmindedness, of candor and thoroughness has pervaded all our deliberations. In the spirit which lived in the councils of earlier ages, and brought to the defence and protection of the slave, of the child, of the poor and of woman, the moral power of the Christian religion, which led the way to representative government and parliamentary rule, the American bishops, living in a country where slavery has ceased to exist, where the child is held in reverence, woman in honor, and the poor are cared for, have turned their thoughts to the giving of new impulses to the forces which work for the cause of God in the world, which is also the cause of man. And, first of all, they feel that what is most necessary to individuals and to nations is the strength which comes of true religious faith, by which we are held in living and loving communion with the Author of our being, the Source of life and truth and goodness. Such faith is the support of noble aims and the vital principle of worthy deeds; it is the safeguard of morals and the best incentive to efforts to improve both ourselves and the society in which we live; and so it becomes the foundation of national prosperity.

History teaches that epochs of faith are epochs of progress, while in the atmosphere of skepticism the intellects and consciences of men are darkened and weakened, and the way to general decay is prepared. Hence the Fathers of the Council know that in seeking to create an intenser and more living faith in God and His Church, they are laboring not only to fit men for an immortal and God-like destiny, but are also giving necessary aid to whatever tends to make the earthly life of man more worthy and blessed. And since the Christian religion, like all religions that have left a deep and lasting impress upon the peoples which they have influenced, is essentially sacerdotal, the Fathers of this Council have turned their thoughts first of all to the priesthood itself, and by the enactment of laws which have been drawn up and discussed with the greatest care, they have sought to regulate the relations of bishops and of priests, and priests and people, in a way which will bring about more perfect harmony, more complete sympathy, and a nearer approach to the ideal upheld by the Saviour when He said: 'By this shall men know that you are My disciples, if you love one another.'

The character of the true priest demands that he possess both great virtue and great knowledge. The bishops, therefore, have labored not only to inspire a deeper love of holiness, a more ardent zeal and a stricter observance of the ecclesiastical discipline, which is the practical expression of the wisdom of the saints in many lands and many ages, but they have also given most serious thought and consideration to plans and methods whereby the standard of priestly education may be raised. They have not been slow to give expression to their conviction that only the best discipline and cultivation of mind can fit the priest in an age and country like our own to be the accomplished and effective teacher of divine truth. They have adopted measures which will insure a more thorough elementary education of candidates for the priesthood. They have lengthened and deepened the course of philosophy and theology, and have emphasized the importance and necessity even of literary and scientific acquirements. And in this connection they have laid the foundation of what they believe will in due time grow to be a real American Catholic University. But their attention has not been confined to sacerdotal education. They perceive and affirm the fact that all men need education, but they hold to the principle that a system of education which fails to recognize that religion is essential both to right thinking and right living is necessarily defective. Hence they have sought to organize and perfect our system of parochial schools, so that our children may there receive not only proper training of the heart and conscience, but may also enjoy opportunities for the improvement of the mind equal to those afforded in the best schools of the country. They have also insisted that it is the urgent duty of priests and people to provide Catholic schools for Catholic children.

A Catholic congregation without a Catholic school is like a family without a mother. The formal service may be there, but the deep heart of love and wisdom, with power to shape and mold character, is wanting; and in due time, the showy temple will become only a monumental mockery standing in the midst of an unbelieving generation. Man is a religious being, and a system of education which excludes the teaching of religious truth and morality, rests upon unsound principles, and must prove hurtful to the strength and permanency of free government.

In Europe, who are the advocates of secular education? Are they not almost without exception the enemies of positive religion? Bring together the infidels of the world of every shade of opinion, from the teachers of naked atheism and materialism to the professors of the various forms of deism, and you will find that in the midst of a thousand conflicting and contradictory tenets they all agree in their opposition to religious education. And they, and they alone, are logical in taking up this position. Since they reject all positive religious doctrines as superstitious and absurd, they are consistent in seeking to exclude them from the class-room.

The originators of the public school system of this country certainly had no irreligious intention, and the purely secular character of this system is the result of circumstances rather than of a deliberate purpose. But this does not affect the necessary tendency of such education to produce religious indifference, and consequently to destroy the power and influence of religion: and hence whatever may be the intention or purpose of those who maintain this system, they are in point of fact the most effective allies of the propagators of unbelief. The Fathers of the Council are not opposed to universal education, or to free education, or to taxation for the support of schools, or to methods and contrivances of whatever kind, by which knowledge and enlightenment may be diffused through the masses of the people: but they are opposed, necessarily and unalterably opposed, to any and all systems of education which either ignore or exclude religious knowledge, since they believe and hold this knowledge to be the primal and most essential element of true human culture: and consequently that it should form the basis of instruction and discipline in the school as in the family and in the Church. The work of developing and moulding human character is difficult enough when these three centres of influence are in harmony and co-operate; but to throw them into antagonism is to undermine the work of each; and in a society where this state of things exists, the Church will lose its sacredness, the family its authority, and the school, acting upon the intellectual faculties alone, will but serve to show how little and helpless man is when his life is not breathed upon by love and hope and faith in higher things.

The Fathers of the Council have not been unmindful of the intimate relations of the school with the family, or of their duty to watch over and foster that first and more sacred school—the Christian Home—which springs from the Sacrament of Matrimony, and rests upon the unity and indissolubility of marriage, and which consequently is the out-growth of Catholic teaching, practice and influence. More than by any other agency the characters of men are moulded by their home-life. When this is religious, pure and sweet, the virtues that sanctify and adorn life blossom like the flowers in the warm and gentle air of spring, but when the tender bud of childhood is blighted in this, its earliest sanctuary, all hope of fragrant bloom and ripe fruit is lost. The relations of the Church to conjugal and domestic society are essential and intimate; and whenever Catholics are permitted to lose sight of this truth, religious zeal and practical piety decay. "All paternity," says St. Paul, "in heaven and on earth, derives its name from God:" and hence marriage, in its essence, its ends and its authority, as well as from the fact of its institution, is sacred and of divine origin; and in the religion of Christ, it is also a Sacrament. If the presence of God is not recognized and confessed at the home fireside, the spirit of Christian faith and filial piety dies out of the family; and irreverence and indifference take possession of the hearts of the young. Indeed, if the family be suffered to lose its religious character, it were folly to think that even the best system of Catholic schools can prevent the decay of faith and the ruin of souls. The first and most indispensable school, that which is the basis of all others, which lays the foundation of character, moulds the heart, gives to the mind its original turn, to the imagination its primal and ineffaceable tinge, is the family: and if it is secular, or pagan, or religiously divided, or indifferent, what hope can there be of saving the children to the Church and to God? We hold it as a principle that he who wishes to enter the priesthood should try himself and be tried through a long course of years, lest he unworthily or rashly assume a ministry in which he shall have to answer for the souls of men, redeemed by the Blood of Christ; but the all-wise and all-just Judge will not first or chiefly hold the priest accountable. He will demand the soul of the child first of all from the father and the mother, through whom it was brought into the world. When we look around us, it is difficult to believe that Catholics realize this truth; so thoughtlessly, so frivolously, do they take upon themselves the greatest of responsibilities. Too often, like unbelievers, they act, as though they were free, in this matter, to follow their whims and fancies without regard to the divine law or the commandments of the Church. Their present passion is their only guide, and in many instances, a life of misery and a death of modified despair, is the penalty. Of the existence of this evil the Fathers of the Council, consider that there is no more lamentable proof, than the custom, for such it has grown to be with us, of intermarrying with those who have no faith or a religion different from our own. Such marriages are, in their very nature, unchristian, and have in all ages been so regarded by the Church; and if a sort of forced consent is given, it is as a mother, who despairs of offering effective opposition, consents to the marriage of a daughter with one who she knows will break the heart of her child.

How can people who disagree concerning interests which are eternal, absolute, of infinite moment, and nearest to the most sensitive and central nature of the soul, be truly united in anything? The greatest evil, however, in this marriage of people, who, in regard to their soul's faith, stand on opposite sides of a chasm which neither is likely to pass over, is not in the fact that, in such marriage, there can be no perfect union of heart, no complete sympathy, no entire revelation of each to each, and consequently not that peace and contentment which the marriage union should bring; but it is found in this other fact, that in such wedlock, deep religion and earnest piety are almost impossible, while the children of these religiously divided families, grow up in indifference, and sooner or later fall away from the faith. The bishops of the Plenary Council therefore call upon Catholics to bear ever in mind that marriage is a holy state; that to be good it should be consecrated by sacramental grace; and since it is permanent and durable as life, it should be entered into with serious thought and reverent intention. Let them remember that fatherhood and motherhood which spring from this sacred union, are a kind of priesthood which imposes upon parents the duty of constant watchfulness over their children: for, to quote the words of the great Apostle: "If any one have not care of his own, especially those of his own household, he has denied the faith and is become worse than an infidel." From the society of the family, the Fathers of the Council have gone on to consider other associations, and they have approved and encouraged all societies, which based upon true principles of faith and reason, have for their object, the promotion of the cause of religion and morality, the protection and defence of the weak and the wronged, or the correction of abuses which are harmful to the growth of the Church, and to the permanence of free and just government. In an especial manner have they spoken in commendation of the Catholic Temperance Societies, which are laboring with zeal and not without good results to diminish the evils of drunkenness and to lead men to the beauty, dignity and freedom of a sober life. The many and great evils which flow from the vice of intemperance are not unknown to any of us. More than any other, this vice disrupts families, makes orphans, digs untimely graves, breaks mothers' hearts, takes bread from hungry mouths, fills asylums, peoples prisons, and drives its unhappy victims along the highway which leads to shame, despair and the loss of God. In the presence of all this, the pastors of Christ's flock may not be silent. *Vae mihi*, says St. Paul, *si non predicarero*. It is hard to understand how any one can love the Church and not be zealous against the vice of drunkenness: for though there are other sins which doubtless are more grievous, there is none which brings so much obloquy upon our holy faith or which so much retard its progress in this country.

It is the unfortunate tendency of this vice to parade its hideous features before the public gaze, to multiply itself, to seek evil company and to combine with evil-doers; to be noisy and to create disturbance, to advertise itself by oaths, blasphemies, quarrels, rows, assaults and murders. It enters into the general history of crime: and its loud breath rising from the slums and purlieus that surround the police court, is perceptible also in higher circles, throwing its unmistakable odor over the daily calendar of embezzlement, fraudulent bankruptcy, seduction and divorce. And in this connection, the American bishops, with a deep sense of the intimate relations of free government with morality, have urged Catholics to cultivate the spirit of obedience to the laws of their country, and to hold in reverence those who are clothed with civil authority, which, not less than religious authority, comes from God. Let them set their faces against all abuses which tend to deaden the public conscience and to lower the standard of conduct. Let them bear in mind that the faithful observance of the Lord's Day is not only of vital importance to our religious life, but scarcely of less importance to the prosperity of our country.

The bishops have also approved and commended certain associations whose object is to protect and guide the immigrants who come in such multitudes to our shores, and appeal to us in the name of Him who said: "I was a stranger and you took Me in." They have also given their approval to societies formed for the purpose of assisting our poor people who are huddled together in the squalid quarters of great cities and manufacturing towns, to get homes in the country, where bodily life is healthier and moral life is purer. But since associations may be made the instruments of evil not less than of good, the Fathers of the Council have raised their voice to warn Catholics of the dangers of societies whose object is immoral or unlawful, or whose rules and constitutions are not framed in accordance with sound Catholic principles.

So enlightened a body as this could not fail to recognize the great services which the press is capable of rendering to the cause of religion: and hence the bishops have considered the means by which the influence and circulation of Catholic newspapers may be extended. A few good journals will render greater help than a multitude of inferior newspapers, and they have therefore determined that each ecclesiastical province shall create or build up some one Catholic journal, to which all may look as an able and enlightened advocate of the Church. Careful and serious attention has also been given to the claims upon our Christian sympathy and help of the colored people and the Indians. They are our countrymen, our brethren, redeemed by the Blood of Christ, and if we can do aught to soften the hardships of their lot, or to lighten the weight of the wrongs by which they have so long been oppressed—above all, if we can point out some surer way to a higher and better world, we shall thank God for the opportunity of so beneficent and holy a mission.

Thus have I briefly and lightly touched some of the questions which have engaged the thoughts of the Fathers of this third Plenary Council of Baltimore, which doubtless will mark an epoch in the history of the Church in the United States.

No age seems wonderful to those who live in it; no work seems great to him who does it; but in other centuries men will look back not without gratitude to what has been accomplished here. Who can look upon the uprising of the Church in this New World without comforting thoughts, without a sense of deeper trust and higher courage? As from amidst sullen waves and swollen clouds, the sun breaks forth to run his heavenly course, so, from the darkness, as of the grave, in which throughout the English speaking world, the Church had been buried for centuries, she comes forth again all luminous and young, to lead anew, in this other world, the life which for two thousand years has been the fountainhead of truth, of goodness, of peace to men. Ah! surely there is here some higher vital principle, some divine source of energy, some heavenly guidance, which enables the Church to renew her strength and to walk forever young amid the graves and ruins of the generations that die.

Rt. Rev. R. Gilmour, D.D.

Rt. Rev. J. J. Conroy, D.D.

Rt. Rev. H. J. Richter, D.D.

Rt. Rev. L. De Goesbriand, D.D.

Rt. Rev. Francis Mora, D.D.

Rt. Rev. C. H. Borgess, D.D.

Rt. Rev. Joseph Dwenger, D.D.

Rt. Rev. Francis S. Chatard, D.D.

Rt. Rev. M. J. O'Farrell, D.D.

Our Lady, Patroness of the Union.

SERMON OF RIGHT REV. F. S. CHATARD. D.D.,

BISHOP OF VINCENNES.

IN the ages of faith, when men fought and died for their belief, shedding around their race a supernatural halo from noble and brilliant deeds done to roll back the flood of Mohammedan invasion, and rescue from desecration the holy sepulchre of our Lord, it was a pious custom to invoke the patronage of God's saints, and to fight under the inspiring influence of their names. The gallant hosts of France invoked St. Denis; the chivalrous knights of Spain called upon St. James; the fleets and soldiers of Venice fought under the banner of St. Mark; while the cry of St. George for England animated the brave warriors of the Isle of Saints. It was a wholesome and noble idea, besides being one intensely Christian. The world has changed much since then. The coins of some once truly Catholic peoples still are found, now and then, with an image, or an inscription, that recalls the memory of the custom; but it is not the fashion now for nations to stand before the world as clients of any saint. How could this be expected, when the tendency is to set aside the God of sanctity Himself? So, far from invoking the saints, the world of to-day, if it do no more, smiles at what it calls the poetic credulity of the past, and scoffs at any attempt to revive what it has concluded to look upon as antiquated and superstitious. It is not my purpose, dearly beloved friends, to demonstrate at length the correctness of the practice of our forefathers in the faith, in their veneration of the saints and in their devotion to them. But I cannot, in passing, withhold saying a word on the subject. Consult the records of the human race, and everywhere you will find a tendency to honor heroes, to deify them, and to believe in their protection. Call it what you will, it is there, and an evidence of a universal inclination of the human mind; and where such universal disposition exists, the germ of it comes from the Creator of nature Himself. It rests therefore on a truth,—the truth of the immortality of the soul, and of the power of the good with God; and this truth the revealed religion of Jesus Christ has vindicated most splendidly. The teaching, therefore, of revelation came to direct and exalt this natural tendency, and render it a most powerful and beneficial influence in the social life of nations. In doing this God's Church had to battle with the inborn superstition of the human race, even as now; a superstition which has its reason of being in facts that convince men of the existence of agencies above nature, and which more or less always shows itself; just as it does now in the consultation of departed spirits, and in seeking from creatures of another order knowledge and power men cannot otherwise have. Witness the result in the number of unfortunate occurrences, of mental perversion, of insanity, and of death even, familiar to all readers of the daily press. The Church of God, which is given us as "a light in a dark place," to use the expressive phrase of the great Apostle (II Peter, i, 19), separates the truth from the falsehood, the fact from the superstition. She points to the passages of Holy Writ where the intercessory power of the angels is affirmed; where holy men are shown "to pray much for the people" (II Macc., xv, 14), and where supernatural aid was vouchsafed the hosts that fought for the true God. She bids us look to those remains of antiquity which have been providentially preserved, to let us see what was the belief and practice of those centuries, which even the most violent of her opponents are forced to acknowledge as pure in faith. In the subterranean crypts of the Roman Campagna she has found treasures of antiquity, and these demonstrate the honor in which the early Christians held God's saints; how they invoked them—asked their help. The eloquent appeals of those who chose to be laid to rest near the martyrs, as we read them on their tablets, the prayers to St. Petronilla, to Januarius, and to others; the prayers of fathers and mothers, of brothers and of sisters to their dear departed, "because they know they are in Christ," awaken not alone the sense of faith in the great doctrine of the Communion of Saints, but stir the well-spring in the heart of those high and beautiful feelings of Christian love, which ennoble the soul and raise it up to follow after that which is lofty, holy, and sublime.

Of all the saints in whom God has manifested the wonders of His power and of His grace, no one will deny that the greatest is she whom He chose to be the Mother of His divine Son, and adorned with all the beautiful prerogatives that befit her unspeakably exalted dignity,—the ever Blessed Virgin Mary.

It is a signally fortunate circumstance that by the unanimous choice of the bishops of the sixth Provincial Council of the Church in the United States, and by the act of the Sovereign Pontiff, Pius IX, of holy memory, she was named to be the Patroness of the Church of the United States; and I think, dearly beloved brethren, you will agree with me when you will have heard the reasons on which I base the assertion.

In the first place, we should consider what is meant by the custom of having a patron for a nation, a church, a diocese, or even a parish. It is not merely to have a name, not merely to have a special feast, to have an advocate to look to in time of need. It is more properly to have a bright and beautiful example of Christian virtue; a hero, who, though in all like unto ourselves, met and overcame the same obstacles, the same dangers, the same opposition we find in our daily life, and before which we so often fall. The life of every saint is a gift God makes to the world to draw men to Him, and stimulate them to ways of virtue. We in America, being young as a people, with institutions not perfect certainly in every respect, but which are so favorable to the development of the best qualities of men in every position, where human nature, under healthy influence of true freedom, is full of promise, which we pray may, under the fostering care of God and His Church, be realized in its budding forth and bearing flowers and fruits acceptable to God; we, I say, may be pardoned for looking on ourselves as a providential people, of the foremost, destined to show, as perhaps none other has done, what Christian civilization and Christian liberty can do with man. To effect this, however, a high ideal must be reached, and the ideal of the highest life of virtue we have in her to whom we are bid direct our eyes as to our model and patroness—in Mary Immaculate, Mother of God. All Christian antiquity unites, dearly beloved brethren, in extolling her as the perfect realization of all beautiful virtue. An old work of the Egyptian or Coptic Christians salutes Mary in these words, than which nothing can more fully speak her excellence: "Hail glory of the angels! Hail Thou! chosen above the hosts of heaven and of earth, above every cherubim." (Passaglia, "De Immaculato Conceptu," t. III, p. 1158.)

An old Father of the Church, Petrus Cellensis, writes, (Book ix, Epistle 9): "Every privilege is to be granted the Blessed Virgin which it is not proven was positively and efficaciously denied her; and every presumed assertion of excellence is to be held as good unless the contrary be proven." The greatest of theologians, known as the Angelic Doctor, St. Thomas Aquinas, approves this rule, and in his work, 3 Sent. dist. 2, q. 1, art. 1, says: "It is by all means to be believed that every gift was bestowed on Mary that could have been conferred." Therefore, we can never imagine anything too good or too holy in the Immaculate Virgin. Is it not a cause for congratulation that such a model should in a special way be placed before our growing people to make them aim at something of the perfection we see in Mary? In fact, as man comes from the hand of God, and as his ultimate perfection consists in attaining the end for which God has made him, the possession of truth itself and of the sovereign good, which is God, it follows that man's highest development is inseparably bound up with his advancement in moral excellence. The proposition is self-evident. For moral excellence is the observance of the natural law—the law of conscience which recognizes God and obeys His precepts. The sanction of that law is ignorance and the slavery of passion. The observance of it brings as its result and reward the elevation and the development of the mind, and manly self-control which enables us to coerce any inclination hostile to the development of the mind and to the rectitude of the heart; while it aids us to select and use those means which are adapted to the attainment of an intellectual and moral perfection. Even the pagans saw this, and appreciated it. Seneca, in his book of Controversies, recommends to studious youth a moral life, and goes on to say that there is nothing so fatal to intellects as luxury or vice. Cicero, in his work on the republic, speaks in praise of the deeply-laid foundation of modest reserve in the youthful heart. Before these, the great Aristotle developed the same idea. (Caprara, "Dissertatio ad Legem Codicis de Professoribus.") These heathen writers, by the light of mere natural wisdom, understood the value of a life of virtue as a requisite for the attainment of the culture man can acquire. It is with the greatest reason then, my dear friends, that we should hail most thankfully the presentation to us, as a national patroness and model, of one who is the glory of the moral order; for in imitating her we do that which is most conducive to individual progress of mind and heart; for that progress requires as a condition the imitation of the resplendent virtue of the Immaculate Virgin Mary.

But not only to the individual is the patronage of this great type of moral worth useful; it is especially so to our people in a social sense. On the excellence of womanhood undoubtedly rests the good and stability of society. As long as the woman is good just so long will morality hold its sway undisputed. Let woman become corrupt, and the social fabric, too, becomes rotten to the core. For it is on woman that the education of man depends. The lips of the mother are the first to teach the child the lessons that are to guide its steps in life, and those lessons are the most deeply impressed on a man's mind, and the most influential in their bearing on his after life. Who of us does not recall with fond affection, and filial reverence, the admonitions we received from her whom we loved to address with the beautiful name of mother? Who of us but must recall the many times her words have returned to chide or encourage us in our journey through life? How many of us must attribute our success in life to the wise and loving counsels we had from her! I remember reading the words of a gifted and exemplary Cardinal of the Holy Church, his Eminence the Archbishop of Westminster, spoken on two occasions of solemnity at an interval of eight or ten years. He was preaching at the obsequies of those two most estimable prelates—the Right Rev. Dr. Goss, of Liverpool, and the Right Rev. Dr. Vaughn, of Plymouth. He wove the panegyric of their virtue and good works, and gave his audience the source whence they came: "It was," he exclaimed, "because he had a good mother!"

Since such is the undoubted and acknowledged influence of a mother on her children, the paramount importance of the correct moral training of woman cannot be exaggerated. Any influence that can be brought to further so desirable an end is a great boon to society. If we needed anything to convince us of this it would be to see how all the false systems of worship of past and present times, and how the secret societies of to-day in Europe, have labored and do labor to get possession of the female mind, and hold up as a model to the young some one of whom the doctrines of Christianity cannot approve.

Simon Magus had as his aid in disseminating his anti-Christian teaching her whom he styled the Wisdom of the Divinity. Mohammed degraded woman while wielding the terrible power that came from her degradation. Luther overthrew the beautiful type of the Christian virgin and gave his following as a model an apostate nun, whom he chose as his companion. Henry VIII, like him, trod under foot every precept of the inspired Word, and by his licentious example destroyed the veneration in which holy purity had been held in England. Heresy and treason to God's Church thus show an instinctive horror of holy virginity, and too often set up idols of abomination for the worship of youth with the most fatal result to society. And the reason of this is, that as only the grace of God can make man curb his strong passions, so the act of casting off relations with God's Church, the only source of grace, loosens the reins of those passions, and man is carried on irresistibly to spiritual destruction.

How different and consoling the effect of holding to that faith once delivered to the saints! And how the heart warms with gratitude to God that He should have given us the fruit of His work in the world, the spotless example of Mary, to teach us how to live, and so correct the evil tendency of corrupt nature! The Church presents us in her the type of the maiden pure and undefiled; of the spouse faithful, humble and obedient; of the mother loving, solicitous, strong and full of sublime virtue. Oh, how this day of ours needs the teaching of this varied and exhaustive example, suiting every condition of womanhood! What a blessing to our young Christian maidens that they should have their eyes directed always to that greatest of creatures, Mary Immaculate. What a benefactress to our whole people does not the Church show herself to be in insisting on the development of that education which places Mary in the school-room as the guardian of innocence and as the model of life. How the perfumes of Mary's virtue linger in the memory of the Catholic child on whom, in her studies, the loving eyes of her Blessed Mother looked down from the picture on the wall, rude it may be, but like a pre-Raphaelite, though inexact in detail, possessing a soul that spoke to hers. The life of Mary enters in this manner into every circumstance of woman's daily life. As a child, she teaches by her example obedience, industry, prayer; as a maiden, modesty, purity, humility; as a wife, obedience to her husband, patience, attention to the duties of her household and of hospitality; as a mother we see in her every virtue that makes a mother worthy of admiration, for she devotes herself without reserve to the welfare of her Offspring, suffering every hardship for His sake, and even shares in His ignominy as He hangs on a gibbet. Let Christian mothers learn from her to love their children and not seek to avoid the cares of motherhood, or throw their burden of duty on strangers. Let them recognize that theirs is a most sacred obligation to watch over the budding mind of the child, to see that in its soul no seeds of evil shall fall and no weed of vice spring up through her carelessness. For no one so represents the authority and the love of God for His creature as a mother to whom God has given that love of her child in order that she may preserve it for Himself. No Rachel mourns her lost ones as the Heart of God weeps over the child that has strayed away, and of a mother will He demand a strict account.

But useful as is the influence of Mary's virtues, on the individual and on society, there is a greater benefit still, which flows from the patronage of Mary under the title of Immaculate Conception. The will is a blind power and is directed by the mind. It is the will which is engaged in the practice of that virtue which makes life happy and beautiful. The office of the mind is to recognize first what virtue is, in what its beauty consists, and why the will should love it and go after it. Everything, therefore, depends on the mind, on its synderesis, on the principles that bind it and compel it to conclude what is to be done practically; and that conscience is to be followed. Now, what is so powerful in this as the principle of faith? And what is so essential to the very idea of faith as the supernatural? Acceptance, therefore, of the existence of the supernatural is an essential condition of faith. In believing in the Immaculate Conception of

Mary we profess in the most solemn and effective manner our acceptance of this supernatural order. What, in fact, is the doctrine of the Immaculate Conception if not a reiteration of the doctrine of St. Paul, that we have all sinned in Adam, as the exception in her case but confirms the rule? She alone of all men was preserved from original sin through the merits of her divine Son. And, therefore, as we proclaim Mary immaculate, we hold her up to a material world as a type of the supernatural. The great want of the day is the belief in the supernatural. Men are engulfed in matter, they wish to think of nothing save what tends to the pleasure and prosperity of life, and the writers whose works are most read are they whose opinions are most grossly positivist and material. Men of the highest position, on whom rests the responsibility of leading society, have been known to declare, in the midst of a people claiming to be Christian, that all men are born good. There are days when the most obscuring and fatal forms of Pelagianism, so valiantly opposed by the great African Doctor, St. Augustine, and so triumphantly dispelled by the rays of the sun of truth shining through the decisions of the councils of the Church, find favor with the people everywhere and destroy utterly all hope of spiritual life. To meet and overcome this hurtful and lethargic error that like an Upas tree is blighting the higher life of our people, whose teachers continually show that the idea of the supernatural is obliterated from their minds, the Church of God has recourse to her of whom we sing: "Thou, alone, hast destroyed all heresies throughout the whole world." Once more the words are verified, and her privilege convicts the world of heresy and of unbelief.

Permit me, my dear friends, briefly to place before you what is involved in the doctrine of the Immaculate Conception of Mary, that you may the better appreciate the unspeakable benefits that flow from it, and more directly to us who are under the sweet influence of its protection. The world was astounded when, in 1854, on the 8th day of December, that great Pontiff of holy memory, Pius IX, gave to the Church his dogmatic definition, to the glory of the Mother of God and to the greater exalting of God's power. Most men did not understand it, and with blind prejudice assailed the Pope and the bishops with every term of hate and denunciation. Others did understand it, and in proportion to their leaning to the current theories of the day, attacked that authority which dared to mark their favorite ideas with the stigma of error and of ignorance. Good reason had they to cry out, for the doctrine of Immaculate Conception was the reassertion of God's empire in the world, of the havoc wrought by the spirit of evil and by sin in mankind. What had the Sovereign Pontiff, the Doctor of the Universal Church, said? He had solemnly declared: "To the honor of the Most Holy and Undivided Trinity; to the ornament and glory of the Virgin Mother of God; to the exaltation of the Catholic faith, and to the increase of the Christian religion, that the doctrine which holds the Blessed Virgin Mary, in the very first instance of her conception, was by a singular grace and privilege of Almighty God, in view of the merits of Jesus Christ, the Redeemer of the human race, preserved free from all stain of original sin, has been revealed by God, and is, therefore, to be firmly and perpetually believed by all the faithful."

In making this solemn declaration the Pope took his stand on the tradition of the Church of which he is the divinely appointed judge, and relied on that assistance, vouchsafed him by the Holy Ghost, in virtue of the prayer of Christ: "Rogavi pro te ut non deficiat fides tua," and whom God sent down on the Apostles on the day of Pentecost, "the Spirit of Truth, who was to abide with them forever" (John xiv, 17), and "bring all things to their mind whatsoever He had told them" (John v, 26).

In casting a glance over the writings of the Fathers and the Liturgies of the Church, we are not surprised to find them speaking in the terms of unlimited admiration of the holiness of the Mother of God, especially when we bear in mind the rule of Petrus Cellensis, and of the Angelic Doctor, of which I spoke a few moments ago: "It is by all means to be believed that every gift was bestowed on Mary that could have been conferred." The Sovereign Pontiff, therefore, had no difficulty in finding innumerable passages that show the belief of past ages, from the beginning, that there was no spot or stain in Mary; that the foe of mankind never had dominion over her. Thus, for example, if we take the verse of the XLIV Psalm: "The Most High has sanctified His Own Tabernacle"—words which apply primarily to Jerusalem, then prophetically to the Church—we find these words used, by accommodation, with reference to the Mother of God, by many Fathers. Methodius, speaking of Simon and Anna (Passaglia, "De Immaculato Conceptu," t. II, p. 735), says of Mary: "Thou among all created things, visible and invisible, far beyond all, shinest with honor. Happy the root of Jesse, and blessed the house of David in which thou didst bud forth. God is in the thee and thou shalt not be moved; for the Most High hath sanctified His Tabernacle."

John, Bishop of Eubea, celebrating the Blessed Virgin's own conception, says: "Sing, exult, and praise! Lo! the devil is overcome, who had reduced our nature to his tyranny. Behold a throne is erected on earth more admirable than that of the cherubim, of which it is written: God is in the midst of it, and it shall not be moved."

In like manner writes Germanus, the Bishop of Constantinople. St. John Damascene calls her "something new under the sun," and others apply the verse to Mary. The Greek Church also speaks, in its turn, of Mary as the tabernacle of the Most High, and ends with the exclamation: "O, Lady in every way immaculate!"

The Jesuit Fathers, in their work on the Immaculate Conception, the direction of which was given to Professor Passaglia, one of their number, thus sum up the words of the Fathers and the testimonies of the Greek Church quoted:

"The Fathers have taught: I. That when Mary was conceived a throne was prepared more admirable than that of the cherubim. II. That Mary first existed as a temple built by the spiritual Solomon, and as a city aided by God lest it should be taken. III. That she came as something new under the sun, as the miracle of miracles, as abounding with grace, wholly beautiful and next to God. IV. That Mary, not created other than as Eve, came from the very hands of God. V. That no dishonor attached to God from the creation of Mary, because she was brought into existence as a work pleasing to God. VI. That the triumph over Satan, to be fully achieved by Christ, began with the origin and primodial existence of Mary."

The Sovereign Pontiff moreover had the support of the public opinion of the Church, in which as a soul the Holy Ghost dwells, making all of one mind, and that public opinion was in accordance with the writings and testimony of learned and pious Fathers. As teacher of the Church, his power of unerring, authoritative ex cathedra decision in matters of controversy has been gloriously vindicated by the Œcumenical Council of the Vatican, and it is a point of Catholic faith that he has that assistance of the Holy Ghost whereby the Church is infallible.

But this regards only the statement of the doctrine; we have to do with the effects of it—its influence on the world, and especially on our country, of which Mary Immaculate is the Patroness. What is that effect? To condemn naturalism and to exalt the supernatural; to make all understand the absolute necessity of the spiritual life.

Our Most Holy Father, Pope Leo XIII, in his recent Encyclical has, with great care and precision, noted the existence of naturalism, its characteristics and tendencies, and with equal firmness, and with inexorable, logical conclusion, has condemned it. It is the evil of the day. It is to be found everywhere. More especially is it to be encountered where education is most advanced and most widespread. It has enthroned itself in the great universities of non-Catholic countries, as the legitimate outcome of so-called free thought. I say *so-called*, for I will not concede the sacred name of freedom to rebellion against God and against reason; and if ever there has been rebellion against God and against reason, it was when the principle of private judgment in matters of faith was asserted: for the teachings of faith came from God, and reason tells us to accept without question what we know God reveals. From non-Catholic universities naturalism has spread to Catholic peoples and even to what were once Catholic universities, but which now, under the influence of the ideas fostered by European Freemasonry, the great teacher and propagator of naturalism, have become arch-professors of error; denying the existence of the supernatural, and consequently of grace. From the universities, naturalism has spread to the press, and the press has popularized it nowhere more than here in America, till you can hardly take up any great daily without finding it openly taught, or lurking in articles written with every beauty of style, and on subjects that vividly interest. And as the direct consequence of naturalism is to destroy the idea of sin, so you find the writers of these articles speaking with light raillery of sin, and insiduously undermining the ideas most essential to Christian morality. Especially is this the case with regard to holy purity; and the result is that not only do young persons of both sexes laugh at the assertion that impure thought is sinful, but they even declare openly that the most shameful vices are not sins at all. This is a very terrible state of things; but I have put the case most temperately, as any one who has had the experience that even I had, must say. What the future of society is to be with such ideas gaining ground, it makes one shudder to think of. What is the remedy? Where is the counteracting influence? The Catholic faith with its clear definitions, its fearless and consistent preaching of the supernatural order, and especially in its presenting to the people types of virtue in the saints, and pre-eminently in the definition of the Immaculate Conception of Mary, which not only epitomizes the teachings of the supernatural order, but gives us a type of moral beauty and of the spiritual life of grace, so excellent, that the human intellect is not adequate to grasp it. The Immaculate Conception epitomizes the teachings of the supernatural order, because it reaffirms the existence of original sin, and its universal incurrence, the Mother of God being the only exception; it reaffirms the necessity of justification, and that through the merits of Jesus Christ alone; and as a consequence, it reaffirms the existence of the grace of God, and the need we all have of it; finally, it reaffirms all the teachings of St. Augustine in the fourth century, and of the second Council of Orange in the sixth, against Pelagianism and Semi-Pelagianism; the former of which denied the existence of grace, and the latter attributed the beginnings of conversion to man, contrary to what Christ Himself said: "No man can come to Me save My Father draw him." (John vi.) "Without Me you can do nothing." While the great inspired Apostle, St. Paul, writes: "What hast thou that thou hast not received; and if thou hast received it, why dost thou glory as if thou hadst not received it?"

That the doctrine of the Immaculate Conception presents us a supernatural type of moral beauty, of spotless purity, and of a spiritual life of grace, does not need demonstration after what I have said. With the Church we can speak of this Immaculate Virgin as "Candor lucis eternæ et speculum sine macula," as the reflected "brightness of eternal light and the mirror without spot!" What the effect on the mind and heart of such a perfect, brilliant and beautiful model is, you and I, dearly beloved brethren, know. Oh! what a blessing to have Mary before our eyes, the thought of her holiness in our minds, the perfume of her virtues ever drawing us on; "in odorem unguentorum tuorum currimus;" so that we run in the ways of the Lord whither that delightful odor leads us! Let us give devout thanks to God, that we are especially placed under her protection. May that protection ever hover over this beloved country of ours; may its benign influence ever foster in it everything that is true, everything that is beautiful, everything that is holy! Amen.

PASTORAL LETTER

—OF THE—

THIRD PLENARY COUNCIL

OF BALTIMORE.

V. Rev. Bonaventure Frey, O.M.Cap.

Very Rev. D. Ruesing, O.S.F.

Very Rev. Hyacinth Epp, O.M.Cap.

Very Rev. James McGrath, O.M.I.

Very Rev. A. Aiguepersse, S.P.M.

Rt. Rev. F. Conrad, O.S.B.

Rt. Rev. A. Edelbrock, O.S.B.

Rt. Rev. F. Mundwiler, O.S.B.

Rt. Rev. B. Wimmer, O.S.B.

PASTORAL LETTER

— OF THE —

ARCHBISHOPS AND BISHOPS OF THE UNITED STATES

— ASSEMBLED IN THE —

THIRD PLENARY COUNCIL OF BALTIMORE,

TO THE CLERGY AND LAITY OF THEIR CHARGE.

The Archbishops and Bishops of the United States, in Third Plenary Council assembled, to their clergy and faithful people—"Grace unto you and peace from God our Father, and from the Lord Jesus Christ."

VENERABLE BRETHREN OF THE CLERGY,
        BELOVED CHILDREN OF THE LAITY:

Full eighteen years have elapsed since our predecessors were assembled in Plenary Council to promote uniformity of discipline, to provide for the exigencies of the day, to devise new means for the maintenance and diffusion of our holy religion, which should be adequate to the great increase of the Catholic population. In the interval, the prelates, clergy and faithful have been taught by a wholesome experience to appreciate the zeal, piety and prudence that inspired the decrees of those venerable Fathers and to listen with cheerful submission to their authoritative voice, whether uttered in warning, in exhortation or positive enactment. And the whole American Church deeply feels and cordially proclaims her gratitude for the treasure bequeathed to us by their wise and timely legislation. Its framers, in great part, have gone before us with the sign of Faith and now sleep the sleep of peace. But their work, after following them (Apoc.) to the dread tribunal of the great Judge to plead in their behalf and insure their reward, has remained upon earth a safe-guide and rich blessing for the clergy and people of their generation.

Since that time, however, the body of our clergy and religious has grown to wonderful dimensions, our Catholic institutions have been multiplied tenfold, with a corresponding increase in the number of our faithful laity. The territory, likewise, over which they are spread, has been greatly enlarged. The land of the far West, that was once desolate and impassable, through God's providential mercy, now rejoices and flourishes like the lily. Under His guiding hand, it has been taught to bud forth and blossom and rejoice with joy and praise. The wilderness has exchanged its solitude for the hum of busy life and industry; and the steps of our missionaries and Catholic settlers have invariably either preceded or accompanied the westward progress of civilization. Forests have given away to cities, where Catholic temples re-echo the praises of the Most High, where the priceless perfume of the "Clean Oblation," foretold by Malachi, daily ascends to heaven, and where the life-giving sacraments of Holy Church are dispensed by a devoted clergy. In view of this great progress of our holy religion, this marvellous widening of the tabernacles of Jacob, it has been judged wise and expedient, if not absolutely necessary, to examine anew the legislation of our predecessors, not with any purpose of radical change, much less of abrogation, but to preserve and perfect its spirit by adapting it to our altered circumstances. And as every day gives birth to new errors, and lapse of time or distance of place allows abuses to gradually creep into regular discipline, we have judged it the duty of our pastoral office to check the latter by recalling and enforcing established law, and to guard our flock against the former by timely words of paternal admonition.

Such, too, has been the expressed wish and injunction of our Holy Father Leo XIII, happily reigning, to whom, as Supreme Pontiff and successor of the Prince of the Apostles, by inherent right belongs the power of convoking this our Third National or Plenary Council, and of appointing (as he has graciously done) an Apostolic Delegate to preside over its deliberations.

One of the most important events that our age has witnessed was the assembling by Pius IX, of happy memory, of the General Council of the Vatican. It was held three years after the close of our Second Plenary

Council, and all, or nearly all, of its members, and many besides of the prelates now assembled in this Third Plenary Council, enjoyed the rare privilege of sitting with the other Princes of the Church in the only Ecumenical Synod vouchsafed these latter ages. Its appointed task was to condemn the most influential and insidious errors of the day, and to complete the legislation on weighty matters of discipline that had been contemplated and discussed, but left undecided, by the Council of Trent. Like its predecessor, the Council of the Vatican was interrupted by the disturbed condition of Europe; and the Fathers, leaving the work of their deliberations unfinished, returned to their homes, some to this Western continent, others to remote regions of the East. But we would fain cherish the hope, and lift up to heaven our earnest prayer, that the Father of mercies and God of all consolation, who is ever ready to comfort His Church in all her tribulations, who holds in His hand the counsels of princes and the devices of peoples, may deign, in His own good time, to reunite the prelates, or their successors, over the tomb of St. Peter or elsewhere, as may seem best to His infinite wisdom. The Vatican Council, however, during its short session of seven months, gave solemn, authoritative utterance to some great truths which the Church had unvaryingly held from the days of Christ and His Apostles; but which she found it once more necessary to recall and inculcate against the widespread skepticism and unbelief of our day. Besides condemning the philosophy, no less wicked than false and teeming with contradictions, of the last two centuries, and especially of our own times, she had to uphold (such is the lamentable downward course of those who rebelled against her divine commission to teach all nations!) the truth and divinity of the Sacred Books against the very children of those, who once appealed to Scripture to disprove her teachings, and to maintain the dignity and value of human reason against the lineal descendants of those, who once claimed reason as the supreme and only guide in picking out from her creed what mysteries they would retain, what mysteries they would reject. Nobly did she perform her duty and assert in the face of a forgetful or unbelieving world that reason is God's highest and best gift to man in the natural order, and that this most salutary aid of his weakness is not only not impaired, but strengthened, supplemented and ennobled by the supernatural gift of Divine revelation.

We have no reason to fear that you, beloved brethren, are likely to be carried away by these or other false doctrines condemned by the Vatican Council, such as materialism or the denial of God's power to create, to reveal to mankind His hidden truths, to display by miracles His almighty power in this world which is the work of His hands. But neither can we close our eyes to the fact that teachers of skepticism and irreligion are at work in our country. They have crept into the leading educational institutions of our non-Catholic fellow-citizens, they have (though rarely) made their appearance in the public press and even in the pulpit. Could we rely fully on the innate good sense of the American people and on that habitual reverence for God and religion which has so far been their just pride and glory, there might seem comparatively little danger of the general diffusion of those wild theories which reject or ignore Revelation, undermine morality, and end not unfrequently by banishing God from His own creation. But when we take into account the daily signs of growing unbelief, and see how its heralds not only seek to mould the youthful mind in our colleges and seats of learning, but are also actively working amongst the masses, we cannot but shudder at the dangers that threaten us in the future. When to this we add the rapid growth of that false civilization which hides its foulness under the name of enlightenment—involving, as it does, the undisguised worship of mammon, the anxious search after every ease, comfort and luxury for man's physical well-being, the all-absorbing desire to promote his material interests, the unconcern or rather contempt for those of his higher and better nature—we cannot but feel that out of all this must grow a heartless materialism, which is the best soil to receive the seeds of unbelief and irreligion, which threaten to desolate the country at no distant day. The first thing to perish will be our liberties. For men, who know not God or religion, can never respect the inalienable rights which man has received from His Creator. The State in such case must become a despotism, whether its power be lodged in the hands of one or many.

To you, beloved brethren, who possess the treasure of Catholic faith, we may safely address the reiterated injunctions of the Lord to the chosen leader of His people.

"Take courage and be strong . . . take courage and be very valiant. . . . Behold I command thee, take courage and be strong. Fear not and be not dismayed, because the Lord thy God is with thee."[1] The latter clause gives the reason why we should take courage and be strong. An intermediate verse gives the means of securing God's assistance: "Let not the book of this law depart from thy mouth, but thou shalt meditate on it day and night, that thou mayest observe and do the things that are written in it." Keep, then, day and night, before your eyes the Law of God and His teachings through that Holy Church that He has appointed mother and mistress of all men. Fly the reading of all infidel books, and keep them from your children, as you would the poison of asp or basilisk.

[1] Josue, 1, 6, 7, 8, 9.

Teach them that you and they, in listening to Holy Church, have the guidance of Him who said, "I am the way, the truth and the life." Let others doubt or deny, but with the Apostle, you know whom you have believed, and you are certain that He will make good the trust you have reposed in Him.[1]

Christ our Lord commissioned His Apostles to teach mankind the truths they had been taught by Him. They received no commandment to write on any doctrine, much less to draw up a body of articles of faith such as our children now learn from the catechism. They preached and taught by word of mouth; or, when occasion offered itself, they wrote as the Divine Spirit prompted them. What they wrote and what they delivered by oral instruction are equally God's Word. And this two-fold Word, written and unwritten, is the Deposit of divine truth, committed to the keeping of the Catholic Church, and chiefly to him on whom the Church was built—the only Apostle who, in the full sense of the words, yet lives and rules in the person of his successors, and from his unfailing chair imparts to all who seek it the truth of Christian faith.[2] It is his office to confirm his brethren, and the history of the Church exhibits him, from the beginning and through all ages, as faithfully fulfilling the charge entrusted to him by his Master.[3] From the earliest ages down to our own, the voice of Peter has been foremost in condemning all deviations from apostolic doctrine. No threats of worldly power could subdue or silence that voice. To such threats Peter, through his successors, has ever given the same answer that he gave at Jerusalem to the assembled priests and ancients.[4] No pleading of princes and potentates could ever win Rome's sympathy for error; no heresy under false semblance of Catholic truth ever yet eluded her vigilant eye.[5] As soon as any novelty appeared, all hearts and eyes were turned towards the Chair of Peter, and when that Chair gave its decision, the Christian people yielded obedience. Those who would not were cut off from the communion of the Church, and became thenceforth as the heathen and the publican.

This doctrine, therefore, which had so thoroughly wrought itself into the life and action of the Church, the Vatican Council deemed proper to consecrate by a solemn definition. Hence, that no one in future may craftily pretend not to know, how and whence to ascertain what the Church officially teaches; above all, that no one may henceforth scatter the baneful seeds of false doctrine with impunity, under the mask of an appeal from the judgment of the Holy See (whether it be to learned universities,

---

[1] II. Tim., i, 12. [2] Luke, xii, 32.
[3] See Epist. S. Petri Chrysologi inter Epp. S. Leonis M. [4] Acts, iv, 19-20.
[5] Cf. St. Cyprian, Ep. lix.

or State tribunals, or future councils, particular or general, as was done by Luther and the Jansenists), the Church of the living God, through the Fathers of the Vatican Council, has unequivocally declared that her authentic spokesman is the successor of St. Peter in the Apostolic See of Rome, and that what he, as Head of the Church, officially decides is part of the Deposit of Faith intrusted to her keeping by Christ Our Lord, and hence subject to neither denial, doubt nor revision, but to be implicitly received and believed by all.

In this authoritative declaration there is nothing new, nothing to give cause for wonder. It is only setting the solemn seal of definition upon what has always been the belief and practice of the Church. Yet "the gates of Hell," the powers of darkness that forever assail the Church built on Peter—though knowing (for the very devils believe and tremble in believing)[1] that they cannot prevail against it nor make void God's promise[2]—seem to have been stirred to their very depths by the proclamation of this great truth. And their impotent rage has found its echo upon earth. The definition evoked a storm of fierce obloquy and reckless vituperation, such as has been seldom witnessed amongst our opponents. And a wretched handful of apostate Catholics "went out from us, but they were not of us."[3]

But, what was far more serious, the kings of the earth stood up and the princes assembled together against the Lord[4] and against His annointed Vicar, because of the definition. They revived the old war-cry raised by the Jews against our Saviour[5] and so often renewed by the persecutors of the Church. They pretended that by defining the infallibility of St. Peter's successor, she had made herself the enemy of Cæsar. Herein we see plainly verified the strong language of Scripture: "Iniquity hath lied to itself."[6] The Pope, even after the proclamation of his infallibility, is no more the enemy of Cæsar and of human governments, than was the infallible Peter the enemy of Nero, or Christ our Lord, who is infallible truth itself, the enemy of Augustus and Tiberius under whom He was born into the world, taught and suffered. The governments by which, three centuries ago, the new tenets of Luther, Zwingli and Calvin had been imposed on reluctant peoples by the sword, were the first, indeed the only ones, to again unsheathe it against Catholic believers, and especially against the bishops and clergy. It was their purpose to exterminate by degrees the Catholic hierarchy, and replace it by a servile priesthood that would subordinate its preaching and ministry to the will of the State. To do this

---

[1] Credunt et contremiscunt, James ii, 19.
[2] Matth., xvi, 18.
[3] John, ii, 19.
[4] Acts, iv, 26.
[5] John, xix, 12, 15.
[6] Ps., xxvi, 12.

they had to trample on solemn treaties and organic laws. But the Catholics of Prussia, clergy and people, while proving themselves most devoted and faithful to their country's laws, stood up like a wall of adamant against the tyranny of its rulers. With generous vigor and admirable constancy, they availed themselves of every legal and constitutional means to check the advances of despotism and save their own freedom and that of their country. They have given to the world a glorious example, which it is to be hoped the victims of tyrannous Liberalism in Catholic countries may some day have the wisdom or the courage to imitate. The struggle has now lasted fourteen years; but the very friends of this persecuting legislation have been driven at last to acknowledge that it has proved to be a miserable failure; and no better proof of it could be found than the fact, that the rulers of Prussia have had to fall back on the patriotism of the Catholic body to stay the threatening march of socialism and revolution. In Switzerland, too, the persecution has yielded to the policy of mildness and conciliation adopted by Our Holy Father, Leo XIII.

Beloved brethren, we have no need to encourage you to hold steadfastly to this doctrine of the Vatican Council; for you were trained from infancy to believe it, as were your fathers before you, while it was not yet invested with the formalities of a definition, just as the early Christians held firmly to the divinity of the Son and of the Holy Ghost three hundred years before the Church found it necessary to define them in the Councils of Nice and Byzantium.

And in our own country, writers and speakers who know the Church only by the caricatures drawn by prejudice, have occasionally re-echoed the same charge; but despite local and temporary excitements, the good sense of the American people has always prevailed against the calumny. We think we can claim to be acquainted both with the laws, institutions and spirit of the Catholic Church, and with the laws, institutions and spirit of our country; and we emphatically declare that there is no antagonism between them. A Catholic finds himself at home in the United States; for the influence of his Church has constantly been exercised in behalf of individual rights and popular liberties. And the right-minded American nowhere finds himself more at home than in the Catholic Church, for nowhere else can he breathe more freely that atmosphere of Divine truth, which alone can make him free.[1]

We repudiate with equal earnestness the assertion that we need to lay aside any of our devotedness to our Church, to be true Americans; the insinuation that we need to abate any of our love for our

[1] John, viii. 32.

country's principles and institutions, to be faithful Catholics. To argue that the Catholic Church is hostile to our great Republic, because she teaches that "there is no power but from God;"[1] because, therefore, back of the events which led to the formation of the Republic, she sees the Providence of God leading to that issue, and back of our country's laws the authority of God as their sanction,—this is evidently so illogical and contradictory an accusation, that we are astonished to hear it advanced by persons of ordinary intelligence. We believe that our country's heroes were the instruments of the God of Nations in establishing this home of freedom; to both the Almighty and to His instruments in the work, we look with grateful reverence; and to maintain the inheritance of freedom which they have left us, should it ever—which God forbid— be imperilled, our Catholic citizens will be found to stand forward, as one man ready to pledge anew "their lives, their fortunes, and their sacred honor."

No less illogical would be the notion, that there is aught in the free spirit of our American institutions, incompatible with perfect docility to the Church of Christ. The spirit of American freedom is not one of anarchy or license. It essentially involves love of order, respect for rightful authority, and obedience to just laws. There is nothing in the character of the most liberty-loving American, which could hinder his reverential submission to the Divine authority of Our Lord, or to the like authority delegated by Him to His Apostles and His Church. Nor are there in the world more devoted adherents of the Catholic Church, the See of Peter, and the Vicar of Christ, than the Catholics of the United States. Narrow, insular, national views and jealousies concerning ecclesiastical authority and Church organization, may have sprung naturally enough from the selfish policy of certain rulers and nations in by-gone times; but they find no sympathy in the spirit of the true American Catholic. His natural instincts, no less than his religious training, would forbid him to submit in matters of faith to the dictation of the State or to any merely human authority whatsoever. He accepts the religion and the Church that are from God, and he knows well that these are universal, not national or local,—for all the children of men, not for any special tribe or tongue. We glory that we are, and, with God's blessing, shall continue to be, not the American Church, nor the Church of the United States, nor a Church in any other sense exclusive or limited, but an integral part of the one, holy, Catholic and Apostolic Church of Jesus Christ, which is the Body of Christ, in which there is no distinction of classes and nationalities,—in which all are one in Christ Jesus.[2]

[1] Rom., xiii, 1.   [2] Gal., iii, 28.

While the assaults of calumny and persecution directed against the Church since the Vatican Council have abundantly shown how angry the powers of evil have been at the Council's luminous utterances of Divine truth, our Holy Father the Pope has been, naturally enough, the main object of attack. And Divine Providence has been pleased to leave him, for a while at the mercy of his enemies, in order that their impious violence might work out the demonstration of its own injustice; that the true character and the indestructibility of the office of St. Peter might be made manifest to the world; that the wisdom of the Providence which has guarded the independence of that office in the past, might be vindicated and reaffirmed for the future. The great and beloved Pius IX died the "Prisoner of the Vatican," and Leo XIII has inherited his Apostolic trials, together with his Apostolic office. Day after day he has seen the consecrated patrimony of religion and charity swept into Cæsar's coffers by the ruthless hand of spoliation and confiscation. At this moment, he sees that same grasp laid upon the property of the Propaganda, piously set apart for spreading the Gospel of Jesus Christ throughout the missionary countries of the world. So utterly unjustifiable an act has called forth a cry of indignant protest from the Catholics of all countries, and from no country has the cry gone forth clearer and louder than from our own. We thank our government for the action that saved the American College from confiscation; and we hope that the protest and appeal of all governments and peoples that "love justice and hate iniquity" may yet shame the spoiler into honesty. Meanwhile the hearts of all Catholics go out all the more lovingly towards their persecuted Chief Pastor; and from their worldly means, be they abundant or scanty, they gladly supply him with the means necessary for carrying on the administration of his high office. Such has been your liberality in the past, beloved brethren, that we hardly need exhort you to generosity in the collection for the Holy Father, which will continue to be made annually throughout all the dioceses of the country. Let your devoted affection be shown by your deeds, and the persistency of injustice be more than matched by the constancy of your faithful and generous love.

While enduring with the heroism of a martyr the trials which beset him, and trustfully awaiting the Almighty's day of deliverance, the energy and wisdom of Leo XIII are felt to the ends of the earth. He is carrying on with the governments of Europe the negotiations which promise soon to bring peace to the Church. In the East he is preparing the way for the return to Catholic unity of the millions whom the Greek schism has so long deprived of communion with the See of Peter, and is following the progress of exploration in lands hitherto unknown or inaccessible with corresponding advances of Catholic missions. To the whole world his voice has again and again been gone forth in counsels of eloquence and wisdom, pointing out the path to the acquisition of truth in the important domain of philosophy and history—the best means for the improvement of human life in all its phases, individual, domestic and social—the ways in which the children of God should walk—"that all flesh may see the salvation of God."

But in all the wide circle of his great responsibility, the progress of the Church in these United States forms, in a special manner, both a source of joy and an object of solicitude to the Holy Father. With loving care his predecessors watched and encouraged her first feeble beginnings. They cheered and fostered her development in the pure atmosphere of freedom, when the name of Carroll shone with equal lustre at the head of her new-born Hierarchy, and on the roll of our country's patriots. Step by step they directed her progress, as with marvellous rapidity, the clergy and the dioceses have multiplied; the hundreds of the faithful have increased to thousands and to millions; her churches, schools, asylums, hospitals, academies and colleges, have covered the land with homes of divine truth and Christian charity. Not yet a century has elapsed since the work was inaugurated by the appointment of the first Bishop of Baltimore, in 1789; and as we gaze upon the results already reached we must exclaim: "By the Lord hath this been done, and it is wonderful in our eyes."[1]

In all this astonishing development, from the rude beginnings of pioneer missionary toil, along the nearer and nearer approaches to the beauteous symmetry of the Church's perfect organization, the advance so gradual yet so rapid has been safely guided in the lines of Catholic and Apostolic tradition, by the combined efforts and wisdom of our local Hierarchy and of the successors of St. Peter. It was in order to take counsel with the representatives of the American Hierarchy concerning the important interests of religion in this country, that the Holy Father, last year, invited the Archbishops of the United States to Rome. And the object of the present council is to put into practical shape the means of religious improvement then resolved upon or suggested.

EDUCATION OF THE CLERGY.

One of our first cares has been to provide for the more perfect education of aspirants to the holy Priesthood. It has always been the Church's endeavor that her clergy should be eminent in learning. For she has

[1] Matt., xxi. 42; Ps., cxvii. 23.

always considered that nothing less than this is required by their sacred office of guarding and dispensing Divine truth. "The lips of the priest shall keep knowledge," says the Most High, "and the people shall seek the law at his mouth." This is true in all times; for no advance in secular knowledge, no diffusion of popular education, can do away with the office of the teaching ministry, which Our Lord has declared shall last forever. In every age it is and shall be the duty of God's priests to proclaim the salutary truths which our Heavenly Father has given to the world through His Divine Son; to present them to each generation in the way that will move their minds and hearts to embrace and love them; to defend them, when necessary, against every attack of error. From this it is obvious that the priest should have a wide acquaintance with every department of learning that has a bearing on religious truth. Hence in our age, when so many misleading theories are put forth on every side, when every department of natural truth and fact is actively explored for objections against revealed religion, it is evident how extensive and thorough should be the knowledge of the minister of the Divine Word, that he may be able to show forth worthily the beauty, the superiority, the necessity of the Christian religion, and to prove that there is nothing in all that God has made to contradict anything that God has taught.

Hence the priest who has the noble ambition of attaining to the high level of his holy office, may well consider himself a student all his life; and of the leisure hours which he can find amid the duties of his ministry, he will have very few that he can spare for miscellaneous reading, and none at all to waste. And hence, too, the evident duty devolving on us, to see that the course of education in our ecclesiastical colleges and seminaries be as perfect as it can be made. During the century of extraordinary growth now closing, the care of the Church in this country has been to send forth as rapidly as possible holy, zealous, hard-working priests, to supply the needs of the multitudes calling for the ministrations of religion. She has not on that account neglected to prepare them for their divine work by a suitable education, as her numerous and admirable seminaries testify; but the course of study was often more rapid and restricted than she desired. At present our improved circumstances make it practicable both to lengthen and widen the course, and for this the Council has duly provided.

We are confident, beloved brethren, that you feel as deeply interested as ourselves in the accomplishment of these great results. This you have hitherto manifested by the zealous liberality by which you have enabled us to build and support our seminaries; and we are well assured that you will not be found wanting, should even greater efforts be necessary, to enable us to make the education and usefulness of the clergy as perfect as we desire. In the future, as in the past, look upon your annual contribution to the Seminary fund as one of your most important duties as Catholics, and let your generosity be proportioned to the dignity and sacredness of the object for which you offer it.

And here we remind those among our Catholic people to whom God has been pleased to give wealth, that it is their duty and their privilege to consider themselves the Lord's stewards, in the use of what His Providence has placed in their hands; that they should be foremost in helping on the work of the Church of Christ during life, and make sure to have God among their heirs when they die; and we recommend to them as specially useful the founding of scholarships, either in their diocesan or provincial Seminaries, or in the American College in Rome, or elsewhere, as circumstances may suggest.

PASTORAL RIGHTS.

No small portion of our attention has been bestowed on the framing of such legislation as will best secure the rights and interests of your pastors, and of all ranks of the clergy in this country. It is but natural, beloved brethren, that the first and dearest object of our solicitude should be our venerable clergy. They are our dearest brethren, bound to us by ties more sacred than those of flesh and blood. Our elevation to a higher office only draws them to us more closely, since their happiness and welfare are thereby made the first object of our responsibility, and since upon their devoted labors must mainly depend the welfare of the souls entrusted to our charge. We need not tell you, beloved brethren, how admirably they fulfil their sacred trust. You are witnesses to their lives of toil and sacrifice. And to them we can truly say in the words of St. Paul, "You are our glory and our joy."[1]

The rights of the clergy have reference chiefly to their exercising the sacred ministry in their missions, to the fixity of their tenure of office and to the inviolableness of their pastoral authority within proper limits. It is the spirit of the Church that the various grades of authority in her organization should in no wise be in rivalry or conflict, but orderly and harmonious. This she has secured by her wise laws, based upon the experience of centuries, and representing the perfection of Church organization. It is obvious that in countries like our own, where from rudimentary beginnings our organization is only gradually advancing towards perfection, the full application of these laws is impracticable; but in proportion as

[1] I. Thes., ii, 20.

they become practicable, it is our desire, not less than that of the Holy See, that they should go into effect. For we have the fullest confidence in the wisdom with which the Church devised these laws, and we heartily rejoice at every approach towards perfect organization in the portion of the vineyard over which we have jurisdiction. This has been to some degree accomplished by regulations enacted during recent years, and still more by the decrees of the present Council.

But while it is our desire to do all on our part that both justice and affection can prompt, for fully securing all proper rights and privileges to our priests, let us remind you, beloved brethren, that on your conduct must their happiness chiefly depend. A grateful and pious flock is sure to make a happy pastor. But if the people do not respond to their pastor's zeal, if they are cold and ungrateful or disedifying, then indeed is his lot sad and pitiable. Since, therefore, the Priests of God leave all things to devote themselves to your spiritual welfare, show by your affection, by your co-operation with their efforts for your spiritual improvement, and even by your care for their physical comfort, that you appreciate their devotedness and the reciprocal obligation which it imposes. Look upon your priests as your best friends, your trustiest advisers, your surest guides. If duty sometimes calls upon them to admonish or rebuke you, remember that the reproof is meant for your good, and take it in the spirit in which it is given. And if perchance they have to speak to you oftener than is pleasant about church finances and the demands of charity, understand that it must be at least as disagreeable to them as it is to you; that it is not for themselves, but for the needs of the parish church or school, which are intended for your benefit, or of the parish poor, who are your charge, that they have to plead; and that, while they are to bear in mind the advisability of speaking of money as seldom as possible, you must be mindful to make your generosity equal to the need, and thereby save both your pastors and yourselves the painful necessity of frequent appeals.

And here we deem it proper to say a few words concerning church properties and church debts. The manner of holding the legal title to these properties is different in different places, according to the requirements of local civil laws; but whether the title be held by the bishop, or by boards of diocesan or parish trustees, it always remains true that the properties are held in trust for the Church for the benefit of the people. One generation buys or builds, another generation improves and adorns, and each generation uses and transmits for the use of others yet to come,— bishops and priests having the burden of the administration and being sacredly responsible for its faithful performance.

In the discharge of this duty it often becomes necessary to contract church debts. Where the multiplication of the Catholic population has been so rapid, rapid work had to be done in erecting churches and schools. And if, under such circumstances, pastors had to wait till all the funds were in hand before beginning the work, a generation would be left without necessary spiritual aids, and might be lost to the Church and to God. We fully recognize, beloved brethren, how strictly we are bound to prevent the contraction of debts without real necessity; and this we have endeavored to secure by careful legislation. Still, despite all our efforts, it must inevitably happen that the burden imposed on us by our gigantic task of providing for the spiritual wants of the present and the rising generation will always be heavy, and will weigh upon us all. But the special Providence of God towards our country, which has made the work and the need so great, has never failed hitherto to inspire our people with a zeal equal to the demand. You have rivaled your pastors in the ardor of their desire for the building up of the Church of Christ and the extension of His Kingdom; and we are confident that you will preserve your zeal unto the end, and transmit it undiminished to your descendants. It is our earnest wish that existing debts should be liquidated as soon as possible, in order that the money now consumed in paying interest may be employed in the great improvements still to be made, and especially in helping on the glorious work of Christian education.

CHRISTIAN EDUCATION.

Scarcely, if at all, secondary to the Church's desire for the education of the clergy, is her solicitude for the education of the laity. It is not for themselves, but for the people, that the Church wishes her clergy to be learned, as it is not for themselves only, but for the people that they are priests. Popular education has always been a chief object of the Church's care; in fact, it is not too much to say that the history of civilization and education is the history of the Church's work. In the rude ages, when semi-barbarous chieftains boasted of their illiteracy, she succeeded in diffusing that love of learning which covered Europe with schools and universities; and thus from the barbarous tribes of the early middle ages, she built up the civilized nations of modern times. Even subsequent to the religious dissensions of the sixteenth century, whatever progress has been made in education is mainly due to the impetus which she had previously given. In our own country notwithstanding the many difficulties attendant on first beginnings and unexampled growth, we already find her schools, academies and colleges everywhere, built and sustained by voluntary contributions, even at the cost of great sacrifices, and comparing favorably with the best educational institutions in the land.

These facts abundantly attest the Church's desire for popular instruction. The beauty of truth, the refining and elevating influences of knowledge, are meant for all, and she wishes them to be brought within the reach of all. Knowledge enlarges our capacity both for self-improvement and for promoting the welfare of our fellow-men; and in so noble a work the Church wishes every hand to be busy. Knowledge, too, is the best weapon against pernicious errors. It is only "a little learning" that is "a dangerous thing." In days like ours, when error is so pretentious and aggressive, every one needs to be as completely armed as possible with sound knowledge,—not only the clergy, but the people also that they may be able to withstand the noxious influences of popularized irreligion. In the great coming combat between truth and error, between Faith and Agnosticism, an important part of the fray must be borne by the laity, and woe to them if they are not well prepared. And if, in the olden days of vassalage and serfdom, the Church honored every individual, no matter how humble his position, and labored to give him the enlightenment that would qualify him for future responsibilities, much more now, in the era of popular rights and liberties, when every individual is an active and influential factor in the body politic, does she desire that all should be fitted by suitable training for an intelligent and conscientious discharge of the important duties that will devolve upon them.

Few, if any, will deny that a sound civilization must depend upon sound popular education. But education, in order to be sound and to produce beneficial results, must develop what is best in man, and make him not only clever but good. A one-sided education will develop a one-sided life; and such a life will surely topple over, and so will every social system that is built up of such lives. True civilization requires that not only the physical and intellectual, but also the moral and religious, well-being of the people should be promoted, and at least with equal care. Take away religion from a people, and morality would soon follow; morality gone, even their physical condition will ere long degenerate into corruption which breeds decrepitude, while their intellectual attainments would only serve as a light to guide them to deeper depths of vice and ruin. This has been so often demonstrated in the history of the past, and is, in fact, so self-evident, that one is amazed to find any difference of opinion about it. A civilization without religion, would be a civilization of "the struggle for existence, and the survival of the fittest," in which cunning and strength would become the substitutes for principle, virtue, conscience and duty. As a matter of fact, there never has been a civilization worthy of the name without religion; and from the facts of history the laws of human nature can easily be inferred.

Hence education, in order to foster civilization, must foster religion. Now the three great educational agencies are the home, the Church, and the school. These mould men and shape society. Therefore each of them, to do its part well, must foster religion. But many, unfortunately, while avowing that religion should be the light and the atmosphere of the home and of the Church, are content to see it excluded from the school, and even advocate as the best school system that which necessarily excludes religion. Few surely will deny that childhood and youth are the periods of life when the character ought especially to be subjected to religious influences. Nor can we ignore the palpable fact that the school is an important factor in the forming of childhood and youth,—so important that its influence often outweighs that of home and Church. It cannot, therefore, be desirable or advantageous that religion should be excluded from the school. On the contrary, it ought there to be one of the chief agencies for moulding the young life to all that is true and virtuous, and holy. To shut religion out of the school, and keep it for home and the Church, is, logically, to train up a generation that will consider religion good for home and the Church, but not for the practical business of real life. But a more false and pernicious notion could not be imagined. Religion, in order to elevate a people, should inspire their whole life and rule their relations with one another. A life is not dwarfed, but ennobled by being lived in the presence of God. Therefore the school, which principally gives the knowledge fitting for practical life, ought to be pre-eminently under the holy influence of religion. From the shelter of home and school, the youth must soon go out into the busy ways of trade or traffic or professional practice. In all these, the principles of religion should animate and direct him. But he cannot expect to learn these principles in the work-shop or the office or the counting-room. Therefore let him be well and thoroughly imbued with them by the joint influences of home and school, before he is launched out on the dangerous sea of life.

All denominations of Christians are now awaking to this great truth, which the Catholic Church has never ceased to maintain. Reason and experience are forcing them to recognize that the only practical way to secure a Christian people, is to give the youth a Christian education. The avowed enemies of Christianity in some European countries are banishing religion from the schools, in order gradually to eliminate it from among the people. In this they are logical, and we may well profit by the lesson. Hence the cry for Christian education is going up from all religious bodies throughout the land. And this is no narrowness and "sectarianism" on their part; it is an honest and logical endeavor to preserve Christian truth and morality among the people by fostering religion in the young. Nor is it any antagonism to the State; on the contrary, it is an honest endeavor to give to the State better citizens, by making them better Christians. The friends of Christian education do not condemn the State for not imparting religious instruction in the public schools as they are now organized; because they well know it does not lie within the province of the State to teach religion. They simply follow their conscience by sending their children to denominational schools, where religion can have its rightful place and influence.

Two objects therefore, dear brethren, we have in view, to multiply our schools, and to perfect them. We must multiply them, till every Catholic child in the land shall have within its reach the means of education. There is still much to do ere this be attained. There are still thousands of Catholic children in the United States deprived of the benefit of a Catholic school. Pastors and parents should not rest till this defect be remedied. No parish is complete till it has schools adequate to the needs of its children, and the pastor and people of such a parish should feel that they have not accomplished their entire duty until the want is supplied.

But then, we must also perfect our schools. We repudiate the idea that the Catholic school need be in any respect inferior to any other school whatsoever. And if hitherto, in some places, our people have acted on the principle that it is better to have an imperfect Catholic school than to have none, let them now push their praiseworthy ambition still further, and not relax their efforts till their schools be elevated to the highest educational excellence. And we implore parents not to hasten to take their children from school, but to give them all the time and all the advantages that they have the capacity to profit by, so that, in after life, their children may "rise up and call them blessed."

THE CHRISTIAN HOME.

We need hardly remind you, beloved brethren, that while home life would not, as a rule, be sufficient to supply the absence of good or counteract the evil of dangerous influences in the school, it is equally true, that all that the Christian school could accomplish would be inadequate without the co-operation of the Christian home. Christian schools sow the seed, but Christian homes must first prepare the soil, and afterwards foster the seed and bring it to maturity.

1. *Christian Marriage.*—The basis of the Christian home is Christian marriage; that is, marriage entered into according to religion, and cemented by God's blessing. So great is the importance of marriage to the temporal and eternal welfare of mankind, that, as it had God for its Founder in the Old Law, so, in the New Law, it was raised by Our Divine Lord to the dignity of a sacrament of the Christian religion. Natural likings and instincts have their own value and weight; but they ought not by themselves be a decisive motive in so important a step as Christian marriage; nor are they a safe guarantee for the proper fulfillment of the high ends for which marriage was ordained. That Christian hearts and lives may be wisely and rightly joined, God must join them, and religion sanctify the union; and though the Church sometimes permits the contraction of mixed marriages, she never does so without regret and without a feeling of anxiety for the future happiness of that union and for the eternal salvation of its offspring.

2. *The Indissolubility of Marriage.*—The security of the Christian home is in the indissolubility of the marriage tie. Christian marriage, once consummated, can never be dissolved save by death. Let it be well understood that even adultery, though it may justify "separation from bed and board," cannot loose the marriage tie, so that either of the parties may marry again during the life of the other. Nor has "legal divorce" the slightest power, before God, to loose the bond of marriage and to make a subsequent marriage valid. "Whom God hath joined together, let not man put asunder."[1] In common with all Christian believers and friends of civilization, we deplore the havoc wrought by the divorce-laws of our country. These laws are fast loosening the foundations of society. Let Catholics, at least remember that such divorces are powerless in conscience. Let them enter into marriage only through worthy and holy motives, and with the blessings of religion, especially with the blessing of the Nuptial Mass. And then, far from wishing for means of escape from their union, they will rejoice that it cannot be divided but by death.

3. *Home Virtues.*—The pervading atmosphere of the Christian home should be Christian charity—the love of God and of the neighbor. It should be the ambition and study of Christian parents to make their home a sanctuary, in which no harsh or angry, no indelicate or profane word, should be uttered,—in which truth, unselfishness, self-control, should be carefully cultivated, in which the thought of God, the desire to please God, should be, sweetly and naturally, held before the children as their habitual motives. From the home sanctuary, the incense of prayer should ascend as a most sweet morning and evening sacrifice to the Lord.

[1] Matt., xix, 6.

How beautiful and rich in blessings is the assembling of parents and children for morning and evening prayer! Our hearts are filled with consolation when, in the course of our pastoral visits, we meet families in which this holy practice is faithfully observed. In such families, we are sure to find proofs of the special benedictions of heaven. Faith, religion and virtue are there fostered to luxuriant growth, and final perseverance almost assured. We earnestly exhort all parents to this salutary custom. And if it be not always feasible in the morning, at least every evening, at a fixed hour, let the entire family be assembled for night prayers, followed by a short reading from the Holy Scriptures, the Following of Christ, or some other pious book.

4. *Good Reading.*—Let the adornments of home be chaste and holy pictures, and, still more, sound, interesting, and profitable books. No indelicate representation should ever be tolerated in a Christian home. Artistic merit in the work is no excuse for the danger thus presented. No child ought to be subjected to temptation by its own parents and in its own home. But let the walls be beautified with what will keep the inmates in mind of our Divine Lord, and of his saints, and with such other pictures of the great and the good as will be incentives to civic and religious virtue.

The same remark applies equally to books and periodicals. Not only should the immoral, the vulgar, the sensational novel, the indecently illustrated newspaper, and publications tending to weaken faith in the religion and the Church of Jesus Christ, be absolutely excluded from every Christian home, but the dangerously exciting and morbidly emotional, whatever, in a word, is calculated to impair or lower the tone of faith or morals in the youthful mind and heart, should be carefully banished. Parents would be sure to warn and withhold their children from anything that would poison or sicken their bodies; let them be at least as watchful against intellectual and moral poison. But let the family book-shelves be well supplied with what is both pleasant and wholesome. Happily, the store of Catholic literature, as well as works which, though not written by Catholics nor treating of religion, are pure, instructive and elevating, is now so large that there can be no excuse for running risk or wasting one's time with what is inferior, tainted, or suspicious. Remember, Christian parents, that the development of the youthful character is intimately connected with the development of the taste for reading. To books as well as to associations may be applied the wise saying: "Show me your company and I will tell you what you are." See, then, that none but good books and newspapers, as well as none but good companions, be admitted to your homes. Train your children to a love of history and biography. Inspire them with the ambition to become so well acquainted with the history and doctrines of the Church as to be able to give an intelligent answer to any honest inquiry. Should their surroundings call for it, encourage them, as they grow older, to acquire such knowledge of popularly mooted questions of a scientific or philosophical character as will suffice to make them firm in their faith and proof against sophistry. We should be glad to see thoroughly solid and popular works on these important subjects, from able Catholic writers, become more numerous. Teach your children to take a special interest in the history of our own country. We consider the establishment of our country's independence, the shaping of its liberties and laws as a work of special Providence, its framers "building wiser than they knew," the Almighty's hand guiding them. And if ever the glorious fabric is subverted or impaired it will be by men forgetful of the sacrifices of the heroes that reared it, the virtues that cemented it, and the principles on which it rests, or ready to sacrifice principle and virtue to the interests of self or party. As we desire therefore that the history of the United States should be carefully taught in all our Catholic schools, and have directed that it be specially dwelt upon in the education of the young ecclesiastical students in our preparatory seminaries; so also we desire that it form a favorite part of the home library and home reading. We must keep firm and solid the liberties of our country by keeping fresh the noble memories of the past, and thus sending forth from our Catholic homes into the arena of public life not partisans but patriots.

5. *The Holy Scriptures.*—But it can hardly be necessary for us to remind you, beloved brethren, that the most highly valued treasure of every family library, and the most frequently and lovingly made use of, should be the Holy Scriptures. Doubtless you have often read A'Kempis's burning thanksgiving to our Lord for having bestowed on us not only the adorable treasure of His Body in the Holy Eucharist, but also that of the Holy Scriptures, "the Holy Books, for the comfort and direction of our life."[1] And you have before your eyes, prefixed to the Douay version of the Holy Bible, the exhortation of Pope Pius the Sixth in his letter to the Archbishop of Florence, that "the faithful should be moved to the reading of the Holy Scriptures; for these," he says, "are most abundant sources which ought to be left open to every one to draw from them purity of morals and of doctrine, to eradicate the errors which are so widely disseminated in these corrupt times." And St. Paul declares that "what things soever were written, were written for our learning; that through

[1] Fol. of Christ, B. 4, c. 11.

patience and the comfort of the Scriptures we might have hope."[1] We hope that no family can be found amongst us without a correct version of the Holy Scriptures. Among other versions, we recommend the Douay, which is venerable as used by our forefathers for three centuries, which comes down to us sanctioned by innumerable authorizations, and which was suitably annotated by the learned Bishop Challoner, by Canon Haydock, and especially by the late Archbishop Kenrick.

But in your reading remember the admonition of A'Kempis: "The Holy Scriptures must be read in the same spirit in which they were written; if thou wilt derive profit, read with humility, simplicity and faith."[2] And keep ever before your mind the principle laid down by St. Peter in the first chapter of his second Epistle: "Understanding this first, that no prophecy of Scripture is made by private interpretation, for prophecy came not by the will of man at any time, but the holy men of God spoke, inspired by the Holy Ghost." And this other given by St. John, in the fourth chapter of his first Epistle, in the name of the Apostolic teaching Church: "Dearly beloved, believe not every spirit, but try the spirits if they be of God. We are of God; he that knoweth God heareth us; he that is not of God heareth us not; by this we know the spirit of truth and the spirit of error." In these two divinely inspired rules you have aways a sure safe-guard against the danger of error.

6. *The Catholic Press.*—Finally, Christian parents, let us beg your earnest consideration of this important truth, that upon you, singly and individually, must practically depend the solution of the question, whether or not the Catholic press is to accomplish the great work which Providence and the Church expect of it at this time. So frequently and so forcibly has the providential mission of the press been dwelt upon by Popes and prelates and distinguished Catholic writers, and so assiduously have their utterances been quoted and requoted everywhere, that no one certainly stands in need of arguments to be convinced of this truth. But all this will be only words in the air, unless it can be brought home to each parent and made practical in each household. If the head of each Catholic family will recognize it as his privilege and his duty to contribute towards supporting the Catholic press, by subscribing for one or more Catholic periodicals, and keeping himself well acquainted with the information they impart, then the Catholic press will be sure to attain to its rightful development and to accomplish its destined mission. But choose a journal that is thoroughly Catholic, instructive and edifying; not one that would be, while Catholic in name or pretence, uncatholic in tone

---

[1] Rom. xv.   [2] B. 1, c. v.

and spirit, disrespectful to constituted authority, or biting and uncharitable to Catholic brethren.

Beloved brethren, a great social revolution is sweeping over the world. Its purpose, hidden or avowed, is to dethrone Christ and religion. The ripples of the movement have been observed in our country; God grant that its tidal wave may not break over us. Upon you, Christian parents, it mainly depends whether it shall or not; for, such as our homes are, such shall our people be. We beseech you, therefore, to ponder carefully all that we have said concerning the various constituents of a true Christian home, and, to the utmost of your ability, to carry them into effect. And we entreat all pastors of souls to bear unceasingly in mind, that upon the Christian school and the Christian homes in their parishes must mainly depend the fruit of their priestly labors. Let them concentrate their efforts on these two points,—to make the schools and the homes what they ought to be;—then indeed will they carry to the Lord of the harvest full and ripe sheaves, and the future generation will bless them for transmitting unimpaired the priceless gifts of faith and religion.

THE LORD'S DAY.

There are many sad facts in the experience of nations, which we may well store up as lessons of practical wisdom. Not the least important of these is the fact that one of the surest marks and measures of the decay of religion in a people, is their non-observance of the Lord's Day. In travelling through some European countries, a Christian's heart is pained by the almost unabated rush of toil and traffic on Sunday. First, grasping avarice thought it could not afford to spare the day to God; then unwise governments, yielding to the pressure of mammon, relaxed the laws which for many centuries had guarded the day's sacredness,—forgetting that there are certain fundamental principles, which ought not to be sacrificed to popular caprice or greed. And when, as usually happens, neglect of religion had passed, by lapse of time, into hostility to religion, this growing neglect of the Lord's Day was easily made use of as a means to bring religion itself into contempt. The Church mourned, protested, struggled, but was almost powerless to resist the combined forces of popular avarice and Cæsar's influence, arrayed on the side of irreligion. The result is the lamentable desecration which all Christians must deplore.

And the consequences of this desecration are as manifest as the desecration itself. The Lord's Day is the poor man's day of rest; it has been taken from him,—and the laboring classes are a seething volcano of social discontent. The Lord's Day is the home day, drawing closer the sweet domestic ties, by giving the toiler a day with wife and children; but it has been turned into a day of labor,—and home ties are fast losing their sweetness and their hold. The Lord's Day is the church-day, strengthening and consecrating the bond of brotherhood among all men, by their kneeling together around the altars of the one Father in heaven; but men are drawn away from this blessed communion of Saints,—and as a natural consequence they are lured into the counterfeit communion of Socialism, and other wild and destructive systems. The Lord's Day is God's Day, rendering ever nearer and more intimate the union between the creature and his Creator, and thus ennobling human life in all its relations; and where this bond is weakened, an effort is made to cut man loose from God entirely, and to leave him, according to the expression of St. Paul, "without God in this world."[1] The profanation of the Lord's Day, whatever be its pretext, is a defrauding both of God and His creatures, and retribution is not slow.

In this country, there are tendencies and influences at work to bring about a similar result; and it behooves all who love God and care for society, to see that they be checked. As usual, greed for gain lies at the bottom of the movement. Even when the pretence put forward is popular convenience or popular amusement, the clamor for larger liberty does not come so much from those who desire the convenience or the amusement, as from those who hope to enrich themselves by supplying it. Now far be it from us to advocate such Sunday-laws as would hinder necessary work, or prohibit such popular enjoyments as are consistent with the sacredness of the day. It is well known, however, that the tendency is to rush far beyond the bounds of necessity and propriety, and to allege these reasons only as an excuse for virtually ignoring the sacredness of the day altogether. But no community can afford to have either gain or amusement at such a cost. To turn the Lord's Day into a day of toil, is a blighting curse to a country; to turn it into a day of dissipation would be worse. We earnestly appeal, therefore, to all Catholics without distinction, not only to take no part in any movement tending toward a relaxation of the observance of Sunday, but to use their influence and power as citizens to resist in the opposite direction.

There is one way of profaning the Lord's Day which is so prolific of evil results, that we consider it our duty to utter against it a special condemnation. This is the practice of selling beer or other liquors on Sunday, or of frequenting places where they are sold. This practice tends more than any other to turn the Day of the Lord into a day of dissipation, to use it as an occasion for breeding intemperance. While we hope

---

[1] Ephes., ii, 12.

that Sunday-laws on this point will not be relaxed, but even more rigidly enforced, we implore all Catholics, for the love of God and of country, never to take part in such Sunday traffic, nor to patronize or countenance it. And we not only direct the attention of all pastors to the repression of this abuse, but we also call upon them to induce all of their flocks that may be engaged in the sale of liquors to abandon as soon as they can the dangerous traffic, and to embrace a more becoming way of making a living.

And here it behooves us to remind our workingmen, the bone and sinew of the people and the specially beloved children of the Church, that if they wish to observe Sunday as they ought, they must keep away from drinking places on Saturday night. Carry your wages home to your families, where they rightfully belong. Turn a deaf ear, therefore, to every temptation; and then Sunday will be a bright day for all the family. How much better this than to make it a day of sin for yourselves, and of gloom and wretchedness for your homes, by a Saturday night's folly or debauch. No wonder that the Prelates of the Second Plenary Council declared that "the most shocking scandals which we have to deplore spring from intemperance." No wonder that they gave a special approval to the zeal of those who, the better to avoid excess, or in order to give bright example, pledge themselves to total abstinence. Like them we invoke a blessing on the cause of temperance, and on all who are laboring for its advancement in a true Christian spirit. Let the exertions of our Catholic Temperance Societies meet with the hearty co-operation of pastors and people; and not only will they go far towards strangling the monstrous evil of intemperance, but they will also put a powerful check on the desecration of the Lord's Day, and on the evil influences now striving for its total profanation.

Let all our people "remember to keep holy the Lord's Day." Let them make it not only a day of rest, but also a day of prayer. Let them sanctify it by assisting at the adorable Sacrifice of the Mass. Besides the privilege of the morning Mass, let them also give their souls the sweet enjoyment of the Vesper service and the Benediction of the Blessed Sacrament. See that the children not only hear Mass, but also attend the Sunday-school. It will help them to grow up more practical Catholics. In country places, and especially in those which the priest cannot visit every Sunday, the Sunday-school ought to be the favorite place of reunion for young and old. It will keep them from going astray, and will strengthen them in the faith. How many children have been lost to the Church in country districts, because parents neglected to see that they observed the Sunday properly at home and at Sunday-school, and allowed them to fall under dangerous influences!

FORBIDDEN SOCIETIES.

One of the most striking characteristics of our times is the universal tendency to band together in societies for the promotion of all sorts of purposes. This tendency is the natural outgrowth of an age of popular rights and representative institutions. It is also in accordance with the spirit of the Church, whose aim, as indicated by her name Catholic, is to unite all mankind in brotherhood. It is consonant also with the spirit of Christ, who came to break down all walls of division, and to gather all in the one family of the one heavenly Father.

But there are few good things which have not their counterfeits, and few tendencies which have not their dangers. It is obvious to any reflecting mind that men form bad and rash as well as good and wise designs; and that they may band together for carrying out evil or dangerous as well as laudable and useful purposes. And this does not necessarily imply deliberate malice, because, while it is unquestionably true that there are powers at work in the world which deliberately antagonize the cause of Christian truth and virtue, still the evil or the danger of purposes and associations need not always spring from so bad a root. Honest but weak and erring human nature is apt to be so taken up with one side of a question as to do injustice to the other; to be so enamored of favorite principles as to carry them to unjustifiable extremes; to be so intent upon securing some laudable end as to ignore the rules of prudence, and bring about ruin instead of restoration. But no intention, no matter how honest, can make lawful what is unlawful. For it is a fundamental rule of Christian morals that "evil must not be done that good may come of it," and "the end can never justify the means," if the means are evil. Hence it is the evident duty of every reasonable man, before allowing himself to be drawn into any society, to make sure that both its ends and its means are consistent with truth, justice and conscience.

In making such a decision, every Catholic ought to be convinced that his surest guide is the Church of Christ. She has in her custody the sacred deposit of Christian truth and morals; she has the experience of all ages and all nations; she has at heart the true welfare of mankind; she has the perpetual guidance of the Holy Ghost in her authoritative decisions. In her teaching and her warnings therefore, we are sure to hear the voice of wisdom, prudence, justice and charity. From the hill-top of her Divine mission and her world-wide experience, she sees events and their consequences far more clearly than they who are down in the tangled plain of daily life. She has seen associations that were once praiseworthy, become pernicious by change of circumstances. She has seen others, which won the admiration of the world by their early achievements, corrupted by power or passion or evil guidance, and she has been forced to condemn them. She has beheld associations which had their origin in the spirit of the Ages of Faith, transformed by lapse of time, and loss of faith, and the manipulation of designing leaders, into the open or hidden enemies of religion and human weal. Thus our Holy Father Leo XIII has lately shown that the Masonic and kindred societies,—although the offspring of the ancient Guilds, which aimed at sanctifying trades and tradesmen with the blessings of religion; and although retaining, perhaps, in their "ritual," much that tells of the religiousness of their origin; and although in some countries still professing entire friendliness toward the Christian religion,—have nevertheless already gone so far, in many countries, as to array themselves in avowed hostility against Christianity, and against the Catholic Church as its embodiment; that they virtually aim at substituting a world-wide fraternity of their own, for the universal brotherhood of Jesus Christ, and at disseminating mere Naturalism for the supernatural revealed religion bestowed upon mankind by the Saviour of the world. He has shown, too, that, even in countries where they are as yet far from acknowledging such purposes, they nevertheless have in them the germs, which, under favorable circumstances, would inevitably blossom forth in similar results. The Church, consequently, forbids her children to have any connection with such societies, because they are either an open evil to be shunned or a hidden danger to be avoided. She would fail in her duty if she did not speak the word of warning, and her children would equally fail in theirs, if they did not heed it.

Whenever, therefore, the Church has spoken authoritatively with regard to any society, her decision ought to be final for every Catholic. He ought to know that the Church has not acted hastily or unwisely, or mistakenly; he should be convinced that any worldly advantages which he might derive from his membership of such society, would be a poor substitute for the membership, the sacraments, and the blessings of the Church of Christ; he should have the courage of his religious convictions, and stand firm to faith and conscience. But if he be inclined or asked to join a society on which the Church has passed no sentence, then let him, as a reasonable and Christian man, examine into it carefully, and not join the society until he is satisfied as to its lawful character.

There is one characteristic which is always a strong presumption against a society, and that is secrecy. Our Divine Lord Himself has laid down the rule: "Every one that doth evil, hateth the light and cometh not to the light, that his works may not be reproved. But he that doth truth cometh to the light that his works may be made manifest, because they are done in God."[1] When, therefore, associations veil themselves in secrecy and darkness, the presumption is against them, and it rests with them to prove that there is nothing evil in them.

But if any society's obligation be such as to bind its members to secrecy, even when rightly questioned by competent authority, then such a society puts itself outside the limits of approval; and no one can be a member of it and at the same time be admitted to the sacraments of the Catholic Church. The same is true of any organization that binds its members to a promise of blind obedience—to accept in advance and to obey whatsoever orders, lawful or unlawful, that may emanate from its chief authorities; because such a promise is contrary both to reason and conscience. And if a society works or plots, either openly or in secret, against the Church, or against lawful authorities, then to be a member of it is to be excluded from the membership of the Catholic Church.

These authoritative rules, therefore, ought to be the guide of all Catholics in their relations with societies. No Catholic can conscientiously join, or continue in, a body in which he knows that any of these condemned features exist. If he has joined it in good faith and the objectionable features become known to him afterwards, or if any of these evil elements creep into a society which was originally good, it becomes his duty to leave it at once. And even if he were to suffer loss or run risk by leaving such a society or refusing to join it, he should do his duty and brave the consequences regardless of human considerations.

To these laws of the Church, the justice of which must be manifest to all impartial minds, we deem it necessary to add the following admonition of the Second Plenary Council:[2] "Care must be taken lest workingmen's societies, under the pretext of mutual assistance and protection, should commit any of the evils of condemned societies; and lest the members should be induced by the artifices of designing men to break the laws of justice, by withholding labor to which they are rightfully bound, or by otherwise unlawfully violating the rights of their employers."

But while the Church is thus careful to guard her children against whatever is contrary to Christian duty, she is no less careful that no injustice should be done to any association, however unintentionally. While therefore the Church, before prohibiting any society, will take every precaution to ascertain its true nature, we positively forbid any pastor, or other ecclesiastic, to pass sentence on any association, or to impose eccle-

---

[1] John, III, 20, 21. [2] No. 519.

siastical penalties or disabilities on its members without the previous explicit authorization of the rightful authorities.

CATHOLIC SOCIETIES.

It is not enough for Catholics to shun bad or dangerous societies, they ought to take part in good and useful ones. If there ever was a time when merely negative goodness would not suffice, such assuredly is the age in which we live. This is pre-eminently an age of action, and what we need to-day is active virtue and energetic piety. Again and again has the voice of the Vicar of Christ been heard, giving approval and encouragement to many kinds of Catholic associations, not only as a safeguard against the allurements of dangerous societies, but also as a powerful means of accomplishing much of the good that our times stand in need of. Not only should the pastors of the Church be hard at work in building up "the spiritual house,"[1] "the tabernacle of God with men,"[2] but every hand among the people of God should share in the labor.

In the first place, we hope that in every parish in the land there is some sodality or confraternity to foster piety among the people. We therefore heartily endorse anew all approbations previously given to our many time-honored and cherished confraternities, such as those of the Sacred Heart of Jesus, of the Blessed Sacrament, and of the Blessed Virgin.

Next come the various associations for works of Christian zeal and charity: the Society for the Propagation of the Faith, and the Holy Childhood, than which there are none more deserving; societies for the support of Catholic education; Christian doctrine societies for the work of Sunday-schools; societies for improving the condition of the poor, among which stands pre-eminent the Society of St. Vincent de Paul; church-debt societies; societies for supplying poor churches with vestments and other altar requirements; local sanctuary societies; and other methods of uniting the efforts of the people of the parish for useful and holy purposes. It ought to be the comfort and the honest pride of every Catholic to take an active part in these good works; and if any are hindered from contributing a portion of their time and labor, they should contribute as liberally as they can out of their pecuniary resources.

Then there are associations for the checking of immorality, prominent among which are our Catholic Temperance Societies. These should be encouraged and aided by all who deplore the scandal given and the spiritual ruin wrought by intemperance. It is a mistake to imagine that such societies are made up of the reformed victims of intemperance. They should be, and we trust that they everywhere are largely composed of zealous

---

[1] I. Pet., ii, 5.   [2] Apoc., xxi, 3.

Catholics who never were tainted by that vice, but who mourn over the great evil and are energetically endeavoring to correct it.

We likewise consider as worthy of particular encouragement associations for the promotion of healthful social union among Catholics,—and especially those, whose aim is to guard our Catholic young men against dangerous influences, and to supply them with the means of innocent amusement and mental culture. It is obvious that our young men are exposed to the greatest dangers, and therefore need the most abundant helps. Hence, in the spirit of our Holy Father Leo XIII, we desire to see the number of thoroughly Catholic and well organized associations for their benefit greatly increased, especially in our large cities; we exhort pastors to consider the formation and careful direction of such societies as one of their most important duties; and we appeal to our young men to put to good profit, the best years of their lives, by banding together, under the direction of their pastors, for mutual improvement and encouragement in the paths of faith and virtue.

And in order to acknowledge the great amount of good that the "Catholic Young Men's National Union" has already accomplished, to promote the growth of the Union and to stimulate its members to greater efforts in the future, we cordially bless their aims and endeavors and recommend the Union to all our Catholic young men.

We also esteem as a very important element in practical Catholicity, the various forms of Catholic beneficial societies and kindred associations of Catholic workingmen. It ought to be, and we trust is everywhere their aim to encourage habits of industry, thrift, and sobriety; to guard the members against the dangerous attractions of condemned or suspicious organizations; and to secure the faithful practice of their religious duties, on which their temporal as well as their eternal welfare so largely depends.

With paternal affection we bestow our blessing upon all those various forms of combined Catholic action for useful and holy purposes. We desire to see their number multiplied and their organization perfected. We beseech them to remember that their success and usefulness must rest in a great measure, upon their fidelity to the spirit of the Church, and on their guarding carefully against influences that might make them disloyal. The more closely pastors and people are united in good works, the more abundantly will those associations be blessed and their ends accomplished, the more perfectly will all Christians be united in fraternal charity, and the more widely and firmly will the Kingdom of Christ on the earth be established.

HOME AND FOREIGN MISSIO.

The duties of a Christian begin with his own household and his own parish; but they do not end there. The charity and zeal in his heart must be like that in the heart of the Church, whose very name is Catholic,—like that in the heart of Christ, who "died for all men, and gave Himself a redemption for all."[1] The Divine commission to the Church stands forever: "Go, teach all nations; preach the Gospel to every creature;"[2] and every one who desires the salvation of souls, should yearn for its fulfillment, and consider it a privilege to take part in its realization. The more we appreciate the gift of faith, the more must we long to have it imparted to others. The heart of every true Catholic must glow as he reads of the heroic labors of our missionaries among heathen nations in every part of the world, and especially among the Indian tribes of our country. The missionary spirit is one of the glories of the Church and one of the chief characteristics of Christian zeal.

In nearly all European countries there are Foreign Mission Colleges, and also associations of the faithful for the support of the missions by their contributions. Hitherto we have had to strain every nerve in order to carry on the missions of our own country, and we were unable to take any important part in aiding the missions abroad. But we must beware lest our local burdens should make our zeal narrow and uncatholic. There are hundreds of millions of souls in heathen lands to whom the light of the Gospel has not yet been carried, and their condition appeals to the charity of every Christian heart. Among our own Indian tribes, for whom we have a special responsibility, there are still many thousands in the same darkness of heathenism, and the missions among our thousands of Catholic Indians must equally look to our charity for support. Moreover, out of the six millions of our colored population there is a very large multitude, who stand sorely in need of Christian instruction and missionary labor; and it is evident that in the poor dioceses in which they are mostly found, it is most difficult to bestow on them the care they need, without the generous co-operation of our Catholic people in more prosperous localities. We have therefore urged the establishment of the Society for the Propagation of the Faith in every parish in which it is not yet erected, and also ordered a collection to be made yearly in all the dioceses, for the foreign missions and the missions among our Indians and Negroes. We have done this through a deep sense of duty, and we trust that our noble-hearted people will not regard it as a burden imposed on them, but as an opportunity presented to them of co-operating in a work which must be specially dear to the Heart of our Divine Saviour.

[1] II. Cor., v. 15; I. Tim., ii. 6.   [2] Mat., xxviii, 19; Mark, xvi, 15.

These are the leading matters, venerable and beloved brethren, which have engaged our attention during this Council. The objects of our deliberations have been the same that have occupied the energies of the Church and her pastors ever since the days of the Apostles,—namely, the extension of the kingdom of God, the building up the Body of Christ, the giving greater "glory to God in the highest, and peace on earth to men of good will," by shedding abroad more abundantly the blessings of religion, and the graces of redemption. Our legislation is not intended to impose burdens or limitations upon you, but, on the contrary, to enlarge and secure to you "the liberty of the children of God." The path of duty and virtue is clearly marked and pointed out, not to restrain your freedom, but that you may journey safely, that you may live wisely and virtuously, that you may have happiness temporal and eternal.

And now we write you these things, that you may be partners in our solicitude, that every heart may cry out "Thy Kingdom come," that every hand may be active in establishing and extending it. Accept with willing and loving minds these lessons which spring from hearts full of love for you, and entirely consecrated to your service. Give joy to us and to our Divine Lord by putting them faithfully in practice. And may the blessing of Almighty God, the Father, the Son, and the Holy Ghost, descend upon you abundantly, and abide with you forever.

Given at Baltimore, in the Plenary Council, on the 7th day of December, in the year of our Lord 1884.

In his own name and in the name of all the Fathers,

✠ JAMES GIBBONS,
Archbishop of Baltimore and Apostolic Delegate.

THE CATHEDRAL ORGAN.

As the new organ which was placed in the Cathedral just before the opening of the council ranks amongst the most remarkable, if not the largest in the world, we deem it of sufficient interest to herewith present a cut of its exterior, and a few words descriptive of its most important features. It is indeed a magnificent instrument, and the latest triumph by Mr. Hilborne L. Roosevelt, in the art of organ building.

The instrument is located in the transept gallery at the north side of the dome, in the same position that the old organ occupied, though it covers more floor space and is of greater height. The old organ was built in 1821 by Thomas Hall, who was then a leading organ builder of New York City, and, at the date of its construction, was one of the largest and finest instruments in America, containing what were then considered many novelties, and an unusually complete Pedal Organ. Its grand and rich old case, with the addition of new wings at each side, has been renovated and repaired, and now contains the new instrument. The organ contains three Manuals and a Pedal Organ, and includes in its specification 37 speaking stops, 7 Couplers, 5 Mechanical Accessories, 11 "Roosevelt Adjustable Combination Pistons," and 5 Pedal Movements, making a grand total of 65 stops and appliances, the pipes numbering in all 2,340. The complete control of the instrument by means of its wonderful and perfect mechanism, the great delicacy and characteristic quality of tone in the different stops, the dignified power of "full organ" without harshness, and the perfect blending of the whole into an agreeable and massive tone, yet not lacking in brilliancy, were all demonstrated most satisfactorily to the public on October 23d by Mr. Frederic Archer, the well-known organist, who gave a most delightful recital in the evening of that day.

One of the most noticeable musical effects mechanically obtained is the *crescendo* and *diminuendo* of startling intensity produced by the Swell Pedals, owing to the fact that, in addition to the amplitude of the Swell Organ, the Choir Organ is independently enclosed in another Swell-box, which also contains the mutation work and reeds of the great organ, and which it would be impossible to produce under other circumstances. Considering the manual stops, this places 24 out of the total 32 under the influence of the two Swell Pedals, which are conveniently located so that they can be operated independently or simultaneously by either foot.

The "Roosevelt Adjustable Combination Action" is another novelty which affords the organist the most absolute and complete control of the instrument. By these means he can manipulate his stops in any manner he may see fit with the aid of the 11 Combination Pistons and 2 pedals, which are adjustable in a manner which our space will admit us to describe. The adjustability which enables the organist to arrange his combinations specially to suit every piece he plays has never been attempted by any other builder, and is here most eminently successful.

The Wind chests throughout the organ are not such as the other builders use, but are a form invented and used exclusively by Mr. Roosevelt. They afford a separate pallet for every pipe, and have many advantages over the slide chests

The Cathedral Organ Used During the Council.

ordinarily employed, such as not being affected by changes in the condition of the atmosphere, and producing even a more perfect repetition than that of a grand piano, while the touch is most agreeable, light and elastic.

The wind system is also far better than that usually met with, the supply being copious and *absolutely steady*, owing to the use of "regulators" and "lungs." The Feeders are operated by a "Jacques Hydraulic Engine," placed in the cellar beneath.

Everything is easy of access, and the keyboards and their surroundings, which are indeed a work of art, are so arranged as to afford the most convenient control to the organist. Wherever one looks in the organ, one cannot help being impressed by the perfection and superiority of the workmanship and materials in every detail.

www.ingramcontent.com/pod-product-compliance
Lightning Source LLC
Chambersburg PA
CBHW051844300426
44117CB00006B/261